A PROSE ENGLISH TRANSLATION OF MARKANDEYA PURANAM

A PROSE ENGLISH TRANSLATION OF MARKANDEYA PURANAM

Editor

MANMATHA NATH DUTT

GYAN

Published by

GYAN

Gyan Publishing House
5, Ansari Road
Daryaganj, New Delhi-110002
Phone: 011-47034999, 9811692060
E-mail: books@gyanbooks.com

Distribution Network
gyanbooks.com
India, USA, Canada, UK, Australia

ISBN: 978-93-7169-122-2 (PB)

First Published, 1896

2nd Impression 2025

Printed at: Gyan Press, Delhi.

A PROSE ENGLISH TRANSLATION OF MARKANDEYA PURANAM
Editor: MANMATHA NATH DUTT

A

PROSE ENGLISH TRANSLATION

OF

MARKANDEYA PURANAM.

EDITED AND PUBLISHED BY

MANMATHA NATH DUTT, M.A., M.R.A.S.

RECTOR, KESHUB ACADEMY;

Author of the English Translations of the Ramayana, Srimad-bhagavatam, Mahabharata, Bhagavat-Gita and other works.

CALCUTTA:

PRINTED BY H. C. DASS,

ELYSIUM PRESS, 65/2 BEADON STREET.

1896.

INTRODUCTION.

---:o:---

General Character.

THE different works known by the name of Puranas (or old) are evidently derived from the mytho-heroic stage of Hindu belief. They deal with five characteristic topics, which, as Mr. Colebrooke mentions are (1) Primary creation (2) Secondary creation (3) the Genealogy of gods and patriarchs (4) reigns of the Manus and (5) history or such particulars as have been preserved of the princes of the solar or lunar races and of their descendants to modern times. Siva and Vishnu, under one or other form, are almost the sole objects that claim homage of the Hindus in the Puranas. These are the characteristics of the Puranas as given by Amar Sinha, the great lexicographer. But the Puranas, which we see in the present, do not conform to this description. The reason is not far to seek. There has been a considerable addition of subject matter in the shape of interpolation. Sanskrit scholars in India never cared for their own name. But to preserve what is considered by one as his best production in letters is a human instinct. Thus we find fine literary compositions, emanating from the pens of Sanskrit Pundits, time to time shelved in the bulk of great leterary works. These interpolations in the original body of a work, made at different periods, present it to us as a completely different book. It is for this reason we find so many heterogenous things in old Sanskrit works. Whatever may be the value of the Puranas as a history or a record of the knowledge of the ancient Hindus their importance as books of religious instruction is undoubtedly very great.

Style.

The invariable form of the Puranas is that of a dialogue in which some person relates its contents in reply to the enquiries of another. This dialogue is interwoven with others which are repeated as having been held on other occasions between different individuals. The immediate narrator is commonly Lomaharshana, the disciple of

Vyasa who is supposed to communicate what was imparted to him by his preceptor.

Division.

The Puranas are commonly stated to be eighteen in number. It is said there are also eighteen *Upa* or Minor Puranas—but the names of all these are not found. The principal eighteen Puranas are Brahma, Padma, Vishnu, Saiva, Bhagavat, Naradiya, Markandeya, Agni, Bhavishya, Brahma Vaivarta, Linga, Varaha, Skanda, Vamana, Kurma, Matsya, Garuda and Brahmanda.

All these Puranas are classed into three groups according to the qualities which prevail in them. The Matsya Puran remarks that those in which glory of Hari or Vishnu prevails are Satwika; those in which the legends of Agni or Siva predominate are Tamasa and those which dwell most on the stories of Brahma are Rajasa. The two representative works of the first group namely Vishnupuran and Bhagavatpuran we have already translated. Markandeya Puran, the subject of our present translation, is the representative of the last group. Truly does professor Wilson remark that the Rajasa Puranas lean to the Sakta division of the Hindus, the worshippers of Sakti or the female principle.

Contents of the Markandeya.

"That Purana in which beginning with the story of the birds that were acquainted with right and wrong everything is narrated fully by Markandeya, as it was explained by holy sages, in reply to the question of the Muni, is called the Markandeya containing nine thousand verses." This is the account given of it in the Matsya Puran. Although according to this account as well as that of other Puranas the original work is said to consist of nine thousand verses, the text, that is now seen, consists only of six thousand and nine hundred verses.

Date.

It is very difficult to ascertain the date of these works. Internal evidence—Jaimini applies to Markandeya for an explanation of some of the incidents described in Mahabharata—establishes the priority of the Mahabharata to the Markandeya Purana. This in not of a piece with the tradition that having finished the Puranas Vyasa wrote the poem.

Markandeya Puran is classed in the same category with the Vedas and described as an immediate production from Brahma's mouth. Although a Purana it is not attributed to Vyasa who is considered as the author of all works bearing that appellation. The Markandeya does not acknowledge him as its composer, editor or compiler. It claims equal honour with the Vedas themselves. It is clearly seen from the Bengal Manuscripts that the Markandeya presents a singular exception to this hackneyed enumeration of the eighteen Puranas and the celebration of Vyasa's name as the author of them all.

Authorship and antiquity.

The following is a synopsis of the work. When Markandeya was asked by Jaimini to explain some incidents in the Mahabharata he refers them to some birds living on the Vindhya mountain of a celestial origin and profoundly versed in the Vedas and the knowledge of spiritual truths. Jaimini accordingly goes to them and puts to them the following questions "Why was Vasudeva born as a man ? How was it that Draupad was the queen of the five Pandavas ? Why did Baladeva expiate Brahmanicide. And why were the children of Draupadi killed when they had Krishna and Arjuna to help them." These are the some incidents—the missing links as it were in the Mahabharata—described in the first portion of this Purana. Besides its independent merit as a work of art imparting moral instructions it has an additional value of fllling up the gap in the great epic.

Synopsis.

Legends of Vitrasura's death, Baladeva's penance, Harishchandra's ascension to heaven and the quarrel between Vishwamitra and Vasishtha are followed by a discussion regarding birth, death and sin. This is follwed by a far more extensive account of hells. It gives a description of the Vedas and the origin of the patriarchal families. There is an account of the Manwantaras which is followed by a series of legends, some old and some new, relating to the sun and his prosperity continued to Vaivaswata Manu and his sons, terminating with Dhama, the son of Narisyanta.

The most important section or the episode of the Markandeya Purana is the Chandipatha : a work in very great estimation throughout Bengal, with the votaries of the goddess Kali and other deities to whom

Chandi.

sangunary sacrifices are offered. The tittle *Saptasati* or seven hundred is attached to it because it consists of seven hundred verses. The whole poem is a detail of the actions and transfigurations of the goddess during her dreadful combats with the demons and dark spirits for the mastery of the universe, which ends with the goddess annihilating their power and restoring the vanquished gods to their respective dominions.

Characteristics.

This Purana has a character quite different from that of the other Puranas. It is entirely shorn of that sectarian spirit which is seen in other Puranas. There are rarely to be seen prayers and invocations to any deity. Its leading feature is narrative and it abounds in a number of beautifully written legends.

MARKANDEYA PURANAM.

CHAPTER I.

OM! Salutation unto the Divine Vāsudeva. May those two lotus feet of Hari, capable of dissipating the affliction consequent upon the fear of existence, which, being got at, are adored by the ascetics of composed minds, and which, coming into view, have in order enveloped heaven and earth and the nether region, purify you. May he, who is capable of destroying all sins, who reposed on the serpent (Ananta) living in the interior of the Milky ocean, and in whose company, the ocean, although having the billows of its waters rendered terrific by its breath, seemed to dance, protect you.

Having saluted the Supreme Deity (Nārāyana), and the highest of male beings (Nara) as also the goddess of learning, Saraswati, let us cry success. The highly energetic Jaimini, the disciple of Vyasa, asked the great ascetic Mārkandeya, engaged in hard austerities and the study of the Vedas (1). "O Reverend Sir, the story of *Bhârata,* that has been related by the high-souled Vyasa, is full of many brilliant expressions collected from various scriptures, and consists of divine metres and figures of speech, excellent words, questions and their solutions (2—3). As Vishnu is amongst the celestials, a Brāhmana amongst men, the peerless jewel amongst all ornaments, the thunder-bolt amongst all weapons and mind amongst all organs, so is the most excellent *Mahâbhârata* amongst all sacred writings (4—5). In it are described both collectively and separately wealth, virtue desire and liberation (6). It is the foremost of all religious scriptures, the most excellent of all treatises treating of wealth, the foremost of all works relating to desire and the best of all discoursing on liberation (7). O great Sir, in it have been described by the intelligent Veda Vyasa, the practices, mode of living and the attainment of object belonging to the four conditions (of life) (8). O Sir, this has been so composed by the generous Vyasa that this great scripture, albeit very extensive, is not assailed by contradictions (9). The earth has been freed from dust by the watery billows of Vyasa's words coming down from the mount of the *Vedas* and capable of destroying the trees of false arguments (10). The huge lake of the Vedas composed by Krishna (Dwaipāyana Vyasa) has the sweet words for its big swans, the great stories for its excellent lotuses and the saying for expansive water (11). Being desirous of learning (from you) faithfully this story of *Bhârata* instinct with deep import and full of *Srutis* I have approached you, O reverend Sir (12). Why did Janārdana, the son of Vasudeva, although devoid of qualities, assume a human form for the creation, preservation and destruction of this universe? (13). Why did Krishnā, the daughter of Drupada, alone become the queen of the five sons of Pandu? I have a great doubt in this (14). How did the highly-powerful Balarāma, having a plough for his weapon, atone for the sin of Brāhmanacide by visiting holy shrines? (15). Why did the mighty car-warriors, the high-souled sons of Draupadi, having the Pāndavas as their lords, die before they were married like forlorn (persons)? (16). It behoves you to describe all this in detail to me, for you always enlighten ignorant people" (17). Hearing those his words, the great ascetic Mārkandeya, freed from the eighteen shortcomings* addressed himself to speak (18).

MARKANDEYA said :—"O foremost of Munis, the hour for performing my rites is present; this is not the proper time for describing it in detail (19). I shall name now some birds, O Jaimini, that shall describe (this to you) and remove your doubt (20). Those best of birds, conversant with true knowledge, who always think upon scriptures, and whose understanding is ever free in entering into the knowledge of the Vedic scriptures, Drona's sons, Pingāksha, Vibodha, Suputra and Sumukha are living in a cave of the Vindhya (mountain); go there and ask them (about what you seek to learn)" (21—22). Being thus accosted by the intelligent Mārkandeya, that best of ascetics, having his eyes expanded with wonderment, replied (23).

JAIMINI said :—"Highly wonderful it is, O Brahman, that birds speak like men (and greater it is) that they should attain to knowledge which it is so difficult to acquire (24). If they have sprung from the species of birds wherefrom have they attained to this knowledge? Where are these birds called the sons of Drona? (25). Who again is Drona who has these four sons born to him? How did these high-souled and accomplished ones acquire knowledge of righteousness?" (26).

MARKANDEYA said :— "Listen attentively to what took place in Nandana (the garden of gods) when Sakra, Nārada and Apsarās met (27). Nārada saw Sakra, the king of the celestials, in the midst of the courtesans with his looks firmly fixed upon their faces (28). As soon as he was espied by that best of ascetics, Sachi's lord (Indra) at once rose up and respectfully offered him his own seat (29). Beholding that destroyer of Vala and Vitra rise up, the celestial damsels, bending low with humility, bowed to that

---

* Sleep, lassitude, fear, anger, stupefaction, pride insanity, negligence, surprise, doubt, covetousness, malice, envy, insincerity, falsehood, faithlessness, partiality and ignorance.

celestial saint (30). Being honored by them and on the performer of hundred sacrifices taking his seat, (the ascetic), duly welcomed, started a pleasant conversation. After it had ended, the performer of hundred sacrifices said to the great ascetic (31).

SAKRA said:—"Command, let one of them, whom you like, dance—Rambhā, Misrakesi, Urvasi Tilottamā, Ghritāchi, Menakā, or (any one else) whom you choose" (32). Hearing the words of Sakra, Nārada, the foremost of the twice-born, thinking (for a while) said to the Apsarās who stood (before him) (33). "Let her, amongst you, who considers herself as superior in beauty and nobility—dance before me (34). One, devoid of beauty and accomplishments, cannot attain to consummation in dancing. A dancing which is accompanied by gestures is (real) dancing—any thing else is but infliction"(35).

MARKANDEYA said:—Immediately after he had spoken this, each, bowing, said:—"I am superior in accomplishments" while the other said "not you, not you" (36). Seeing their bewilderment the Divine chastiser of Pāka said:—"Ask you the ascetic and he will say who amongst you is superior in accomplishments" (37). Hear from me, O Jaimini, what Nārada then said on being asked by them, following the direction of Sakra (38). "I shall consider her to be the foremost in accomplishments, who, by her charm, shall agitate the foremost of ascetics Durvāsa, carrying on hard austerities on the mountain-chief" (39). Hearing his words, they all, shaking their heads said "We are all incapable of doing this" (40). Amongst them one Apsarā, by name Vapu, proud of (her capability) to agitate the sage, said:—"I shall go where the anchoret is (41). I shall make to-day that driver (of the chariot) of the body who has controlled the horses of the senses, lose the hold of reins and become an unskilled driver (42). Even if Brahmā, Janārdana, and the blue-red (deity Siva) come to me I shall make to-day their hearts pierced with the shafts of desire" (43). Having said this

Vapu then went to the mount Praleya, (where) by the power of the ascetic's penances the ferocious beasts and asylums were rendered quiet (44). Remaining at a distance of two miles from where the great ascetic was, that excellent Apsarā, having the sweet voice of a male coel, began to sing (45). Hearing her music, the ascetic, having his mind filled with surprise, went where that damsel of sweet voice was (46). Beholding her, all whose limbs were graceful, the ascetic, controlling his mind and knowing that she had come to agitate it, was filled with wrath and indignation. Then the great sage, of hard austerities, told her the following (47). "Since, O ranger of the sky, O you intoxicated with pride, you have come to cause me woe and to put impediments in my austerity acquired by pain, you shall, therefore, O you of vicious understanding, sullied by my wrath, be born in the species of birds (and remain such) for sixteen years (48—49). O wretch of an Apsarā, renouncing own form and assuming that of a bird four sons will be born to you (50). And not obtaining delight in them, and purified by (the stroke of an) weapon you shall again acquire your residence in heaven. There is nothing for you to say in reply" (51). Making that damsel of tremulous bangles, hear of this unbearable speech, that Brāhmana, of eyes reddened with anger, leaving the earth containing the Gangā of liquid waves, went to the celestial Gangā endued with well-known virtues. (52).

CHAPTER II.

MARKANDEYA said :—There was a king of birds, by name Garuda, the son of Arishthanemi : he had a son, known as Sampāti (1). He had a heroic son, Supārshwa, endued with the velocity of the wind : Supārshwa's son was Kumbhi and Kumbhi's son was Pralolupa (2). He had two sons, Kanka and Kandhara (3). Kanka saw on the summit of the Kailāsa, a Rākshasa, having eyes like lotus petals, the follower of the god of riches, known as Vidyudrupa (4). Wearing a brilliant garland and raiment and seated with his spouse on a beautiful clean marble slab he was engaged in drinking (5). As soon as he was seen by Kanka, that Raksha, filled with anger, said :—"Whence have you come here, O wretched oviparous ? (6). Why do you come to me who am waiting here with my wife ? Such is not the procedure of the intelligent in things sacred to secrecy ?" (7). Kanka said :—"This mountain-chief is common property, it belongs to you, me and other creatures ; what special attachment have you for it ?" (8). Mārkandeya said :—Being thus accosted by Kanka the Rākshasa cut him down : he looked frightful with blood gushing out ; and deprived of consciousness he rolled about (9). Hearing Kanka slain, Kandhara, the king of the oviparous ones, beside himself with ire, made up his mind for the destruction of Vidyudrupa (10). Then repairing to the summit of the Kailāsa where Kanka lay slain, that sky-ranger (bird) performed the obsequies of his elder brother. Then with his eyes rolling in ire and indignation and sighing like a serpent he went, where the Rākshasa, the slayer of his brother, was. Then agitating the huge mountains with the mighty wind of his wings, and scattering the clouds with great vehimence, that destroyer of his enemies, with reddened eyes, in a moment, attacked the mountain with his wings (11—13). He saw there the night-ranger, engaged in drinking with countenance and eyes rendered coppery and seated on a golden sofa; having his head encircled with wreaths adorned with Hari sandal, and furnished with a countenance highly terrific with teeth resembling the inlying leaves of Ketaki (14—15). He saw also his wife, by name Madanikā, of large eyes and gifted with the sweet notes of a male coel, seated on his left thigh (16).

Thereupon having his mind filled with wrath, Kandhara said to him who was waiting in that mountain cave "O wretch, give me battle (17). As my eldest brother, (always) confiding, has been slain by you I shall therefore despatch you, possessed by pride, to the abode of Yama (18). Being slain by me to-day you shall go to the hells designed for those who destroy the confiding, women and children" (19).

MARKANDEYA said:—Being thus addressed by the king of birds in the presence of his wife the Raksha replied to the bird who was filled with anger (20). "If I have killed your brother forsooth I have displayed my prowess: I shall also slay you, O bird, with this sword of mine (21). Wait a moment, O wretch of a bird, and you shall not go hence living." Saying this he took up a shining sword resembling a mass of collyrum (22). There arose an unequalled encounter between the king of birds and the follower of the king of Yakshas like that between Garuda and Sakra (23). Then in great anger, taking up vehemently the sword having the hue of extinguished charcoal the Rākshasa hurled it at the king of birds (24). As Garuda (takes up) a snake, the king of birds, raising the sword a little up from the ground, took it by his beak (25). Then breaking it with beak and talons that oviparous one was worked up with anger; on the sword being thus snapped there ensued a hand to hand encounter (26). Then striking the Rākshasa on his breast the king of birds severed his entrails, feet, hands and head (from his body) (27). On his being thus slain, his wife sought refuge with the bird; and being terrified a little she said. "I will be your wife" (28). Then taking her that foremost of birds went back to his own house; and by destroying Vidyudrupa, he was relieved (of the sorrow consequent upon the death) of his brother (29). Going to the abode of Kandhara, that daughter of Menakā, having fair eye-brows and capable of assuming forms at will, took that of a female bird (30). He then begat on her that best of Apsarās, a daughter named Tārkshi—sullied by the imprecation of the ascetic—and the bird gave her the name of Tārkshi (31). Mandapāla had four highly intelligent sons, the foremost of the twice-born, Jarita and others ending with Drona (32). The youngest of them, virtuous-souled and conversant with the Vedas and its branches, espoused the fair Tārkshi, by the permission of Kandhara (33). After some time Tārkshi conceived and when the conception passed over seven fortnights she went to Kurukshetra (34). The dreadful combat between the Kurus and Pāndavas going on at that time, she, from the inevitable course of actions, entered into the thick of battle (35). There she beheld the encounter between Bhagadatta and Kiriti, by the continued discharge of whose arrows the sky was filled as if with locusts (36). There a shaft, dark-blue like a serpent, discharged from the bow of Pārtha and coursing vehemently, severed the skin of her abdomen (37). On the abdomen being riven, four eggs, endued with the lustre of the moon, being destined to live, dropped to the earth like a mass of cotton (38). And simultaneously with their fall the huge bell fell down from that best of elephants, Supratika, having its tie cut by an arrow (39). Although it dropped down at the same time along with the eggs riving the face of the earth, (yet) the eggs of the bird were covered by it above the parts where the embryos were (40). After that lord of men, the king Bhagadatta, had been slain, the battle between the armies of the Kurus and Pândavas went on for many a day (41). After the close of the battle, Dharma's son (Yudhisthira) went to the son of Sântanu (Bhisma) to hear from the high-souled (Bhisma) an exhaustive discourse on religion (42). A self-controlled ascetic, the foremost of the twice-born by name Shamika, came, in search of them where the eggs lay under the bell (43). There he heard the indistinct cries which, though they had full knowledge, the embryos were emmitting on account of their infancy (44). Then the sage, filled with surprise, along with his disciples, took up the bell and saw there the young ones having no parents (45). Seeing them in that way on the ground the divine ascetic Shamika, filled with surprise, said to the twice-born who were following him (46). "Beholding the army of the Daityas assailed by the celestials, well did that foremost of the twice-born Sukra, the son of Usanâ, say:—(47). "Desist, you should not go—where do you go in fear? Wherever you may go renouncing fame and heroism you must not die (48). As you have been created by the Deity, so long he wishes you must live whether you fight or not (49). Some die in their own homes, others while flying away, and others perish while taking food or drinking water (50). Others (again), enjoying the sweets of life, possessing good health, and having their persons not wounded by weapons, come under the subjection of the lord of the dead (51). Others, engaged in hard austerities, are carried away by the followers of the king of the dead; even those who practise *Yoga* can never attain to immortality (52). Formerly the thunder-bolt was hurled by the holder of thunder (Indra) at Samvara; he was wounded at the chest and still the Asura did not die (53). But when the time came, with the self-same thunder-bolt and by the same Indra the Daityas immediately met with destruction (54). Knowing this you should not be afraid and do you return." Thereupon casting off the fear of death the Daityas desisted (55). The words of Sukra have been verified by these excellent birds for they did not meet with death even in that superhuman battle(56). O Vipras, what was the fall of birds and what was the simultaneous dropping of the bell ? And what again was this battle covering the earth with flesh, fat and blood ? (57). O Vipras, who all these (birds) may be—they are not ordinary birds ; the favour of the Deity sometimes displays good luck in this world (58). Having said this and seeing them he again spoke " Stop, go to the hermitage taking with you these young ones of the bird (59). Keep these oviparous ones at a place where cats, rats, hawks or murgooses may not come (60). What is the use of over care, O twice-born ones ? As creatures live or die by their own actions, so it will be with these young ones of the bird (61). Still a man should put forth his endeavour in all that he does ; if he does not employ his energy he is censured by the good" (62). Thus commanded by the ascetic the sons of the Munis, taking the birds, went to the hermitage, beautified with the presence of saints and black bees swarming round the branches of trees (63). Collecting, as he liked, roots, fruits, flowers, and *Kuça* grass, the twice-born one performed various religious rites, sanctioned by the *Sruti*, in honor of the holder of discus (Vishnu), Rudra, (Siva), Brahmā, Indra, Yama, the god of fire, the lord of waters, the lord of speech, the god of wealth, the wind-god, Dhātā, Vidhātā and Vishwadeva (64—65).

CHAPTER III.

MARKANDEYA said:—O foremost of Vipras, day after day that great ascetic protected and reared those young ones with food and water (1). Within a month they, gazed at by the sons of the ascetics, with eyes expanded with curiosity, began to fly about in the course of the sun's car (sky) (2). Having gone round the earth, resembling the wheel of a car, abounding in cities, seas, and great rivers, those high-minded ones, not born of any female, with their minds and bodies exhausted, returned to the hermitage (3). By the potency of the ascetics their knowledge became manifest at that place (4). While the Rishi (Shamika), for favouring his disciples, was discoursing on the certain truths of religion, they, circumambulating him, bowed to his feet (5). (They) said :—"O ascetic, we have been saved by you from a dreadful death; by giving us shelter, food and water, you have proved to be our father and preceptor (6). Our mother died when we were in the womb and no father has brought us up; you have given us our life, for you have protected us in our infancy (7). O you of undeteriorating energy, taking away the bell of the elephant, you did remove our misery while we, on the earth, were drying up like so many earth-worms (8). 'When will these poor (young ones) grow up? When shall I see them strong? When shall I see them go to the tree from the earth and fly about from one tree to another? (9). When shall the native lustre of my body meet with destruction by the dust raised by the wind of the wings of these ones, ranging about me?' (10). Thinking in this wise, O father, we have been brought up by you. We have now grown up and our understanding has increased, what shall we do now?" (11). Hearing those their distinct words resembling those of a refined speech, surrounded by all his disciples and his son Sringi, the ascetic, stricken with curiosity and with his hairs standing erect, said :—"Tell me truly how you can utter speech (12—13). It behoves you to speak to us by whose imprecation you have come by this change in your form and speech" (14). The birds said :—"Formerly there was a great ascetic well-known by the name of Vipulāswan. He had two sons born to him, Srikrishna and Tamvaru (15). Of the self-controlled ascetic Srikrishna we are the four sons, always conducting ourselves with humility and bending low with reverence (16). While he was engaged in hard austerities, according to his will, with his senses restrained, we used to collect for him sacrificial fuel, flowers and other requisites (17). Thus we all living there in that forest, came to us once the king of the celestials assuming the form of a huge, broken-winged and a decrepit bird, having coppery eyes and trembling body, for imprecating a curse on us and asking (something) of that foremost of Rishis endued with truthfulness, purity, forgiveness, good conduct and nobleness of mind (18—20). He said:—'O foremost of the twice-born, you should save me, who am stricken with hunger, I seek for food, O great one, and be you my help (21). While living on the summit of the Vindhya mountain, I was thrown down, O great one, by the violent wind generated by wings of the bird (Garuda) (22). Possessed by bewilderment I lay on the ground for seven days and on the eighth day I regained my consciousness (23). Regaining consciousness, stricken with hunger, desirous of food, with delight gone and a suffering mind I seek refuge with you (24). Therefore, O you of pure mind, do you firmly make up your mind to save me; O Brāhmana saint, give me such food as may sustain my life (25).' Being thus accosted he replied to Indra in the form of a bird:—'I shall give you such food by which you may sustain your life' (26). Having said this that foremost of the twice-born again asked. 'What food shall I procure for you.' Whereto he replied:—'I find great delight in the flesh of men' (27).

THE RISHI said:—'O oviparous one, your childhood is gone as well as your youth; forsooth, old age is now with you, when the endless desires of men come to an end. Why then even in your old age you are so very cruel? (28—29). What is human flesh? What is the end of your life?

The desires of the wicked never meet with perfect pacification? (30). And what is the use of my speaking this? We should now think that what has been promised must be given' (31). Having said this to him that best of the Vipras, making up his mind, speedily sent for us. And praising each according to his merit, that ascetic of aggrieved heart, addressed highly cruel words to us all who were bending low with humility, filled with devotion and had our hands joined (32—33). 'O foremost of the twice-born, you have subdued yourself and have been freed from your debts along with me. O twice born ones, as you are my offsprings, you have begotten excellent children (34). If I am your preceptor, worshipful and your father, worthy of your reverence, then do you satisfy my words with a good spirit' (35). As soon as we were addressed by him affectionately with these words we said:—'Think what you have said to us as already accomplished' (36).

THE RISHI said:—'This bird, stricken with hunger and thirst, has sought refuge with me. Do you soon do that by which he may obtain satisfaction with your flesh and slake his thirst with your blood (37). Thereupon pained and trembling with great fear we said, 'Alas! Alas! this cannot be done by us (38). Why should a wise man destroy his own body for the sake of others; one's own body is like one's own son (39). A son, as mentioned, satisfies the debts of the ancestral manes, deities and human beings but he never gives his body (40). Therefore we shall not do this; nor those, that have passed away, did it; a person, living, attains to well-being; a person, living, performs pious deeds (41). A person, dying, loses his body and all his religious merit comes to an end; the virtuous men have said:—'Protect thy life by all means' (42). Hearing these words of ours, the ascetic, as if burning in anger and consuming us with his eyes, again addressed us saying (43):—'Promising to me as you do not satisfy my words, so burnt down by my imprecation you shall be born as birds' (44).

Having said this to us and performed his own funeral rites according to the ordinances he said to the bird (45). 'O foremost of birds, do you eat me up confidingly; I have converted this body of mine into food for you (46). O best of the birds, as long as a Brâhmana observes truth so long his [Brâhmanahood is maintained (47). A Brâhmana does not acquire piety so much by sacrifice, gift or any other act as he does by observing truth' (48). Hearing these words of the Rishi, Sakra, under the guise of a bird, having his mind filled with surprise, replied to the ascetic (49). 'O foremost of Vipras, resorting to *Yoga*, renounce your own body—I do not feed upon living animals, O best of Brâhmanas (50). Hearing his words the ascetic engaged in *Yoga*. Then knowing his determination and assuming his own form Sakra said:—(51). 'O best of Vipras, O intelligent one, do you understand, by your intelligence what should be understood. O sinless one, for trying you, I have committed this offence by you (52). O you of pure mind, either forgive me, therefore, or do what you will; I have been highly pleased with you for satisfying your promise (53). From to-day you shall have knowledge of Indra and there will be no disturbance to your religious penance' (54). After Sakra had departed having said this, we, saluting our sire filled with anger, thus addressed the great ascetic (55). 'O noble-minded one, you should forgive us, poor as we are, who have been afraid of death; (certainly) we do love our life (56). We cherish attachment for this body which is made of skin, bones, and flesh and filled with pus and blood, for which no attachment should be cherished (57). Hear, O great one, how people become infatuated, losing all control over themselves, by the powerful enemies—the vices, lust, anger, &c., (58). The king, *Purusha*, endowed with consciousness, lives in the great city (body) encircled by the ramparts of wisdom, having bones for its support, a strong foundation of skin, pasted with flesh and blood, having nine entrances, (the flood-gates) of mighty miseries surrounded on all sides with nerves (59—60). He has two ministers, intellect and mind opposed to each other; and each of these tries to destroy his enemy (61). The king has four enemies, who are always desirous of killing him—namely, lust, anger, covetousness and the other enemy is stupefaction (62). When the king lives closing those entrances, then only he is strong, healthy and freed from anxiety (63). Then attachment grows in him and he is not overcome by his enemies (64). But while he throws open all the doors, then the enemy attachment gets holds of the entrances of his eyes, etc. (65). He is all-pervading, highly powerful and is capable of entering through five doors. And following him enter the other three dreadful foes (66). Thereupon entering there through the doors designated as organs of sense, attachment attains to unification with mind and the rest (67). Subjugating the mind and the senses and occupying the entrances that dreadful one destroys the ramparts. Beholding mind under his subjugation, intellect immediately meets with destruction (68). Having no councillors, renounced by the inmates of his house, and with enemy acquiring the possession of his house that king meets with death (69). In this way those wicked ones, attachment, stupefaction, covetousness and anger, go about destroying the recollection of men (70). From attachment originates anger, from anger covetousness; from covetousness springs stupefaction and from it the weakness of memory. From the impairment of memory originates loss of intellect and from loss of intellect follows the destruction of one's own self (71). O foremost of men, do you extend your grace to such persons who have lost their intellect, are following attachment and covetousness and cherish a desire for life (72). May the curse, that has been imprecated on us by you, the divine sage, may not prove true, and O foremost of ascetics, we may not come by the painful state generated by the quality of darkness (73).'

THE RISHI said :—' What have I said can never be falsified. O my sons, to this day, I have never spoken an untruth (74). I consider destiny in this as supreme ; Oh fie on useless manliness ! by which perforce I have unthinkingly perpetrated an iniquity (75). Since you have propitiated me by bowing to me, you shall even, when born as birds, attain to knowledge (76). Having ways discovered by your knowledge and your distressing sins washed away through my grace, you shall unhesitatingly attain to most excellent *Siddhi* (accomplished piety) (77). When, O my sons, you shall begin speaking (in answer to) Jaimini's questions about his doubts you will then be freed from my curse. This is the favour I extend to you (78).' O worshipful Sir, in this way we were formerly imprecated by our sire under the influence of destiny and after a lapse of time we have been born in another species (79). We have been born in a battle-field and brought up by you. O foremost of the twice-born, in this way we have come by the state of birds (80). There is no such (person) in this world who is not governed by destiny—all the actions of the creatures are subject to destiny (81)."

MARKANDEYA said :—O reverend Sir, hearing their words, the great ascetic Shamika said to the twice-born ones who were around him (82). I have already spoken to you all that they are not ordinary birds ; they must be some great twice-born ones for they did not meet with death in that superhuman battle (83). Then obtaining permission from that high-souled one who was glad at heart, they repaired to that best of mountains Vindhya filled with trees and creepers (84). Even up to the present day those pious birds live in that mountain being engaged in hard austerities and the study of the *Vedas* and firmly determined upon (carrying on) the contemplation of mind (85). Having thus received good behaviour from that ascetic, those sons, of the anchorite, who came by the state of birds, live with minds controlled in the woods of that best of mountain in the Vindhya range, (abounding in) high sacred streams (86).

CHAPTER IV.

MARKANDEYA said:—Thus did the sons of Droṇa, the birds, obtain knowledge. They live in the Vindhya mountain; do you adore them and ask them (regarding your question) (1). Hearing the words of the saint Markandeya, Jaimini went to the summit of the Vindhya where the pious birds were (2). Approaching that mountain he heard the sound of reading and at this filled with surprise Jaimini thought (3). "The foremost ones of the twice-born are reciting the Vedas with proper accent and emphasis, controlling their breaths, without any fatigue, with distinctness and without any fault. (4). Me-thinks it is a wonder that the goddess of learning has not forsaken these sons of the anchorite who have come by a different birth (5). Friends and acquaintances, leaving one according to their will, go to another house but the goddess of learning never forsakes him (6)." Thinking this he entered the mountain cave; and entering there he saw the twice-born ones seated on a mountain slab (7). Beholding them recite (the Vedas) without any distortion of the face, he, filled with delight and sorrow, said to them all (8). "May good betide you, O eminent twice-born ones, know me as Jaimini, the disciple of Vyāsa who have come here to see you (9). You should not be sorry for being born as birds and for being imprecated by your sire in great anger: this is all destiny (10). O foremost twice-born ones, some intelligent persons, born in an affluent family, were comforted, on the loss of wealth, by a barbarian (11). Some persons giving (their all) go about begging; others killing (some) are themselves killed; some bringing down (others) are themselves prostrated: all this springs from the wane of asceticism (12). Many such contraries have been seen by me: the world is perpetually disturbed with these contending chances and mischances (13). Thinking this in your mind you should not grieve: this is the fruit of knowledge not influenced by joy or grief (14)." Then welcoming Jaimini with water to wash feet and an offering of *Kuça* grass they all, bowing to the great ascetic, enquired about his well-being (15). Then all those birds said to the ascetic, the disciple of Vyāsa, seated at ease, and relieved of fatigue by the wind of their wings (16). "Blessed is our birth to-day and our life has proved to be a good life since we have seen the pair of your lotus feet worshipped even by the celestials (17). O Vipra, that, which originating from our father's anger, exists in our bodies has been quenched to-day with the water of your presence (18). At your asylum, O Brahman, is it all well with birds and beasts, trees, creepers, groves consisting of bark only, grass and others of the same origin? (19). Or perhaps we have not made a proper enquiry, regarded by you as we are; how can they, who are with you, suffer misfortune? (20). Do you favour us and tell us the cause of your coming: your noble presence is like the company of the celestials. By what great good luck you have been brought within the range of our vision (21)." Jaimini said:—"Hear, O you the foremost of the twice-born ones, why I have come to this charming hollow of the Vindhya watered by the river Reva (22). I have come here to ask you about some doubts in the scripture *Bhârata*. Formerly asking the high-souled Mārkandeya, the best of the Bhrigu race, I came across some doubtful points in *Bhârata*. I have been told by him 'There are in the great mountain Vindhya the high-souled sons of Drona: they will speak to you (on this) at length' (23—24). Following his words I have come to this great mountain: do you hear them exhaustively and explain them to me" (25). The birds said:—"We shall tell you if it be a (worthy) subject, do you hear it, shorn of fear. And why should we not speak out what has come within the range of our intellect? (26). And although, O foremost of the Brâhmanas, our intellect ranges over the four Vedas, the scriptural works, all its branches and others recognised by the Vedas still we cannot pledge ourselves to any promise (about it) (27—28). Communicate to us confidingly if you have any doubts in *Bhârata* and we shall explain them to you, O you conversant with virtue, unless we are overpowered by stupefaction (29)."

JAIMINI said:—O you of pure souls, hear what doubtful points I have in *Bhârata* and hearing them you should explain (30). Although devoid of qualities, why did Janārdana, the son of Vasudeva, the stay of the universe and the cause of all causes, come by the state of a man? (31). Why did Krishnā, the daughter of Drupada, become the one queen of the five sons of Pāndu? I have a great doubt in this (32). How did the highly powerful Valadeva, having a ploughshare for his weapon, expiate the sin of Brâhmanicide by visiting holy shrines (33). Why did the mighty car-warriors, the high-souled sons of Draupadi, having the Pândavas for their lord, meet with death, before they entered upon matrimonial life, like those who have none to help them (34). Explain all these my doubts anent *Bhârata*, which I have spoken, so that accomplishing my object I may return to my own hermitage (35).

THE BIRDS said:—Saluting the lord of the celestials, the highly powerful Vishnu, the Purusha of incomparable (energy), the eternal and undecaying, identical with four *Vyuhas*, the three-fold qualities and shorn of them, who is most excellent, most powerful, worshipful and immortal; him, than whom there is nothing greater or smaller, by whom, unborn and the beginning of the world, this universe has been permeated;

him, who appears and disappears, who is seen and not seen, who is the creator and the destroyer of all in the end; bowing with a controlled mind to the Prime deity Brahmā who, bringing out from his mouth *Rik* and *Sâman*, purified the three worlds (36—40). Saluting Içāna, defeated by whose single arrow the Asuras cannot put in obstacles in the sacrifices of the sacrificers (41); we shall describe, at length, the moral truths which have been revealed in *Bhârata* by Vyāsa of wondrous deeds (42). Water has been called *Nâra* by the ascetics seeing the true essence of things: he who reposed on it, in the beginning is called *Nârâyana* (43). O Brahman, the divine lord Nārāyana, permeating all, exists in four fold forms, (either) endued with qualities or being devoid therefrom (44). One of these forms cannot be defined; the wise behold it as white; this form, called Vāsudeva, is seen as being engarlanded by effulgence, the principal stay of the *Yogis*, distant yet near, above the attributes and shorn of all attachments (45—46). Form, color *etc* do not really belong to it, but are the work of imagination. Its form is one, eternal, pure and glorious (47). The second form, known as Sesha, remaining underneath, holds the earth. It is pervaded by the quality of ignorance and is accordingly called as belonging to the brute creation (48). The third goes through actions, being engaged in protecting people; it is permeated by the quality of goodness and is known as establishing righteousness (49). The fourth lies within water resting on a serpent bed: darkness is its attribute and it always carries on the work of creation (50). That third form of Hari, which is engaged in protecting people, always establishes righteousness on earth (51). Slaying the rising Asuras who always disturb virtue, it protects the deities and other pious men always intent upon protecting virtue (52). At all times, O Jamini, whenever the virtue has suffered deterioration this form has been incarnated for raising righteousness (53). Formerly assuming the form of a boar, and dividing the water with the projection of the mouth, it, with one tooth, raised up the earth like a lotus (54). Assuming the form of man-lion he slew Hiranyakaçipu and other Dānavas headed by Viprachitti (55). Dwarf and various other forms of his—I do not like to enumerate. The present one is his Mathurā incarnation (5). When the form permeated by the quality of goodness was incarnated it engaged in the work of preservation under the name of Pradyumna (57). Either born as a celestial, a human being or a beast, Vāsudeva, according to his will, assumes the nature of the form (in which he is born) (58). All this has been described; now hear next, how the lord Vishnu, although attaining to perfect success, assumed the form of a man (59).

CHAPTER V.

THE BIRDS said :—Formerly the Patriarch Tashtā had a son by name Triçirā; (once) performing auterities with his head downwards he was slain by Sakra in fear (1). O Brahman, Tashtā's son being slain, Indra's energy suffered impairment being greatly assailed by the sin of Brāhmanicide (2). On account of this iniquity Sakra's energy entered into righteousness—and his energy having entered into righteousness Sakra became shorn of it (3). Thereupon hearing of the destruction of his son the Patriarch Tashtā, worked with anger, tore a matted-lock and said :—(4). "Let the three worlds with the deities behold my prowess to-day; let also the wicked-minded chastiser of Pāka, who has slain a Brāhmana, witness it also, by whom my son, engaged in his own penances, has been killed." Saying this, he, having his eyes reddened with anger, offered the matted-locks to fire (5—6). Thereupon arose a mighty, huge-bodied Asura, Vritra, engarlanded by flames, having huge teeth and resembling a mass of crushed collyrum (7). Being impregnated by the energy of Tashtā, the highly powerful enemy of Indra, of incomparable energy, daily grew in strength like the course of an arrow (8). Beholding the mighty Asura Vritra for his own destruction, Sakra, stricken with fear, sent the seven Rishis for making a peace (9). The sages, ever engaged in the well-being of all creatures with a glad heart, arranged for a conditional treaty between him and Vritra (10). When disregarding the condition Vritra was slain by Indra, his strength became enfeebled on account of his being assailed by the sin of Vritra's destruction (11). The strength driven out of Sakra's body entered into air, all-spreading, invisible and the deity presiding over all prowess (12). When assuming the form of Goutama, Sakra, the lord of the celestials, ravished Ahalyā, his beauty disappeared (13). The grace of his limbs which was highly charming, leaving the wicked king of the deities, resorted to Nāsatyas (the twin sons of Aswini) (14). Knowing that the king of the celestials was shorn of virtue and energy and deprived of strength and beauty the Daityas addressed themselves for vanquishing him (15). O great ascetic, being desirous of vanquishing the king of the celestials, the highly powerful Daityas were born in the races of mighty monarchs (16). Once on a time, the earth, assailed by her load, went to the summit of the mount Meru where there was an assembly of the celestials (17). She, distressed with a heavy load, communicated to them the cause of her affliction arising from the Daityas, the sons of Dānu (18). "All those powerful Daityas, who had been destroyed by you, have been born in the region of men in the houses of the kings (19). They are great many Akshouhini (in number)—distressed by them I am going down;

do you so arrange therefore, O celestials, that I may attain to peace (20)."

THE BIRDS said:—Thereupon dividing their energy the celestials descended on earth from their own region for protecting creatures and relieving the earth of her burden. (21). Then the deity Dharma put the energy of Indra's body in Kunti and then was born the highly energetic king Yudhisthira (22). The God of Wind gave away his energy and Bhima was born; and Pārtha (Arjuna) the conqueror of the god of riches was born from a half of Sakra's energy (23). The highly effulgent twins resembling Sakra were born from Mādri. In these five ways did the Divine performer of hundred sacrifices incarnate himself (24). His great wife came out from fire as Krishnā (25). Krishnā was the wife of Sakra and of none else. The great *Yogis* can convert their body into many (26). We have thus described to you how one became the wife of the five. Hear how Valadeva went to the Saraswati.

CHAPTER VI.

——oo——

THE BIRDS said:—Knowing that Krishna had a great love for Pārtha, Rāma, having the plough for his weapon, thought much as to what should be done (1). "Without Krishna I shall not go to the side of Duryodhana and how can I, siding with the Pāndavas, slay the king Duryodhana, my son-in-law, disciple and lord of men? (2—3). Therefore I shall purify myself by visiting holy shrines so long as the Kurus and Pāndavas do not exterminate each other (4)." Thus greeting

Hrishikeça, Pārtha and Duryyodhana, Valarāma (Souri) surrounded by his soldiers went to Dwarkā (5). Going to Dwarkā filled with contented and healthy men, Rāma, holding plough as weapon, began to drink on the day preceding his departure to holy shrines (6). Then finishing his glass and holding by the hand the proud Revati, resembling an Apsarā he went to the rich garden of Raivata (7). Encircled by a bevy of damsels, he, inebriete as he was, reeled as he went along. The heroe then saw the highly charming wood, rich with fruits and flowers of all seasons, filled with monkeys, holy and abounding in lotus groves and lakes (8—9). He heard many maddening notes emitted by birds creating delight, pleasant to the ears and greatly sweet (10). He saw those trees, loaded with the fruits of all seasons and shining with the flowers of all seasons, echoed with the notes of birds (11); mangoes, hog-plums, Bhavyas, cocoanuts, *Satindakas*, jeeras, promegranates, Vijapurakas, Panasas, Lakuchas, Mochas, highly charming Nipas, Pārāvatas; Kankolas, lotuses, Amlavetasas, Bhallātaka, Amalakas, Tindakas having big fruits, Ingudas, Karamardas, Haritakas, Vibhitakas—that descendant of Yadu saw these and other trees. He saw also Açokas, Punāgas, Ketakis, Vakulas, Champakas, Sataparnas, Karnikāras, Mālatis, Pārijātas, Kovidāras, Mandāras, Jujubes, flowery Pātalas, Devadāru trees, Sālas, Tālas, Tamālas, Kinçukas, and Vanjulas, the foremost of trees, filled with sweet strains, pleasing to the ears, of Chakoras, Satapatras, black-bees, parrots, male coels, sparrows, Hāritas, Jivajivakas, Pryaputras, Chātakas and various other birds (12—19). (He saw there) also charming lakes of delightful waters overspread with lilies, lotuses, auspicious red lotuses, Kalhāras, and filled with Kadamvas, Chacravākas, water-fowls, Karandavas, Plavas, swans, tortoises, shags and other acquatic animals (20—22). Surveying this charming forest, one by one, Souri, followed by women, went to an excellent grove of creepers (23). He saw there the twice-born ohes versed in the Vedas and their branches, Kouçikas, Bhārgavas, the descendants of Bhwaradāja with those of Goutama and other eminent twice-born ones born in various races, who, seated on *Kuça* sheets, on spacious black deer skins and other seats of the ascetics, were listening with attention. Amongst them, Suta was discoursing on themes, relating to Purānas, on the character of the original celestial saints (24—26). Beholding Rāma with eyes reddened with drink and considering him to be inebriate all the twice-born hurriedly stood up (27). They all welcomed the holder of plough, except him who was born in the race of Suta (28). Thereat the highly powerful holder of plough, filled with anger, and his eyes rolling, who had slain numberless Dānavas, killed Suta (29). Suta, being slain, attained to the dignity of Brahmā ; and all the twice-born, clad in antelope skin, went away from the forest (30). Considering himself sullied, the holder of plough thought:—"A great iniquity has been perpetrated by me (31). I have slain Suta who has attained to the dignity of Brahmā ; and seeing me all these twice-born ones have gone away (32). The smell of my body, hard as iron, is creating uneasiness. I have degraded my own-self cursed with the destruction of a Brāhmana (33). Fie on spite, drink, egoism and rashness, possessed by which I have perpetrated this mighty iniquity (34). For expiating my sin, I shall observe a vow extending over twelve years by washing away my deed and making an excellent atonement (35). In this visit of the holy shrines which I have undertaken I shall go to *Pratilomâ* Saraswati" (36). Thereupon Rāma repaired to *Pratilomâ* Saraswati ; hear next the narration concerning the Pāndavas (37).

4

CHAPTER VII.

——oo——

THE BIRDS said :—Formerly in the Tretā age, there was a royal saint by name Harishchandra: that ruler of the earth was virtuous, renowned for good deeds and of a handsome person (1). During his rule there was no famine or disease or untimely death amongst men ; nor his citizens used to take delight in impious deeds (2). They were not proud of their riches, prowess and asceticism ; and no woman ever gave birth to children before she attained her youth (3). Once on a time it so happened, that as that mighty-armed one was engaged in pursuing a deer in the forest he heard the cries of "Save me" coming from a certain women (4). Then leaving the deer the king said "No fear; what wicked person is engaged in doing wrong during my regeme ?" (5). He (then) proceeded to the direction of cries: in the interval, the dreadful Deity of impediments, who puts in obstacles in the beginning of every thing, thought (6) : "Carrying on unequalled devout penances the highly powerful Viçwāmitra, observing a vow, is striving to acquire various learnings of Bhava and others never before acquired by any (7). They, being accomplished by the ascetic, endued with forgiveness, silence and self-control, and assailed by fear, are (now) crying. What should I do now ? (8). The foremost of Kouçikas is energetic and we are greatly weak: assailed with fear they are crying; this appears as incomprehensible to me (9). I have got here the king exclaiming for the moment, 'Do not fear.' Entering into his body I shall accomplish what I desire" (10). Thinking thus, the dreadful Deity of impediments possessed the king who wrathfully said (11);—"Who is this simple man who ties up the fire with the ends of his cloth, while I, the king, burning with strength and energy, am present here (12)? Who, to-day, pierced all over with shafts discharged from my bow, lighting up all quarters, shall enter into a long sleep"? (13) Thereupon hearing the words of the king, Viçwāmitra was enraged; and that foremost of Rishis having been exercised with anger, all those forms of learning immediately disappeared (14). Beholding all on a sudden the ascetic Viçwāmitra, the king, stricken with fear, began to tremble like a leaf of an *Açoka* tree (15). When the ascetic said "Stay! O wicked-minded man," the king, bowing down with humility, said (16). "O reverend Sir, this is my duty! O lord! there is no folly of mine. O ascetic, you should not be angry with me who have followed my own duties (17). A virtuous king should perform charities and protect (people); and in pursuance of scripture he should fight lifting up his bow" (18).

VISHWAMITRA said:—"Whom should you confer upon (a thing), whom should you protect and with whom should you fight, O king? Tell me this speedily, if you fear unrighteousness" (19). Harishchandra said:—"Gifts should be made to the foremost of Vipras and those whose business does not pay them; those that are afraid should be protected and robbers should always be fought with" (20). Viçwāmitra said:—"If, O king, you observe fully all the duties of a king, I appear before you as a Brāhmana desirous of begging something: give me my desired-for gift" (21). The birds said:—Hearing those words, the king, having his inner heart filled with delight, considered himself to have been born again and said to Kouçika (22). Harishchandra said:—"Tell me freely, O reverend Sir, what I shall have to give you; and even it be difficult to procure know it as already given to you, (23)—be it silver, gold, son, wife, body, life, kingdom, fortune or any other thing that you may like to have" (24). Viçwāmitra said:—"Consider, O king, what you have said as accepted by me. First give me the Dakshinā of the Rājashuya sacrifice," (25). The king said:—"I shall confer this Dakshinā upon you, O Brahman. Tell me, O foremost of the twice-born, what it is that I shall give you." Whereto Viçwāmitra replied:—"This earth with its seas, lands and cities, all your kingdom, O hero, consisting of cars, steeds and elephants, your treasury with all your wealth and whatever else of which you are the owner, except your wife, son and your own body, O sinless one, even your piety, O you conversant with all virtues, that follows one after his death—what is the use of speaking more—you give me all this" (26—29.)

THE BIRDS said:—Hearing the words of the Rishi, the king, without any change on his countenance and with a delighted heart, said "so be it" with joined hands (30).

VISHWAMITRA said:—"If, O royal saint, you have given away to me your kingdom, earth and forces who then is the king of them all, myself being engaged in austerities"? (31). Harishchandra said:—"From the time I have given over to you this earth with kingdom, you are the lord and king of the earth, O reverend Sir" (32). Viçwāmitra said:—"If you have conferred upon me, O king, the entire earth and if this be my property, then do you, leaving off all your ornaments, the thread round your waist and wearing bark, go out from this place with your wife and son" (33—34).

THE BIRDS said:—Saying 'so be it' the king addressed himself for departure along with his wife Saivyā and his son—a boy (35). As he was going away he (Viçwāmitra) obstructing his path said to the king—"Where do you go without giving me the Dakshinā of Rājashuya?" (36). Harishchandra said "O reverend Sir, I have conferred upon you this kingdom freed of all thorns and I have reserved to me, O Brahman, these three bodies of mine" (37). Viçwāmitra said:—"Still you should confer upon me the sacrificial Dakshinā; if what has been promised to the Brāhmanas in particular be not given every thing is destroyed (38). As long as the Brāhmanas are not satisfied in the Rājashuya sacrifice, O king, so long gifts of Râjashuya should be given (39). You had promised before that you would give what you promised, fight with the robbers and protect the distressed" (40). Harishchandra said :—"O reverend Sir, I have nothing at present but I shall give you in time; favour me, O Brâhmana saint, cherishing good feelings towards me" (41). Viçwâmitra said :—"How long shall I wait, O lord of men; tell me speedily or the fire of imprecation shall consume you" (42). Harischandra said :—"Within a month I shall confer upon you the Dakshinâ, O Brâhmana saint: at present I have nothing; you should permit me (therefore)" (43). Viçwâmitra said :— "Go! go! O foremost of men and satisfy your duties; may you fare well on the way and may not the robbers disturb you" (44).

THE BIRDS said :—Then permitted with saying 'go' that foremost of royal saints, the lord of the earth, having his mind possessed by wonderment, departed. His wife, unused to walking, followed him (45). Beholding that foremost of kings issue out of the city with his wife and son, the citizens following, began to lament (46);—"O lord, why do you leave us distressed and oppressed by others? O king, you have always acted piously and been kind to the citizens. If you observe virtue, O royal saint, take us (also with you) (47). Wait for a moment, O best of kings, we shall drink your lotus countenance with these black bees of eyes! When shall we see you again? (48). The wife, taking the boy son (with her) follows him, whom, when going before, the kings used to follow (49). The self-same Harishchandra, the foremost of kings, whose servants mounted on elephants used to precede him, is now going on foot (50). O king, how shall your beautiful face, having a fair nose and eye-brows, be sullied with dust on your way? (51). Wait! wait! O best of kings, satisfy your own duty; compassion is the best of virtues especially for the Kshatryas (52). Of what avail are the wives and the sons? What is the use of riches and corns?

Leaving all these we will follow you like your shadow (53). O lord ! O great king ! O master ! why do you renounce us? Wherever you will be we will go ; wherever you live there is our happiness ; wherever you reside there is our city—where the king is there is our heaven" (54). Hearing the bewailings of the citizens, the king, possessed by sorrow and having compassion, stopped on the way (55). Seeing him agitated by the words of the citizens and approaching there Viçwāmitra, having his eyes expanded with anger and indignation, said :—(56) "Fie on you ! who are wicked, speak false and utter untruths ; having given your kingdom to me you wish to take it back" (57). Thus addressed by him with harsh words he began to tremble and saying "I go" he speedily went away taking his wife by the hand (58). While his tender wife, exhausted with fatigue, was thus drawn, Viçwāmitra all on a sudden struck her with a chastising rod (59). Beholding her thus struck, Harishchandra, the lord of the earth, stricken with grief, said "I am going" and did not utter any thing else (60). Seeing Harishchandra, the lord of men, thus circumstanced, the five Viçwadevas, moved with pity, said :—(61) "To what region this greatly sinful Viçwāmitra attain by whom this one, the foremost of those performing sacrifices, has been deprived of his own kingdom ? (62). And drinking whose *Soma* sanctified by reverence and offered in great sacrifice with *Mantras* shall we attain to great delight ?" (63).

Hearing those their words, the son of Kuçika, filled with great anger, imprecated them, saying 'Do you all become human beings" (64). Being propitiated by them the great ascetic again said :—"Although born as men you will not get children nor wives, nor there will be ill-feeling for you. Being shorn of lust and anger you shall again become celestials" (65—66). Thereupon all those deities, with their own virtues, were incarnated in the house of the Kurus as the five sons of the Pāndavas sprung from the womb of Draupadi (67).

It is for this reason by the imprecation of the great ascetic the mighty car-warriors, the sons of the Pāndavas, did not obtain wives (68). Thus we have described to you every thing relating to the history of the sons of the Pāndavas and the four questions. What more do you wish to hear? (69).

CHAPTER VIII.

JAIMINI said:—"All this you have described to me in order of my questions. But I have a great curiosity as to the story of Harishchandra (1). Alas! a great misfortune befell that high-souled one, but did he, O foremost of the twice-born one, ever attain to felicity like before?" (2).

THE BIRDS said:—Hearing the words of Viçwāmitra, the poor king, accompanied by his wife Saivyā and the boy son, duly proceeded (3). He thought 'This city is above the enjoyment of human beings being created by the trident-handed deity (Siva)' (4), and then going to the celestial city Vārānashi (Benares) he stricken with grief proceeded on foot along with his obedient wife but at the entrance of the city he saw Viçwāmitra present (5). Seeing him present he bowed down with humility, then folding his hands Harishchandra said to the great ascetic (6). "This is my life! this is my son and this is my wife, O ascetic. Do you take one of these which you like best and require at present. You should also command me what else can we do for you?" (7—8).

VISHWAMITRA said:—"The month is complete, O royal saint; give me my Dakshinā relative to Rājashuya if you remember your own words" (9).

HARISHCHANDRA said :—O Brahman, O effulgent saint! to-day the month will be complete! Wait half a day more; you shall not have to wait long (10).

VISHWAMITRA said :—Let it be so, O great king, I come again. If you do not give me to-day I shall curse you. (11.)

THE BIRDS said :—Saying this the Brāhmana went away and the king thought :—" What Dakshinā shall I give him which I have promised? Where can I get substantial friends? (12). And where can I get wealth? If I do not redeem my promise I shall come by perdition? (13). Shall I give up my life? Where shall I go? If I meet with destruction by not giving what I had promised, I shall, being guilty of robbing a Brāhmana of his wealth, become a worm, the vilest of vile (14). It is better that selling myself I shall enter into servitude" (15). (Then) his wife, with words suppressed with grief, said to the poor and anxious king thinking with his head hanging down (16). "Give up thought, O great king, and satisfy your promise : a man, who has been driven out from the range of truth, should be shunned like a cremation-ground (17). They say there is no other duty greater for a man, than the satisfaction of one's own promise, O foremost of men (18). The perpetual maintenance of a sacred fire, the study of religious books, all the pious acts, charity and others become fruitless for him whose words are barren (19). Persons, versed in religious scriptures, hold that truth greatly leads to salvation whereas untruth brings down those who have not controlled their own selves (20). Having performed seven horse sacrifices you have celebrated the Rājashuya sacrifice. O king, for one single untruth should you be cast down from heaven? (21). O king! I have borne children." Saying this she began to weep. Then the king having his eyes filled with tears said (22).

HARISHCHANDRA said :—" Renounce your grief, O fair one! this boy waits here; speak out if you want to say anything more, O you endued with the gait of an elephant" (23). The wife said :—" O king, I have borne children ; the virtuous marry for having sons : therefore selling me for money, give the Dakshinā to the Brāhmana" (24.)

THE BIRDS said:—Hearing this the Lord of the earth swooned away: regaining his consciousness he bewailed piteously (25). " Mighty is my grief, O fair one, that you speak this to me, have I, a sinner as I am, forgotten your smiling conversation? (26). Alas! Alas! how could you speak this, O you of pure smiles? And how can I carry this word so hard to utter?" (27). Saying this that foremost of men again and again exclaimed, " Oh fie on me! fie on me!" and fell down on the earth, deprived of consciousness (28). Seeing Harishchandra, the king of the earth, lying down on earth, the queen, greatly stricken with grief, gave vent to these piteous accents (29). " Alas! O great king, what a circumstance, beyond conception, is present, since you, used to the coverlets of Ranku deer skin, are lying down on earth (30). The king, my husband, who conferred upon Brāhmanas ten million of precious kine, sleeps on the ground (31). Oh, what a great misery! O God! what did this king commit by you that he, resembling Indra or Upendra, has been reduced to this strait" (32). Having said this, that one of fair hips, assailed with the unbearable affliction of her husband, swooned away and fell down on earth (33). Seeing his parents thus lying down on earth, the boy, greatly assailed with hunger and sorrow, said (34). " Father, father, give me food! mother, mother, give me food! my hunger is growing powerful and the top of my tongue is dried up" (35).

THE BIRDS said:—In the interval Viçwāmitra of hard austerities came there. Seeing Harishchandra lying down on earth bereft of consciousness and washing him with water, he said to the king:—" Rise! Rise! O best of kings, give me my Dakshinā. The misery of a man who is in debt (always) multiplies" (36—37).

Having been washed by ice-cold water the king regained his consciousness; but seeing Viçwāmitra he again lost it and the ascetic was worked up with anger (38). Consoling the king that foremost of the twice-born said:—"If you wish to observe piety, give me that Dakshinā (39). By truth the sun gives its rays, in truth the earth exists; truth is spoken of as the great virtue and heaven (itself) is established in truth (40). A thousand horse-sacrifices and truth being weighed in the same balance, truth weighs heavier than thousand horse-sacrifices (41). What is the use of speaking these sweet words to you, who, although a powerful king, are now a dishonourable, vicious-designed, cunning and untruthful man? Hear this, what I speak candidly (42). If, O king, you do not give me my Dakshinā to-day, I shall forsooth imprecate a curse on you, on the sun going to the setting hill" (43). Saying this the Brāhmana went away and the king remained assailed with fear (thinking) "Reduced to such a degraded state, without any means and oppressed by the rich where shall I go?" (44). His wife again said: "Act up to my words. Burnt down by the fire of his imprecation, do not meet with death" (45). Urged on repeatedly by his wife the king said:—"I shall shorn of shame even sell you, O fair one (46). I shall do even what the heartless cannot, provided that I can utter such a word which it is so hard to speak out" (47). Having said this to his wife with his throat and eyes obstructed with tears and going to the city, the grief-stricken king said (48). "O ye citizens, hear ye all my words. Why do you ask me? I am a merciless one, not even a man (49). I am a veritable demon, hard-hearted or even viler than it, for I am ready to sell my beloved wife and not renounce my own life (50). If any one of you would require her as a maid-servant who is dearer than my life itself, let him speak out quickly before I put an end to my life" (51).

THE BIRDS said:—Thereupon advancing a little an aged

Brāhmana said to the king:—"Give me this maid-servant I shall buy her giving the price (52). I have profuse wealth and highly tender is my beloved wife; she cannot do the work of household, so you give her to me (53). Your wife is one of those that are active, young, fair, and good-natured: give me the woman and take this fair price" (54). Being addressed by the Brāhmana the mind of the king Harishchandra was sundered by grief and he could not speak any thing (55.) Then having tied fast the money with the corner of the king's bark the Brāhmana began to drag the queen holding her by the hair (56). Seeing his mother thus drawn the boy Rohitāswa, having locks on his head, began to cry pulling the cloth by his hands (57). The queen said;—"Leave me, leave me, till I have seen the child. O my boy, it will be very difficult for you to see me again (58). Behold, behold your mother, O boy, who have become a slave. But do not touch me, O prince, I am unworthy of being touched by you" (59). Then seeing all on a sudden his mother thus drawn, the boy, with eyes overflowing with tears, followed her crying "mother!" (60). The twice-born one in anger kicked him with foot who was then coming but still he kept up crying "mother" and did not let his mother go (61). The queen said:—"O master, show me this favour, do you also buy up this boy; although bought, I shall be of no use to you without him (62). Unfortunate as I am, be you kind to me. Link me with him as a cow is united with its calf" (63). The Brāhmana said:—"Take this money and give me your boy. Persons, conversant with scriptures, have settled the value of both a man and a woman at a hundred, a thousand, a ten thousand and a ten million coin" (64). Then tying the money in his cloth (the Brāhmana) took the boy along with his mother and bound them together (65). Seeing them, his wife and boy, thus taken away, the king, greatly stricken with grief, began to lament sighing hot again and again (66). "That my wife, whom even the wind, the sun and the moon or any man whatever did not see before, has now come by the condition of a slave (67). Descended from the solar race, this my boy, having tender fingers, has been sold. Oh! fie on me! Fie on my perverted sense! (68). Oh dear! O my child! through my unfair conduct, who am a dishonourable man it is, that you have come by this state under the influence of destiny; still I do not die; Oh! fie on me" (69). While the king was thus bewailing, the Brāhmana, taking those two, quickly disappeared in the midst of trees and houses (70). Immediately after Viçwāmitra came there to the king and asked for the money; and accordingly Harishchandra handed over to him the money (71). Finding the money that came from the sale of his wife, to be small, Kouçika, enraged, said to the king who was overwhelmed with sorrow (72). "O wretch of a Kshatrya, if you consider this to be fit for my sacrificial gift, then behold to-day the great strength of my hard austerities, unalloyed Brahma energy, terrific prowess and pure studies" (73—74). Harishchandra said:—"I shall confer upon you other gifts, O reverend Sir, tarry for a moment. At present I have nothing, I have sold my wife and son" (75). Viçwāmitra said, "O king, a fourth of the day remains; I shall wait till then, but you should not give any other reply" (76).

THE BIRDS continued:—Having thus addressed that best of kings with cruel and merciless words, the son of Kuçika, taking the money, speedily went away (77). Viçwāmitra having departed, the king, drowned in the middle of the oceans of fear and sorrow, determining every thing, cried aloud with his face bent downwards (78). "Let him, that would buy me as his slave for money, declare his intention speedily before the sun sets" (79). Then came there quickly the Deity of virtue under the guise of a Chandāla smelling bad, deformed, rough, bearded, large-toothed, of a dreadful look, black, with a huge abdomen, of twany dreadful eyes, harsh-speeched, carrying a number of birds, adorned with a garland of dead bodies, with a skull in hand, huge-faced, terrific, always speaking, surrounded by a pack of dogs, of a fearful look, with a rod in his hand and appearing to have no form (80—82). He said :—" I want you, tell me quickly how much do you want for your service, small or great, by which I may buy you up" (83). The birds said :—Beholding him in that form, of terrible looks, highly ruthless words and of dreadfully bad ways, the king asked: "who are you" (84). The Chandāla replied :— "I am a Chandāla, known in this most excellent city as Pravira—I am the executioner of those that are sentenced to death and take the blankets from the corpses" (85). Harishchandra said :—"I will not be a servant of a Chandāla so highly degraded. Rather I would be consumed by the fire of imprecation than be a slave of a Chandāla (86)". The birds said :—While he was thus giving out the great ascetic Viçwāmitra, his eyes rolling in anger and indignation, came there and said to the king :—(87). "This Chandāla has come here to give you plenty of money. Why do you not give me in full the sacrificial gift? (88). Harishchandra said :— "O reverend Sir, O son of Kuçika, I know me as descended from the solar race. Desirous of money, how can I enter into the service of a Chandāla ?" (89). Viçwāmitra replied :— " If you do not give me the Chandāla's money that you will get by selling yourself, forsooth shall I, when the time comes, imprecate a curse on you" (90).

THE BIRDS said :—Thereupon the king Harishchandra, bewildered by anxiety and sorrow, held the ascestic's feet saying " Favour me" (91). Harishchandra said :—" I shall be your slave, I am afflicted, I am affrighted ; I am particularly your devoted votary. Favour me, O Brāhmana saint; to serve a Chandāla is a misery (92). With all my wealth gone I shall serve you, performing every sort of work. O foremost of ascetics, I shall be your servant satisfying every desire of yours" (93). Viçwāmitra said :—" If you are my servant, I make you over to this Chandāla for the consideration of a hundred million coin" (94).

THE BIRDS said:—When he had said this the Swapāka,* delightedly giving the money to Viçwāmitra and finding the king who was greatly trembling on being beaten by the rod, whose senses were agitated, who was disconsolated, for being divorced from all that was dear to him and his friends, took him to his own house (95—96). Living in the house of the Chandāla, the king Harishchandra, every morning, noon and evening, sang (97). " Seeing her boy poorly before her, the damsel, seated with an woe-begone countenance, remembers me (thinking) 'the king shall liberate us both, by earning wealth and giving it profusely to the Brāhmana" (98). That one, having the eyes of a young deer, does not know that I have fallen into worse misfortune (99). Alas ! a series of misfortune has (befallen me)—the loss of kingdom, the renunciation of friends, the selling off of the wife and child and my coming by the state of a Chandāla"! (100) Thus living there, deprived of all and stricken with grief he used to remember daily his beloved son and his wife devoted to him (101). After a length of time, the king Harishchandra, brought under this (Chandāla's) control, was engaged in stripping the corpses of clothes at the cremation ground (102). He was instructed by the Chandāla, engaged in robbing the dead of clothes, 'Wait here day and night watching the arrival of dead bodies (103). For every corpse a sixth of the proceeds is to be given to the king, three are mine and two are your wages 104).' Thus advised he went to the house of the dead, then

---

* Man of a degraded or outcaste type, son of a Ugra woman by a Kshatriya father and classed with the Chandala with whom he is to live outside the town, to feed from broken vessels, to wear the clothes of the dead, to possess no other property than asses and dogs and to be excluded from all intercourse with other tribes. He can only be employed as a public executioner or in carrying the bodies of those who die without kindred.

situated to the south of Vārānashi (105)—to the cremation ground, filled with terrible sounds, a pack of jackals, scattered with the skulls of the corpses, giving out a detestable smell, filled with profuse smoke, abounding in malevolent spirits, ghosts, goblins, female imps and Yakshas, swarming with vultures and jackals, strewn with bones smelling horribly and filled with heart-rending cries of the relatives of the dead. "O son, O friend, O kinsman, O brother, O child, O my dear husband, O sister, O mother's father, O father, O grandson, O relative, where are you gone? Come here,' there a number of men were crying in this way; (105—110) there it was filled with the cracking sounds of burning flesh, fat and marrow; there half-burnt and darkened corpses, showing their rows of teeth, seemed to laugh in the midst of fires as if to say. 'This is the end of the body'; (111) there were heard the cracking sounds of flames accompanied by the cries of birds in the midst of the collection of bones, the bewailings of friends and the cheering sounds of the Pukkasas (Chandālas); and were heard the hideous songs of ghosts, goblins, malignant spirits and demons resembling the roars of the universal dissolution; there the collection of the dung of cows and buffaloes, surrounded by heaps of bones mixed with flames and diverse presents of garlands and lights (to the dead) and offerings to the crows, made the cremation ground, filled with various noises, resemble the hell (112—116). Filled with the loud cries of the ominous jackals of burning mouths and as well as with those of others living in caves, the fearful cremation ground, full of lamentations, seemed to strike terror even into the heart of Fear (117). The king, going there, filled with grief, began to mourn :—"O god, where are those servants, councillors, Brāhmanas and the kingdom gone? (118). O Saivyā, O my boy, forsaking me, who am wretched where have you gone through Viçwāmitra's imprecation?" (119). Thus did he think again and again by the Chandālas. Pale, with his body rough all over, with (profuse) hair, smelling (bad) with a braid of hair as well as a staff, looking like the very destroyers he rushed about crying, " Here is the corpse, this is the price that I have received. This is mine. This is the king's. This is the ignorant Chandāla's." Thus going about hither and thither, the king seemed to have undergone a change of existence (20—22). He was clad in blanket made of rags stitched together; his face, arms and chest were covered with the ashes of the funeral pyres; and his fingers were besmeared with fat, marrow and ashes. Sighing he lived upon the food offered to the numberless dead and was contented therewith (122—124). He adorned his head with their garlands. He did not sleep in the night or in the day but always cried " Alas! Alas!" (125). Thus did the twelve months appear like a hundred years. Once on a time that foremost of kings, separated from his friends and having a rough body, was fatigued and possessed by sleep. He slept motionless. Sleeping there he saw a highly wonderful dream in consequence of his habit of living in a cremation ground or through the influence of powerful destiny. Having conferred on his preceptor his Dakshinā in another body and undergone miseries extending over twelve years he has been liberated. He saw himself born of the womb of a *Pukkashi* (a female Chandāla). Remaining there the king thought " Having come out of it I shall practise virtues and charities" (126—130). Afterwards when he was born as the son of a Pukkasa he was always engaged in the performance of purifactory rites of the dead in the cremation ground (131). When he became seven years old he saw the dead dody of a poor but accomplished Brāhmana brought to the cremation ground by his friends (132). Being chastised by him demanding the fee, the Brāhmanas said:— " This is Viçwāmitra's action (133). Do this unrighteous act, O sinful wretch. Formerly the king Harishchandra, you, having your piety destroyed by your not giving to a Brāhmana what you promised, have been reduced to a Pukkasa by Viçwāmitra (134)." Because he did not show them any consideration he was imprecated by them in anger "O wretch of a man, go you immediately to a dreadfull hell (135)." As soon as this had been said the dreaming king beheld the messengers of Yama with nooses in their hands (136). He then saw himself carried forcibly by them. Greatly pained he exclaimed "O father, O mother? Where are you to-day?" (137). As soon as he said this, he was thrown into a hell of boiling oil (138). Severed with a saw, sharp as a razor on the lower part of his body, he, tormented, began to feed on pus and blood in darkness (139). Born as a Pukkasa, in the seventh year, he found himself, when dead, burnt and boiled every day in hell (140). Here was he depressed and there penitent and elsewhere beaten and tortured; plunged in waters and burnt and assailed by severe cold and winds (141). In the hell one day appeared like a hundred years. Then from the guards in the hell he heard that a hundred years had passed away (142). Then he was thrown on earth and was born as a dog living on excretion. Feeding on refuses, he assailed by cold, died within a month (143). He then saw himself in the body of an ass, an elephant, a monkey, a beast, a goat, a cat, a heron, a cow, a ram, a bird, a worm, a fish, a tortoise, a boar, a deer, a cock, a male parrot, a female parrot, a serpent and other immobile objects. Daily born in the species of various creatures and assailed by sorrow, he considered a day to be a hundred years (144—146). After hundred years had passed away in his being born as those cursed animals, the king saw himself one day in his own race. (147). While he was living there he was deprived of his kingdom through gambling; then losing wife and son he alone went to woods (148). He saw there a dreadful lion with his mouth wide open coming forward along with a Sarabha* to devour him (149). Devoured

* A gigantic fabulous animal with eight legs.

by him he lamented for his wife (crying) "O Saivyā ! where do you go now leaving me here in danger (?)" Again he saw his wife along with his son (crying) "Save us, O Harishchandra, no more with gambling (150—151). Your son, with your wife Saivyā, has been reduced to a miserable plight—" He ran about hither and thither but could not see them (152). Then stationed in the sky the king again saw her, distressed and naked with dishevelled hair, carried away forcibly and exclaiming "Alas ! alas ! save me." He then saw some persons stationed in the sky at the command of the king of righteousness exclaiming "Come, O king, Yama has been commanded for you by Viçwāmitra" (153—155). Having been thus accosted the king was forcibly carried away with a noose of serpents being informed that this was the doing of Viçwāmitra (156). Still no pious thoughts did arise in his mind. All these miseries, which he had seen in dream, he suffered for twelve years. After the expiry of twelve years he was taken away by the emissaries (of Yama) (157—158). He saw there Yama in his own form who said to the lord of men. "This is the irrepressible wrath of the high-souled Viçwāmitra (159). Kauçika will even bring about the death of your son. Go you to the world of men and go through the remaining sufferings. Going there, O king, you shall meet with your well-being (160). After the expiration of the twelfth year there will be an end of your miseries, O king." Then pushed by Yama's emissaries he fell down from the sky (161). Then dropping down from the region of Yama he awoke from an excess of terror and thought—"Alas ! what a misery, it is sprinkling salt over a sore (162). In a dream I have seen a great misery, the end of which I do not get at ; but have twelve years passed away while I was seeing this in dream"—in great fear he asked the Pukkasas who were waiting there. Of them some said 'no' others 'yes' (163—164). Hearing this, the king, stricken with grief, sought refuge with the gods, saying "O deities, grant me, Savyā and my boy, good fortune (165). Salutation unto the Great Dharma, salutation unto Krishna, the Disposer, salutation unto the Prime of prime, the holy, the ancient and undecaying (166). Salutation unto thee, O Vrihaspati and unto Vāsava." Having said this the king engaged in the work of a Pukkasa and the settlement of funeral fees, like one who had lost recollection of all things. The king became dirty and dusky : his hairs became matted, he had a staff and his senses were bewildered (167—168). Then neither his son nor his wife came within the range of recollection ; and dispirited on account of his having lost his kingdom he lived in the cremation ground (169). One day taking her own dead son, bitten by a serpent, came there bewailing the wife of that king (170). She repeatedly exclaimed :—" O my son ! O my child !" She was lean, discoloured, absent-minded and had her hairs covered with ashes (171). The king's wife said :—" See, O king, to-day, a moon on earth, your son, whom you saw before playing, bitten by a mighty serpent and dead (172)." Hearing her lamentations, the king, thinking " I shall get the blanket of the dead" speedily went there (173). The king could not recognise his bewailing wife stricken with sorrow consequent upon living long in a foreign country and seeming to have been born again (174). And the princess too could not recognise the king formerly wearing beautiful ringlets but now with matted locks looking like a withered tree (175). Beholding that boy beaten by a deadly serpent covered in black and endued with the marks of royalty the king thought :—" Oh what misfortune ! born in the race of what king, this infant has been reduced to such a condition by the wicked-minded Destroyer (176—177). Seeing this boy lying on the lap of his mother I remember my boy the lotus-eyed Rohitāshwa (178). If he had not been brought to its control by the Dreadful Death he must have also come at this age" (879). The queen said :—"O my boy, by the malignant desire of what sinful man, this dreadful misfortune has overtaken us the end of which I do not get at? (180). O lord, O king, without solacing me who am assailed by grief how and where do you remain in security? (181). O Destiny, what have you not done to the royal saint, Harishchandra, the destruction of kingdom, the renunciation of friends and the selling off of the wife and son" (182). Hearing those her words the king, recognising his beloved wife and dead son, dropped down from his place (183). "Oh! painful! this is Saivyā, this is my boy" cried he; thus stricken with grief he wept and swooned away (184). Recognising him and seeing him in that plight she fell into a trance, and stricken with grief dropped down on earth motionless (185). Then regaining consciousness both the king and the queen began to lament, being greatly stricken with sorrow and laden with the weight of sorrow (186). The king said:—"Oh my boy, seeing your pale face, tender and having beautiful eyes, eye-brows and a nose why does not my heart rend? (187). Clasping whom, coming of himself to me with sweet "Papa! Papa!" shall I call "O my child!" out of love? (188). With the twany dust of whose thighs shall my scarf, lap and limbs be covered? (189) Descended from my loins, you, the delight of my mind and heart, were sold like a chattel, O my child, by this worthless father of yours? (190). Having robbed me of my vast territories, possessions and wealth, the ruthless serpent of destiny has bitten my child (191). Casting my looks upon the lotus face of my son bitten by the serpent of Destiny I have been blinded by the dreadful venom" (192). Having said this he, with his voice choked with the vapour of grief, embraced his son, swooned away and dropped down motionless (193).

THE QUEEN said:—"Forsooth, from his voice he appears to be that best of men Harishchandra, the moon of the minds of the learned (194). Like his nose it is high and curved downward at the top. Like those of the illustrious high-souled one his teeth resemble the buds (195). But why has that lord of men come to the cremation ground?" Then casting off the grief consequent upon the death of his son she looked upon her fallen husband (196). The exalted (queen), pale, filled with surprise and assailed by the grief of her son and husband, casting her looks, saw the hateful rod of her husband (197). (Crying out) "I am *Swapaka*" that one of expansive eyes fell into a swoon. And regaining consciousness within a short time she said with a heavy voice (198). "Fie on you, O Destiny, who are greatly hard, hateful and devoid of dignity, by whom this king, resembling an immortal, has been reduced to the state of a *Swapaka* (199). Having brought about the destruction of his kingdom, the renunciation of friends, the sale of wife and son, you have not released him; this king has been made a Chandāla (200). Why do you not, raising me from the earth who am burning in grief, say, O king, 'get upon this bed!' (201). I do not see to-day your umbrella or your *Bhringâra** or chowrie or fan. What is the change brought about by Destiny (202). That best of kings, before whom, formerly while going out, the kings used to do the work of menials and make the earth freed from dust with their scarps, that one, under the influence of misfortune, is now living in the cremation-ground filled with earthen water-pots and vessels coming in contact with human skulls, dreadful with profuse hairs sticking to the threads of the wreaths of the dead, covered with greese and dry faggots, terrific with a mixture of ashes, charcoal, half-burnt bones, and marrow; from which small birds, terrified by vultures and jackals, have fled away; darkened all over by the flames of the funeral phyres; and where the night-rangers are brimful with delight by eating the flesh" (203—207). Having said this and clapsed the neck of the kings the princess, the object of numberless miseries and afflictions, began to lament in piteous accents (208).

---

* A golden vessel used on the occasion of royal ceremonials.

THE QUEEN said :—"O king, is this a dream or a reality; tell me what you think, O great one; my mind is stupified (209). If this be so, O you conversant with morality, virtue is of no avail; and there is no merit in worshipping the Brāhmanas, the deities and in protecting the earth (210). There is then no truth, sincerity or kindness, since you, so pious, have been deprived of your kingdom" (211). Hearing her words, heavy and accompanied by hot sighs (he) described to that damsel of slender make how he had become a *Swapaka* (212). Weeping long, sighing hot, that timid lady, stricken with grief, described duly to him the death of her son (213).

THE KING said :—"O dear, I do not like to undergo this misery for a long time. O slender-made lady, behold my misfortune that I am not (even) a master of own self (214). If without obtaining permission from the Chandāla I enter into fire, I shall, in another birth, become the slave of one (such) (215)). Or I shall fall into a hell as an insect feeding on earth-worms; or I shall fall into *Vaitarini* filled with profuse pus, fat, blood and muscle (216). Or going to a forest of sword-blades I shall be sorely cut; or going to *Raurava* or *Mahâ Raurava* I shall suffer misery (217). If a man is drowned in a sea of miseries he can come to an end by giving up his life. The only boy, a son on whom depended the perpetuation of the race, even he is drowned by the powerful tide of destiny. A wretched slave as I am, how can I relinquish my life? (218—219). But a distressed and troubled person does not care for sin. Not even in being born as a beast, nor in the forest of sword blades or in *Vaitarini* is that misery which comes from the loss of a son (220). O slender-made lady, I shall throw myself into the fire blazing with the body of my son; you should pardon me for this iniquity (221). Permitted by me, go you to the house of the Brāhmana, O you of fair smiles, and consider my words with a concentrated mind (222). If I have practised charities, if I have performed sacrifies, if I have pleased my spiritual guide, I shall again, in another world, be united with you and my son (223). What is the possibility of my object being secured in this world? I should therefore, with you, wend the way of my son (224). If, O you of fair smiles, I have said anything indecent in private (even) by way of jest, you should pardon me, who am begging (225). Out of haughtiness that you are a queen, you should not disregard the twice born one; but O fair one, you should please him even like a husband or a deity" (226). The queen said :—" O royal saint, even this very day I shall enter into this burning fire with the load of grief in your company" (227).

THE BIRDS said :—Then making a funeral phyre and placing his son thereon, the king, with his wife, began to meditate upon the supreme spirit, the Lord Nārāyana, Hari, living in the cave of heart, Vāsudeva, the lord of the celestials, without beginning and end, Brahmā, or the holy deity clad in yellow raiment (Krishna) (228—229). While he was thus thinking, all the deities with Vāsava, taking Dharma before them, came there speedily (230). They, all coming there, said :—" Hear, hear, O king, O lord, here is the grand-father (Brahmā), here is the reverend Dharma and these are the *Sâdhyas*, the *Vishwas*, the Maruts, and the Lokapālas with their respective conveyances, Nāgās, *Siddhas*, with the *Gandharvas*, Rudras, as well as *Aswinis*; these and others as well as Viçwāmitra, of whom the three worlds could not make a friend, are anxious, for their behoof, to have you as their friend." Then Sakra, Dharma and Gadhi's son came before him (231—234). Dharma said :—" Be not rash, O king; I am Dharma who have come to you having been pleased with your qualities of forgiveness, self-control, truthfulness and others" (235). Indra said :—"O great Harishchandra, I am Sakra and have come to you. You have along with your wife and son gained the eternal region (236). Go to the celestial region, O king, accompanied by your wife and son which is hard to be got at by other people but you have acquired it by your acts" (237).

THE BIRDS said:—The Lord Indra, who had come there, at the funeral phyre, created a nectarine shower from the sky capable of destroying violent deaths (238). He caused a great shower of blossoms and huge celestial drums to be sounded. Then in that assembly of celestials, assembled in parties, the son of the high-souled king rose up, with a tender body, healthy and with sprightly senses and mien (239—240). Then immediately embracing his son, the king Harishchandra, along with his wife, was covered with grace and adorned with celestial garlands and raiments (241). He then became comforted with his mind entirely filled with great felicity. Immediately Indra again said (242): "You shall with your wife and son attain to great bliss. O great one, rise up in consequence of your own acts" (243). Harishchandra said:—"O king of the celestials, without being permitted by my master *Swapaka* and obtaining a release from him I cannot go to the region of the celestials" (244). Dharma said:—Coming to know of your future sufferings by my own power I had brought myself to the state of a *Swapaka* and displayed that fickleness (245). Indra said:—"Harishchandra, ascend the region of the pious men, the most exalted station, which all men on earth seek (246). Harishchandra said:—Salutation unto you, O lord of the celestials, hear these my words, which favoured by you, I shall speak to you with a delighted countenance on account of your having been pleased (247). People are living in the city of Koçala with their minds sunk in my grief. Leaving them (behind) now can I go to the celestial region? (248). The renunciation of a devoted follower is equally as mighty a sin as that of the destruction of a Brāhmana, a preceptor, a cow and a woman (249). There is no happiness, either here or hereafter for him who renounces a devoted and innocent follower. Therefore, O Sakra, go you to heaven (250). If, O lord of the celestials, they go to heaven with me, I shall go there or I shall go to hell along with them (251). Indra said:—"Various and diversified are their virtues and iniquities. How can you go to heaven along with so many?", (252). Harishchandra said:—O Sakra, it is through the energy of his dependents that a king enjoys his kingdom and celebrates great sacrifices and Purtta acts * (253). I shall never forsake them through the desire of getting heaven, them, my benefactors, by whose help I have performed everything (254). O lord of the celestials, let whatever small merit, therefore, I may have acquired by gifts, performance of sacrifices and recitation of religious formulæ, be in common with them (255). And through your favour let me, with them, in one day, enjoy the fruit of my acts which is to last for a long time (256).

THE BIRDS said:—Then saying "so it shall be" Sakra, the king of the three worlds, with a delighted heart, Dharma, and Gādhi's son, Viçwāmitra came down from heaven to earth abounding in million of cars and said to the people of Ayodhyā, "Do you come up to heaven" (257—258). Hearing Indra's words and pleased with the king, Viçwāmitra, of hard austerities, brought Rohitāshwa and sprinkled the prince in the charming city of Ayodhyā. And the celestials, with the ascetics and Siddhas sprinkled that lord of men (259—260). Then in the company of the king, all those fat and contented people, together with their wives and sons, went to the celestial region (261). And men began to move from one car to another with an accession of delight. The king Harishchandra, the lord of men, (going to heaven) in a car, obtained immense wealth and lived in a city fortified by walls and battlements (262—263). Seeing his prosperity, the great preceptor Ushanā, versed in all branches of learning, hymned the following verses (264),

* Acts of pious liberality such as digging a well or tank.

SUKRA said :—There has never been, nor will be, a king like Harishchandra. Whoever, assailed by grief, listens to it, shall attain to great felicity (265). One, aspiring after heaven, obtains heaven ; one, desirous of children, obtains children ; one, desirous of a wife, gets wife ; and one, longing for kingdom, gets kingdom (266). Oh the force of patience, Oh the mighty result of charity, for Harishchandra has attained heaven and the dignity of Indra (267).

THE BIRDS said ;—We have thus described to you in detail all the actions of Harishchandra ; hear the remaining, O leading ascetics (268) ; the disturbance of the Rājashuya sacrifice, which led to the destruction of the earth as well as the great battle between Ari and (the heron) that originated from that disturbance (269).

CHAPTER IX.

THE BIRDS said :—On Harishchandra having been deprived of his kingdom and gone to the region of the celestials, his highly effulgent priest come out of his watery habitation, on the expiration of the twelve years which he spent on the Ganges. The ascetic Vashistha learnt everything about the work of Viçwāmitra, the misfortune of the liberal king Harishchandra, his being reduced to the condition of a Chandāla and the sale of his wife and son (1—3). Hearing this, that energetic and great one, who was delighted with the king, became offended with the ascetic Vçiwāmitra (4). Vishistha said :—My hundred sons were destroyed by Viçwāmitra ; even in that I was not offended so much as I have been to-day, hearing that this high-souled and greatly meritorious king, given to the adoration of the deities and the Brāhmanas, has been deprived of his kingdom (5—6). As the truthful and the self-controlled king, having no ill-will even towards his enemies, meaning no harm, virtuous-souled, careful, and our support, has been reduced to this state along with his wife, servants and son, and has been deprived of his kingdom and subjected to various miseries, that vicious-souled hater of a Brāhmana, that one, foolish and shorn of wisdom, imprecated by me, shall become a heron (7—9). The birds said :—Hearing of the imprecation, the highly energetic Viçwāmitra, the son of Kuçika, cursed him in return saying " Be you an *Ari*" (10.). And in accordance with each other's curse, both Vashistha and the highly energetic Viçwāmitra, the son of Kuçika, although endowed with great effulgence, came by inferior births (11). Although born in other species they both of incomparable energy and endued with mighty strength and prowess, being greatly enraged, fought with each other (12). O Brāhmana, the *Ari* was two thousand *Yojanas* high and the heron was three thousand and ninety-six *Yojanas* high (13). Endued with great strength, they, srtiking each other with their wings, created exceeding fear of creatures (14). Shaking his wings, the heron, with reddened eyes, struck *Ari* and the latter too, uplifting its neck, attacked the heron with its legs (15). Dashed with the wind of their wings, the mountain dropped down on earth, and assailed by the downfall of the mountain the earth shook (16). The earth shaking, the ocean, overleaping its bounds, flooded the earth; and sinking on one side the earth was going to seek the nether region (17). Some by the fall of the mountain, some with the waters of the ocean, and some with the shaking of the earth, all creatures met with destruction (18). All greatly agitated and deprived of their consciousness began to exclaim *Oh* and *Alas*. The universe was greatly agitated and the terrestrial round was all confused (9). " Oh child! O husband! O infant! Fly. I am in this plight. O my dear, O my husband, the mountain falls down. Do ye fly at once." Thus did the creatures, overwhelmed with fear, cry at that time. Then came the Grandfather (Brahmā) encircled by all the celestials (20—21). The Lord of the Universe addressed them both who were greatly worked up with anger ;—" Do you both desist from fight and let the creatures get respite" (22). Although hearing the words of self-sprung Brahmā, they, possessed by anger and spite, fought on and did not desist (23). Thereat beholding the destruction of creatures the Deity, the Grandfather, wishing the well-being of them both, romoved their beast-hood (23). Those two best of ascetics, Kauçika and Vashistha, regaining their former forms on the destruction of the condition pervaded by ignorance, the Deity Brahmā said :—(25). "My child Vashistha, O you foremost of the Kouçikas, desist trom this conflict having its origin from the quality of ignorance (26). This conflict of yours obstructs the Rājashuya of king Harishchandra and brings destruction of earth (27). Nor has this foremost of Kouçikas committed any wrong to the king; but (on the other hand) being instrumental to his attainment of heaven proved a benefactor to him (28). Having come under the control of anger you have been the agents in obstructing asceticism. May good betide you, cast it off. Brahman is highly powerful" (29). Being thus addressed by him both of them were ashamed; embracing each other affectionately they forgave each other (30). Thereupon worshipped by the celestials Brahmā repaired to his own region. Vashistha wended his way to his own habitation and Kouçika to his own hermitage (31). This conflict between *Ari* and heron and the story of Harishchandra, as soon as heard, become free from sin those mortals who hear as well as those who narrate; nor any impediments fall in the way of their action.

CHAPTER X.

——oo——

JAIMINI said :—O eminent twice-born ones, do you remove my doubt, who ask you regarding the birth and death of creatures obtaining (in this world) (1) Why is a creature born, why does it grow up, why with its body assailed by sufferings does it live in the womb? (2) Why coming out of the womb does it attain growth? And why at the time of death is it deprived of consciousness? (3) Verily does a man while dying reap the fruit of both his good and bad actions? How does an act produce its fruit? (4) Why in the womb of a female, where is digested the food which is hard of digestion, is not a small lump of flesh digested? (5) Do you explain to me all this so that all my doubts may be removed. This is a great mystery wherein all creatures are stupified (6).

THE BIRDS said :—The question, that you have put to us, is a difficult one, though of very great interest; referring to the existence or otherwise of all creatures it is not within the range of easy comprehension (7). O great one, hear, what formerly a highly virtuous son, by name Sumati said to his father (8) A certain high-minded Brāhmana, born in the race of Bhrigu, said to his gentle son Sumati, resembling one void of sense at the time of his investiture with sacred thread (9). "Study the Vedas, O Sumati, in due order being intent upon serving your preceptor and depending upon alms (10). Then entering the life of a house-holder do you celebrate excellent sacrifices and beget desirable offspring and then enter into woods (11). When you shall live in the forest, O child, and leaving the company of your wife, lead the life of a mendicant, you will attain to that *Brahman*, approaching whom no one grieves (12)." The birds said :—Although accosted thus in many ways (the son) could not say anything on account of his decrepitude ; but the father, out of affection addressed him again and again on many topics (13). Being thus urged on by his father out of parental affection with nectarine words, he, smiling, said:—(14) "O father, all that you advise me to study has been exhaustively read by me together with various other branches of learning and diverse mechanical arts (15). Ten thousand births more come to my recollection. I was conversant with happiness and misery and was engaged in destruction, progress and prosperity (16). I had union with enemies, friends, and wives, as well as separation from them. I saw many a mother as well as many a father (17). I experienced thousands of miseries and happiness. I had a great many friends and different kinds of father (18). I lived in a female womb sullied by urine and excreta and I suffered from severe diseases and ailments in thousands (19). I suffered numberless miseries in the womb in infancy and youth and in old age ; all these I now recollect (20). I was born as a Brāhmana, a Kshatriya, a Vaisya and a Sudra and again as a beast, a worm, a deer and a bird (21). I was born in the houses of the royal retainers and war-like kings, as I have been born in your house (22). I became servants and slaves of many men and I came by mastery, lordship, and poverty (23). I slew many and in turn was slain and struck down by them. My wealth was given away by many to others and I also gave away much (24). I was always pleased by fathers, mothers, friends, brothers and wives ; and when I became poor I bathed my countenance with tears (25). Thus revolving on the perilous wheel of the world, I have attained to this knowledge, O father, which is instrumental to the attainment of liberation (26). Acquiring this knowledge all the actions sanctioned by *Rik, Yajus* and *Sâma* appear to me as shorn of any virtue and inadequate (27). Therefore of what use are the *Vedas* to me who have acquired understanding, have been satiated with the wisdom of the preceptor, am devoid or exertion and am fond of the soul? (28). I shall attain that most excellent Brahma state which is shorn of the six kinds of action, misery, happiness, delight, sentiment, and attributes (29). Therefore I shall go, O father, renouncing the collection of evils, as is well-known, originating from sentiment, joy, fear, anxiety, anger, spite, decrepitude, and casting off the three Vedas which are like the Kimpāka fruit and lead to demerit (30—31)."

THE BIRDS said:—Hearing his words, the great father with delighted heart said to his own son, being filled with joy and wonder (32):—"What is it that you say, O my son? Whence has this your knowledge come? By what your previous dullness been changed into wisdom? (33). Is it that on the wane of the curse of an ascetic or a deity, your knowledge that was once lost to you has come back? (34). I wish to hear all this; great is my curiosity. Tell me O my child, all that you did formerly" (35). The son replied:—"Hear, O father, my history, the origin of happiness and misery as to what I was in another birth and what took place thereafter (36). I was formerly a Brāhmana having my soul consigned to the Supreme Spirit; I acquired eminence in discussion relating to self-knowledge (37). Being always engaged in Yoga in that birth, I, from practising integrity of conduct, companionship of the pious, from passing a righteous course, from reforming the ordinances, attained great delight and acquired the position of a preceptor being eminently fitted to remove the doubts of the disciples (38—39). Thereupon after a long time I attained highest concentration. But the tranquility of mind being disturbed through ignorance, I, by my carelessness, fell into peril (40). But till the time of my death my memory did not fail me; and I remember all the days of my life which I have told (41). By virtue of my previous practice, O father I shall, controlling my senses, so endeavour to work that the same thing might not befall me again (42). This my recollection of the previous births which is the fruit of knowledge and gift, is not acquired by men engaged in duties laid down by the three Vedas (43). Resorting to the virtue of intense, whole-minded concentration, acquired in previous birth I shall exert myself for acquiring emancipation (44). Tell me therefore, O great one, the doubts which exist in your mind. Encompassing your pleasure on this head I shall be freed from the debts that I owe you" (45). The birds said:—Reverencing his words, the father asked the son of the same thing that you have enquired of me—the birth and death of creatures (46). The son said:—Hear, O father, a true account of what I have experienced again and again. This wheel of an world is undecaying, still it has no existence (47). Commanded by you, O father, I shall communicate to you all from the time coming out, which no one else can speak (48). In this body, the bile,* growing angry, being fanned by a strong wind and flaming, although nearly no fuel, pierces the (very) vitals (49). Then the wind named *Udâna*† moves over it and obstructs the passage of the meat and drink taken (50). Only those persons, that have given away food and drink to others, enjoy comfort at that precious moment (51). He, who has given away food with a meat purified by reverence, obtains satisfaction even without food (52). He who has never uttered a falsehood, he who has not made a distinction of love, he who believes in God and who is reverential, meets with happy death (52). Those who are intent upon adoring the deities and Brâhmanas, who are free from spite, who are pure in spirit, are liberal and bashful, meet with easy death (54). He who does not forsake virtue through lust, anger or spite, he who keeps his promise and is gentle, meets with easy death (55). But he who

---

* Air, bile and phlegms are according to the Hindu system the essential ingredients of a human body.

† These are the five vital breaths in the body—namely Prana, Apana Samana, Udana and Vyana.

does not give water to one who is thirsty, food to one who is hungry, are assailed by them when death presents itself (56). Those who give fuel conquer cold, those who give sandal conquer heat; but those, who afflict people, come by a dreaful pain destroying (the very) life (57). Those worst of men, who cause ignorance and stupefaction, attain great fear and are crushed by fierce pangs (58). Those, that give false evidence, or speak false, or satisfy the orders of a wicked man, or disregard the Vedas, die in ignorance (59). The dreadful and vicious-souled followers of Yama, breathing hellish smell around, with nooses and maces in hands; approach them (60). And when they come within the range of their vision they all tremble and continually bewail for their brothers, mothers and sons" (61). Then their speech becomes indistinct, O father, and is composed of one letter; their eyes roll and their faces are dried up with fear and sighs (62). Then with breath running high, sight dimmed and assailed by pain he renounces his body (63). Then going before the body, for undergoing affliction consequent upon his acts he assumes another body not sprung from a father or a mother but which has the same age, condition and habitation as assigned to the other body (64). Then the emissaries of Yama quikly bind him with dreadful nooses and drag him to the south, trembling with the stroke of the rod (65). Then he is dragged by the emissaries of Yama sending out dreadful, inauspicious yells through grounds rough with Kusa, thorns, ant-hills, pins and stones, glowing with flames at places, covered with pits, blazing with the heat of the sun and burning with its rays—(66—67). Dragged by the dreadful (emissaries) and eaten by hundreds of jackals, the sinful person goes to Yama's house through a fearful passage (68). But those, who have distributed umbrellas and shoes, those who have given away cloth, and as well as those who have given away food, go easily by that way (69). Going through such sufferings, losing all control over self and assailed by sin a man is taken, on the twelfth day, to the city of Dharma (70). When his body is burnt he experiences a great burning sensation ; and when his body is beaten or cut he feels a great pain (71). His body being thus destroyed, a creature, although walking into another body, suffers eternal misery on account of his own adverse actions (72). Going there he feeds on the sesame and water or the ball of boiled rice offered by his descendants (73). A person receives comforts from his relations rubbing their bodies with oil, from their kneading their limbs and from their taking their food (74). He enjoys rest by his relations lying down on the ground. A dead man is pleased with his relations by his performance of charitable works (75). Taken to his own home on the twelfth day he sees it and feeds on the *Pinda* and water that are offered on the earth (76). After the twelfth day, being drawn, a man beholds the dreadful and terrible-looking iron city of Yama (77). As soon as he enters there he beholds Yama in the midst of the Destroyer, Death and others having blood-red eyes, and resembling a mass of crushed collyrium, with face with dreadful teeth, and a dreadful frowning countenance ;—the lord, encircled by hundreds of distempers having disfigured and dreadful visages, carrying his rod, mighty-armed, with the noose in his hand and highly fearful to look at. A creature attains to a state, good or bad, assigned by him (78—80). One giving false evidence or uttering falsehood goes to Raurava. Hear now, I will give what is the true description of Raurava (81). It measures two thousand *Yoyanas*. There is a pit which is knee-deep and difficult of being crossed (82). Levelled with heaps of flaming charcoal it is heated by a piece of land burning dreadfully with coal (83). Into it the followers of Yama throw the perpetrator of impious deeds. And burnt by the dreadful fire he runs about (84). His feet get torn and injured at every step and within a day and night he can but once take away his feet (85). When he thus goes over a thousand Yoyanas he is let alone. Then to have his sins washed off he is taken to another such hell (86). After having gone through all the hells the sinner takes upon a beastly life. Then going through the lives of worms, insects, and flies, beasts of prey, knats, elephants, trees, horses, cows, and through diverse other sinful and miserable lives, he, coming to the race of men, is born as a hunch-back, or an ugly person or a dwarf or a Chandāla Pukkasa (87—89). Then carrying the remnant of his virtue and vice he goes up gradually to the higher caste, Sudras, Vaishyas, Kshatriyas, Brāhmanas, and the sate of the king of gods; sometimes perpetrating iniquites he falls into the hell beneath (90—91). Hear, I shall now describe, how virtuous people proceed. These persons follow the pious course laid down by Yama (92). With Gandharvas singing, Apsaras dancing, wearing many a beautiful and shining garlands they proceed in excellent cars embellished with chains, bangles and other beautiful ornaments (93). Coming down therefore they are born in the families of other high-souled kings and protect people engaged in noble works (94). After having enjoyed all the best things of life they go upward; but if they go down they fare as before (95). I have thus described to you all about the sufferings of creatures. Hear now, O Brāhmana saint, how embryos are created (96).

—:o:—

CHAPTER XI.

THE SON said :—As soon as the male seed is mixed with female blood one, released from heaven or hell, enters into it (1). O father, the two kinds of seed being influenced by him he attains stability. He then grows into protoplasm, next into a bubble and then into a lump of flesh (2). The germ that grows up in the lumps of flesh is called Ankura and then are gradually produced the five limbs (3). Then the minor limbs, fingers, eyes, nose, face, and ears are developed from (principal) limbs and from them the nails, &c. (4). Then hairs grow on the skin and then those on the head. Thus does the embryo grow up along with the uterns (5). As a cocoanut fruit grows along with its case so does this increase along with its case, with is face bent downwards (6). It grows keeping its hands downwards to its thighs and sides; the thumbs are placed on the thighs and the other fingers before them (7). The eyes are behind the thighs and the nose is within the thighs. The hips are between the two heels; the arms and legs remain outside (8). Thus a creature, lying in the womb of a female, grows up gradually; the embroys of other creatures lie in the womb according to their forms (9). It gets hardened by fire and lives by what is eaten and drunk; the embryo exists in the womb depending upon virtue and vice (10). The entrail called *Apyayani* fixed to its navel is attached to the entrail of the female and it grows there (11). Having its body nourished while in the womb, by the food and drink a creature gradually grows up (12). It then gets the recollection of its many births and then pushed hither and thither it comes to entertain a distaste (for such a state) (13). Having been released from the womb— "I shall never do it again—I shall so strive that I shall not have to enter into the womb any more"—thus does it think remembering a hundred miseries of births originating from destiny which he had experienced before (14—15). Then in the course of time, the creature, with its face bent downwards, turns itself and is then born in the ninth or the tenth month (16). And coming out it is assailed by the *Prajapatya* wind and tormented by the grief that is in its heart it bewails (17). Coming out of the womb it falls into an unbearable trance; it regains its consciousness when it feels the (surrounding) air (18). Then the enchanting illusion of Vishnu takes possession of it; having its soul possessed by it, it sustains a bewilderment of sense (19). With the loss of sense the creature comes of infancy, boyhood, youth and old age (20). A man repeatedly goes through a cycle of births and deaths. In this way, he rolls like a clock on the wheel of the world (21). Sometimes a man attains heaven, sometimes he goes to hell and sometimes a dead man reaps both heaven and hell (22). And sometimes born again in this earth he reaps the fruits of his own acts. And sometimes enjoying the fruits of his own acts within a short time he breathes his last (23). Sometimes, O best of Brāhmanas, living in heaven or hell for a short time on account of his limited merit or demerit he is born in this earth (24). O father, the dwellers of heaven are seen by them to enjoy happiness—and then those, brought down to perdition, think that there is a great misery in hell (25). Even in heaven there is incomparable misery for from the time of ascension every one conceives in his mind. "I shall fall" (26). Beholding the people of hell, they attain to mighty misery thinking day and night "I shall be brought to this condition" (27). Mighty is the pain of living in the womb, of being born from a female, of the infancy of one when born, and that of decrepitude as well (28). There is also great misery in youth influenced by lust, malice and anger; old age is also full of miseries and the culmination of this is death (29). Mighty is the pain of those who are carried away by force by the emissaries of Yama and thrown into hell; then again is birth in the womb and death and hell (30). In this wise bound by the fetters of nature the creatures revolve on the wheel of the world like a clock and suffer miseries (31) O father, there is not the least happiness in this world abonding in a hundred miseries. Why then shall I, exerting for emancipation, follow the three Vedas? (32).

CHAPTER XII.

THE FATHER said :—Glory be to you, O my child ; in the shape of imparting instructions, you have given a highly useful discourse on the wilderness of the world (1). In this you have described Raurava and all the other hells. Do you describe them now at length, O you of great intelligence (2). The son said :—I have first described to you the hell called *Raurava* ; then hear of the hell, O father, known as *Maharaurava* (3). It extends, on all sides, over twelve thonsand Yoyanas. There the ground is coppery and underneath is the flaming fire (4). Heated by that fire, all the ground, having the resplendance of the rising moon, appears dreadful to look at or feel (5). There the sinner, bound hand and foot, is left by the envoy of Yama and he rolls in it (6). Being eaten by crows, herons, owls, scorpions, knats and vultures he is pulled by them on the way (7) Being bewildered and greatly agitated he continually cries out, "O father, O mother, O brother, O child" and does not obtain any respite (8). It is after Ayuta and Ayuta of years that the wicked sinners find release from those (sufferings) (9). There is another hell called *Tama*, bitterly cold by nature ; it is as spacious as *Maharaurava* and enshrouded by darkness (10). Stricken with cold people run about in that dreadful drakness and remain clasping each other (11). Stricken with cold and trembling their teeth break up and they suffer from hunger, thirst and other afflictions (12). A dreadful wind, blowing over the cold tract, cuts assunder their bones ; and they, assailed by hunger, feed on the fat and blood coming out therefrom. And they, collected together, while licking it, are whirled away (13). In this way, O best of Brāhmanas, do the people suffer greatly so long their sins are not washed away (14). There is another principal hell called *Nikrintana*; in it, O father, potters' wheels are continually rolling (15). Getting upon them people are cut off from the soles of their feet to their heads by the dreadful threads held by the fingers of Yama's envoy (16). These do not however perish, O foremost of the twice-born, and the portions of their bodies, sundered into hundreds, are again combined. Thus the sinners are sundered for a thousand years, so long their sin is not completely washed off (18). Hear, I shall now describe the hell, *Apratishtha*; living in it, people suffer afflictions hard to bear (19). There are wheels at places—and the clocks at others—the instruments of affiictions to persons of impious deeds (20). Some men, fast fixed on the wheels, are whirled on and they cannot come out even for a thousand years (21). Firmly fixed on the machinery of the clock even as a clock is fixed in water, people are whirled on, continually vomitting blood. (22) Vomitting forth blood through their mouths and having eyes overflowing with tears these creatures suffer intolerable afflictions (23). Hear again, I shall describe another hell, the forest of sword blades, which is all fire, covering the earth for a thousand Yoyanas (24). Scorched by the terrible and fierce rays of the sun, creatures, dwelling in hell, always drop there (25). In it there is a beautiful forest covered with cool foliage. The leaves and fruits thereof, O foremost of the twice-born, consist of sword blades (26). There bark a million of powerful dogs, with large mouth, huge teeth and dreadful like tigers to look at (27). Beholding before them the forest covered with dews and shades, creatures, afflicted with thirst, rush towards it (28). Having their feet burnt by the fire raging underneath, they, greatly afflicted, cry out, "O father, O mather!" (29). As soon as they reach there, the wind blows, shaking the sword leaves and the swords fall on them (30). They then drop down on earth—here a collection of fire and there all ablaze with flames spreading all over the surface (31). The dreadful dogs then quickly tear into pieces their bodies and numberless limbs as they cry in agony (32). I have described to you, O father, the forest of sword-blades. Hear, now from me, of the far more dreadful *Taptakumbha* (33). It has all around it heated pans, encircled by flames of fire, filled with iron dust and boiling oil resembling flames (34). In these vessels are thrown by the envoys of Yame perpetrators of wicked deeds with their faces bent towards the ground ; they are fried there with their bodies bursting and rendered foul with fatty excretions (35). With their heads, eyes and bones coming out they are forcibly taken up by ferocious vultures and are again thrown into them (39). Then accompanied by hissing sounds and converted into liquid their heads, bodies, tendons, flesh, skin and bones are mixed up with oil (37). Then the perpetrators of iniquities are pounded in these volumes of eddying oil with a laddle by the emissaries of Yama (38). Thus I have described to you at length, O father, the hell *Taptakumbha* (39.

—:o:—

CHAPTER XIII.

THE SON said :—In the seventh birth preceding this, I was born in the Vaishya race. Formerly I obstructed the approach of kine, to a reservoir (1). From that adverse action, I was thrown into a dreadful hell, terrific with flames and abounding in iron-beaked birds (2) ; covered with mire of the streams of blood coming out from bodies crushed by instruments (of torture) and filled with the cries of sinners dropping down sundered (3). Thrown there and oppressed by powerful heat and thirst and burning I remained a hundred years and more (4). It so happened that one day came to me a fresh cool breeze delighting my heart, flowing from an earthen vessel filled with meals mixed with curds (5). By its touch the numberless afflictions of the people were brought to a close and I too attained that excellent joy which is enjoyed by the inhabitauts of the celestial region (6). (Thinking) 'What is this, with eyes expanded and shaking with joy we saw near us a most excellent man, the jewel of the race) (7). A dreadful emissary of Yama, resplendent like lightning, with a rod in his hand, waited before him showing him the way and saying 'come this way' (8). Beholding the hell abounding in a hundred miseries, he, filled with compassion, said to the follower of Yama :— (9). "Tell me, O emissary of Yama, what iniquity did I commit before by which I have been consigned to this dreadful hell filled with terrible afflictions (10). I was celebrated for my erudition in the family of my fore-fathers. Born in Vedaha, I governed well the people (11). Performing many sacrifices I righteously protected the earth; I never did turn away from fight nor did any guest go away disappointed (from my house)? (12). I never dishonored my manes, the celestial saints, or the servants. And never did I covet another's wife or wealth (13). As kine come to at rough so the manes come of themselves to a man during a Parva, and deities on lunar days. (14). The *Ishth* and *Purtha* acts of a householder become fruitless from whose house they go away disappointed (15). The sighs of the departed manes destroy the religious merit of seven generations and forsooth those of deities destroy that of three generations (16). For this, I always tried to encompass the pleasure of the manes and the deities. Therefore have I been doomed to this highly dreadful hell?" (17).

CHAPTER XIV.

THE SON said :—Thus addressed by that high-souled one in our hearing, the dreadful emissary of Yama replied in soft words :—(1). "You have spoken the truth, O great king, there is no doubt about it. I shall now remind you of a small amount of sin committed by you (2). You had a wife born in Vidharbha named Pivari. When she was in menses you made them go fruitless (3). You had your heart then attached to the highly beautiful Kaikeyi; and in consequence of your making her menses fruitless you have been consigned to this dreadful hell (4). As at the time of a Homa (sacrifice) the fire expects sacrificial offerings so does the Lord of creatures expect seed at the time of menses (5). A person, however virtuous he may be, who disregards this injunction and desires for another woman, falls into a hell on account of his sin (for not satisfying) the ancestral debts (6). This is your sin and nothing more; come then, O king, for enjoying the fruits of your virtue" (7). The king said :— "I shall go, O emissary of the deity (Yama) wherever you will take me; I shall ask you something and you should speak to me the truth (8). These crows, having beaks like adamant, are plucking out the eyes of men; but they are regaining their eyes again and again (9). Tell me what an iniquity they had perpetrated? These (crows) are also taking out their tongues growing anew again and again (10). Why are these unfortunate men being severed by saws? And why thrown in oil are they being boiled in earthen vessels filled with meal mixed with curd? (11). Tell me why are these afflicted having the joints of their bodies loosened and been dragged by iron-beaked birds? And why are they uttering shrieks (of pain)? (12). Having their bodies cut all over with the iron and afflicted these men are suffering day and night; what iniquity had they perpetrated? (13). Describe to me at length by what adverse actions these sinful men are undergoing miseries which I see?" (14). The emissary of Yama said :—" O king, you have asked me regarding the consequences of sinful actions; I shall duly describe them to you in brief (15). A person reaps the fruit of virtue or vice by turns; and when the fruit of virtue or vice is reaped it is spent (16). Without reaping the fruits of good or bad actions a person is not released therefrom in the least: the extinction (of an action) originates from the reaping (of the fruit) (17). Hear me explaining virtue and vice; wretched sinners are visited by famine upon famine, pain upon pain, fear upon fear and death upon death; by the fetters of action creatures come by various conditions (18—19). Persons, cherishing reverence, controlling their souls, distributing wealth and performing auspicious acts, enjoy festivities after festivities, heaven after heaven and happiness after happiness (20). But sinners, assailed by iniquities, are doomed to places filled with beasts of prey, elephants, serpents, razors and other dreadful things. What more for pious men? (21). Wearing fragrant garlands, clad in good raiments, driving on beautiful cars, feeding on savouring viands and eulogised by sacred hymns they repair to sacred groves (22). In this way virtue and vice, of men gathered through hundreds and hundreds, thousands and thousands of births, become the seeds of happiness and misery (23). As a seed expects a shower, O king, so virtue and vice are dependent upon time, place and action as the cause (24). If a person commits a slight sin generated by place and time, he suffers such an affliction as is derived from treading upon thorns (25). A greater sin in the same way leads to greater suffering such as a piece of land filled with darts and pins and unbearable head diseases (26). At the time of their being united with fruits the sins mutually expect the instruments of unwholesome food, cold, heat, fatigue and burning (27). In the like manner greater iniquities bring long enduring diseases and other evils and sufferings from arms,fire and chains (28). Even a slight virtue easily gives agreeable odours, touch, sound, taste and form (29). But greater virtue leads to higher enjoyments (30). Thus the poople live here, reaping happiness and misery from virtue and vice originating from repeated births (31). The fruits, of knowledge and ignorance confined by caste and place, remain combined in the soul (32). Performing a sinful deed, either by body, mind or speech a person is never established in virtue (33). Whatever a person attains, happiness or misery, greater or small, it agitates his mind (34). Like a food eaten, his virtue or vice finds extinction by being reaped (35). In this way, these men, living in the heart of hell, are spending away their mighty sins by undergoing horrible sufferings day and night (36). In the same way, O king, in the celestial region, men, in the company of immortals, enjoy bliss listening to the songs of the Gandharvas, Siddhas and Apsarās (37). A creature, either born as a deity, a human being or a beast, reaps good or evil originating from virtue or vice characterised as happiness or misery (38). You have questioned me, O king, for what sins are these sinners going through these miseries; I shall describe it at length (39). The adamant-beaked birds pluck out the eyes of those wretched men who look at others' wives with evil eyes as well as those of covetous people who desire others' property with impious thoughts; and their eyes grow again and again (40—41). They will suffer from their eyes as many thousand years as these men had winks when they perpetrated the crime (42). For so many years the dreadful adamant-beaked birds will pluck out the tongues growing anew again and again of those persons who, for destroying çompletely the spiritual sight of the enemies, instructed people in bad scriptures, gave dishonest counsels, explained the scriptures falsely, uttered untruths, reviled the Vedas, the deities, the twice-born ones and the preceptors (43—45.)

Behold, O king, those wretched men severed by saws, who brought about dissension amongst friends, separation of a father from his son, that amongst relatives, that between a priest and a sacrificer,that of a mother from her son,that of companions (from each other) or that between a husband and a wife (46—47). Those who afflict others, those who obstruct the enjoyment of others, those who deprive people of palmyra fans, air-passages, sandal, Uçira (a fragrant grass) and those wretched people who bring sufferings destroying (even) life, on innocent persons, reap their sins by being placed on sand vessels full of meals mixed with curds (48—49). Those persons, who being invited by others, feed on the *Sraddha* performed by another, either for the ancestral manes or deities, are dragged by these birds in two (opposite) directions (50). Those, who pierce the vitals of the pious with their own hands, have their own in return pierced, without any obstruction, by these birds (51). He, who by his perverted mind and word, commits an iniquity, has his tongue severed in twain by sharpened razors (52). Those, that through haughtiness of heart, disregard their fathers, or mothers, or preceptors, are plunged, with their faces bent downwards, into pits filled with pus, urine and excretion (53). Those wicked people, that take their food, before the deities, guests, servants, new comers, ancestral manes, the fires and birds are fed, are born as Suchimukhas (birds) huge as hills and take delight in eating pus and dung (54—55). Those, who, while observing a vow, feed with partiality the Brāhmanas and persons born of any other order, feed on dung like these (56). Those, who take their food, without treating the poor and beggars and those who drive the same interest, feed, like these, on phlegm. (57). O lord of men, those who while unclean from eating, touch kine, Brāhmanas or fire, have their hands burnt in this flaming fit (58). Those who, while unclean with eating, willingly see the sun, moon or stars, have their eyes cast into fire by the envoys of Yama and are purified there (59). Those men, that have with their feet touched kine, fire, their mothers, Vipras, their elder brothers, fathers, sisters, good wives, preceptors or elderly men, have their limbs bound by chains of heated fire; and being placed in heaps of burning coal, burn up to their knees (60—61). Behold those sinful men, who have eaten Pāyāça, *Kiçara*, goat's flesh or any food given to the deity after having desecrated it, brought down to the earth looking with rolling eyes that are being drawn out with teeth in the mouth of Yama's followers (62—63). Those wretched sinners, who have suffered their preceptors, deities, Brāhmanas and the Vedas to be villified and have taken delight in that, have, although crying, iron pins, showering fire, driven repeatedly into ears (64---65). Those, that possessed by anger and covetousness, have broken and demolished watering places, images, houses of the Brāhmanas, temples, magnificent assembly halls, although crying repeatedly, have their skin separated from their body with sharpened weapons by the highly terrific messengers of Yama (66—67). Those men, that pass urine or excretien in the way of kine, Brāhmanas or the sun, have their entrails extracted by crows through their anus (68.) He, that having given away his daughter to one again gives her to a second man, being sundered into pieces, is thrown into a river of alkali. (69). Those, that possessed by anger forsake helpless sons, servants, wives or friends on the occasion of a famine or any calamity, being thus sundered by Yama's retainers, feed on their own flesh in hunger and again gorge it out (70—71). He, who forsakes out of cupidity dependants living upon service, is assailed with engines, by the servants, of Yama (72). Those persons, who sell their religious merit acquired all through their lives , are pressed with stones like those perpetrators of iniquities (73). Those, who misappropiate deposit money, bound all over, are constrained to feed day and night on worms, scorpions, crows and owls (74). Those sinful persons, who visit women by day or who live with others' wives, are subject to afflictions and have their tongues and palates dried up with hunger and thirst (75). See, they have been fixed on *Shalmali* trees with long iron pins and their bodies have been severed and are bathed in streams of blood (76). And see, O foremost of men, those, who ravished others' wives, killed by Yama's servants being thrown in crucibles (77). The man, who putting his preceptor to shame or striking him dumb, receives lessons or learns any mechanical art from him, suffers misery by carrying stones on his head and is greatly assailed in the way of men; he suffers day and night from hunger and fatigue and his head aches for carrying the load (78—79). Those, that discharge urine, phlegm, stool &c,. in water, are doomed to this hell filled with the bad smell of phlegm, excreta and urine (80). Those, who never treated before each other with hospitality, are now possessed by hunger eating each others' flesh (81). Those, that villified the Vedas and those that, lighting sacrificial fire, disregarded it, are repeatedly being thrown down from mountain peaks (82). Those, who passed their days as the husbands of widows, being emaciated, are reduced to those worms that are being eaten up by ants (83). Those, who accept gifts from an out-caste, who officiate as his priests and those who serve him, become worms living inside the rocks (84). Those, who take sweets in the presence of their servants, friends, and guests, have got to swallow burning coal down their throat (85). O king, those who feed on the flesh of another's back, has his own daily eaten by dreadful wolves (86). The cursed men, who turn ungrateful to persons who do them good, roam about, being stricken with hunger, or being blind, deaf and dumb (87). This highly vicious-minded, ungrateful wretch, injuring his friends, is thrown into a heated vessel and pounded there (88). He is then tortured by the engines in the sand vessels containing milk with curd and is then severed with saws in the forest of sword-blades (89). He will be then hewn by the thread of time; thus undergoing various afflictions I do not know how he will be freed therefrom (90). Those wicked Brāhmanas, leaping over one another, ate the food of a *Sraddha*. They now drink the foam coming out from all their limbs (91). That stealer of gold, that killer of a Brāhmana, that consumer of strong drinks, and that ravisher of his preceptor's wife, are being burnt for many thousand years by a fire flaming above and below: these are again born as men marked with leprosy, consumption and other diseases (92—93). When dead they go to hell and are again born in the same manner. O king, they will suffer from diseases till the end of Kalpa (94). One, who kills a cow, goes to hell for three successive births—this is also the fate of the perpetrators of minor crimes (95). Hear, I shall describe the respective births which persons coming out from hell, take, ordained by their sins (96).

CHAPTER XV.

——oo——

YAMA'S servant said:—Taking gifts from a fallen person a Brāhmana becomes an ass: the priest, of a fallen person, being liberated from hell, is born as an earth-worm (1). A twice-born one who plays his preceptor false, or desires for his wife or covets his property, forsooth becomes a dog (2). If a person disregards his parents, he becomes an ass; if he is angry with his father and mother he is born as a female parrot (3). If a person insults his brother's wife he comes by the state of a pigeon; oppressing her he is born as a tortoise (4). He, who, taking the food of his master, does not seek his welfare, is possessed by stupefaction and is born as a monkey when dead (5). He who appropriates money held in trust, is born as an earth-worm when liberated from hell; and he, who is given to calumny when freed from hell, becomes a Rākshasa (6). A treacherous man is born as a fish. He that steals paddy, barley, sesame seeds, *másha Kulathatha*, mustard, oats, *Kaláyá*, *Kalama*, *Mudga*, wheat, *atasi* or any other kind of grain, being bereft of his sense, is born as a long-faced rat resembling a mungoose. He, who ravishes another's wife, is by and by born as a dreadful wolf, a dog, a jackal, a vulture, a serpent and a heron. That one of perverted sense, who lives with his brother's wife, becomes a male coil on his being freed from hell (7—10.) That lustful person, who violates the wife of a friend, or of a preçeptor or of a king, is born as swine (11). He, who obstructs sacrifices, gifts or a wedding, becomes an earth worm. He that gives away his daughter for the second time is born as an earth worm (12). He who takes his food without (first) giving it to the deities, the ancestral manes and the Brāhmanas on being freed from hell, is born as a crow (13). He, who disregards his elder brother who is like a father to him, on being freed from hell, is born as a Krauncha (14). A Sudra, who lives with a Brāhmana woman, is born as an earth-worm, and begetting children on her he becomes a worm living inside a wood, a hog, an earth-worm, a shag and a Chandāla. An ungrateful and degraded man, on being liberated from hell, is by turns born as an earth-worm, a worm, an insect a centipede, a fish, a cow, a tortoise and a Pukkasa (15—17). Slaying an unarmed man one is born as an ass; the destroyer of a woman or that of a child is born as an earth worm (18). By stealing food a man is born as a fly. There is something particular about food; hear it (19). By stealing rice, one, on being freed from hell, is born as a cat. He, who steals rice mixed with sesame and Pinyaka, is born as a rat (20). By stealing clarified butter a man becomes a mungoose, by stealing goat's flesh he becomes a *Madgu* or a crow. A person that steals flesh or meat becomes a crow; one that steals the meat of a deer becomes a hawk (21). He who steals salt becomes a water-crow and he that steals curds becomes an earth worm; by stealing milk one becomes a crane (22). He who steals oil becomes a cock-roach; by stealing honey a man becomes a gad-fly and by stealing flowers an ant (23). By stealing *nishpava* one becomes a house lizard. By stealing wine one is born as a tittiri (24). The sinful man, stealing iron, is born as a crow; by stealing bell-metal one becomes a wood pigeon and by stealing silver vessel, a pigeon (25). By stealing a golden vessel one is born as an earth-worm; by stealing a silken cloth one becomes a partridge (26). By stealing a satin cloth one is born as a chrysalis. The sinful man, who steals gold-embroidered satin, a fine cloth made of goat's hair or linen, is born as a male-parrot. By stealing cotton cloth, one is born as a *Krauncha* and by stealing bark a heron (27—28). By stealing a paint or *Sákapatra* one is born as a peacock; a person stealing a red cloth becomes a peasant (29). By stealing scents one is born as a mole; and by stealing a dress a hare. By stealing fruits one becomes a bull and by stealing wood a wood-worm (30). One stealing flowers becomes poor and one stealing a conveyance lame. One stealing potherbs becomes a wood pigeon and one stealing water becomes a *Chátaka* (31). Going to dreadful hells Raurava and others the stealer of land becomes successively grass, shrubs, creepers, plants and trees with only barks on, and his sins growing less and weakened he becomes a man (32). Then he is born as an earth-worm, an insect, a grass hopper, an aquatic fowl, a deer, a cow and a cursed Chandāla or a Pukksa (33). He is then born as a cripple, as a blind man, as a deaf man, as a leper and as one suffering from phthysis; he is assailed by diseases of mouth, eyes and stomach (34). He becomes epileptic and is born as a Sudra (35). These are the successive states, to which are reduced the stealers of cow and gold or those that steal learning or lands held rent free by their preceptors (36). The fool, who gives away one's wife to another, being freed from the various pains is born as a bull (37). The man, who offers oblations to fire not perfectly lighted up, is assailed by the disease of indigestion and becomes dyspeptic (38). Calumny, ingratitude, giving pain to another's mind, cruelty, impudence, adultery, robbing one of his own, impurity, vilifying the gods, deceiving people, miserliness, man slaughter these and other forbidden acts and a constant tendency towards them all speak that (the authors) have just come out of the hell; (whereas) kindness for creatures, the bringing of good news, service to the people of the other region, truthfulness, words for the behoof of creatures, the evidence of the Vedas, the worship of the preceptors, celestial saints and Siddhas, companionship with the pious, the practice of good works, friendliness—these and various other recognised good and moral works are considered by a learned man as the marks of pious men just coming out from heaven (39—44.) Thus I have described to you, O king, everything about men reaping the fruits of their acts—pious or sinful (45). We shall now go to another place; you have seen everything. You have seen hell; let us go elsewhere (46).

THE SON said:—Then placing him ahead the king addressed himself for going. Then all men, suffering from agonies, cried aloud (47). "Favour us, O king, wait for a moment. The wind touching your limbs delights our hearts (48). O foremost of men, (it) drives completely the heat of our bodies as well as diseases and ailments; favour us, therefore O king," (49). Hearing these their words, the king asked the envoy of Yama:—"Why do these people delight in my stay? (50). Tell me, what greatly pious action did I perform in the region of mortals which showers delight on them" (51). The emissary of Yama said:—"Your body attained to nourishment by the remnant of the food offered to the ancestral manes, guests and servants and because your mind was always devoted to them, therefore the wind, touching your limbs, gives them delight and these sinners do not feel the pain, O king, (52—53). Because you duly performed horse sacrifices and others, therefore seeing you and thwarted by your energy, these intruments of Yama, engines and weapons, and fires and crows—the causes of affliction, wounds, burning and other great sufferings, have become milder (in their action)" (54—55). The king said:—" The happiness, that one enjoys by affording relief to creatures in distress, is not obtained by men either in heaven or in the region of Brāhma—this is my conviction (56). If for my coming near them they do not suffer torments, I shall, O fair mouthed one, live here motionless like an inanimate object (57)." The envoy of Yama said:—" Come O king, we shall go; leaving the sinners with their sufferings do you enjoy happiness reaped by your pious acts (58)."

THE King said:—"As long these will remain greatly stricken with grief I shall not go; the dwellers of hell become happy by my living near them (59). Cursed is the life of that man who does not know mercy towards the distressed seeking refuge with him, even if they for certan belong to the side of the enemies (60). Sacrifices, gifts, asceticism do not bear him fruit either in this world or in the next who has not his mind bent upon relieving distress (61). I do not consider him a man, whose hard heart is not drawn to children, the distressed and the old—rather he is a Rākshasa (62). If by living near them do I suffer miseries of hell—the heat of fire, piercing effluvia, hunger, thirst and any other great afflction, depriving one of his consciousness, I shall consider my act of affording them relief greater than the felicity of heaven (63—64). If many, in distress, secure happiness by my being in it, what have I not obtained? So you go without any delay (65)." The envoy of Yama said:—"Here are Dharma and Sakra come to take you away; so you must go and therefore come, O king (66)" Dharma said:—" I shall take you to heaven for I have been duly adored by you. Get upon this chariot; come, do not delay (67)."

THE KING said:—Thousands of men are suffering in the hell, O Dharma. They are crying to me in distress "save us." I shall not go (68). Indra said:—By their acts these sinners have come to hell; and you, O king, by your pious acts, should go to heaven (69). The king said:—If I am to know you as Dharma and if I am to know you as Sachi's lord you should tell me the extent of my religious merit (70). Dharma said:—Like drops of water in the ocean, like stars in the firmament, like showers pouring like sands on the Ganga and like countless particles in water, O great king, your religious merit cannot be enumerated (71—72). And this compassion, which you have extended to-day to the dwellers of hell, has multiplied your religious merit a hundred and thousand fold (73). Therefore, go, O you the foremost of kings, to the region of immortals for enjoying it; and let them expiate in hell the sin begotten by their own actions (74). The king said:—Why do those men long for my companionship if they are not elevated by my living near them? (75). If I have done any pious act, O king of heaven, then let these sinners, suffering from torments, be released from hell (76).

INDRA said:—From this you have obtained a higher region, O king and behold these sinners released from hell (77).

THE SON said:—Then flowers were showered upon the king; and placing him upon his car Hari took him to his own region (78). Myself and others there being freed from sufferings came by other births appointed by our own actions (79). I have thus described to you, O foremost of the twice-born, all the hells; and I have described to you, all as seen before by me, all the births taken in parsuance of (their) respective sins; (I have given you) a truthful account based on my previous experience; what more shall I tell you, O great one? (80—81).

CHAPTER XVI.

——oo——

THE FATHER said:—My son, you have described to me truly the most hateful order of the world, going on perpetually like a clock; I have fully learnt all this. Such being the case, tell me what I should do (1—2).

THE SON said:—If you, O father, unhestitatingly rely on my words, then renonncing the condition of a house-holder enter into woods (3). Duly entering upon this life, giving up sacrificial fire, severing all ties and being freed from dissession concentrate your mind upon self (4). Taking your food every alternate day, controlling your mind, become a mendicant shaking off inaction. And there when becoming intent upon Yoga you shall be above the external influence you will then obtain that Yoga which is the remedy of the miseries of existence, the means of liberation, incomparable, and indescribable, and which is not acquired in company and obtaining which you will no more be related to matter (5—6)

THE FATHER said:—Describe to me, O my son, Yoga which is the best means to emanapation, by which I shall not attain to misery for my again being united with matter (7). Explain to me that Yoga, which is unattached and by which my soul, greatly attached, may not be fettered by worldly bonds, (8). Do you sprinkle the cool water of speech regarding the knowlege of Brahma on my body and mind assailed and bewildered by the heat of the sun of a world (9). By making me drink your nectarine words do you revive me who am dead again by being beaten by the black serpent of ignorance and possessed by its venom (10). By opening speedily the gate of love and knowlege do you release me who am fettered by the chains of son, wife, house and field (11). The son said:—Listen properly, O father, to Yoga which was described fully by the intelligent Dattātreya to Alarka when formerly questioned by him (12). The father said:—Whose son was Dattātreya? Why did he explain Yoga? Who was the great Alarka who questioned (him) about Yoga? (13) The son said:—There was a certain Brāhmana, Kauçika, in the city of Prathisthāna, who, in consequence of his pristine sins, was assailed by leprosy (14). His wife served her deseased husband as if he was a deity, by shampooing his feet and limbs, bathing him, clothing him, feeding him, washing off his phlegm, urine, feces and blood, by serving him in solitude and treating him with sweet words (15—16). Although always served by her with humility that highly irascible and cruel (Brāhmana) used to rebuke her angrily (17). Still the humble wife considered him as a deity and regarded that horrible one as the best of men (18). Although incapable of moving about that foremost of the twice-born one day said to his wife:—"Take me to the house of the courtezan living by the road; she lives in my heart, O you conversant with virtue (19—20). I saw that girl at sun-rise and it is now night—from the time of seeing her she does not disappear from my heart (21). If that one of a slender make, perfectly beautiful with plump hips and breasts, does not embrace me you will see me dead (22). Kama, (the god of love) is hostile to men. and she is solicited by many; I am incapable of moving about; it appears hopeless to me (23)." Hearing these words of her husband stricken with lust, his high-minded and devoted wife, born in a noble-family, making a firm resolution, taking profuse money and carrying her husband on her shoulders, proceeded slowly (24—25). It was night; the sky was covered with clouds. That Brāhmana's wife, wishing to encompass the pleasure of her husband, went along the highway discovered by the flash of lightning (26). On the way in darkness that twice-born one of the race of Kuçika, mounted on his wife's shoulders, pushed Mandavya who was greatly suffering from agony having been placed on a dart for being suspected as a thief although he was not so. Being enraged for having been pushed with feet Mandavya said to him (27—28). "That sinful wretch of a man, by whom, I sorely afflicted and reduced to a miserable plight, have been pushed with feet, shall forsooth be deprived of his life at the sun rise. As soon as he will see the rays of the sun he will meet with destruction" (29—30). Thereupon hearing that dreadful curse, his wife, greatly afflicted, said "The sun shall not rise". (31) Therefore the sun not rising there was a continuous night extending over many days and accordingly the celestials were terrified (32). They thought "How can this entire universe, shorn of Vedic recitations and those of *Vashat*, *Swaha* and *Swadha*, be saved from being utterly ruined? (33). Without the division of day and night that of months and seasons will cease and from its being destroyed the summer and the winter solistice cannot be known (34). Without a knowledge of solistice how can the time be measured by a year? And without year no knowledge of time can be had (35). At the words of that faithful wife the sun will not rise and without the rising of the sun bathing, gifts and such other acts cannot take place (36). There is no lighting of the sacrificial fire and the want of sacrifices is observed. And no gratification of ours can accrue but from oblations to fire (37). Being duly gratified by the mortals with our due share in the sacrifices we favour men with rain for the growth of corn (38). On oshadhis having been procured the mortals worship us with sacrifices; and being adored by sacrifices and others we grant them their desires (39). We shower down and the mortals shower up—we with water and men with clarified butter (40). The wicked and the greedy do not perform the daily rites for us but they devour the sacrificial shares themselves (41). For the destruction of these sinful and wicked men we vitiate water, the sun, fire, air and earth (42). By their partaking of the vitiated water many highly dreadful symptoms appear for the destruction of those sinful men (43). But we confer holy regions upon those high-souled men, who, satisfying us all first, feed themselves upon the remnant (44), But nothing of this exists now; how can creation be preserved? How can day appear again?" Thus did the celestials confer with one another (45). Hearing the words of the celestials assembled there and afraid at the stoppage of sacrifices the god Prajāpati (Brahmā) said:—(46). "Energy is pacified by energy and asceticism by asceticism; hear, O ye immortals, my words (47). For the glorification of the chaste wife the sun will not rise; and for his not rising, you and the mortals (are so anxious) (48). If you wish that the sun should rise you should propitiate Atri's wife, the ascetic and devotedly chaste Anusuā" (49). The son said:—Being propitiated by them she said "Tell me what do you wish to have." The deities then begged of her that there might be day as formerly (50). Anusuā said:—"The glory of a chaste woman never suffers decrease. Honoring this pious lady, therefore, I shall create day, O celestials (51). So that there may be again day and night and that the husband of that righteous lady may not meet with destruction" (52). The son said:—Having said this to the celestials that auspicious lady repaired to her house and enquired of the welfare and virtue of herself and her husband (53). Anusuā said:—"O auspicious lady, do you find delight from seeing the face of your husband? Do you regard your husband more than all the deities taken together? (54). It is by serving my husband that I have attained this great fruit; and for my having obtained the fruit of every desire all impediments have disappeared (55). O chaste lady, a man should always pay five kinds of debts and should amass riches in consonance with the duties of his own order (56). He should then duly give away his accumulated wealth to proper recepients. He should always practise truth, sincerity, asceticism and kindness (57). Being shorn of anger and malice he should always perform acts laid down by scriptures with reverence and accompanied by gifts as much as lies in his power (58). O chaste lady, it is by very great toil that a man attains to regions appointed for his own order and then gradually to that of Brahmâ and others (59). But by serving her husband a woman obtains a moity of the religious merit acquired by a man with hardships (60). A woman has not separate sacrifics, Srâddhas or fasts; by serving their husbands they attain to wished for regions (61). As the husband is the most excellent course for women, you should, O chaste and noble lady, always set your heart upon serving your husband (62). Being whole-mindedly intent upon serving her husband a woman reaps the religious merit earned by a man by worshipping deities, his ancestral manes and guests and by the performance of pious rites" (63). The son said:—Hearing her words and honoring them duly, she spoke to Atri's wife Anusuâ (64). "Blessed and favoured I am, O you auspicious by nature, since the celestials have looked upon me and you (have endeavoured) to increase my reverence again (65). I know full well that there is no better refuge to women than their husbands—devotion to them leads to their benefit both in this world and in the next (66). The husband being pleased with her, a woman becomes glorious both in this world and in the region of the dead and attains to felicity; the husband is like a deity to women (67). Tell me, O fair one, what shall myself and my worshipful husband do for you, worthy of reverence, who have come to our house" (68). Anusuâ said:—"The distinction of day and night and pious acts having ceased at your words, all the deities with Indra, stricken with grief, have come to me and solicit the favour of your so ordering that the day and night may be same as before. It is for this that I have come to you. Listen to my words (69—70). For the want of day there is a stoppage of all sacrifices. O female ascetic, for want of them, the celestials do not receive any nourishment

(71). From the disappearance of day there is the extinction of all pious observances; from the draught that arises from this extinction the universe will be annihilated (72). If you wish to deliver the universe from this calamity, be you pleased with people, O chaste lady, and let the sun rise as before" (73). The wife of the Brāhmana said:—"My lord, my husband, has been cursed by the great Māndavya, in anger saying "you will meet with destruction at the sun rise" (74). Anusuā said:—"If you wish, O gentle one, at your words I shall make your husband youthful having a body as before (75). O fair one, I always regard the power of the chastity of women and therefore honour you" (76). The son said:—Thereat she agreeing to it, the ascetic Anusuā, taking up the *Arghya*, began to invoke the sun. It was then night for ten nights together (77). Then the divine Vivaswan (sun) resembling a full blown lotus and having a big disc rose on the rising hill (78). In the interval her husband, divorced from life, dropped on the ground and while falling was taken up by her (79).

ANUSUA said:—"You should not grieve, O gentle lady, and behold now without delay my ascetic power acquired by my serving my husband (80). In beauty, character, intelligence, speech and grace and other accomplishments I have not seen any other person equal to my husband—by that truth let this Vipra, freed from disease, regain his life and be again a help to his wife for a hundred years (81—82). As I have not considered even a deity equal to my husband by that truth let this Brāhmana revive without hinderance (83). I have always been intent upon adoring my husband with my deeds, mind and words, by that let the twice-born one revive" (84). The son said:—Thereupon the Brāhmana rose up freed from disease and regaining his youth, and lighting up the room with his native effulgence like a celestial never touched by decrepitude (85). Then fell showers of blossoms and celestial instruments were sounded; the deities then delightedly said to Anusuā (86). "Pray for a boon, O auspicious lady, you have done a great work for the deities, and they are ready, O anchorite,to confer a boon" (87). Anusuā said:—"If the celestials headed by Brahmā are propitiated with me and are prepared to give me a boon and If am deemed by you worthy of it, then let Brahmā, Vishnu and Maheswara be born as my sons; and may I with my husband acquire Yoga leading to the liberation from miseries" (88—89). Thereupon, Brahmā, Vishnu, Siva, and other gods said 'so be it." Then honoring that female ascetic they repaired to their respective habitations (90).

CHAPTER XVII.

—:o:—

THE SON said:—Thereupon after a long time Brahmā's son the divine Atri cast his look upon his own wife Anusuā (1); bathed after her course having all her limbs purified and an excellent form worthy of being coveted by all. Having his mind stricken with desire that ascetic thought in his mind of that one of a blameless person (2). Engrossed by her thought he discharged his vital fluid and the powerful wind carried it upwards and indirectly (3). Falling on all sides that white fluid, with Brahma energy, covered the ten cardinal quarters in the shape of the moon (4). The moon, the stay of the life of all creatures, was born as the mind begotten son of the patriarch Atri (5). Well-pleased the high-souled Vishnu was born from his own body as the best of the twice-born, Dattātreya permeated by the quality of goodness (6). Incarnating himself Vishnu was born as the second son of Atri known under the name of Dattātreya who sucked the breast of Anusuā (7). Getting angry he got out of his mother's womb within a week. Seeing the haughty, perverse and guilty king of Haihayas and getting angry, enraged as he was before with the vexation and trouble of living in the womb, he made up his mind for killing that Haihaya (8—9). Then was born Durvāsā, a portion of Rudra impregnated with the quality of darkness. Thus Brahmā Vishnu, and Siva were born as her three sons (10). By virtue of the boon conferred upon her by the celestials Brahmā was born as the moon, Vishnu as Dattātreya and Sankara as Durvāsā (11). The patriarch Soma (moon), nursing with his own cool rays plants, herbs and men, always resides in the firmament (heaven) (12). Dattātreya, a portion of Vishnu, protects the creatures by destroying the wicked demons and favouring the good people (13). Assuming a body (impregnated by the energy of Rudra) the divine unborn Durvāsā, of dreadful looks, thoughts and words, burns down those who insult him (14). The Patriarch Brahmā became born in the family of Atri as Soma (the moon). Hari, born as Dattātreya and engaged in Yoga, began to enjoy the worldly objects (15). Forsaking his father and mother and resorting to the most excellent vow, *Unmatha* or madness he wandered over the earth (16). The ascetic Dattātreya was always encircled by the sons of ascetics ; but desiring for dis-association that lord lived sunk in a lake for a long time (17). Still those boys living on the banks of the lake did not leave the noble ascetic of an extremely handsome look (18). And even on the completion of a hundred celestial years the sons of the ascetics did not leave the bank of the lake out of love for him (19). Thereupon arose from the water the ascetic taking with him an auspicious lady, clad in a celestial raiment, and gifted with beautiful breast and hips (20), thinking "the sons of ascetics will leave me on seeing me in the company of a woman and then I shall live disassociated"

(21). Still the boys did not leave the ascetic and then he began to drink wine in the company of the woman (22). But even then those sons of the ascetics did not leave him although engaged in drinking wine with his wife. Although he was sullied by the enjoyment of carnal pleasure, singing, music and the company of a woman, and even by drinking wine still he was regarded (by them) as one having a great soul (22—23). Nor did that great ascetic commit any sin by drinking wine like air blowing in the house of a Chandâla (24). Drinking wine, that one conversant with Yoga, practised austerities in the company of his wife. That master of Yogis was worthy of being contemplated by them desirous of emancipation (25).

CHAPTER XVIII.

:o:

THE SON said:—Some time after Kritavirrya had gone to heaven, the citizens together with the councillors and priests called his son Arjuna with a view to install him on the throne and he then said:—"I shall not govern my kingdom, O ministers, which leads to hell. If that for which a king takes revenues is not done it goes for nothing (1—2). By giving over to the king a twelfth of their proceeds the merchants can go along roads protected by the police from the robbers (3). The cow-herds give a sixth part of the clarified butter, whey or whatever they get and the cultivator also a sixth. If they give more than the share and if the king accepts it from traders, it leads to the destruction of *Ishtha* and *Purtha* acts and that king acts like a thief (4—5). If they, having paid their revenue, are protected by others, the king, receiving the sixth part of the outturn as revenue, certainly goes to hell (6). This has been fixed by the former sages as the remuneration of the king for protecting them; if he fails to protect them he becomes guilty of theft (7). If therefore by practising hard austerities I can attain to the state of a Yogi which I wish, I shall be the one king of the earth endued with the power of protecting the world (8); bearing arms, honored by all and gifted with prosperity. I shall not make me a sharer in sin (9)." The son said:—Learning his decision, the highly intelligent and elderly ascetic by name Garga, seated in the midst of the ministers, said (10). "If for governing your kingdom well, you wish to do this, O prince, then listen to my words and act according to them (11), Worship, O king, the great Dattātreya, a refuge unto all, who* living in the valley of the Sahya mountain, protects the three worlds; immersed in Yoga, noble, impartial towards all, a portion of Vishnu, incarnated on earth for releasing the world; adoring whom the thousand-eyed Deity (Indra) regained his own station robbed by the wicked-souled Daityas and slew the sons of Diti" (12—14).

ARJUNA said:—"How did the celestials adore the powerful Dattātreya? How did Vāsava regain the dignity of Indra which had been robbed (by the Daityas)?" (15).

GARGA said:—"There arose a dreaful battle between the celestials and the Dānavas; the lord of the Daityas was Jambha and that of the celestials the husband of Sachi (Indra) (16). While they were fighting a celestial year passed away and then the celestials were defeated and the Daityas came off victorious (17). Then defeated by the Dānavas and depressed on account of the success of the enemies the celestials headed by Viprachitti addressed themselves for flying (18). Desirous of routing the demonaic

---

* It may also mean "a bark in endurance" from *Sahya*, patience and *Dronis*, a boat.

host Vrihaspati came there and began to consult with those Rishis called Vâlikhilyas (19).

VRIHASHPATI said :—" You should with devotion gratify the great ascetic Dattâtreya, the high-souled son of Atri of uncommon ways (20). A giver of boons as he is, he will confer one for the destruction of the Daityas and then the deities all assembled will slay the Daityas and Dânavas" (21). Garga said :—Thus addressed the celestials then repaired to the hermitage of Dattâtreya and saw the high-souled (ascetic) in company with Lakshmi hymned by the Gandharvas and engaged in drinking wine. Going there they bowing prayed to him for effecting what ought to be done (22—23). They sang his praises and provided meats, drinks and garlands for him. The celestials waited when he waited and moved when he moved. And when he sat on the cushion they worshipped him, having seated themselves below (24). Dattâtreya then said to the celestials who bowed to him " What do you expect of me that you are serving me thus" (25). The deities said :—" O foremost of ascetics, by the demons headed by Jambha invading the three worlds we have been deprived of Bhur, Bhuva &c , and of all our shares in sacrifices (26). We pray for your grace ; concert some plan, O god, for their destruction and our safety so that we may regain the celestial region" (27). Dattâtreya said .—" I am addicted to drink and am impure—I am not master of myself. Why do you, O celestials, expect from me a defeat of you enemies" (28). The deities said :—" O sinless one, thou art the lord of one universe—no impurity can attach to thee whose mind has been washed and purified by learning resplendent with the rays of knowledge (29). Dattâtreya said :—" True it is O celestials, that I, looking upon all things with impartiality, have knowledge—but associating with this woman I have been sullied (30). The association with a woman being bent on enjoyment leads to inquity." Thus addressed the deities again said (31). " O foremost of the twice-born, this sinless mother of the universe is never polluted like the rays of the sun equally touching a twice-born one and a Chandāla" (32). Garga said :—Thereupon being thus addressed by the deities Dattātreya, smiling, said to the celestials :—" If this be your opinion, O celestials, then inviting all the Daityas to battle speedily bring them within the range of my vision (33—34). Being seen by me and having their strength and energy enfeebled by the fire of my looks they all, numberless as they are, will meet with destruction" (35). Hearing his words the mighty Daityas were challenged to fight by the celestials and in anger rushed against them (36). Being slain by those Daityas, the celestials, stricken with fear, all speedily went to the hermitage of Dattātreya seeking his protection (37). Slaying the celestials the Daityas too entered there and saw the greatly powerful and high-souled Dattātreya (38); with his wife seated at the left, the welfare and the wished-for of the entire universe, beautiful of all limbs—Lakshmi, having a moon-like countenance; (39). with beautiful eyes like the petals of a blue-lotus, with graceful hips and breast, speaking in sweet words and endued with all the accomplishments of a female (40). Beholding her before them the Daityas had their minds stricken with desire; and thus assailed they could not with a patient mind bear the rising (desire) (41). Leaving off the celestials, they having their energy enfeebled, became desirous of stealing that damsel ; assailed (by desire) and overwhelmed by sin, they thus said :—(42). " If we can secure this jewel of a damsel, the essence of the three worlds, we shall then be crowned with success—even this is our conviction (43). Then placing her on a palanquin, O you the repressors of the celestials, let us all go to our habitations—this is our determination" (44). Possessed by desire they thus spoke amongst themselves. Then placing the chaste damsel on a palanquin and carrying it on their heads the Daityas and Danavas, assailed by lust, proceeded towards their habitations (45—46). Then smiling Dattātreya said to the celestials:—"Fortunately you will prosper; since Lakshmi, passing by the seven other places, has got on the heads of those Daityas, she will seek a new man" (47). The deities said:—"Tell us, O lord of the Universe, stationed in what places she confers what fruits upon men or brings about their destruction" (48). Dattātreya said:—"When placed on the foot of a man she confers upon him a house; when on the thigh she gives clothes and diverse riches (49). When placed at the organ of excretion she gives wife and when on the lap she gives offspring; and when in the heart she gratifies the desires of men (50). When the best Lakshmi is placed on the throat of those endued with prosperity she gives an ornament of the throat, union with beloved friends and wives living in foreign countries, cultured words, grace and makes his commands always carried out. When she, sprung from the ocean, is placed on the mouth she gives the power of a poet (51—52). When she is placed on the head she forsakes (the man) and seeks refuge elsewhere. She is now on their heads and will immediately renounce them (53). Do you all take up your weapons and strike those enemies of the celestials. These should not be greatly feared by you for they have been robbed of their energy by me. By ravishing another's wife all their pieties have been consumed and their prowess has been destroyed (54). Therefore those enemies of the gods should be killed with various weapons. While Lakshmi has occupied their heads they will meet with destruction. This has been heard by us" (55). Then eulogized by the celestials who were all filled with delight in consequence of the destruction of the Daityas, Lakshmi leaped down (therefrom) and went to the great ascetic Dattātreya (56). Thereupon saluting the intelligent Dattātreya, the deities, freed from anxiety as before, repaired to the celestial region (57). If, O foremost of kings, you wish to have your desired-for, matchless wealth, do you speedily worship him.

CHAPTER XIX.

THE SON said :—Repairing to the hermitage of Dattātreya at the words of the Rishi, Kārtaviryya, the king of men, adored him with devotion (1). By shampooing his legs and otherwise, by collecting honey, etc., by bringing for him garlands, sandal, scents, water and fruits, by arranging for his meals, and taking away the refuses, he gratified the ascetic. As the deities had been addressed by him formerly in the same way he said to him (the king) describing him as polluted by the drinking of wine :—"This woman is always beside me—and I have been contaminated by her company. You should not request me who am incapable. Do you seek another who is capable," (2—5). The son said—Thus addressed by the ascetic and remembering the words of Garga, Kritaviryya's son, Arjuna, bowing, replied (6). Arjuna said :—" Stationed in your own illusive energy, why do you delude me, O god? You are sinless and likewise is the goddess, the mother of all creatures." (7). Thereat thus addressed and delighted, the god said to the great Kārtaviryya, by whom the entire earth had been subjugated (8). " Pray for a boon, since you have been able to perceive my true form, I have been greatly pleased with you, O king (9). Encompassing their great delight I confer wives, sons and wealth upon those men who worship me along with Lakshmi with fragrant wreaths and others, with presents of wine and meals, with sweetmeats and clarified butter accompanied by the adorations of the Brāhmanas, songs and the charming music of Vinā, flute, conch and bugle. And I bring about their sudden deaths who disregard me (10—12.) May good betide you; do you pray for a desired-for boon; by your singing my secret glories I have been ready to extend my grace to you (13). Kārtaviryya said:—"If thou art propitiated with me, O deity, do thou cenfer upon me such excellent prosperity by which I may protect my subjects and be not touched by impiety (14). I may read the intentions of others, may have none to match me in battle and I wish to have a thousand arms and light-handedness (15). I may go unobstructed every where—on mountains, in water, on earth, in sky and the nether region and I may meet with death from one who is mightier (than I) (16). I may point out good ways to them who always wend wrong ways and may my guests be gratified with gifts of endless riches (17). By recollecting me let no one loose his property in my kingdom and may I have whole minded devotion in thee" (18). Dattātreya said:—"You will get all the boons you have begged and by my favour you will be the Lord Paramount" (19). The son said:—Thereupon saluting Dattātreya and summoning together all his subjects he duly received installation (20). Then by the favour of Dattātreya, bringing all articles of installation came there all the leading Gandharvas, Apsarās, the Rishis headed by Vasistha, the mountains headed by Maru, the rivers headed by the Ganges, the oceans full of waters, Plaksha and other trees, the celestials headed by Vāsava, the birds headed by Tārkshya, the citizens and villagers. The celestial Brahmā and others engaged in conversation with one another. For the destruction of impiety and the protection of virtue he was installed by Nārayana in the form of Dattātreya by the rivers and oceans with the sprinkling of water and by the Rishis (21—25). Established in his kingdom and endued with strength for obtaining great prosperity from Dattātreya that Haihaya made a proclamation (26). "Whoever, save me, shall take up a weapon, from to-day and a robber and one intent upon injuring others shall be slain by me" (27). With the issue of the ploclamation there was no holder of weapon in that kingdom save that foremost of men gifted with great prowess (28). He alone was the protector of villages, of beasts, of fields as well as of the twice-born (29). He became the protector of the ascetics as well as that of traders. And that slayer of hostile heroes, as soon as he was thought of, used to release people stricken with fear of robbers, beasts of pray, fire, or weapons, those drowned in the occean or those assailed by other calamities (30—31). While he ruled the earth no body lost his property. He celebrated many sacrifices accompanied by profuse gifts (32). He undertook many battles and performed hard austerities. Beholding his prosperity and intelligence the ascetic Angirā said: (33). "Forsooth, kings will never be able to equal Kārtaviryya in sacrifices, in gifts, in asceticism and great energy in battle" (34). That king used to celebrate a sacrifice in honor of Dattātreya, on that day on which from him he obtained prosperity (35). And there beholding the great prosperity of the king the subjects too, with devotion, used to celebrate sacrifices in his honour (36). Such is the glory of the intelligent Dattātreya. The incarnations, of the great, eternal Vishnu, the preceptor of the mobile and immobile creation, incomparable and the holder of the Sranga bow, conch, mace and club, have been described in the Puranās (37—38). The man, who meditates upon this most excellent form, becomes happy and is freed forever from worldliness (39). Why shall not men seek refuge with him who always says: "I am easily attainable unto the votaries of Vishnu by devotion" (40). For the destruction of impiety and protection of virtue the deity, without beginning or end, carries on the work of creation and preservation (41). I shall now relate to you the birth of Alarka. Dattātreya described Yoga to that high-souled royal saint Alarka devoted to his sire (42).

CHAPTER XX.

THE SON said :—There was a highly energetic king in the days of yore, by name Shatrujit in whose sacrifice drinking Soma Purandara was gratified (1). His son became greatly energetic and capable of smiting his enemies and in intelligence, prowess and grace, was equal to the preceptor Sukra or Aswini (2). The prince was always encircled by other princes of equal age, intelligence, energy, prowess and exertion (3). They sometimes used to engage themselves in scriptural discussions, sometimes in the criticism of poems, dramas and music, sometimes in the pleasurable game at dice, sometimes in learning the use of arms and the art of warfare and sometimes in riding elephants, horses, or in driving cars (4—5). Thus did the prince, filled with delight, sported day and night in the company of other princes (6). While they sported there many sons of the Brāhmanas, Kshatriyas and Vaisyas of the same age delightedly joined them (7). After some time two Nāga princes, sons of Ashwatara, came to the earth from the region of the Nāgas (8). These two youthful and beautiful (Nāgas) disguised as Brāhmanas, remained there, sporting delightedly in diverse ways with those princes and other Brāhmana boys. All those princes, the sons of the Brāhmanas, Kshatriyas, Vaisyas, and the sons of the Nāga used to bathe together, rub their bodies, put on their clothes, paste their bodies with unguents and take their meals (9—11). Out of love for the prince those two Nāga princes used to come there delightedly every day (12). With various sports, merriment and conversation the prince too attained to great satisfaction from them (13). Without them he could not take his food, bathe, or drink honey; nor could he enjoy or read scriptures for the improvement of his own self (14). And without that high-souled one they too used to spend night in the nether region sighing heavily and used to come away every day (15) After a long time the father asked the two sons :—" To whom in the region of mortals are you so attached, O my sons? (16). You two, beautiful as you are, have not been seen by me for many days during the day time in the nether region, I see you only in the night" (17).

THE SON said :—Thus addressed by their sire and bowing with folded palms those two great sons of the king of serpents replied :—(18). "O father, there is a son of Shatrujit celebrated by the name of Hritadhwaja, endued with beauty and simplicity, heroic, honourable and sweet speeched ; he does not speak uncalled for, is an expert in speaking, learned friendly and a mine of accomplishments ; he honours the honourable, is intelligent, modest and has humility for ornament ; our minds have been pilfered by his good behaviour and love and we have no attachment, O father, either for the region of Nāgas or the region Bhuva (19—21). In his separation even the nether region does not appear cool but produces affliction from heat, in his company even the rays of the sun give delight" (22). The father said :—" Blessed is that son of a pious man whose accomplishments are being sung even in his absence by accomplished beings like yourselves (23). Persons, well-read in scriptures, (sometimes) behave themselves bad (whereas) there are ignorant men who behave well ; O my sons, I consider him more blessed who has a good character as well as a knowledge of scriptures (24). His father has a true son whose friends speak of his qualities as a friend and whose enemies speak highly of his prowess (25.) For the satisfaction of the mind of that your benefactor, have you ever accomplished his desired for objects ? (26). He is blessed and blessed is his life and birth from whom persons, expecting something, do not go away disappointed and who is never weak in doing good to his friends (27). You can without hesitation confer upon him whatever he likes of gold, jewels, conveyances and seats that are in my house (28). Cursed is the life of that man, who, without returning the benefit of friends doing good, thinks, 'I am living" (29). People desire for the perpetual advancement of that wise man, who, like a cloud, showers benefits upon his friends and injuries on enemies" (30). The sons said :—" What can we do for him who always does what should be done and in whose house persons are always united with their desired-for objects (31). Where are in the nether region those jewels, seats, conveyances, dresses and ornaments that are in his house? (32). The knowledge that exists in him is not to be seen elsewhere. O father, he is the foremost of those who sever the doubts of the wise (33). There is one thing to be done by him which it is impossible for us to accomplish—only Brahmā, Vishnu, Maheswara and others can do it" (34). The father said :—"Whether it is within my power or not I wish to hear of that excellent work of his. What is there which the learned cannot do? (35). Those who have a firm perseverence can get by all they desire—the dignity of a god, that of the king of immortals or that which even they worship (36). For the energetic men who have controlled their minds and senses there is nothing unknownable, unapproachable and unattainable either in this world or in the celestial region (37). While moving on an ant goes to the length of a thousand yoyanas and if he does not like to go, Garuda even cannot stir out a footstep (38). There is nowhere to go or not to go for inactive men. Where is the earth and the region of Dhruva, which the king Uttanapada's son Druva attained to although living on earth (39). Tell me, O sons, therefore what you can do for the great prince by which you may be freed from his debt" (40). The sons said :—"What had befallen that one of good conduct in his boyhood was described by that high-souled one, O father (41). Once came to the king Shatrujit a leading and prosperous twice-born one by name Gālava, taking an excellent horse (42). He said to the king :— "Coming to my hermitage, O king, a sinful wretch of a demon is devastating it (43). Assuming the forms of a lion, elephant and of other small wild animals day and night he uselessly so obstructs me who am inmersed in concentration and meditation and am observant of the vow of silence, that my mind is agitated (44—45.) I am capable of consuming him immediately with the fire of anger, but I do not like to waste, O king, my hard earned austerities (46). O king, once on a time, being distressed by him, while I was sighing heavily with a depressed heart on seeing that demon, this horse was immediately dropped down from the sky and words were uttered not by bodily beings. Hear them, (47—48). "To you is given this most excellent horse, which, without exertion, is capable of going round the circumference of the entire earth along with the sun (49). It shall have its course unobstructed in the nether region, in the firmament or in the water and and its motion shall not be broken even while going to all the quarters or the mountains (50). Since it is capable of going round the circumference of the earth without any exertion it shall be known on earth by the name of Kuvalaya (51). O foremost of the twice-born, riding on this horse Hritadwaja, the son of the king Satrujit, shall destroy that sinful wretch of a demon who is distressing you day and night. And obtaining this jem of a horse he will be well-known through it (52—53)." For this I have come to you ; subdue him, O king, who throws impediments in the way of asceticism. A king too is entitled to a due share of ascetic merit (54). I dedicate, O king, this jem of a horse to you. Do you order your son so that virtue may not disappear" (55). At his words the virtuous-souled king, placing his son Hritadwaja on that jem of a horse and performing benedictory rites, despatched him with Gālava. Taking him the ascetic too repaired to his exalted hermitage (56—57).

CHAPTER XXI.

THE FATHER said :—Wonderful is your story, O sons, tell me what was done by the prince proceeding along with Gālava (1). The sons said :—Residing in the charming hermitage of Gālava the son of the king removed all the impediments of those conversant with Brahman (2). That wretch of a Dānava, beside himself with vanity, could not perceive that the heroe Kuvalayāswa was living in the hermitage of Gālava (3). Thereupon one day, to inflict the Brāhmana Gālava, engaged in evening prayers, he came there assuming the form of a boar (4). Then the disciples of the ascetic crying aloud, the prince, riding quickly on his horse and taking up the bow, pursued the boar (5). And stretching his strong and beautifully painted bow he struck him with a bow lustrous like the crescent (6). Being pierced by the arrow and anxious to save his life the beast entered into a huge forest abounding in hilly trees (7). Then spurred on by the prince engaged in satisfying the command of his father, the horse, fleet as the mind, quickly pursued him (8). Then passing over quickly a thousand yoyanas the boar fell into a pit on the face of the earth (9). And following him immediately the prince too, with the horse, fell into that huge pit covered with darkness (10). The prince could not see him there : he then saw the light and nether region, but could not see him (11). He saw there a city resembling that of Purandara, surrounded by ramparts and abounding in a number of golden palaces (12). Entering into that city he did not see any man—and then while retracing his steps quickly he espied a damsel (13). Thereat that one of a slender make was asked by him. "To whom and for what are you going?" The damsel said nothing and went up to a palace (14). Binding the horse somewhere the prince fearlessly followed her having his eyes expanded with wonderment (15). He then saw a damsel like Rati, the companion of Kâma, lying on a highly spacious bed-stead all made of gold (16). Her countenance was like that of the moon: eye-brows fair, hips and breast round; her lips were like Vimva fruits; she was thin built and her eyes were like red lotuses (17). Her nails were dark-blue and a little high; her body was dark-blue and tender and her hands and legs were coppery; her thighs were like the trunks of an elephant—she had beautiful teeth and her curling locks were dark-blue, thin and firm set (18). Beholding her with every limb fair like the tender creeper (wife) around the body of the bodiless (god of love) the prince took her to be a goddess of the nether region (19). Beholding him too with dark-blue locks, with well-built thighs, arms and shoulders that fair one also took him for Madana (the god of love) (20). Having her mind agitated that noble lady, of a slender make, rose up but immediately yielded to the control of bashfulness, wonder and restlessness (21). (She thought) "Who is he? Is he a god, a Yaksha, a Gandharva, a serpent, a Vidyadhara or a man who practised virtues only that has come here?" (22). Indulging in this way in various thoughts, sighing heavily and stting on the earth, that one, of inebriete eyes, fell into a trance (23). Assailed by the shafts of Cupid the prince too, approaching, consoled her and said "Do not fear" (24). Taking up a palmyra fan, the damsel, who had been seen before by the high-souled one, began to fan her anxiously (25). Then soothing her he enquired into the cause of her trance and the damsel, a little abashed, described every thing through her companion (26). She described to the prince at length, that the trance was owing to her seeing him, as she had been commissioned by her mistress (27). The woman said:—"O prince, she is the daughter of the king of Gandharvas living in the celestial region celebrated by the name of

Vishawavasu. This one, of fair eye-brows, is known as Madalasā (28). The fierce Dānava, capable of riving the enemies, known as Pātālaketu, the son of Vajraketu, lives in the nether region (29). When she came to the garden without me that vicious-souled one, resorting to his illusive energy begotten of darkness, carried her away (30). The Asura shall espouse her on the thirteenth lunar day. He does not deserve this fair one as a Sudra is not entitled to read the Vedas (31). While at the end of the day this lady was about to lay violent hands upon her own life Surabhi said to her :—" The wretch of a Dānava shall not be able to get you. (32). O great lady, the one, who will pierce him with shafts when gone to the region of mortals, shall soon become your husband. (33). I am her loving companion by name Kundalā, daughter of Vindhyavān and the wife of Veerapushkaramālin. (34). My husband being slain by Shumbha I am observing a vow and bent upon going to the next world roaming about from one shrine to another by virtue of my celestial gait. (35). The vicious-souled Pātālaketu, assuming the form of a boar, has been pierced with an arrow by some one for protecting the ascetics. (36). For learning the truth I have come here speedily, for certain that wretch of a Dānava has been struck by some body. (37). Listen, now to the cause of her falling into a trace. O conferrer of honors, from the very moment she saw you she fell in love with you. (38). You are like the son of a god and gifted with sweet speech and other accomplishments. She is the wife of that one by whom this Dānava has been pierced. (39). For this reason she has fallen into a great trance. Will this spare.built damsel go through life-long mesiries? (40). She has been attached to you whereas another will be her husband and then her misery will last for life; Surabhi's word can never be otherwise. (41). I have been stricken with grief, O lord. For my love for her I have come here: there is no particular difference between one's own body and her companion (42). If this fair one can get a desired-for heroic husband, I can then carry on my hard austerities with a mind shorn of anxiety (43). O you great one, who are you and for what have you come here? Are you a deity, a Daitya, a Gandharva, a Pannaga or a Kinnara? (44). For such is not a human body nor can he come here. Do you therefore speak to me the truth as I have told you" (45). Kuvalayāshwa said:—"You have asked me, O you conversant with virtue, who I am and for what I have come. Listen, O you of unsullied understanding, I shall relate all from the very beginning (46). I am the son of the king Satrujit. Despatched by my sire, O fair one, for protecting the ascetics I came to the hermitage of Gālava (47). While I engaged in protecting the ascetics of pious observances some body, assuming the form of a boar, came to obstruct them (48). Being struck by me with an arrow resplendent like the crescent he fled away quickly and, I on horse back, followed him (49). Both he and my horse all on a sudden fell into a pit. And I, on horse back, alone roamed about in darkness (50). Then while I got light I saw you. But when asked by me you gave no reply (51). Following you then I entered into this most excellent palace. I have thus spoken to you the truth—I am neither a god nor a Dānava; (52) nor a Pannaga, nor a Gandharva nor a Kinnara, O you of pure smiles. All these deities and others, O Kundalā, are worthy of my veneration. I am a man and you should not fear me" (53).

THE SONS said:—Then filled with delight that damsel became inert with bashfulness. She kept gazing on the most beautiful countenance of her companion and could not speak anything else (54). Her companion (Kundalā) delighted with hearing that all that he said was compatible with the words of Surabhi, replied. Kundalā said (55). "O hero, you have spoken the truth—there is no doubt about your words. Her heart shall not go elsewhere. Seeing you she has been pacified (56). Supreme grace seeks refuge with the moon, the rays with the sun, prosperity with the lucky, endurance with the heroe and forgiveness with the good (57). Undoubtedly that sinful wretch of a Dānava has been struck by you. Why should Surabhi, the mother of kine, speak falsehood? (58) Blessed and fortunate is she by having you near her; do you, O hero, duly perform what should be done now" (59). The sons said:—O father, the prince then said to her;—"I am not my master; how can I espouse this damsel without obtaining permission?" (Kundalā said):—Don't speak like this. She is really the daughter of a god. Marry her." Thus addressed by her he agreed to marry her. (Kundalā) then thought of Tumvuru, her family priest. He too, for his love for Madalasā and reverence for Kundalā, immediately came there with *Samit* and *Kuçā* in his hands. Lighting up fire, offering oblation consecrated with Mantras, performing the benedictory rites, and celebrating duly the nuptials of the girl that intelligent (ascetic) repaired to his hermitage for carrying on his asceticism (60—64). She (Kundalā) then said to her companion "I have been satisfied, O fair one, seeing you, beautiful as you are, connected with him (65). Now with an undisturbed mind I shall engage in matchless austerities. I shall have my sins washed by the water of the holy river and then I shall not be so again (66)." She then, desirous of going away, bending low with humility and with words suppressed by the love for her companion, said to the prince (67). Kundalā said:—"Even men cannot instruct persons like you, O you of matchless wisdom, how can women? So I do not impart instructions upon you. (68). But my heart has been attracted by love for this youthful damsel and you too trust me. Therefore I do remind you, O slayer of enemies (69); that a husband should always maintain and protect his wife. A wife always helps a husband in the acquirement of virtue, profit and desire (70). When a husband and a wife are attached to each other then is the union of three-fold objects, namely, virtue, profit and desire (is brought about) (71). How can a man, O lord, acquire virtue without wife or how can he get profit or desire—for these three are established in a wife (72.) And in the same way a wife, without her husband, is not capable of acquiring virtue etc for the accomplishment of three fold objects is dependant upon the conjugal relation (73). O prince, without wife a man cannot adore the gods, the ancestral manes, the servants and the guests (74). In the absence of a wife or when united with a bad wife, the wealth, even when acquired by men and brought to their house, is spent away (75). It is directly seen that men cannot accomplish their desired for objects without wives. The husband and wife, when they jointly carry on pious observances, attain to three fold virtues (76). As a man satisfies his ancestral manes with offspring, the guests with food and the immortals with adoration, so with all these should he protect his chaste wife (77). The wife too, without her husband, cannot acquire, virtue, desire, wealth and offspring for these three-fold objects follow only the conjugal, relation (78). I have thus said this to you both. I shall now go to my wished for place. Do you advance with her in prosperity, offspring and happiness (79).

THE SONS said:—Having said this, embraced her companion and saluted him, she, with her celestial motion, went away where she liked (80). Having placed her on the horse while Satrujit's son was about to come out of the nether region, the offspring, of Danu, informed of it, all on a sudden cried out:—"He is stealing away that jem of a girl which had been brought from heaven by Pātālaketu (81—82). Then with Parighas, Nishtringshas, maces, darts, arrows and other weapons the host of the Dānavas came there along with Pātālaketu (83). Then exclaiming "Wait! wait!" those leading Dānavas made a downpour of arrows and darts upon the prince (84). Then the highly powerful son of Satrujit easily, as if smiling, sundered all those weapons with a network of arrows (85). Cut into pieces by his arrows the mass of swords, Saktis, Hrishthis and daggers of (the Daityas) covered, in no time, the surface of the nether region (86). Then taking up the weapon Tashtra he discharged it at the Dānavas. By it, greatly fierce like a garland of flames, all the Dānavas, with Pātālaketu, were consumed, with their bones reduccd to ashes like the sons of Sagara by the energy of Kapila (87—88). Having slain the leading Asuras, the prince, on horse back in company with that jem of a female, went to his father's city (89).

Having saluted him he communicated to his father all—his going to the nether region and meeting with Kundalā (90); his obtaining Madalasā, his encounter with the Dānavas, their destruction by arms and as well as his return (91). Hearing of the adventure of that one of a charming disposition his father was exceedingly pleased; then embracing his son he said to him son (92). "Worthy and high-souled as you are, O son, you have redeemed my promise and releaved from fear the ascetics practising their own pious observances (93). The fame, that had been established by my forefathers, and had been spread by me, has been magnified by you, O heroe, endued with prowess as you are (94). The person, who does not destroy the fame, wealth or prestige acquired by his father, is considered as of mediocre worth (95). And the wise designate him as the best of men, who, by virtue of his inherent might, increases the influence (96). And that one, who decreases the wealth, power or fame acquired by his father, is called the worst of men (97). I had rescured Brāhmanas as you have done; but you have, O my son, O foremost of men, in addition to this gone to the nether region and destroyed the Asuras (98). Blessed are you therefore, O my son; and obtaining you who have excelled all in virtues I am worthy of being applauded even by the virtuous (99). The man, who is not excelled by his son in generosity, wisdom and prowess does not experience, me-thinks, the joy of having a son (100). Oh fie on the life of a man, who is known in this world through his father and blessed is his birth who, through his son, obtains fame (101). He, who is known through himself, is fortunate, he who is known through his father or grand-father is middling but the worst of all is the man who gains renown through his mother or maternal relations (102). Do you therefore, O my son, flourish in riches, power and happiness. Never do you forsake this daughter of Gandharvas" (103). Having thus addressed him repeatedly with many sweet words and embraced him the father sent his son along with his wife to his house (104). And in company with his wife he began to sport in the palace of his father as well as in other places, in gardens, woods and slopes of the mountains (105). Saluting the feet of her father-in-law and mother-in-law every morning, that fair and youthful damsel disported with him (106).

—:o:—

CHAPTER XXII.

THE SONS said:—Then after a considerable time the king again addressed his son "Go now and wander over the world for the deliverance of the Brahmanas (1). Mounting on this horse, in the morning you should, every day, be intent upon ever seeing that the leading Brāhmanas may not meet with obstacles (2). There are hundreds of wicked Dānavas born from sinful sources. Do you so act that the ascetics may not meet with hindrances from them (3). Then the prince did as he was commanded by his father.

Day after day the king's son, at the early part of the day, ranged over the entire earth and then saluted the feet of his sire; and the remaining portion of the day he passed merrily with the dainty-waisted damsel (4—5). It so happened that once on a time while he was passing along the banks of the Yamunā he espied Pātālaketu's younger brother Tālaketu, who was living in a hermitage at that place (6). That Dānava, of illusive powers, remained there assuming the form of an ascetic. Remembering former enemity he said to the prince (7). "O prince, if you wish, do what I tell you; O you of truthful vows, you should not disregard the prayer of one (8). For acquiring virtue I shall celebrate a sacrifice and shall also perform the *Ishtis*. For this I shall have to make necessary fires but I have no sacrificial presents to give (9). Therefore for my gold, give me, O heroe, the ornament that is around your neck, and protect my hermitage so long I do not come back speedily, after having, under water, propitiated the deity Varuna, the lord of acquatic animals, with Vedic formulæ relating to Varuna conducive to the well-being of the creatures." When he had said this the prince saluting conferred upon him his own ornament (10—12). He said to him, "Go you with a heart free from anxiety and I shall remain near your hermitage as commanded by you until your return. Myself remaining here no one will present any obstacle. Confiding in me, O Brahman, carry-out your desire" (13—14). Thus addressed by him he entered into the water of the river and he too protected his asylum created by illusion (15). Then going from the water to Madalasā Tālaketu said to her in the presence of others :— (16). "While protecting the ascetics near my asylum, the heroic Kuvalayāshwa, fighting to the best of his power and destroying in battle the enemies of the Brāhmanas, was struck on his breast with a dart by a wicked Daitya resorting to the power of illusion (17—18). While dying he gave this neck ornament to me. He has been cremated in the forest by the Sudra ascetics (19). While his horse, terrified and with tears in its eyes, was neighing distressfully it was carried off by that wicked Dānava (20). This has been witnessed by me, heartless and wicked as I am. After this you should do what ought to be done at this juncture (21). Do you also take this neck ornament capable of giving solace to your heart. What shall we ascetics do with gold?" (22). The sons continued:—Saying this and throwing the ornament on the earth he went away as he had come. And then all, filled with grief and possessed by trance, fell down on earth (23). And immediately regaining consciousness all the females of the king's seraglio, the queen and the king, stricken heavily with grief, began to bewail (24). Beholding that neck ornament and hearing of the death of her husband, Madalasā at once renounced her life (25). And there arose a great noise of lamentations in the houses of the citizens and in the palace (26). Beholding Madalasā dead from the separation of her husband, the king, gaining his mental equilibrium by his judgment, said to all the people:—(27). "You should not mourn. I perceive the unreality of all, of myself and of all connected with me (28). Should I mourn for my daughter-in-law? To consider it properly none of them should be mourned for they have done their duties (29). Having engaged himself in the protection of the Brāhmanas in pursuance of my command my son met with his death. Why should (therefore) that intelligent one be mourned (30)? While he has sacrificed his body, a body which must go, on behalf of the twice-born, it will forsooth lead to his well-being (31). This one born in a noble family has followed her husband. Why should she be mourned? A woman has no other god but husband (32). If she had survived her husband she would have been an object of pity to ourselves, our friends and to other compassionate people (33). Hearing of the destruction of her husband this lady immediately followed him. Why should she be mourned by the wise? (34). Those women who suffer from the loss of their husbands should be mourned and not they who die with them. This grateful lady had not to suffer the loss of her husband (35). How can a woman consider her husband as a man who is the dispenser of happiness of both the worlds, here and hereafter (36)? Thereupon neither he, nor this lady, nor I, nor his mother should be mourned. Having given his life for the interest of the Brâhmanas he has saved us all (37). Having given up his half nourished (youthful) body my noble son has liberated himself from his debts to the Brâhmanas, to virtue and to myself (38). Having cast off his life in battle for the protection of the twice-born he has vindicated his own heroism, his mother's chastity and the purity of my race (39).

THE SON said:—Hearing of her son's destruction and beholding her husband, Kuvalayâshwa's mother followed her husband (40). Saying:—" O king, neither my mother nor my sister experienced such a joy as I have done on hearing of the destruction of my son for the protection of the ascetics (41). In vain did their mothers bear them who die, assailed by deseases and sighing sorrowfully before their friends (42). But those, who while fighting fearlessly for the protection of the kine and the twice-born are wounded and die, are really men on earth (43). The father, of a man who does not turn away from suitors, friends and enemies, has indeed a son in him and his mother has borne a hero (44). When her son is either victorious in battle or slain in battle the mother then considers the misery of carrying a child crowned with good result (45)." The sons said:—The king then performed the funeral obsequies of his daughter-in-law; then issuing out he bathed and offered water to his son (46). Tâlaketu, too coming out of the water of the Yamunâ, said to the prince the following sweet words in love (47). "Go, O prince, I have got the accomplishment of my object through you. You having waited here steadfastly I have been able to accomplish my long cherished work (48), the sacrifice of Varuna, the high-souled king of waters. All this which I had desired has been carried out (49)." Then saluting him the king mounted his steed gifted with the vigor of Suparna or the wind and repaired to the city of his father (50).

CHAPTER XXIII.

THE SONS said:—Then reaching his own city hastily desirous of saluting the feet of his father and beholding Madalasā the prince saw the people filled anxiety and their faces betraying sadness. And immediately he found them overwhelmed with wonderment and their faces indicated joy. He saw some others with eyes expanded exclaiming "Luck! Luck!"; and speaking to one another in joy they said "Long live, O you of great auspiciousness. May your enemies meet with destruction, do you gladden the hearts of your parents and free us also from anxiety" (1—4). Saying this they encircled him on his front and rear. And experiencing instantaneous joy he entered his father's house (5). Embracing him his auspicious mother, father and his other relations conferred upon him blessings (6). Saluting him and filled with surprise he asked his father "What is this all, O father." He too described to him every thing (7). Then hearing of the demise of his beloved consort Madalasā and seeing his parents before him he was sunk in a sea of shame and sorrow (8). He thought:—"Hearing of my death that chaste lady gave up her existence. Oh fie on my cruel heart (9). I am heartless and ignoble. Shameless as I am, I am alive without that one of the eyes of a deer who, for me, met with death (10). Then consoling his mind and driving away his emotion, he, stricken with grief and sighing heavily, again thought (11). "If I resign my life because she is dead on my account, what good can I do to her? This is applauded by the females (only) (12). If I mourn poorly exclaiming again and again "Oh my dear!" this will not lead to my praise for we are men (13). If overcome by grief and stricken with sorrow I throw away my garlands and besmear my body with dirt I shall be the object of the triumph of my enemies (14). My duty is to subdue my enemies and serve the king, my father. My life is at his command, how can I give it up? (15). Then what again do I consider as my duty? Have I done with enjoying women? But that even will not lead to the well-being of that thin-built (lady) (16). Whether good or bad to her I should observe some pledge for her. This even is small in as much as she has given up her life for me (17)."

THE SONS said:—Having thus made up his mind, he performed the ceremony of offering water and other rites. Hritadhwaja again said:—(18) "When that thin-built Madalasā is no longer my wife, no other (woman) shall be my wife in this life (19). Excepting that daughter of a Gandharvā having the eyes of a doe I shall not sport with any other woman. This is the vow I take (20). Leaving that my pious wife moving like a she-elephant I shall not enjoy in the company of any other woman. This is the vow I take" (21).

THE SONS said:—Then, O father, giving up all enjoyments in the company of women, in her separation he began to beguile his time in disporting with companious of the same age gifted with excellent character (22). Who is capable, O father, of accomplishing this great work for him? Even the Deity cannot with difficulty do it, what to speak of others? (23).

THE (INNERT) SON said:—Hearing those their words their father became sorry. Then deliberating over the matter, the king of Nāgas, smiling, said to his sons (24) :—" If by knowing things to be impossible of execution people renounce perseverence in action a great injury will be produced from the absence of perseverence (25). Therefore without giving up manliness a man should engage in actions. The issue of an act depends upon the energy of an individual as well as on the Divinity (26). I shall therefore so exert in this matter that I may in no time come off successful" (27). The (innert) son said :—Having said this the king of Nagas, repairing to the sacred spot *Plakshavatarana* on the mountain Himavān, engaged in hard austerities (28). Then with his mind centered in her, restraining his food and bathing during three twilights he hymned the goddess of learning, Saraswati (29). Aswatara said :—" Desirous of adoring the auspicious goddess who protects the universe, I, bowing down my head, hymn Saraswati sprung from Brahmā (30). All states, real or unreal, fraught with profit or liberation, although unconnected with thee, O goddess, appear as being connected with thee (31). O goddess, thou art the supreme letter in which all is established. And this supreme letter pervades all like an atom (32). The letter is the great Brahman and the universe composed of water. And as fire exists in wood and as the atom pervades the earth so this Brahman as well as the entire universe exist in thee. O goddess, the letter Om, the stable and the unstable, the three measures, the existent and the non-existent are in thee. The three worlds, the three Vedas, the tree branches of learning, the three fires, the three luminous bodies, the three orders, the kinds of morality, the three principles, the three sounds, the three gods, the modes of life, the three kinds of time, the three ages, the ancestral manes, day and night—all these, O goddess, constitute the three measures which are thy form, O Saraswati (33—37). It is by the utterance given by thee, O goddess, that the Brahmvādins can perform the seven kinds of recitations, original and eternal, assigned to Somā, Hari and Paka, laid in Brahmanas for persons of diverse creeds. There is another supreme form of thine in half measure which is not represented, which is divine, and not susceptible of changes, decay or development; this thy supreme form I cannot describe in words. It cannot be described by mouth, tongue or palate. Indras, Vasus, Brahmā, the moon, the sun, and the other constellations, (are thy forms). In thee exist the abode of the universe, the form of the universe, the lord of the universe, the Great Lord, whatever has been mentioned in Sankhya and Vedanta, and has been ascertained by various branches; whatever is without beginning, middle or end, whatever is existent and non-existent, whatever is real; that which is one, that which is many, that which is the root of the difference in creation; and that which goes by the name of six attributes, four objects and which is the root of the three-fold qualities; that which is the essence of various powerful energies; that which is happiness or misery; and that which is supreme felicity is manifest in thee (38—44). Thus thou dost, O goddess, pervade all objects, crude, or manifest. In thee exists Brahmā both in His one and many forms (45). Through thee are properly perceived all objeets that are eternal, that are destructible, the gross, the subtle or supersubtle, that exists in the earth, in the sky, and at any other place. To thee are related all that has no form, all that has a form, that which is perfect, that which is partial, that which is in heaven, that which is on earth, that which is in sky and that which is at any other place. They are known only through thy vowels and consonants" (46—47). Thus hymned by him, the goddess Saraswati, Vishnu's tongue, replied to the high-souled Ashwatara, the king of Nagas (48). "O brother of Kamvala, O king of Nagas, I shall confer upon you a boon. Tell me and I shall give what exists in your mind" (49). Ashwatara said:—"First giving me, O goddess, Kamvala as my help do thou then confer upon me a knowledge of all the musical notes" (50).

SARASWATI said :—"O king of Nāgas, there are seven notes, seven kinds of *Ragas** ; seven classes of songs, seven *Murchanas*† ; forty nine measures and three *Gramas*‡. All this shall you sing as well as Kamvala, O sinless one (51—52). By my favour you will know many other things also, O king of serpents. And I shall confer upon you a knowledge of four *Padas*,§ three *Talas*,‖ three *Layas*,¶ six *Yatis*$ and four *Todyas***. By my favour, O king of serpents, (you will have a knowledge of) all this or more that is included in this or is dependent on this and that is related to vowels and consonants. All this has been exhaustively given to you as well as to Kamvala (53—55). O serpent, on earth and in the nether region, you two shall be the authors of all these—in the nether region, the region of gods, on earth, O you serpents(56). The (inert) son said :—Having said this the lotus-eyed goddess Saraswati, the tougue of all, immediately vanished from the view of the Nāga (57). And as said both the brothers acquired all that knowledge consummate regarding Pada, measure and notes (58). Then singing by notes to the accompaniment of time kept by stringed instru-

---

* *Raga* means the agreeable effect that is produced by a determinate succession of notes. *Raga* is not exactly what is understood by air for one *Raga* may consist of a number of airs. *Ragas* are six in number.

† "A term expressive of the full extent of the Hindu scale of music ; and as this consists of three octaves there are consequently twenty one *Murchanas*."

‡ A series of notes arranged and disposed to certain laws. A *grama* consists of seven principal notes *Sa, Ri, Ga, Ma, Pa,* D*ha, Ni* corresponding to *C, D, E, F, G, A, and B.*

§ *Pada* is of four kinds *Ashtayi* 1st strain, *Antara*, second, *Sanchari*, third and *Abhoga* fourth ; every air must consist of at least two parts.

‖ Musical time or measure.

¶ The stream of time that runs through a piece of composition from the instant of its adoptiou to that when it is dropped. The three kinds of *Laya* are (1) *Madhya* normal, (2) *Vilamvita* next and then (3) *druta*.

$ A stop is rest in music.

** Four kinds of instruments (1) *Tara*, stringed (2) *Anaddha*—made of hide (3) *Sushira*, blowing instruments (4) *Ghana*, metalic instruments.

ments, the Nāgas, with a view to worship the Lord seated on the summit of Kailaça, the best of mountains, the destroyer of Cupid's body with their words and senses restrained and minds concentrated, exerted themselves greatly, morning, night, noon and evening (59—60). Then after a considerable time, the Deity, having the emblem of a bull on his banner, was greatly pleased with their songs and said :—"Pray for a boon" (61). Then bowing to Mahadeva, the sable-throated lord of Umā, Ashwatara, along with Kamvala, said: (62.) "O thou having six sorts of wealth, O god of gods, O thou having three eyes, if thou art propitiated with me then do thou confer upon us the boon we pray for (63). O god, may Kuvalayāshwa's dead wife be born as my daughter at once, attaining to the same age (64). May she, endued with the same beauty, and the recollection of her pristine birth, be born in my house as a Yogini and Yogamāta (the mother of illusion) 65).

MAHADEVA said :—O foremost of Pannagas, by my favour, what you have said shall all come to pass. Listen to this, O serpent (66). At the time of her Srāddha, do you, O foremost of serpents, being pure and of controlled mind, eat the middle *Pinda* (67). After you had eaten it, from your middle hood shall that auspicious damsel spring in the same form in which she died (68). Cherishing this desire in your mind do you offer water to your departed manes; and as soon as you will sigh that one of fair eye-brows, that auspicious damsel, shall come out from your middle hood and in the same shape in which she died (69)." Thereupon hearing this and saluting the great deity those two, filled with delight, again reached Rasātala (70). Then the Nāga, the younger brother of Kamvala, performed the Srāddha and as directed ate the middle Pinda (71). Then cherishing that desire as soon as he drew forth a sigh there sprang from his middle hood that slender-waisted damsel in the same form as before (72). The serpent did not disclose it to any one but secretly kept that one of fine teeth in his seraglio guarded by women (73).

Every day the two Nāga princes, resembling the immortals, sported happily with Hritadwaja (74). One day the snake-king delightedly spoke to his sons:—"Why do you not do what I had said to you before? Why, my sons, do you not bring to me that giver of honors, that prince, the benefactor of yours so that I may render some good to him? (75—76)" Thus addressed by their father affectionately they, going to the city of their friend, sported with that intelligent one (77). Then after having talked on other matters they affectionately invited Kuvalayāshwa to go to their house (78). The prince then said to them "Forsooth this is your house—all these riches, conveyances, clothes and others are yours as they are mine (79). O sons of the twice born, if you love me, confer upon me whatever you like of those riches, gems etc. (80). I have hitherto been disappointed by the wicked destiny since you do not regard my house as your own (81). If you wish to encompass my pleasure, if you wish to favour me then consider these my riches and house as yours (82). What is yours is mine and what is mine is yours. Know this for certain, and you two are my life moving about outside (83). Never again, O best of twice-born one, speak of such a difference. For love for me be favourable. I charge you on my life" (84). Then with their faces bathed with tears of love and somewhat enraged from affection those two Nāga princes said to the king's son:—(85—86). "O Hritadhwaja, there is no doubt in what you have said to us. Even such is our feeling. You need not fear otherwise (87). But our noble father repeatedly told us "I wish to see Kuvalayāshwa (88)." Then rising up from his excellent seat Kuvalayāshwa said:—" My father has said" and then bowed low to the ground.

KUVALAYASHWA said:—" Blessed am I and great is my piety; who else is equal to me for my father is so eager to see me (89). Rise up, I do not like to disregard his command even for a moment; I swear by his feet (90)." The inert (son) said :—Having said this the prince went away with them. And having issued out of the city they reached the holy Gomati (91). The sons of the king and Nāga went along the breast of the river. The prince thought that their house was on the other side of the river (92). Then they pulling him took the prince to the nether region. And there he saw the two Nāga princes shining with the effulgence of the gems crowning their crest and bearing auspicious marks on their breast (93). Beholding them of beautiful persons, the prince, with eyes expanded with wonder, said smilingly out of love :—" Well done, O foremost of the twice-born" (94). Then they communicated it to their father, the king of serpents, the gentle Ashwatara, worshipped even of the celestials (95). Then the prince saw the nether region to be highly charming ; beautified with boys and youths, old people and serpents, daughters of Nāgas bedecked with ear-rings and necklaces, sporting all around as the sky is beautified with stars, filled with songs accompanied by the music of flutes and *Vinas*, with the sounds of *Mridangas*, *Pannavas* and *Atodyas* and abounding in hundreds of beautiful houses (96—97). Casting his looks upon the nether region, that subduer of foes, the son of Satrujit proceeded along with those two loving serpents (98). Then they all entered the palace of the king of serpents and saw the great king seated there with excellent garlands and dress, adorned with ear-rings set with gems, bedecked with chains of transparent pearls—that great one adorned with armlets, and seated on a throne completely made of gold—whose true form had been hidden by the effulgence of rubies, sappires and lapises (99—102). He was then shown by them, saying, "This is our father" and then said to their father. " This is the hero Kuvalāyaswa"(103). He saluted the feet of the king of Nāgas and the king of Nāgas, too, taking him up, embraced him warmly (104). Then smelling his head he said :— " May you live long. With your enemies slain, may you serve your father and mother (105). Fortunate you are O my child, for even in your absence my sons speak of your extraordinary virtues (106). For this you shall grow in mind, speech and energy. The life of an accomplished man is praiseworthy, while one, devoid of accomplishments, is dead even when alive (107). Encompassing the satisfaction of his parents and giving pain to his enemies, a meritorious man, placing his confidence in great men, secures his own well-being (108). Celestials, departed manes, relatives, Brahmanas, friends, suitors and maimed persons all wish for the long life of a meritorious person (109). Blessed is the life of an accomplished man, desisting from calumny, cherishing kindness for all and giving shelter to the distressed" (110). The (inert) son continued:—Having said thus to the heroe,—the serpent, desirous of entertaining Kuvalayāshwa, spoke to his sons (111). "Having finished our bath and other acts duly, drunk wine, enjoyed other pleasures and taken our meals after our heart we shall, with delighted hearts, spend some time with Kuvalayāshwa in conversation resembling the festivity of heart (112—113)." Satrujit's son silently agreed to that. And the noble of king serpents acted accordingly (114). Then that self-controlled and the truthful king, of the powerful serpents, in the company of his sons and the prince, ate and drank, enjoying the climax of pleasure (115).

CHAPTER XXIV.

JARA (inert) said:—After that high-souled king, of those living on air, had finished his meals, he was adored by his sons as well as by the prince (1). Then the great serpent with delightful words pleased the friend of his sons and said :—(2). "You should, O gentle one, renouncing all misgivings, who have come to my house, tell me even as a son speaks to his father, what I can do for you (3). Tell me what would you have, even if it be hard of obtainment—silver gold, raiment, conveyances or seats" (4). Kuvalayâshwa said :—"By your favour, I have gold in my father's house. I have never felt the want of any such article (5). My father having ruled over the world for a thousand years and yourself over the nether region my mind has never been bent on solicitation (6). They are worthy of heaven and religious merit, who, their father living, consider in their youth, a koti of coins as chaff (7). My friends are of the same temparament with me and my body is free from diseases My father is gifted with wealth and I am with youth ; what then have I not ? (8). A man, having no wealth, has his mind bent upon begging. But myself having enough why should my tongue beg ? (9). Blessed are they who depend on the shade of their father's arms without thinking whethere there is wealth in their house or not (10). But they, who having no father, from their boyhood are engaged in maintaining their relatives, have, me-thinks, been deprived of the taste of happiness by the Providence (11). By your favour, out of the wealth amassed by my father and given to me, I, according to my desire, distribute riches amongst the suitors (12). While I have been able to touch your feet with the jewel cresting my crown and while I have touched your body I have secured all these," (13). Jara (inert) said :—Having been thus addressed with humble words that foremost, of serpents out of love, said to the prince, the benefactor of his sons :—(14). "If you do not wish to take jewels or gold from me, tell me what do you like and I shall confer it upon you" (15). Kuvalayâshwa replied :—"By your favour, O reverend sir, every kind of object is in my house ; I have obtained them in particular from seeing you (16). I have accomplished all my objects and my life has been united with fruits, for being a man I have touched your body who is a god (17). While the dust, of your feet, has been placed on my head, what have I not attained, O king of serpents? (18). And still if you wish to confer upon me a desired for boon, let it be that the inclination for the performance of pious acts may not leave my mind (19). Conveyance, house, seats, gold, jewels, precious stones, wife, meats, drinks, sons, beautiful garlands, perfumeries, song, music of instruments and all other desired for things, I think, are but the fruits of the tree of piety (20—21). Therefore every self-controlled man should water the roots of piety ; there is nothing difficult of attainment to those who are devoted to virtue" (22). Ashwatara said :—" O wise man, your mind shall ever be inclined in this way to virtue. Truly as you have said, such is the fruit of virtue (23). Still having come to my house you must accept something which you like and which cannot be secured in the region of men" (24). Hearing his words the prince cast his looks on the faces of the sons of the king of serpents (25). Then bowing, those two heroes communicated plainly to their father what was in the mind of the prince (26). They said :—"Imposed upon by a wicked-souled, vicious and inimical Dānava his beloved spouse, hearing of his destruction, gave up her life—the daughter of the Gandharva king, known by the name of Madalasā (27—28). Thereat this one faithful (to his wife) made this vow " Renouncing Madalasā I shall not take to any other wife" (29). O father, this hero Hritadhwaja is eager to have a look on her, beautiful of all limbs. If you can do this you will do a good service to him (30)."

ASHWATARA said :—" While the elements have been once decomposed how can they be united again except in a dream or by the illusive energy of Samvara" (31.)

JARA (inert) said :—Then saluting the king of serpents Satrujit's son, filled with bashfulness and love, said to that high-souled one :—(32). "If even, O father, you can show me Madalasā created through the power of illusion I shall consider it a favour done to me" (33). Ashwatara said :—"If you wish to behold (her in) illusion, O my child, see her. Though a boy, you are worthy of my reverence as a preceptor for you have come to my house" (34). Jara (inert) said :—Then the king of serpents brought Madalasā protected in her house. With a view to deceive them he uttered loudly a number of words (35). He then showed the auspicious damsel to the prince. "Is she or not your wife Madalasā, O prince"? (36). Beholding that slender-made damsel he, at once throwing off shame, rushed towards her crying "My beloved," and the Nāga Ashwatara prevented him saying :—(37). "My son, this is illusion. Do not touch her. I have already told you that an illusary figure vanishes as soon as it is touched (38)." At once he fell down senseless on earth exclaiming "O my beloved." The fair one thought (39). "Oh! what great affection has the king for me—his mind is firm since he, who brings the enemies to the ground, has been brought down without weapons (40). I have been shown by him (the serpent) as an illusory (figure). It is evident that an unreal illusion is produced by the active energy of air, water, light, earth and ether" (41)

JARA (the inert son) said :—Then comforting Kuvalayāshwa the serpent told him every thing regarding the revival (of Madalasā) (42). Then delighted on obtaining his beloved (the prince) saluting the Nāga thought of his horse which immediately came. Then mounting on it he started for his charming city (43.)

CHAPTER XXV

———oo———

HAVING returned to his own city he communicated every thing to his father how he had obtained that slender built damsel after she had died (1). That auspicious lady bowed down at the feet of her father-in-law and mother-in-law and honoured all her relations with salutations and embraces with reference to propriety and age. And then there was in that city a great festivity of the citizens (2–3). And Hritadhwaja too, for a long time, sported with that slender-waisted damsel near the fountains of the mountains, the banks of the rivers, in charming forests,as well as gardens (4). And desirous of spending her religious merit through the enjoyment of desirable objects she sported with that greatly beloved one at charming places (5). After a long time the king Satrujit, having governed well the earth, breathed his last (6). Then the citizens installed, as king, his son Hritadhwaja, high-souled and of liberal actions and conduct (7). And while he was governing well his subjects as if they were his own begotten children Madalasā gave birth to her first son (8). The father gave to his intelligent son the name of Vikrānta. The servents were greatly delighted and Madalasā laughed (9). One day while her baby, lying at ease on her lap, was crying in indistinct notes, Madalasā, by way of soothing him, said (10) "Thou art pure, O child, and without a name. It is by imagination that a name has been given to thee. This thy body, composed of five elements, is not thine. Nor dost thou belong to it. Wherefore dost thou weep? (11). Or perhaps thou dost not weep—This is a self produed sound coming out through the king's son. Various qualities, good or bad, relating to the elements, have been attributed to thy organs (12) In this world, beings, extremely feeble, acquire their growth by help of the elements, and taking meats and drinks; but thou hast no growth or decay (13). This body is a covering and it will be shattered and still thou wilt live on; therefore thou shouldst not yield to stupefaction in this body. It is by virtue of good and bad acts engendered by stupefaction, caused by pride and other passions that this covering of a body has been fixed on thee (14). The father, the son, the mother, the wife, the relatives and those that are not so, are nothing; thou shouldst not attach too much importance to this collection of elements (15). Those, who have their minds stupified, consider pain as neutralizing pain and enjoyment as leading to pleasure. Ignorant persons, who have their minds possessed by stupefaction, consider pain as pleasure (16). When a woman laughs her bones come out and her two shining eyes throw out anger. Her breast is a mass of flesh and so is her organ. Therefore is not a woman a hell? (17). On earth is the conveyance, in the conveyance is the body—and in the body is placed another person. The sense of *this is mine* does not exist there as it is in the body. Oh fie on the infatuation (18).

CHAPTER XXVI.

As her son, shorn of attachment, grew up day by day the queen taught him knowledge of self in the shape of ministering to him in sickness etc, (1). As he duly acquired strength and the heart of his father he attained to self-knowledge by his mother's words (2). Having been thus instructed from his very birth the wise (son), with his mind shorn of attachments, did not think of entering the life of the house-holder (3). She gave birth to her second son and the father gave him the name of Suvāhu and thereat Madalasā laughed (4). And she soothing him in the same way as before, that highly intelligent one obtained the same kind of knowledge (5). And when after the birth of the third son the king named him Satrumarddana that one, having fair eye-brows, laughed for some time (6). In the same way he was instructed from his boyhood by that slender-waisted damsel. He was without any desire and rendered no pious offices (7). And when the fourth was born, the king, desirous of giving him a name, looked to Madalasā of pure ways who smiled gently. And while she was thus smiling, the king, somewhat stricken with curiosity, said to her (8).—Whenever I was ready to give a name you laughed. Tell me the cause. Vikrānta, Suvāhu and Satrumarddana, the names I gave, I believe are all good names. The Kshatriyas should have names embodying ideas of heroic spirit (9–10). If they do not find room in your mind, O auspicious lady, you assign a name to this fourth son (11). Madalasā said :—What you have said, O great king, I must carry out. I shall give a name to this fourth son (12). This virtuous one shall be celebrated in the world by the name of Alarka. This your youngest son shall also be intelligent (13). Hearing this meaningless name Alarka given to the son by his mother, the lord of the earth, smilingly said :—(14). "O auspicious lady, this name, which you have given to my son,is meaningliss. Why is this O Madalasā?" (15). Madalasā said :—"I have given the name,O great king,out of fancy only but in consonance with custom. Listen, O king, to the meaninglessness of the names given by you (16). The wise describe the soul as omnipresent but *kranti* means *going fram one place to another* (17). But the Lord of the body being omnipresent does not go (from one place to another). So the name of Vikrānta in my view is meaningless (18). O king, 'in consiquence' of the soul having no form, the name of Suvāhu which you have given to your another son, is meaningless (19). The name of Satrumarddana, which you have given to your third son, has also no meaning. Listen to the reason hereof (20). When the self-same soul lives in every body, then O king, who is its enemy and who its friend ? (21). Elements are destroyed by elements. But can that which has no form perish ? On account of the separate existence of anger and others such a conception is meaningless (22). If in pursuance of custom such imaginary names are conceived why does then Alarka appear meaningless to you?" (23). Thus addressed with excellent words by his queen the highly intelligent king said to his beloved spouse who had spoken the truth "this is so" (24). And when the fair-browed lady again engaged in the same way in instructing her son in the knowledge of self the king said (25)—"What are you doing O foolish one ? You are going to bring ill-luck upon this my son as before by initiating him into the knowledge of self (26). If you wish to encompass my pleasure, if you regard my words, then lead this son to the way of desire (27). The road of action should not be destroyed, O reverend lady, nor should the funeral cake be withheld from the manes. In consonance with good or bad actions the ancestral manes go to heaven, are born as lower animals, or as men or in any other life. When they are stricken with hunger or thirst and are weakened accordingly men, by constantly offering them funeral cakes and oblations of water, relieve the ancestral manes. And O fair-browed lady, in the same way they please the deities and guests (29—30). Gods, men, ancestral manes, goblins, ghosts, Guhyakas, birds, worms, insects and all depend on men for their subsistence (31). Therefore, O slender made lady, perfectly instruct my son in the duties of a Kshatrya which may lead to his well-being both in this world and in the next (32)." Thus addressed by her husband that most excellent lady Madalasā instructed her son Alarka by way of consoling him: (33). " Grow, my son, and gratify my lord with acts. Be you for the good of friends and destruction of enemies (34). Blessed are you, O my son, who, freed from your enemies, will govern the earth for a long time. May all enjoy happiness by your rule, and may you, by acquiring religious merit,be immortal (35). You should attentively gratify the Brâhmanas at every Parva, satisfy the desires of your friends, should think of doing good to others and abstain from violating others' wives (36). By celebrating various sacrifices you should gratify the celestials, with profuse wealth you should please the twice-born; you should satisfy the females with numberless articles of enjoyment and your enemies with fight, O heroe (37). In boyhood satisfy your friends, in youth your worshipped relatives by obeying their commands, in manhood the females having ornaments of noble ancestry and in old age, O my son, in the forest, the rangers thereof (38). While ruling you should gratify your friends, protect the pious, celebrate sacrifices, destroy the wicked and enemies in battle on behalf of kine and Brahmânas and then meet with death (39).

CHAPTER XXVII.

JARA (INERT) said :—Thus comforted by his mother every day the one named Alarka grew up in years and intelligence (1). On his attaining to youth and being invested with sacred thread the wise son of Hritadhwaja, bowing to his mother, said (2) :—" Speak to me all who am bowing to you as to what I should do leading to happiness both here and hereafter" (3). Madalasâ said :—O my child, being installed on the throne, a king, without infringing the duties of his own order, should endevour to please his subjects (4). Abandoning evils* which strike at the seven roots† a king by keeping his counsels, should protect himself from his enemies (5.) As from a car of strong wheels one meets with death in eight ways, so does, forsooth, a king, by giving out counsels (6). He should ascertain whether his enemies have corrupted his courtiers or not; and through careful spies he should make himself acquainted with the ways of his enemies (7). A king should not confide in his friends, adherents and kinsmen; and when the necessity comes he should confide even in his enemies (8). Not influenced by lust a king should acquire the knowledge of place, increase and decrease and possess the six attributes (9). First controlling his self, next the ministers, next the servants, next the citizens he should enter into hostilities with his enemies (10). The king of uncontrolled self, who, without first subjugating all these, desires to defeat his enemies, on being defeated by his courtiers, is brought under the control of his enemies (11). Therefore, my child, desires should be conquered first by a king; on them being brought under control success surely attends a king; but if he is conquered by them he meets with destruction (12). The enemies are lust, anger, covetousness, pride, idea of self and joy, and they bring on the ruin of kings (13. Thinking that Pandu was deprived of his life through lust, that Anirudda was deprived of his son through anger, that Aila was deprived of his life through covetousness that Vena was killed by the twice-born through his arrogance, that Anusuā's son Vali was destroyed through his over weening self conceit and that Puranjaya was killed through excess of joy, one should throw off these passions (14—15). Conquering those the high-souled Mārutta subdued the entire

* Hunting, gambling, sleep during the day, calumny, concupiscence, dancing, singing, sporting, useless walking, drinking, violence, creating malice, ill-will, deceipt, cruelty and villifying others.

† Lordship, counsellors, friends, treasury, punishment, kingdom and capital.

earth. Remembering this a king should cast off all these short-comings (16). A king should take his lessons from the crows, Kokilas, the black-bees, the harts, the serpents, the peacocks, the swans, the cocks and the iron.* A king should act like worms towards his enemies and in season, O king, should show the diligence of acts (18). He should spread like the scintillations of fire or like the seeds of the cotton tree. And governing the earth like the sun and the moon a king should learn wisdom from the prostitute, the lotus, the *Sarava* the *Sutika,* the breast of a woman big with child and the milk-woman. (19—20)†. For governing (his subjects) a king should act like Indra, the king of gods, the sun, Yama, the Moon and the wind-god (21). As Indra pleases the creatures of the earth with showers for four months so the king should satisfy his subjects with self-sacrifice (22). As the sun with his rays draws up the water for eight months so the king, with minute means, should collect his revenue (23). As Yama metes out punishment both to those whom he likes and to those whom he hates when the proper time comes, so the king should impartially deal with those whom he loves and whom he dislikes—the good and the wicked (24). That king truly behaves like the Moon in whose regeme all the subjects are happy and experience delight like what persons derive from seeing the

---

* As charity from a crow, perfection from a Kokila, the habit of accumulation from a bee, the habit of not easily going to the clutches of an enemy from the hart; how to bring down a big enemy with a small expedient from a serpent. He should take the good thing and leave off the bad thing as a swan drinks the milk out of water mixed with it. He should learn how to rise early from a cock and should be hard and useful like iron.

† He should learn from the prostitute how to please many; like lotus he should not only be beautiful of person but be accomplished also. The *Sarava* is a strong animal. Like *Sutika* he should entirely kill his enemy. As milk is created in the breast of a woman for the future child so the king should make preparations for the future. As a milk woman can make many things out of milk so the king should do many things.

full moon (25). As the air scretly goes through all creatures so the king, with spies, should read his citizens, courtiers and friends (26). The king, whose mind is not possessed by lust, the desire for wealth, or any other thing, repairs to the celestial region, O my son (27). The king, who brings back to the pale of their own religion those foolish persons who stay away from right paths and fall off from their duties, goes to the celestial region (28). The king, in whose kingdom, O my child, the duties of the various orders and Asramas do not suffer deterioration, attains eternal happiness both in this world and in the next (29). To establish persons in their own religion which is being disturbed by wicked people constitutes the paramount duty of a king and leads to his success (30). By governing his subjects a king accomplishes his end—and by governing them well and assiduously he is entittled to a portion of their piety (31). A king, who protects the four orders, attains to happiness and ranges with Sakra in his own region (32).

---:o:---

CHAPTER XXVIII.

JARA (inert) said:—Hearing the words of his mother Alarka again accosted her regarding the duties of the various orders and conditions of life (1). "O noble body, you have described to me, the duties of the kings. I wish to hear now of those regarding the various orders and conditions of life" (2). Madalasā said:—"Gifts, study and sacrifice are the duties of a Brāhmana; he has not the fourth duty, except carrying on trade for subsistence (3). The adequate means of his livelihood has been described as three-fold, namely tuition, officiating as priests at sacrifices performed in a pure spirit and receiving sanctified gifts (4). The duties of a Kshatrya have been described as three-fold, namely, gifts, study and sacrifice; the administration of the earth and the use of weapons are the means of his livelihood (5). Gifts, study and sacrifiee constitute the three-fold duties of a Vaiçya; trade, tending cattle and agriculture are the means of his livelihood (6). Gifts, sacrifice and serving the twice-born have been described by me as the duties of a Sudra; handicrafts, serving the other orders, keeping cattle and buying and selling are the means of his livelihood. I have described to you the duties of the orders and hear I shall now describe the duties relating to the diverse modes of life (7—8). By observing the duties of his order and not deviating therefrom a person is crowned with success; but when one does a thing which is proscribed he goes to hell (9). So long as a person, belonging to one of the twice-born orders, has not been invested with sacred thread so long he can act, speak or eat according to his will (10). But when the proper ceremony of investiture is gone through he must live in the house of his spiritual guide as a Brahmacharin. Hear, I shall describe his duties (11). The study of the Vedas, and the keeping of sacred fire, going about begging, taking food with the preceptor's permission after having previously dedicated it to him, to satisfy him completely, promptitude in the preceptor's work, to engage in study at his command, devotion to him, concentration of mind upon him (are the duties of a Brahmacharin) (12—13). Having obtained, one, two or all the Vedas from the preceptor's lips, having saluted him and with his permission he should present *Dakshinâ* to the preceptor (14). Then desirous of entering upon the life of a householder one should do it; or he can, according to his desire, enter upon the fourth mode of life, namely *Vânaprashtha* (15). Or the twice-born one may live in his preceptor's house performing hard austereties; shorn of vanity he should live as a Brahmacharin ministering to his son in the absence of the preceptor and to his disciples in the absence of his preceptor's son'. Then returning from his preceptor's house and desirous of entering upon the life of a householder he should, for leading a domestic life, marry a girl of a different race, befitting him, free from disease and having no defective limb (16—18). Then acquiring wealth by his own exertions he should gratify completely the deities, the departed manes and the guests and support his dependants (19). And as much as lies in his power, he should, with food, support his servants, sons, persons in distress, the blind, the fallen, beasts and birds (20). This is the duty of a householder as well as that of living with his wife while in her season. And he should, to the best of his power, celebrate the five sacrifices (21). Respected by all, he should, along with his servants, feed upon what remains, proportionate to his means, after the departed manes, the guests and the kinsmen have eaten (22). Thus have I described to you in full the duties of a householder. Hear, I shall now describe to you the duties of one entering upon the *Vânaprashtha* mode of life (23). Seeing his children and grand children as well as the decay of his own body a wise man should retire to woods for purifying his soul (24). There living on wild fruits he should improve his soul by asceticism. He should sleep on the earth, practise the *Brahmacharyya* mode of life, perform acts on behalf of the departed manes, deities and guests, perform Homa, bathe three times a day, wear bark and matted locks, practise *Yoga* and feed on the wild produces of the forest (25—26). He should thus lead the *Vânaprashtha* mode of life for washing off his sins and improving his soul. The *Vikshu* (mendicant) mode of life is the final stage of a man (27). Hear now from me the true account of the fourth condition of life, as well as the duties thereof, as has been described, O my child, by great men (28). One, in this mode of life, should renounce company, practise *Brahmacharyya*, drive away wrath, mortify his senses, should not live at one place for a long time, withdraw himself from all actions, feed once only on whatever has been got by begging, should acquire the knowledge of self and an insight into his soul (29—30). I have thus described to you the duties of the fourth stage of life. Do you now listen to me, describing, in a general way, the duties of the other orders and modes of life (31). Truth, purity, freedom from malice and the desire of injuring others, forgiveness, kindness, liberality and contentment as the eighth quality—these have been described in brief by me to you as the duties of the various orders and modes of life. Every one should satisfy the duties of his own order and condition (32—33). A king should mete out punishment to him who goes astray transgressing the duties of his own order and stage of life (34). If the king does not punish a man who disregards his own duties his *Ishta* and *Purta* acts come to naught (35). Therefore the king should carefully place all the orders in their respective duties and inflict punishment on them whenever they go astray (36).

———:o:———

CHAPTER XXIX.

ALARKA said :—"Tell me truly, who ask, what acts should be duly performed by a householder, leaving which undone one is fettered and performing which one attains to liberation—that which leads to the well-being of men, that which should be discarded by a good man in his home and that which should be done. Tell me all this duly (1—2)." Madalasā said :—"By adopting the life of a householder, O my son, a man nourishes the entire universe and thereby conquers the wished-for regions (3) The departed manes, the ascetics, the deities, the goblins, men, worms, insects, flies, birds, beasts and demons all depend upon a householder for their subsistence and attain to gratification through him. Thinking 'will give or not' every one looks at his face (4—5). This is the support of all and the cow of the three (Vedas) on which is established the universe and which is recognised as the cause thereof (6). The *Rik* is her back, the *Yayur* is her middle, the *Saman* is the face and neck, *ishtha* and *Purta* are her horns; the sacred *Suktas* are her hairs; *Santi* and *Pushti* are her urine and excreta and the orders and modes of life are her developments. The whole universe is sustained by her. She suffers no deterioration or decay (7—8). My son, *Swaha, Swadha, Vashat, hanta* are her four udders. The deities suck the udder *Swáha*, the departed manes the udder *Swadhā*, the ascetics that of *Vashat* and all save the deities, goblins, Asuras and others—the human beings suck the udder *Hanta*. Thus my son, the cow of the threefold Vedas gratifies all beings 9—11). The man who destroys these is guilty of a mighty iniquity. He is plunged into Tamiçrā and Andhatamiçrā (hell) (12). The person, who, in season, makes her calves, the immortals, drink her milk, attains to the region of the celestials (13). Therefore, O my son, it is incumbent upon every human being to support the deities, the departed manes, men, ghosts as he sustains his own body (14). For this reason having bathed and purified himself, a person, with a concentrated mind, should offer, in due time, oblations of water to deities, departed manes, and Prajāpati (15). After worshipping deities with sandal and incense, a man should worship fire and then offer eatables (16). In a room a person should place to the east and north offerings of food for Brahmā, the Vishwadevas and Dhanyantari (17). The food, intended for Sakra, should be placed in the east and that for Yama in the south, that for Varuna in the west and that for the Moon in the north (18). The food for Dhātā and Vidhātā, should be kept, at night, at the gate of the house and that for the sun should be kept arouud outside the house (19). A person should scatter in the air the food intended for ghosts and night-rangers. Placing one's self towards the south one should offer food to the departed manes (20). Then being up and doing and concentrating his mind well, the householder should take up water for rinsing his mouth (21). Then the wise one should scatter food at different places designed for the deities. Having thus made offerings of food at his house the householder, purifying himself, should offer food to the ghosts for their gratification. He should keep on the ground food intended for dogs, *Swapachas* and birds (22—23). The offering, named Vaishyadeva, should be performed in the morning and evening. Then rinsing his mouth the wise man should look towards the door (24). Then for an eighth part of a *Muhurtta* he should look on in expectation of a guest. And on getting a guest at that place he should, to the best of his might, gratify him with meats and drinks and with fragrant flowers. One should not receive as a guest a friend or a person living in the same village (25—26). A Brāhmana, of unknown name and birth, stricken with hunger, wearied, and destitute, and who comes at that hour and begs for food, has been called a guest and should be entertained by the wise according to their power (27). A learned man should not enquire after the leneage, status or Vedic accomplishments of his guest. Whether beautiful or ugly he should be considered as Prajāpati himself (28). Because a man does not live for ever therefore he is called *Atithi.* And when a guest is gratified the householder is freed from the debt of *Nriyajna* (29). The sinful man, who feeds himself without feeding his guest, is visited by iniquity and lives on dung in the future life (30). The guest, that goes away disappointed from the house of a man, transfers to the householder all his sins and takes away the latter's religious merit (31). To the best of his might a man should entertain his guest with water, herbs or any other thing that he himself takes (32). A person should perform always the *Sraddha* with water and food for the departed manes and feed one or more Brāhmanas (33). Taking off the first portion of rice one should offer it to a Brāhmana and he should offer alms to the begging mendicants and Brahmacharins (34). A mouthful of rice is called *Bhikshâ* and four mouthfuls make an *Arghya* and four *Arghyas* make up a *Hanta*. Thus say the leading twice-born ones (35). Without offering *Hanta*, *Arghya* or *Bhikshâ* according to his own power one should not take meals (36). After having fed guests one should feed his kinsmen, friends, suitors, boys, old people, the diseased, destitute people stricken with hunger and begging food. If he has money he should also feed poor relatives who desire it (37—38). If a person, obtaining a prosperous kinsman, meets with poverty, the sins, committed by him in that state, visit the prosperous kinsman (39). This procedure should also be followed in the evening. When a guest comes at about sunset he should, to the best of one's power, be entertained with a seat, fooding and bed (40). If a person thus bears the burden of a domestic life, the friends, deities, departed manes, great saints, guests, beasts, birds and smallest worms, being gratified, bring about his well-being (41—42). The highly pious Atri sang a hymn in this connection. Hear, O greatly righteous one, the same having the household life for its subject (43). When a house-holder has money, he should, after worshipping the celestials, the departed manes, guests, friends, kinsmen and his spiritual guide, keep food on the ground for birds, *Swapachas* and dogs. The Vaishwadeva ceremony should be performed both in the morning and evening (44—45). A man should not take meat, rice, herbs or any other culinary article, that may be in his house without offering duly a portion of them (to guests) (46).

CHAPTER XXX.

MADALASA said:—The duties of a householder are threefold namely *Nitya* (daily) *Naimittika* (occasional) and *Nityanaimittika*. Hear them, O my son (1). The ceremonies relating to the five sacrifices described to you by me before, are called *Nitya*. The ceremonies that are performed on the birth of a son as well as others are called *Naimittika*. *Sraddhas* on *Parva* days are regarded by the learned as *Nityanaimittika*. The ceremonies, that are performed on the birth of a son, should also be performed in due order on the occasion of his wedding (2—4). In the ceremony called *Nândimukha* the departed manes should be properly worshipped. Sitting with his face turned towards the north or the east the sacrificer should, with his mind concentrated, offer P*indas* (balls) of barley and curds. Some people hold that this ceremony is without Vaishwadeva (5—6). In this ceremony after having circumambulated them a couple of Brāhmanas should be worshipped. This is called *Vriddhi Sraddha Naimittika*. Hear now of the *Aurddha dehika Ekoddishtha* which should be performed on behalf of a person on the day of his demise. In this no worship of the deities, no invocation or oblation to fire is to be made; only *Kuçâ* should be used in it. Near the leavings a *Pinda* should be offered to the spirit of the departed person and remembering his name one should pour water with sesamum seeds. This should be thrown at the spot where the Kusa made Brahmana has been left, saying " May this be without deterioration and may he be gratified with it and they will say. 'We have been gratified." Every month of the year this ceremony should be performed by men. When the year is over or when an opportunity presents itself *Sapindakarana* ceremony should be performed. I shall describe to you the rules of this ceremony (7—12). In it there is no worship of the deties, no offering of oblation to fire and no invocation is to be made. Only an *Arghya* and *Kuça* are to be offered. Placing *Pinda* and water in an opposite direction he should feed an odd number of Brâhmanas (13). The peculiar characterestic of this ceremony is that additional rites should be performed every month. Hear with attention, I shall describe this to you (14). My son, four vessels, containing sesamum seeds and fragrant water, should be kept—three for the ancestral manes and another for the departed (15). An *Arghya* as well as the vessel intended for the departed should be washed over the three vessels and then reciting the Mantras Tesamānâ, the ceremony should be concluded (16). This *ekoddista* has also been laid down for women. But when they have no son they are not entitled to *Sapindakarana* (17). Men should perform *Ekoddishta* every year for females; as in the case of men it should be duly performed on the day of her death (18). In the absence of a son (the ceremony) should be performed by those entitled to offer watery oblation. Those that are a mother's *Sapindas* and those that are a mother's *Sahodakas* should act according to these injunctions; and a person, who is without a son, should have his rites performed by his daughter's son. A daughter's son should thus perform the ceremony for his maternal grandfather (19—20). This rite is called *Dwyamusyayana*. A mother's father and a father's father should be properly worshipped by *Naimittika Sraddhâ* (21). In the absence of any other relatives the wives should perform this rite for their husbands without any *Mantra*. In the absence of wife a king should have the obsequies of the deceased properly performed by one of his own relatives or persons of the same caste. For the king is the friend of all orders (22—23). I have thus described to you, my son, the *Nitya* and *Naimittika* rites; listen now, I shall describe other sorts of *Nitya* and *Naimittika* rites connected with a *Sraddha* (24). The period of the moon's wane is called *Darsa*; this is the time of those rites and indicates their permanence (25).

CHAPTER XXXI.

A FATHER'S grand-father is not entitled to *Sapinda-karana* and being a paternal ancestor of the fourth degree and upwards he is deprived of the paternal *pinda* (1). He is the fourth among them and feeds on the *lepa** and rice offered by the son; he has no relation and is entitled only to the enjoyment of food (2). The father, the grand-father and the great grand-father—these three generations are regarded as being entitled to *pinda* (3). The three ancestral generations, beyond the grand-father's grand-father, can receive only the *lepa*; and of these, the one performing the rite is considered as the seventh (4). This relation of the seven generations has been laid down by the ascetics. Those

* The wipings of the hand which has offered funeral oblations to three ancestors and which are considered as an oblation to ancestors in the 4th, 5th, and 6th degrees.

who precede the sacrificer can receive *anulepa** (5). Listen, O my son, I shall describe now the different *Sraddas* which a sacrificer should duly perform for the gratification of the ancestors preceding them, for those living in the hell, for those born as beasts and those born in other orders of elemental creations (6—7). Those, who are born as *Pishâchas,* obtain gratification from the food that is placed on the ground by men (8). O my young boy, those, that have been converted into trees, are gratified by the drops of water that fall on the earth from wet clothes (9). The drop, of water that falls on the ground from a person's body, brings about the gratification of those that have been born in the order of deities (10), Those, that are born as beasts, obtain gratification from the particles of food that fall down on the ground at the time of the taking up of the *pinda* (11). Those, who although worthy of performing rites, had been burnt in their childhood, without receiving the sanctification, obtain gratification from scattered food and water falling from a broom (12). The others obtain their gratification from water that falls when the Brahmanas rinse their mouths or wash their feet (13). Thus the ancestors, of the persons who perform duly the *Sraddhas* born in other species, are gratified by the food or water, pure or otherwise that is cast by the sacrificer or the twice-born (14). If one performs the *Sraddha* of his ancestor with money obtained from another then the ancestor, born in the order of *Chandalas* or Pukkas, finds gratification therefrom. Thus my child, ancestors born in other species are gratified with meats and drinks that are offered by his kinsmen at the time of a *Sraddha* (15—16). The ancestral manes, in numbers, obtain gratification, from drops of water and particles of food which the kindred cast on the occasion of the performance of *Sraddhas* (17). So a person should duly with devotion perform a *Sraddha,* even with herbs; *Sraddha* being performed no one, born in the race, suffers

* That which is offered after *lepa* is offered.

privation (18). I shall now describe to you the proper time for the performance of *Nitta* and *Naimittika* rites by men. Listen to the procedure thereof described by me (19). On the wane of the Moon Srāddha should be performed during the day of the New Moon as also during the eighth lunar day of the dark half of the month, do you hear from me of the optional seasons (for it) (20). If an excellent Brāhmana is secured and if the articles for the Srāddha are procured, O my son, a Srāddha should be, of one's own accord, celebrated on the ecclipse of the sun or moon during a half year, during the equinox, during the course of the sun through the Zodiac, on the appearance of an evil omen, on the vision of an evil dream, on the ascension of the natal star, or during the malign influence of any planet (21—22). An educated person, a Shrotrio,* a Yogi, one versed in the Vedas and singing the *Yyestha* Saman,† one versed in three *Nachiketas*,‡ one who is versed in the three *Madhus*,§ the three *Suparnas*‖ and the six *Angas*,¶ a daughter's son, a priest a son-in-law, a sister's son, a father-in-law, one who is engaged in the performance of five fire rituals, one engaged in asceticism, a mother's brother, a person devoted to his parents, a disciple, a wife's brother, and a relative,—all these eminent twice-born ones are competent to perform the Srāddha (23—25). A twice-born one, my son, who has not practised Brahmacharyya, who is diseased, who has extra limbs, who has not the natural number of limbs, who is born of a twice-married female, who is without an eye, who is the illegitimate child of a female, whose husband is living or

* A person versed in the study of the Vedas.

† A portion of the Sama Veda, the recitation of which at a sacrifice secures religious merit.

‡ The three Upanishads of Nachiketa.

§ The three classes of spirituous liquors.

‖ Three classes of birds first created by Brahmadikas and included in the daily presentation of water to deceased ancestors.

¶ Six branches of learning.

of a woman whose husband is dead, who has injured his friends, who has diseased nails, who is impotent, who is possessed of dark and twany teeth, who has an ugly form, who has been imprecated by his father, who is crooked-minded or malicious, who sells *soma*, who has sullied his daughter, who practises medicine, who has forsaken his father and preceptor, who teaches for remuneration, who is an enemy, who is the husband of a widow, who has renounced the Veda or fire, who is married to a girl of twelve who has attained her puberty, who is stained,—these, as well as other twice-born ones guilty of transgressions should be forsaken at the performance of the funeral rites of the ancestors (26—29). The above mentioned best of Brahmanas should be invited on the previous day and should be engaged in ceremonies for the ancestral manes and celestials (30). These should keep in restraint all propensities as well as he, that is to perform the Srāddha. The ancestral manes, of a person that visits a woman after distributing gifts in a Srâddha and taking his meal, lie on his semen for a good month (31). The ancestral manes, of a person, who, after knowing a woman, takes his meals or goes to a Srāddha, live on semen and urine for one good month (32). Therefore a wise man should first invite people. Even if (Brahmanas) are not had on that day, those who have associated with women must be renounced (33). After gratifying them with salutation a person should attentively feed the self-controlled ascetics, arrived in due time for alms (34). As the dark half of the month is more liked by the ancestral manes than the light so is the afternoon more liked by them than the morning (35). Adoring duly with welcome the invited guests in the house he should, with hands purified, make them take their seats, after they have rinsed their mouths (36). In a ceremony for the ancestors an odd number of educated Brāhmanas, and in a ceremony for the celestials an even number of educated Brāhmanas should be appointed. But a person, proportionate to his power, may engage a single Brāhmana both in the rites for ancestors and celestials (37). This is also the procedure to be adopted in rites performed for the ancestral manes on the mother's side as also in *Vaishwadevas*. Some people, if they like, may adopt a different procedure in these ceremonies (38). Rites, for the celestials, should be performed by a person with his face towards the east and the rites for the ancestral manes with his face towards the north. This is also the practice in the rites for maternal ancestral manes as laid down by the wise (39). Having handed over Kuça for seats a wise man should adore them with *Arghya* etc ; offering a rope of pack thread a wise twice-born one, with their permission, should invoke the deities with Mantras. Having offered an *arghya* containing barley and water on behalf of the *Vishwadevas* one, after dedicating garlands, incense, lamps, and water, should perform all the ceremonies for ancestral manes on the right side (40–42). Then offering a double quantity of *Darbha* grass and with their leave a wise person should invoke his ancestral manes with the recitation of some Mantras (43). O great one, desirous of gratifying his ancestral manes he should, on the right, dedicate an *arghya* of barley mixed with sesame (44). Thereupon commanded by the twice-born to celebrate the fire rite, with saying "Do it" he should, as directed, offer to the fire rice devoid of curries and ashes (45). (Then saying) "To the bearer of Kavya (offering of food) fire—Swaha" the first oblation should be offered. (Then saying) "To the Moon having Pitris—Swaha" the second oblation should be offered. Then what remains, after the oblations have been offered, should be made over to the vessels of the twice-born (46—47). "Do you to your desire feed on these" with these sweet words spoken to them he should duly offer to them the food placed in their vessels (48) And they, as desired, will intently and silently take the food (49). Tempting them gently and casting off anger a man should gradually offer them the food most liked by them (50). He should then recite the Mantras that are capable of slaying the Rakshasas, and then scatter on earth sesame seeds as well as white mustard for them, for there are many impediments in a Sraddha (51). Then he should address the Brahmanas saying "you have been gratified with nutritious and delightful food" and they should reply "we have been." Then permitted by them a man should scatter rice all over the ground and duly offer water for rinsing their mouths. Then with their permission, he, restraining his body, mind and words, should make a funeral cake containing sesame and place it on a *Darbha* on the southern side, near the leaving, for his ancestral manes (52—54). Then with a concentrated mind he should offer them water from the sacred vessels belonging to the ancestors—he, who, O prince, performs with devotion a sacrifice on behalf of his ancestral manes (55). Then in the same way offering duly *Pindas* for the ancestral manes on his mother's side he should offer water for rinsing, together with perfumeries, garlands etc. (56) Then conferring upon them gifts according to his power he should say "may this prove an agreeable *swadhâ*" and on their, being gratified, saying "So be it" he should make them recite the *Vaishwadeva* Mantras—"O Vishwadevas, be you pleased. May you farewell." And after they have said 'So be it" he should pray for their blessings (57—58). Then with sweet words and saluting them reverentially he should dismiss them: They must be followed to the door; and when they shall bid him adieu he should come back (59). Then the daily rites should be performed and the sacrificer should entertain his guests. Some good people get the daily rites performed for their paternal manes (60). Others say they should not be performed for them. The remaining portion should be gone through in the aforesaid way. Some say there is no necessity of separate cooking in paternal rites, while according to others it must be done (61). Then a man should take that rice along with his servants. O you conversant with piety, in this way or in any other way you should attentively perform the Srāddha of your ancestral manes, so that the leading twice-born ones may be gratified (62—63). In a Srāddha three things are sacred, a maternal grandson, a *Kutapa** and the sesamum seeds; and three according to the leading Brahmanas, are to be cast off, viz anger, walking and hurry (64). My son, in a Srāddha silver vessels are best and silver should be seen and given away (65). It is said on, earth, *Swadhâ* was milched by the ancestral manes with a silver vessel; therefore the silver vessel is acceptable to them and it increases their delight (66).

—:o:—

CHAPTER XXXII.

MADALASA said:—Hear now with reverence, O my son, as to what should be procured for paternal manes and what should be given up on their behalf, and what encompasses their gratification (1). By living on rice mixed with clarified butter one gratifies the paternal manes for a month and by living on meat and fish gratifies them for a couple of months (2). Deer's flesh brings about the gratification of paternal manes for three months; hare's flesh nourishes them for four months (3). Bird's flesh (nourishes) them for five months and boar's flesh for six months; goat's flesh for seven months; *Ena's*† flesh for

* The eigth Muhurtta or a portion of the day. It is an eligible time for the performance of rites for the manes.

† A kind of deer.

eight months (4). Ruru's* flesh certainly gratifies them for nine months and Gavaya's† flesh for ten months (5). Mutton gratifies the paternal manes for eleven months and cow's milk or Pāyaca for twelve months (6). My son, the flesh of the rhinoceros, black hares, honey, flesh offered by a daughter or any descended from the same line, *Gaurisuta*‡ or Srāddha performed at Gayā—these undoubtedly encompass the eternal gratification of paternal manes (7—8). *Syamaka* (3), *Raja-shyamaka* and as well as *Prâsatika*, *Nivara* and *Puskala* these various sorts of rice are agreeable to the paternal manes (9). Besides these, barley, *Vrihi* rice, wheat, sesame, *Mudaga*, mustard, P*ryangu*, *Kovidara* and *Nishpava* can also bring about their gratification (10). M*akala*, *Raja-mansa*, *Knuviprusi*k*a* and *Masuru* should not be used in a Srāddha. Garlic, turnip, onion, carrot, powdered barley mixed with cards, any thing devoid of color and moisture, *Gandharika*, the bottle gourd, salt, treacle and red exudations should be discarded in a Srāddha. Things got by bribe, from a fallen person or obtained by money exacted unfairly by marrying one's daughter, are to be eschewed in a Srāddha. Water that gives out bad odour or that is frothy, that is small in quantity, from which a cow does not obtain gratification, that has been got at night, that has been rejected by every one, that is unfit to be drunk, that has sprung in a *Nipana*§ should, my child, be always eschewed in rites for paternal manes (11—16). A deer's milk, goat's milk, camel's milk, that of an animal with a single hoof, buffaloe's milk, *Chamaru's* milk, the milk of a cow within ten days of her giving birth to a calf, milk that has been got by saying "Do you give me milk for my father's ceremony should not be used in a Srāddha." The earth of a spot that gives out

* Another kind of deer.

† Another kind of deer.

‡ A kind of Sraddha.

§ A ditch near a well.

bad smell, that is filled with worms, rough, or burnt by fire, that is full of disgusting and vicious sounds, must be eschewed in Srāddha (16—19). Those who have disgraced the race, those who have engaged themselves in injuring another's family, those that are nude and that are sinful, injure ceremonies for ancestral manes by their presence there (20). An impotent one cast off by his parents, a cock, a wild boar, a dog and Rakshâsas despoil a *Srâddha* by merely looking on it (21). Therefore well guarded by people should a householder scatter sesame seeds on earth. By doing this, O my son, protection in Srāddha is obtained by both the parties (22). A person, impure for the birth of a child or by the touch of some unclean animal, a valetudinarian, or a fallen, an impure person cannot bring on the nourishment of a paternal gradfathers (23). A woman,in menses, should not be seen, on this occasion; one with his head shaven as well as a drunkard should also be avoided by a sacrificer (24). The food, that has been polluted by the touch of hair or worms, that has been looked at by the dogs, that gives out bad smell, that is stale or that has been touched by the wind of the cloth, must be eschewed in a Srāddha (25). Whatever is dedicated reverentially to the ancestral manes in their name and *gotra*, becomes their food. Therefore in a ceremony for the manes selected articles should be duly kept in a vessel with the object of affording gratification to the ancestral manes (26—27). A learned man should entertain *Yogis* (at a Srāddha). Because the ancestral manes are the receptacles of *Yoga* they should always be entertained (28). If a single *Yogi* is entertained in the place of thousands and thousands of Brāhmanas, he delivers the sacrificer as well as those who feed like a boat which carries people in a river (29). The *Brahmavadins* chant a hymn which had been sung by the manes in honour of the king Aila. "When shall such a good son be born to us who will offer for us funeral cakes on the earth out of the leavings of the *Yogis*, or for affording us gratification every month in *Gaya* offer us excellent Havis in the shape of rhinoceros, black herbs, *tiladhyas* or *Krisara* (30—32). In offering food in the *Vaishwadeva* and *Saumya* ceremonies the flesh of the rhinoceros is considered as the best Havi. When we get the flesh of a rhinoceros having no horns we feed on it so long as the sun is in the sky" (33). On the thirteenth lunar day of either fortnight when *Magha* is in the ascendant one should perform the Srāddha according to the prescribed ritual. And during the southern solistice *Payaça* mixed with honey and clarified butter should be offered (34). With a view to accomplish his object and liberate himself from sins, a man, my son, should reverentially adore his ancestors (35). When the ancestral manes are pleased with a Srāddha they make *Vasus, Rudras, Adityas*, stars, planets and other constellations favourably disposed towards the people (36). When the ancestral manes are pleased with Srāddha they confer longevity, wisdom, riches, learning, heaven, liberation and happiness as well as kingdom (37). Thus, my son, I have described all about the Srāddha ceremony I shall now describe to you the lunar days regarding *Kamya Sráddha* (38).

CHAPTER XXXIII.

—:o:—

MADALASA said :—The first day of the light half of the month is auspicious for the acquirement of riches, the second for prosperity, the third for obtaining boons and the fourth for the destruction of enemies (1). The fifth gives good fortune and the sixth honor. The seventh gives the supremacy over his own people to a man and the seventh finished intellect (2). The ninth confers on him wives and the tenth the accomplishment of all his objects. One, performing a *Sraddha* on the eleventh day, acquires a knowledge of the Vedas (3). One, adoring the ancestral manes on the twelfth day, gains victory, children, intelligence, cattle, prosperity, independence and nourishment (4). If man reverentially performs with rice the *Sráddha* of his ancestral manes on the thirteenth day he certainly comes by a long life and riches. A man, whose ancestral manes died in youth or were slain by weapons, should, to gratify them, perform their rites on the fourteenth day. A man, celebrating with care and purity the *Sráddha* of his father on the day of the new moon, obtains all objects and eternal heaven. A man, by adoring his ancestral manes, on the ascension of *Kirttika*, attains to the region of the celestials (5—8). One, desirous of offspring (should perform it under the influence of) Rohini; one, by performing it during the influence of Saumya, attains energy. A person acquires heroism by performing it during the influence of *Ardra* and he obtains land by performing it during the influence of *Punarvasu* (9). By ever performing the *Sráddha* during the influence of *Pushya* he attains nourishment and by celebrating it during the influence of *Ashlesha* he gets worthy sons. During the influence of *Magha* he gets the lead of his kinsmen and good fortune in that of *Phalguni* (10). During the influence of *Uttara Phalguni* one becomes liberal and gets offspring; and a man, performing the *Sraddha* during the influence of *Hasta*, forsooth attains to excellence (11). Under the ascendancy of *Chitra* one becomes beautiful and gets children. *Swati* gives prosperity in trade and *Vishakha* the accomplishment of the desire of having sons (12). Performing (the *Sraddha* during the influence of) *Anuradha* one attains to the dignity of lord Paramount, supremacy under the influence of *Jyestha* and good health during that of *Mala* (13). During the influence of *Ashâra* one obtains fame, and immunity from grief during *Uttara*; during *sràvana* excellent regions and great riches during *Dhanishthà* (14). By performing the ceremony in *abbijit* one becomes versed in the Vedas and by doing so in *varuna* he becomes a master of medicine; *ajevitha* in *prausthapada* and the Posterior gives infantry (15). In *Revati* one gets metals except silver and gold and horses in *Atwnis*; and performing the *Sràddha* in *Bharani* one obtains good length of life. Thus knowing the truth one should perform the *Kamya Sràddha* during the ascendancy of these stars (16).

CHAPTER XXXIV.

—;o:—

MADALASA said:—Thus, my child, the deities, ancestral manes, guests and friends, goblins, servants, beasts, birds, ants, beggars, suppliants and persons living in the house be entertained with *Havya* and *Kavya* and rice by a pious householder of virtuous ways. One, neglecting the *Nitya* and *Naimittika* rites, is visited by sin (1—3). Alarka said:—"Mother, you have described to me *Nitya, Naimittika* and *Nitya Naimittika*, these threefold rites, the duties of a person (4). O you born in a great race, I wish to hear of the righteous ways by which a person secures happiness both in this world and in the next (5)." Madalasā said:—"A householder should always observe the rules of good conduct. A person, devoid of righteous conduct, does not obtain happiness both in this world and in the next (6). Sacrifice, gift and asceticism on this earth of a man, who acts by disregarding the rules of righteous conduct, do not lead to his well-being (7). An unrighteous person never lives for a good length of time. A man should always exert himself to act righteously; righteous conduct removes ill-luck (8). I will, O my son, describe to you the nature of righteousness. Listening to it with whole-minded attention do you observe it (9).

Every householder should endevour to accomplish the threefold objects of life. If a householder succeeds in this, he achieves success both in this world and in the next (10). A self-controlled man should amass a fourth of what he earns for securing his well-being in the next world; he should spend half for maintaining himself as well as for performing *Nitya* and *Naimittika* rites (11). The remaining one-fourth of his income should be multiplied as the capital for his own-self. If a person behaves in this way, my son, his wealth bears fruit (12). In the same way a learned man should accumulate his religious merit for washing off his sins. Disinterested piety bears fruit in the next world and interested in this (13). From fear of meeting with obstacles one should practise both interested and disinterested piety, so that they may not enter into conflict with each other. Desire has also been described as twofold which never clashes with three other objects of life (14). Think of all these as dependent upon each other. Listen, I shall now describe righteousness, etc., as independent of one another (15). Virtue and morality that is dependant upon it, do not clash with profit. As desire is divided into two kinds by its conjunction with these two, so also virtue and profit divide themselves in combination with desire (16). One should get up at the *Brahma Muhurtta** and engage himself in the contemplation of virtue and worldly profit and the pains of which they are the roots, and in understanding

* A day according to the Hindus is divided into thirty *Muhurttas*. One preceeding the sun rise is called *Brahma*, which is fit for contemplation and recitation.

the true meaning of the Vedas. Then rising up, concetrating his mind, purifying himself, rinsing his mouth and sitting with his face towards the east one should finish his morning prayers (*Sandhyà*) while the stars are still visible in the sky and his evening prayer while the sun is yet shining. One should never disregard it in peaceful times (17—19). O my son (at this time), one should avoid evil talk, falsehood, rough words and the reading of books containing pernicious doctrines, evil discussion and impious service (19). Having controlled himself, every morning and evening, he should offer oblations to the sacrificial fire. He should not look to the solar disc at sunrise and sunset (20). Arranging the hairs, looking in a mirror, cleaning the teeth and offering watery oblations to the celestials, should be performed in the early part of the day (21). One should not pass urine or excreta on a road, passing through a village a dwelling house, a holy spot or a field or a cultivated land or a pasture (22). One should not cast his looks upon a nude woman who is another's wife or on his own stool. And one should not see, touch or talk with a woman in her monthly course (23). A man should not pass urine or excreta in water, nor should he know a woman there. A wise man should not sit on excreta, urine, hair, ashes, potsherds, chaff, embers, bones, torn-out cloth, a rope, a road and the ground (24—25). First, adoring according to his power ancestral manes, celestials, men, and ghosts a householder should afterwards feed himself (26). Sitting with his face to the east or north, he, purifying himself and controlling his speech, should rinse his mouth, and then folding his knees he should sit down and take the rice with his mind concentrated on (the act of eating) (27). Without provocation a wise man should not give out the shortcomings of another and he should not take salt that is seen and overhot rice (28). A self-controlled man should not pass urine or excreta while walking or sitting; nor should he take anything after having rinsed his mouth (29). While impure for his taking food he should not converse or read the Vedas or touch kine, Brāhmanas, fire or his own head (30). He should not, of his own accord, see the sun, the moon, or stars, and should avoid a broken seat, bedstead or vessel (31). Showing his reverence by rising up he should offer seats to his preceptors, should task with them favourably and follow after saluting them; he should never speak to them unfavourably (32). A wise man should not take his food or worship the celestials with a single cloth on, should not make bearers of Brāhamans, pass urine on fire or bathe or lie down in a state of nudity; nor should he itch his heads with both the hands (33—34). Persons should not bathe or always wash their heads without any cause, or rub any limb with oil after having washed their heads (35). He should not recite the Vedas on interdicted days and should never pass urine before Brâhmanas, fire, kine and the sun (36). Facing the north in the day and the south in the night should a person, with ease, pass urine or excreta at a spot free from disturbances (37). One should not communicate (to others) the wrong doings of his parents and he should pacify them when they are angry. He should not hear, if any other man speaks ill of them (38). One should make way for a Brāhmana, a king, one stricken with distress, one more learned than himself, a preceptor's wife, one overburdened although a junior, a dumb, a blind, a deaf man, a mad man, a drunkard, a bawed, an enemy, a boy and a fallen person (39—40). A wise man should circumambulate a temple, a fig-tree, a crossing of the four roads, one more learned than himself, a preceptor and a celestial (41). One should not use the shoes, cloth or garland, worn by another and should discard the holy thread, ornament, and the water-pot (belonging to another) (42). One should abstain from profusely smearing the person with oil, sexual connection on the eighth, fourteenth or fifteenth lunar day, or during a Parva (43). A sensible man should not sit stretching out his legs and feet; one should not cast about his feet, nor should he sit with legs (44). A wise man should avoid cutting another to the quick, giving way to anger or proving cruel to any one. He should not brag, attach too much importance to himself and avoid harsh words (45). He should not mock at an ignorant man, a mad man, one in difficulty, or deformed, a magician, one of defective limbs, one having additional ones (46). He should not inflict punishment on any one else or on his son and disciple under instruction. A wise man should not drag his seat with his foot (47). *Sanyava*, *Kriçara* and meat should not be made ready for one's own self. Entertaining his guests both in the morning and evening he should afterwards take his meal (48). Restraining his words a man should cleanse his teeth with his face towards the east or north. And as a rule, O my son, he should discard a tooth-brush made of forbidden wood (49). One should never sleep with his head towards the north or the west; but one should lie down with his head towards the south or east (50). One should not bathe in foul water or in the night. A person should bathe at night, only when the ecclipse takes place (51). After bathing a man should not rub his body with his cloth or hands; nor should he toss about his hair or cloth (52). Before bathing a wise man should never besmear his person with unguents, nor should he put on a red or black cloth or one of many colors (53). One should not wrongly use his scarf, cloth and ornaments. One should throw away a cloth greatly worn* out and having no ends (54). My child, one should never take rice containing hair or worms, trodden upon, that has been seen or licked by a dog, that has been vitiated for its essence being extracted, the flesh of the back, meat not consecrated, or that should be rejected, or salt placed before (55—56). O my son, rice, that is state or many days old, should be rejected, as well as, O prince, cakes, herbs, sugercane or milk,—or flesh—if the preparation thereof has stood over for days,

* It may also mean polluted. The word in the text is *Apahata*.

should be avoided. One should avoid lying down at sun-rise and sun-set (57—58). One should not lie down after bathing, sleep sitting or lie down absent minded. A person should not sit down on a bed or on the ground sounding it (59). He should not eat with one cloth on or while speaking or without giving away a portion to the spectators. After bathing in the morning and evening a person should take his meals, according to the injunction (60). A wise man should not visit another's wife. The intercourse, of a man with other's wives, destroys *Isthâ* and *purtta* rites and longivity (61). There is no other thing in the world which so much destroys the longivity of a man as is his intercourse with another's wife (62). A man should adore the deities, perform the fire rites and make obeisance to elders. After properly rinsing his mouth a man should take his food (63). Taking with reverence pure water, free from foam, bad smell and dirt, one should rinse his mouth there-with facing the east or the north (64). A man should not take earth from under the water, from his homestead, from an ant hill, from the hole of a rat, or from clay left after performing the act of purification (65). After attentively washing his hands and feet and sprinkling water he should sit folding his knees inward and sip the water three or four times (66). Rubbing twice the corners of his mouth, the cavity thereof and the head, he, being purified, should perform the ceremony after duly sipping water (67), A person should always regardfully perform the ceremonies for the deities, sages and departed manes (68). After having sneezed, spat or put on his dress, a wise man should rinse his mouth with water. After having sneezed, licked, spat, or thrown up, a person should rinse his mouth, touch a cow's back, look at the sun and hold his right ear (69—70). As much as lies in his power he should adopt the after process in the absence of one preceding. In the absence of the former the adoption of the latter is considered favourable (71). One should not gnash his teeth or afflict any part of his body. At the time of two twilights one should avoid lying down, study and eating (72). In the evening one must not engage in a sexual intercourse or start for another place (73). In the forenoon, my son, a man should regardfully adore the celestials, at mid-day human beings and in the afternoon the ancestral manes (74). Washing his head a man should worship the deities and the ancestral manes. One should have his beard shaven facing the east or the north (75). Although born in a good family a bride, that is diseased, that has not got a limb, that is deformed, that is twany coloured, that is talkative and that is full of defects, should be shunned (76). A man, wishing well of himself, should marry a girl that has all the limbs, that has a beautiful nose and is gifted with all auspicious marks (77). He should marry the fifth or the seventh daughter of her parents. He should protect his wife, throw off jealousy, and should not lie down in day and carry on sexual intercourse (78). A man should avoid acts that may give anguish to others and pain to the creatures. Persons, of all the orders, should avoid for four nights women in their menses (79). If a man wishes that a daughter should not be born to him he should also avoid her on the fifth day; he should go to his wife on the sixth night; for a night occuring on an even date is always auspicious, my son (80). If a man knows his wife on the night of an even date he has a son ; whereas one, who visits her on an uneven night, has a daughter (born to him). So if one wishes for a son he should live with his wife on an even night. If a man co-habits in the forenoon he has a son who relinquishes his own religion ; his son becomes a hermaphrodite who does so in the twlight (81). My son, if a man goes through a shaving, if he has thrown up, co-habited or gone to a cremation ground, he should bathe with the cloth on (82). No one should villify the celestials, the Vedas, the twice-born, virtuous and faithful men, noble parents, chaste women, men who perform sacrifices or ascetics; if a proud man cries them down he should not hear him (83—84). A man should not sit down on the bed or seat of either his elder or junior; one should not put on inauspicious raiment or use inauspicious words (85). One should use a white cloth and white flowers. A learned man should not make friends with a proud man, a fool, an insolent fellow, one of a bad character, a thief, a miser, a covetous man, a bawd, the husband of one such, a powerful man, a bad character, one of a scandatous character, one who fears every thing, and one who depends on destiny (86—89). But he should contract friendship with pious persons of good ways, the wise, the powerful and the energetic (90). A wise man should always live with those who are versed in the Vedic lore and who always bathe after the observance of penances. When these six persons, worthy of honor, a friend, one initiated, the king, a *Snátaka*, a father-in-law and a priest themselves come to one's house she should worship them. According to his might one should entertain, carefully with Madhuparka, at the proper time those twice-born ones that have lived for a year. And if one wishes his own well-being he should be obedient to them. He should not quarrel with them even if they remonstrate with him (61—93). Having duly worshipped the house he should at the proper place adore the fire and offer oblations duly to it (94). The first oblation must be offered to Brahmā, the second to Prajāpati, the third to the Guhyakas, the fourth to Kaçyapa and fifth to Anumati (the fifteenth day of the moon) and then he should offer food to the spirits of the air. Then as I told you while explaining to you the daily rites he should make offerings to Vishwadevas. Hear now as to the method from me. Keeping in view the different abodes and the respective shares a man should make separate offerings to the dieties (95—96. He should make three offerings near the clouds, the waters and the earth respectively and also to the air; b-ginning with the east, offer- ings should also be made to each of the cardinal quarter with due order (98); then gradually to Brahman, the sun, the sky, the Vishwadevas and all the elements of the universe 99). Then he should make offerings in the north to Dawn and the king of ghosts. Then reciting *Swadha* and *Namas* he should make offerings to the paternal manes in the south (100). Then wishing to keep the remaining quantity of rice, he should take water out of the vessel by means of the space between his thumb and fore-fiinger and then reciting (the Vedic formula) *Yakshaitatt*, should, as prescribed, offer it in the north-west (101). Then taking out the first portion of the rice of the measure of a *Hantakara** and with *Mantras* for entertaining guests one should duly, according to injunction, offer it to a Brahmana (102). Then with the respective *Tirthas* (parts of the hand) one should duly perform the ceremony. By the help of the *Brahma Tirtha* a man should sip water on behalf of the celestials (103). The line at the base of the thumb of the right hand is called *Brahma Tirtha* and is used for the purpose of rinsing (104). The portion, dividing the thumb and fore finger, is called *Pitri Tirtha*. All offerings, to the paternal manes except Nandimukha,† should be offered through this part (105). *Deva Tirtha* is near the finger tips and with this part the ceremonies for the deities should he performed. At the base of the youngest finger is the *Kàya Tirtha*; with it should the ceremony for Prajāpati be performed (106). In this way ceremonies for the deities and ancestral manes should be celebrated by the help of *Tirthas* and nothing else should be used for this purpose (107). For rinsing *Brahma Tirtha* is the best; with *Pitritirtha* a person should perform ceremonies for the paternal manes; those for the deities

---

* Sixteen handfuls of rice make a *Hantakara*. *Sridhara* in *Vishnupuranam*. It is also called so on account of the word *Hanta* appearing in the *Mantra* that is recited on this occasion.

† This is performed on festive occasions in honor of the departed manes.

should be performed with *Deva Tirtha* and those for Prajāpati with *Kàya Tirtha* (108). He should also offer Pinda and watery oblations to Nandi-mukha progenitors and with Prajāpati *Tirtha* he should perform that for him (109). A discreet man should not hold fire and water at the same time; nor should he stretch out legs in front of dieties or preceptors (110). One should not look to a cow suckling her calf, nor drink water held in the cavity of palms. Serious or otherwise every sort of purificatory rites must be performed promptly; one should not blow on fire with his mouth (111—112). A person, O my son, should not live in a country that has not got a money lender, a physician, a Brahmana versed in the Vedas and a river full of water (113). A wise man should settle permanently in a country where lives a powerful and virtuous king, who has conquered all his enemies. How can happiness be in the country of a bad king? (114). A man secures comfort by living in a country which is ruled by a powerful king, which is fertile, contains self-controlled inhabitants who are just and void of envy (115). A wise man should live in a country, where the husbandmen are not luxurious and where there is a plenty of healing plants (116). A man, O my son, should not live in a country where these are always present, *viz.*, people eager for victory, persons who were once inimical and those always given to festivities (117). A wise man should always live amongst those who have good characters. I have thus, O my son, described to you all this for your well-being (118).

CHAPTER XXXV.

———:o:———

MADALASA said:—Hear, next, of the remedies for things that should be rejected as well those that should be accepted. Stale rice should be always taken after mixing it with oily substances; barley, wheat and curds may however be taken without oily substances. The flesh of a hare, tortoise, inguana, hedgehog, and rhinoceros may be taken, my son; but that of domescated boar or of a domesticated hen should always be avoided. There is no harm of a eating the remnants of a sacrifice to the paternal names and the deities. Nor is there any harm of eating flesh that has been desired by the Brahmanas at a Sradha and which has been purified with water being sprinkled over it, as well as by the recitation of *mantras*, as also what has been prescribed for medicine (1—3). A conch, stone, gold, silver, a rope, a cloth, potherbs, roots, fruits, a basket made of split bamboo, a hide, a ruby, a diamond, a coral, a pearl, or the human body is purified by means of water (4—5). Articles made of iron are purified by means of water; and those made of stone by being rubbed and the purification, of vessels smeared with oil, is made by hot water (6). A winnowing basket, paddy, a deer-skin, a mace, a wooden mortar, clothes and bedding are purified by being sprinkled with water (7). All sorts of barks are purified by water and alkaline substances. Grass, wood and annual plants are purified by sprinkling water (18). When a woolen cloth or one made of hair is dirty it is purified by water mixed with mustard or the husks of sessame (9). When a cotton cloth is unclean, my son, it is purified by water and ashes (10). Things made of inferior metals are purified by water. Wood, teeth, a bone, and a horn is purified with being burnt again. Alms, the hand of a mechanic, commodity of commerce, the face of a female are naturally pure. Things, that have been brought in carriages, that are unknown, that have been carried by servants, that are always spoken of as pure, that have been lying for days together, that are light, that have passed through many hands, are by nature pure. Things in large quantities, a boy, the acts of an old man or of one suffering from disease (are by nature pure) (11—13). A house, where heaps of charcoal are lying about after the performance of a sacrificial rite, is pure, as well as a woman that gives milk to her child, or water that is current, that has no bubble or that does not give out bad smell (14). A ground is purified in time by being burnt, besmeared and with the foot-marks of the kine. A dwelling house is purified by pasting (cow-dung), scraping, washing, sweeping and worship (15). A place or thing, that has been touched by hairs or worms, that has been smelt by kine, that has been infested by fleas, is purified, my son, by water, earth, and ashes (16). A copper vessel is purified by acid, a zinc or leaden vessel by potash and a bell-metalled vessel by ashes and water and the liquid by the process of *plava** (17). And all other things, when they are defiled by polluting substances, are purified on being cleansed with water and earth until the bad smell is removed. All other things are purified when both their hue and bad smell are removed by these two substances (18). The water, that lies in its natural state on the earth, and is capable of satisfying the kine, is pure. The meat, of any beast brought by a *Chandala* or a carnivorous animal, is naturally pure (19). It is said, my son, that cloth and similar things lying on the high way are purified by the air (20). Dust, fire, a horse, a cow, a shade, the solar and lunar day, the wind, the earth, a drop of water,

---

* The process of taking up defiled Ghee with the blade of *Kusa* grass and dropping it in fire.

flies, etc., are not polluted in their coming in contact with vicious things (21). The mouth of a goat or of a horse is clean but that of a calf is not so. The urine and dung of a cow that has given birth to a young one as also the fruits dropped by a bird are pure (22). Like the commodities for sale, a sit, a bed, a vehicle, a boat, a grass growing on the way, are clean for the rays of the sun and moon fall over them and the air passes over them (23). A person should change his dress after walking, bathing, eating, drinking, passing urine and excrata and should rinse his mouth with water (24). If a road, clay, water or anything made of brick and clay is defiled for coming in contact with a polluting substance it is purified by air (25). If a heap of rice is polluted slightly a quantity should be taken from the surface and thrown away. Then by rinsing the mouth with water and sprinkling water on the rest and by earth it is purified (26). If a man unknowingly eats rice that has been defiled he should fast for three nights; but if he does it knowingly he must perform the penance as laid down (27). If a man touches a woman in her menses, a horse, a jackal, a woman, who has of late given birth to a child, the offspring of a *Chandala*, or an undertaker, he should bathe for the purpose of being purified (28). If a person touches a human bone covered with fat he is cleansed by bathing; but if he touches a human bone without fat he should rinse his mouth with water, touch a cow and behold the sun (29). A wise man should not walk over blood or spit or leap over an elevation; nor should he remain in a garden or such like places during a twilight (30). A man should not talk with a woman that has no husband or one who is generally reprehended. A man should throw outside his house leavings, urine, and excreta and water with which his feet have been washed (31). A man should not bathe in another's tank without digging therefrom five lumps of clay; but one should bathe in the Gangā, in any lake or river or natural water (32). If a person touches or talks with a man who villifies the deities, the ancestral manes, the holy books, sacrifices, Mantras, he is purified by looking at the sun (33). If a wise man beholds a woman in her menses, a *Chandala*, a fallen person, a dead body, an unbeliever, a woman who has of late given birth to a child, a hermophrodite, one nude, an offspring of a *Chandala*, those who take out things belonging to a child-birth, an adulterer, he is purified by the same means (34—35). If a man touches forbidden food, a woman just delivered, a hermophrodite, a cat, a rat, a dog, a cock, one fallen, cast off and polluted things, a *Chandala*, an undertaker, a woman in her menses, a domesticated boar, a man unclean for child-birth, he is purified by bathing (36—37). He, in whose house *Nitya* rites are neglected, he, who has been foresken by the Brahmanas, is the worst of men and a sinful wretch (38). Therefore a man should not put a stop to *Nitya* (obligatory) rites. Except on the occasion of birth or death, if he stops it, he is to suffer bondage (39). If a man is impure on account of any birth or death, if a Brâhmana, he should not for ten days make gifts and perform fire-ceremony and other obligatory rites; a Kshatriyâ, for twelve days and a Vaishya, for fifteen days (40). A Sudra should abstain from his own work for a month. After that, each order should perform their respective rites as laid down in holy books (41). The dead body having been cremated outside the house by the persons of the same *gotra*, water should be given to the departed spirit on the first, the fourth, the seventh or the ninth day (42). On the fourth day, the ashes and bones of the dead person should be collected by the persons of the same blood. After such a collection their bodies become touchable (43). After such a collection all the rites should be performed by those who are entitled to offer water. On the day of death, persons, both who can offer Pinda (and who can offer water), may be touched (44). In the event of death being brought about by weapon, water, hanging, fire, poison, fall from an elevated place or by the vow of starvation, or (by mere) starvation, the period of impurity lasts for only a single constellation (45). If one dies in infancy or in a distant country or affer having left his home, impurity disappears on the very day. Some say that the period of impurity lasts for three days (46). If after the death of a *Sapinda* another *Sapinda* dies, all the ceremonies, that are to be performed by the latter, become performable by the *Sapinda* on the expiration of the period of impurity calculated from the date of the first death (47). A similar injunction is followed duly on the birth of a child, both by the *Sapindas* and *Samânodakas* (48). It is enjoined that on the birth of a child, the father should bathe with the (cloth on 49). If after the birth of one, another is born, in that case too the purity is said to take place by counting the days from the first birth (50). On the expiry of ten days, twelve days, fifteen days and thirty days the four orders should duly perform their respective rites (51) On the expiration of such a time the *Ekoddishta* should be performed for the departed spirit. The wise should make presents to the Brahmanas (52). If one wishes to make (these ceremonies eternally (fruitful), he should make presents of whatever object is held in highest esteem in this world and whatever agreeable object is in the house, to the accomplished Brāhmanas (53). After the period of impurity is over, all the orders, touching water, as also the animals they ride or yoke to their cars, weapons, whips and goads, should perform the usual ceremonies (54). Being purified they should perform the ceremonies and acts that are ordained respectively for the various orders for they lead to prosperity both in this world and in the next (55). The three Vedas should be chanted every day and they should behave themselves like the learned. Acquiring riches by lawful means, they should attentively perform the sacrifices (56). O my son, one should fearlessly perform an act which does not bring censure on his own self and which does not require to be concealed from a person worthy of respect (57). Behaving thus, O my dear son, a householder acquires religious merit, worldly profit and desire, and becomes happy both in this world and in the next.

CHAPTER XXXVI.

JARA said :—Thus instructed by his mother, Hritadhwoja's son, on attaining to his youth, duly took to a wife (1). The mighty one begot offspring on her, and adored the celestials with sacrifices, And he satisfied the behest of his father at all times (2). After a considerable time, when he became old, Hritadhwaja installed his son on the throne (3). Then the virtuous-souled one, desirous of practising austerities, entered into woods along with his wife. That great king descended on the earth as the great protector (4). In order to dispell the attachment of her son to the enjoyment of pleasure Madalasā said these pregnant words to him (5). "A householder is always filled with attachment and is therefore the abode of misery. You have adopted the order of a householder. When, while governing your kingdom, you meet with insufferable pain engendered by the separation from dear friends or begotten by the impediments put in by the enemies or produced by the loss of wealth, you should read what is inscribed on this ring in minute letters (6—8).

JARA said :—Having said this, she handed over to him a golden ring and such benedictions as should be followed by one leading the life of a householder (9). Then having made over the kingdom to their son, Kuvalayashawa and his queen retired into forest for carrying on asceticism (10.)

CHAPTER XXXVII.

JARA said :—The righteous-souled Alarka duly governed his subjects as if they were his sons who were all filled with joy and established in the duties of their respective orders (1). He attained great joy by inflicting punishment upon the the wicked and affording protection to the pious. He gratified the deities with great sacrifices (2). To him were born sons who were possessed of great strength and prowess, noble and pious minds and who never trod wrong ways (3). Self-controlled as he was, he acquired wealth by virture and virtue by wealth. He enjoyed all worldly objects without their interfering with each other (4). Thus governing the kingdom, being equally mindful of virtue, worldly profit and desire, many long years passed over his head like a single day (5). Enjoying various sweet objects of life, he did not feel distaste for them; nor was he satiated with the acquisition of virtue and wealth (6). His brother, by name, Suvāhu, living in the forest, heard, that not having been able to control his senses, he was carelessly given to the enjoyment of worldy objects (7). Thinking on this for some time and desiring to awaken him, the king thought that an alliance with the monarch's enemies would be the best means (8). With a view to take away their kingdom, the accomplished (Suvāhu) repeatedly sought the help of the king of Kashi who was a master of an army and powerful animals (19). He made a display of his soldiers against the king and sent messengers to him asking him to make over the kingdom to Suvāhu (10). Fully knowing his own duties, Alarka was reluctant to make over the kingdom at such a command and replied to the envoy of the king of Kashi (11). "Let my elder brother coming to me with brotherly feelings beg the kingdom. From fear of an attack I shall not make over even a small portion of my land (12)." The greatly intelligent Suvāhu did not beg the kingdom of his brother. Begging is not the duty of a Kshatrya. Prowess is his wealth (13). Then encircled by his entire army, the king of Kashi advanced for attacking the kingdom of the monarch Alarka (14). Making alliances with the feudatory chiefs and vassals of the kingdom, the invador, through the servants of those chiefs, attacked Alarka and brought him under his control (15). By well-laid seiges he assailed the army of Alarka and brought the guards of the forts, forest-patrols and wood-men under his subjection (16). And among the feudatory chiefs of Alarka, some were won over by the grant of subsidies, some by creating dissensions and others by conciliation (17). Thus afflicted by the policy of his enemies the king became weakened. His treasury was largely drawn upon and his capital was invaded by the enemy (18). Thus assailed and finding his treasury drawn upon every day the king became greatly cheerless and his mind was very much agitated (19). Overwhelmed by a mighty distress, he thought of the ring about which his mother Madalasā had spoken before (20). Purifying himself by a bath and making some exalted Brāhmanas utter the benedictions, he took out the piece of writing and saw the letters distinctly written on it (21). When the king read aloud the inscription signs of joy appeared on his person and his eyes were expanded with excess of delight (22). (The words were) ;—Association should be renounced with whole heart; if one cannot do it, he should associate with the pious; for the association with the pious is a (powerful) panacea (23). Desire should be renounced with all heart. If one cannot do it, that should be directed towards liberation; for liberation is a powerful medicine for this (24). The king read aloud the words many times and began to think of what leads to the well-being of mankind. Having settled that this can be acquired by liberation and thinking that liberation would spring from association with the pious, the king began to ponder over the subject of association with the pious. Then with a greatly disturbed mind, he went to the highly blessed Dattātreya (25—26). Having presented himself before that high-souled and sinless one, he saluted him; and having adored him with due rites he said (27). "O Brahmana, show your favour to me. You are the refuge of those who seek refuge with you. Remove my sorrow, who am greatly assailed by it and possessed by desire". (28)

DATTATREYA :—"I shall, O king, remove your sorrow this very day. Tell me truly, O monarch, what is that sorrow of yours (29)."

JARA said :—Thus accosted by that greatly intelligent Rishi the king began to reflect. Me-thinks, the abode, of the three kinds* of pain, is self (39). The wise and highly intelligent king, reflecting long and repeatedly upon the self with the help of self, smilingly said (31). "I am not earth; nor water; nor light, nor wind, nor ether. But having been united with the body I desire happiness (32). In this body which is composed of five elements, pleasure and pain vary as regards their measure. If they belong to me, no good will be to me, me that live in some thing else (than body) (33); that have mumberless bodies to go through in the course of eternity and that happens to be up and down on account of the diminution or growth of pleasure and pain When freed from egoism the self appears in its true light (34) Seeing the self in the subtle *Tanmatras* forming the third (stage of Prakriti), what pleasure or pain can attach to me who am sheathed with a body composed of five elements (35). Pain exists in mind. What is called pleasure belongs to the mind also. As I am not my mind, therefore I have neither pleasure nor pain (36). As I am not my conscious-

---

* The three pains according to the *Sankhya* philosophy are 1 *Adhyatmika i.e.*, those proceeding from mind and body 2. *Adhidaivika*—supernatural 3. *Adhibhoutika*—proceeding from accident etc.

ness, as I am not my mind; as I am not my understanding, how can pain, which is begotten by inner faculties and which is alien to me, be mine (37)? As I am neither my body nor my mind, it appears that I am separate both from my mind and body. Therefore whether pleasure or pain exists in the mind or in the body, I have nothing to do with either of them (38). The one born before this body desires to have this kingdom. If this body be only a mass of five elements on account of the tendency of attributes, what have I to do with it? He (my brother) is in it (body). He, however, is different from his body as I am from mine (39). He, that has no hands and various other limbs, he that has no flesh. No bones and no nerves and arteries, what has he to do with elephants, horses and cars and treasures? Man has nothing to do with them (40). I have no enemy, I have no pain, I have no pleasure, I have no city. I have no treasury. I have no army consisting of horses and elephants and others. He has not them. Nor has any one else, as I have not got them (42). As one *Akasha* (space) is seen as manifold, when put into jugs, jars, *Kamandalu* etc., so the self which is one and the same, appears as Suvahu, the king of *Kashis*, and myself, in different bodies, on account of the diversity of bodies.

—:o:—

CHAPTER XXXVIII.

JARA said:—Then having saluted the high-souled Brahmana Dattâtreya, bending low with humility, he said these words in reply (1). "For my seeing correctly, O Brahman, I see that I have no pain. Those who do not see (things) correctly, are always immersed in an ocean of grief (2). To whatever object the mind of a person is attached, it extracts sorrow therefrom and gives it to its owner (3). The measure of sorrow that is felt when a domesticated cock is eaten up by a cat, differs from what is felt at the cat eating up a sparrow or a mouse, because neither is cherished attachment for (4). I am neither miserable nor happy, for I am above Prakriti. The material, which is subjugated by matter, is subject to pleasure or pain* (5)

DATTATREYA said :—O foremost of men, it is even what has been described by you. The consciousness of self is the root of pain, and the absence of it, brings about its cessation (6). From the instant of my questioning, you have acquired such an excellent understanding, that by it the consciousness of self will be dissipated like cotten fibres 7. The mighty tree of ignorance is in the heart; it has originated from the root of *ego*; it has the consciousness of self for its trunk, the house and land for its branches, children, wife etc. for its twigs; wealth and corn are its large leaves; it does not grow up soon; virtue and sin are its flowers; happiness and misery are the great fruits; the relations formed out of ignorance, are the water that nourishes it; it is surrounded by a number of bees in the shape of desire for actions, and it stands in the way of liberation (8—10). How can they attain to emancipation, who, exhausted with walking in the road of the world and subjected to happiness begotten by ignorance, seek the shade of this tree (11)? Those only, who can cut off this tree of self-consciousness with the axe of knowledge whetted well on the stone of the company of the good, can go by this road (12). Reaching the forest of Brahman, cool, freed from dust and thorns, the wise, divorced

* *Prakriti*, according to the Sankhya system of philosophy, is the material nature. *Purusha* is the soul. Sankhya system completely disavows the creation by volition. It is by the union of *Prakriti* (nature) with *Purusha* (soul) that creation is made. The material or *Sthula-Sarira* (body), which is composed of five elements, is subject to pleasure or pain.

from feelings, attain to the most excellent liberation (13). None of us, O king, either yourself or myself, is identical with elements and senses and is gross; nor any one of us is composed of *Tanmatras** or *Manas*† (14) none amongst us, O emperor, do I see identical with *Pradhana*‡; the soul§ transcends the body whereas all other objects, the combination of elements, are composed of *Gunas*‖ (essential ingredients) (15).

ALARKA said:—By your favour, O reverend Sir, I have attained to this most excellent knowledge which creates the notion of distinction between self consciousness and the principle of greatness (17). But my mind being drawn to to the objects of sense I am unable to attain to a state of equipoise. Nor can I make out how shall I liberate myself from the fetters of nature (18). Tell me, O Brahman, how shall I not be subject to re-birth; how shall I be free from *gunas* and how shall I be united with the eternal¶ (19). Tell

---

* The subtle elements that make up the subtle body.

† The intellectual faculties.

‡ According to *Sankhya* teachers *Prakriti* is called Pradhana or the principle of greatness.

§ The word in the text is *Kshetrajna—lit* that which knows the body. This is the soul in the *Sankhya* system.

‖ *Gunas* cannot be properly rendered by quality, or attribute. According to the Sankhya system they enter into the compositiou of a material object. They are equally as essential ingredients in the formation of material objects as the trees for that of a forest. In Sankhya philosophy the *Purusha* or the soul is quite different from the body. There are again two bodies. One is called *Sthula* or gross which is made of elements and the other *linga* or subtle which is made of *Tanmatras* or the subtle immaterial forms.

¶ As this chapter and the succeeding three or four chapters give a description of the Yoga, we think it better to give a brief outline of this system of Hindu philosophy to enable our readers to understand it fully.

The Yoga system of philosophy was propounded by Patanjali; its object is to teach the means by which the human soul may attain complete union with the supreme soul, may be freed from the fetters of Nature and escape re-birth. *Yoga* literally means concentration of mind upon the Divine soul. This concentration can be effected by preventing the modifications of *Chitta*

me, O Brahman, O you of great wisdom, this Yoga. I beg you with humility. Association with the good is always beneficial to mankind (20).

—oo—

CHAPTER XXXIX.

—:o:—

DATTATREYA said:—The separation of a Yogin from ignorance by knowledge is emancipation, and disunion with the essential ingredients of *Prakriti* (nature) is union with Brahman (1). Emancipation springs from Yoga and Yoga from consummate knowledge; O king, knowledge springs from pain which belongs to those whose minds are attached to the consciousness of self (2). Therefore a man, who is desirous of securing emancipation, should cast off attachment; from the absence of attachment proceeds the destruction of the consciousness of self (3). The absence of attachment leads to happiness; from the distaste for the world, the defects, thereof, are perceived; as distaste for the world originates

---

or thinking principle; by the constant habit of keeping the mind in unmodified state and by the practice of *Vairagya* or the complete suppression of passions or the distate for the world. This *Vairagya* can be acquired by the contemplation of the Supreme Being, who is unaffected by works, applications &c. The knowledge of the Supreme Being may be obtained by repeating the monosyllable *Om* accompanied by mental concentration. This *Om* is composed of three letters A. U. M. significant of the Supreme Being as developing himself in the Triad of god, Brahma, Vishnu and Siva. The eight means of mental concentration are (1) *Yama*, forbearance or self-restraint (2) *Niyama*, religious observances (3) *Asana*, postures (4) *Pranayama*, suppression of the breath (5) *Pratyahara*, restraint of senses (6) *Dharana*, steadying of mind (7) *Dhyana*, contemplation (8) *Samadhi*, a state of religious trance, the outcome of profound meditation.

from knowledge, so knowledge also springs from the distaste for the world (4). That is a house wherein a man lives; that is food by which one sustains himself; that is called knowledge which leads to emancipation—any thing else is called ignorance (5). By reaping the fruits of virtue and vice, by performing the daily obligatory rites without any desire, by the dissipation of the acts formerly performed and by not doing new acts, a body is not repeatedly fettered (6—7). Know this, O king, as Yoga, which I have described to you. By acquiring this Yoga a man does not seek refuge with any one else except the eternal Brahman (8). The Yogins should first conquer their selves (by the knowledge of) soul for it is difficult of being conquered by them. You should endeavour to conquer this (self). Hear, I shall describe the means (9). By *Pranayama* he should consume the short-comings, by *Dharana* the sins, by *Pratyahara* the objects of sense, and by *Dhyana* the *Gunas* of the mind which is not controlled (10). As all the impurities of mountain metals are removed by burning, so by the suppression of vital breaths, the impurities of senses are consumed (11). One versed in *yoga* should first undertake the suppression of vital breaths. The suppression of two vital breaths *Prána* and *Apána* is called Prānāyama (12). Prānāyama is of three kinds, namely *Laghu*, *Maddhya*, and *Uttarya*. Hear, O Alarka, I shall explain to you the measure of all these (13). *Laghu*, has twelve *Matras*, *Madhyama* has twice the number and *Uttama* has been described to have thrice the number (14). The time occupied in opening and shutting the eyelids is the measure of a *Matra*. For giving the measure of Prānāyāma, the division called *Laghu* has been described to consist of twelve *Matras* (15). By the first, perspiration should be conquered—by the second, trembling and by the third, the (various) defects such as cheerlessness etc. should be duly conquered (16). As the lion, the tiger and the elephant are quieted down by training, so the *Prána* of *yogis* is brought down to subjection (by these processes) (17). As an elephant trainer brings an infuriated elephant to subjection according to his will (by training it), so the Yogin brings to his subjection the *Prana* (18). As when a lion is trained, it kills only the deer and not men, so when the vital breaths are properly suppressed they destroy the impurities and not the body. Therefore a Yogin should always assiduously practise Prānāyama (19). Hear now, of the fourfold stages of Prānāyama which are the fruits of liberation; O king, they are *Dhvasti*, *prápti*, *Samvit* and *Prasáda*; do you listen in order to their characteristics as I describe them (20—21). The state, in which the fruits of acts, good and bad, are destroyed and along with it the impurities of mind are destroyed is called *Dhvasti* (22). That state extending over all time, in which a Yogin, controls all desires, both of this world and the next, begotten by covetousness and stupefaction, is called *Pràpti* (23). That state of Prānāyāma, in which the Yogin, by virtue of his consummate knowledge, acquiring the same power with the sun, moon, stars and planets, comes to know of the past and future and things not visible and greatly distant, is called *Samvit* (24—25). That state of a Yogin, in which the mental faculties, the five vital breaths, the organs of sense and the objects of sense are purified is called *Prasàda* (26). Hear now, O king, I shall describe the characteristics of Prānāyāma and the postures that are laid down for those who also carry on *Yoga* practices (27). Placing himself in various postures (such as) *padmásana*, *Ardhàsana* and *Swastikásana* and reciting in his mind the mystic syllable 'Om' one should engage in Yoga (28). Seated straight in an even posture contracting his two legs, with the mouth closed and the thighs firmly placed in the front, he should, controlling his mind, so sit that his heels may not touch the organ of generation and testes. He should so raise up his head that one row of teeth may not touch the other (29—30). Fixing his look on the tip of his nose and not diverting it in any other direction, and then obstructing darkness by passion and passion by goodness, and being stationed only in the pure principle of goodness, the Yogin should practice Yoga. Simultaneously withdrawing the senses from their objects, controlling the mental faculties and vital breaths, one should engage in practising *pratyahára*. Like a tortoise withdrawing its limbs he, who, restraining his desires, lives with his mind centered in the soul, sees the Divine soul in the human soul. The same wise man, should, after first purifying his external and internal limbs, from the throat to the navel downwards, and filling thebody with breath, begin practising *pratyahára*. These twelve forms of Prānāyāma are called Dhāranā (31—35). And the two Dhāranas are called *Yoga* by the Yogins acquainted with *Tattwas* or principles. When a Yogin, ever restraining his self, is engaged in Yoga, all his impurities are destroyed and he attains to a peaceful state; and he sees the great Brahman different from the essential ingredients of Nature (36—37); as also the atoms, ether etc., and the pure soul. Thus with restricted diet a Yogin should engage in Prānāyāma (38). He should slowly restrain himself like one ascending a house. Thus when a man cannot conquer the soil (i.e., restrain the bodily faculties) all the passions, diseases and ignorance always multiply. One should not set his foot on a soil which is not conquered* (39). In consequence of restraining the vital breaths it is called *Pranáyáma* (40). It is also called *Dhàraná* for by it the mind is held or restrained. It is also called *Pratyáhára*, for by Yoga, persons who have restrained their self, withdraw the senses from their objects such as sound *etc* (41). The

---

* It is metaphorical. *Soil* here means bodily faculties. Patanjali observes that a man cannot accomplish the union with God, which is the *summum bonum* of his life without restraining the bodily faculties.

expedients have also been pointed out by the great Yogins—the great Rishis, by which, obstacles, such as diseases and others, may not come in their way (42). As a thirsty man drinks slowly water through a vessel or a tube so the Yogin, without any exertion, should inhale air. *Dhàranà* or concentration should be first made on the navel, then on the heart, then on the chest, then on the throat, the mouth, the tip of the nose, the eye, the space between the eye-bows, the head and the last of all on the supreme spirit. This concentration is called the best. These are the ten forms of *Dhàranà* or concentration acquiring which one attains to unification with the Eternal Soul (43—45). If a Yogin, O king, wants to accomplish his purpose he should never engage in practising Yoga when he is hungry, fatigued or unsettled in mind (46). Nor should he, in extreme cold or hot seasons or in other extremes or at a time when the high winds blow, engage in Yoga or meditation (47). In places filled with noise near fire or water, dilapidated cow-sheds, in the crossings of the four roads, on withered leaves, in a river, in cremation grounds filled with reptiles, in dangerous places, on the bank of a well, on tombstones, on ant-hills—in all these places should a wise man renounce the practice of Yoga (48—49). So long as the quality of goodness is not properly developed, (bad) times and places should be avoided. The sight of an impious man does not lead to Yoga and so he should be avoided (50). Those, that through foolishness practise Yoga disregarding the distinctions of time and place, are assailed by shortcomings that impede their Yoga ; hear, I shall describe them (51). Such an ignorant man is afflicted by deafness, decripitude, dumbness, the loss of memory and blindness and fever (52). If the Yogins, through their carelessness, are visited by these evils, hear, I shall describe the remedial 'measures' they should adopt for counteracting (their actions) (53). For the cure of *Gulmas*, caused by (some disorder in the wind) one should eat highly heated *Yavagu* when cooled down and apply it to the afflicted part, to the navel and the stomach (54). *Yavágu* and air counteract all the ills caused by the disorder of the wind. In a similar treatment he should conceive in his mind a huge and motionless mountain (55). On the organ of speech being afflicted by deafness he should think of the organ of hearing, as one, stricken with thirst, thinks that a mangoe fruit is on the organ of taste (56). Then whatever part of the body is deseased the remedy should be applied there—heat for cold and cold for heat (57). Placing a wooden peg on the head strike it with another piece of wood—and the Yogin will immediately regain his lost memory (58). Let him also conceive that the immense space between the earth and heavens is filled with tempest and fire. These are the remedial measures laid down for superhuman impediments (59). If any superhuman creature enters into the Yogin's mind he should consume, it living in his body, by the conception of fire and hurricane (60). Thus O' king, by all means should a Yogin protect his body since it is the root of the accomplishment of virtue, worldly profit, desire and emancipation (61). From the description of the characteristics of propensities and wonderment arises the loss to the Yogin of his knowledge; therefore these should be kept secret (62). The absence of the agitation of the mind, the freedom from diseases and cruelty, fragrant odour, passing occasionally urine and excreta, grace, delight of mind and melody of voice—these are the primary characteristics of the tendency for Yoga (63). The most prominent characteristic of this accomplished state is that people always with love sing his praises in his absence and no creatures fear him (64). He only has attained to perfection who meets with no impediments from extremes of cold and heat and does not fear any thing (65)

CHAPTER XL.

—:o:—

DATTATREYA said :—There are many obstacles to the Yogin's realization of the spirit. Hear I shall describe them briefly (1). He longs for actions of desire, objects of human enjoyment, women, fruits of charity, learning, magical powers, wealth, heaven, the dignity of the celestials, the station of the king of celestials, chemical works, the raising of winds, sacrifics, entrance into fire and water, the fruits of all sorts of gifts and Srāddhas, religious regulations, and as well as that of fasting, the performance of *Purtta* acts, the adoration of the deities and all other pious observances. He longs for all these being surrounded by those impediments (2—4). If his mind is inclined towards this the Yogin should withdraw it; and then uniting his mind with *Brahman* he should liberate it from all these evils (5). All these impediments being remedied, other evils again overtake a *Yogin* orginating from the qualities of goodness, passion and ignorance (6). There are five dreadful impediments which the Yogin meets with in (the way of his) Yoga—they are *Pratibha*, relating to intellect; *Sravana*, relating to the organ of hearing, *Daivi*, belonging to gods, *Bhrama* or wandering, and *Avartta* or whirlpool (7). That by which the meanings of the *Vedas*, of the *Kavyas* (poetical literature) and endless learning and mechanical arts are unfolded to the Yogin is called *Pratibha* (8). That by which one understands the endless meanings of the sounds, and catches sound even from a distance of a thousand *Yojanas* is called *Sràvana* (9). The wise designate that state as *Daiva* in which, he, equal to a deity, sees completely the eight quarters like a mad-man (10). The shortcoming by which the mind of the Yogin wanders about without definite object and trangressing all sacred injunctions, is called *Bhrama* (11). The whirlpool of knowledge, agitated like that of water, destroys (the equanimity of his) mind and this impediment is called *Avartta* (12). All those born in the order of deities, having their Yoga destroyed by these dreadful obstacles, repeatedly turn round and round (13). Thus covering himself with the white blanket of his mind, the Yogin, fixing his mind upon Him, should meditate upon the Great Brahman (14). Restraining his senses and living on restricted food, the Yogin, intent on practising Yoga, should conceive in his head the seven subtile elements* such as earth etc., (15). Let the Yogin meditate upon the earth and he would attain to felicity. He should first conceive himself as earth and then shake off its fetters (16). In the same way he should comprehend the property of savour or taste in *Apas* or water, the property of form or colour in *Tejas* or fire or light, the property of tangibility in *Vàyu* or air, and sound in A*kasa* or ether and he should afterwards cast off these conceptions from his mind (17—18). When again by his mind (*Mana*)† he enters into the minds of all creatures, his mind by such steadying becomes subtle (19). After attaining the intellectual perception of all creatures and

---

* These are the five *Tanmátrás* or subtle elements, particles out of which, the grosser elements are evolved—together with *Buddhi* or intellect and *Ahankára* or the sense of individuality. The first production is the intellectual perception, which again is the source of *Ahankára* or sense of individuality which again produces the five *Tanmàtràs* which are 1 *Akasa*, 'ether' or the substratum of sound; 2, *Vayu*, air with the property of tangibility; 3 *Tejas* fire or light with the property of form or colour 4 *Apas* water with the property of savour or taste; 5, *Prithivi*, earth with the property of odour or smell. Truly does Sir Monier Williams observe "that *Akasa* must not be exactly identified with the modern ether. In some of its properties and functions it more corresponds with the *inane* vacant space of Lucretius."

† The *Manas* can be better rendered by mind or mental faculties. It is with *Ahankára* or 'self 'consciousness the production of *Mahat* or intellectual perception. *Manas*, which is an internal organ of perception, volition and action, according to the Sankhya teachers, stands between the five organs of sense and five organs of action.

then the most subtle intellect, one versed in *Yoga* should cast it off (20). O Alarka, the Yogin, who, after duly comprehending these seven elementary particles, drives them away from his mind, does not suffer from rebirth (21). Observing gradually the subtlety of the seven elementary particles by *Dhāranā* or steadying of mind and dismissing them gradually, the self-controlled Yogin attains to the most accomplished state (22). O king, by being excessively attached to things which he holds dear, he is deceived (23). Thus after comprehending that these subtle elementary particles are connected with each other, the man, who dismisses them, attains to a great state (24). The distaste for elemental creation, engendered in the mind of a man conversant with the knowledge of truth, by the perception of seven elementary particles, leads to his liberation (25). If he becomes attached to smell, etc., he is ruined and is born again and again as a man, remote from Brahman, O king (26). Having thus fixed his mind upon these seven elementary particles, the Yogin, O king, can become absorbed in whatever subtile element he likes (27). He can become absorbed in the bodies of deities, Asuras, Gandharvas, serpents or Rākshasas—but he never becomes attached to anything (28). O king, he attains to eight-fold divine attributes* leading to annihilation—namely, *Animā*, *Laghimā*, *Mahimā*, *Prāpti*, *Prākāmya*, *Ishitya*, *Vashitya* and *Kāmāvasāyitya* (29—30). The state in which one becomes subtler than subtle is called *Animā*; that by which one becomes light-handed and quick

* A Yogin may acquire eight great powers viz., he will have the power of shrinking into the form of the minutest atom; that of assuming a gigantic body; that of becoming extremely light; that of becoming extremely heavy; that of unlimited reach of the organs, as touching the moon with the tip of the finger; that of irresistible will (as, sinking into earth as easily as into water); that of perfect dominion over the inner organs of the body; and that of mastery over all beings, animate and inanimate. These strange effects, attributed to Yoga practices, are the secret of the power which this doctrine has at all times exercised over the Hindu mind.

is called *Laghimá*; that by which one becomes worshipped of the world is called *Mahimá*; that by which everything is obtained is called *Prápti* (31). That by which one becomes omnipresent is *Prákámya*, that by which one becomes the lord of all is called *Ishitya*; that by which one can keep all under his control is called *Vaskitya*—this is the seventh attribute of a Yogin (32). That, which one can move about and do according to his will, is called *Kàmàvasáyita*. By these eight-fold qualities a Yogin can act like the God (33). (The appearance of these qualities) O king, indicates (a Yogin's) liberation and the annihilation of self and that he will neither be born nor increase nor meet with decay (34). He will meet with no metamorphosis or end, and he will not be afflicted by galling pain, burning heat and drying up through elements such as earth, etc. (35). The five elements, sound and other properties, shall not be able to subdue him; he shall not enjoy them nor will be attached to them (36). O king, as a piece of gold, when melted in fire and freed from impurities like a bad metal, is joined with another piece of gold, so when all the evils are consumed by the fire of Yoga, the Yogin attains to unification with Brahman and has no seperate existence (37—38). As fire, when it is thrown into fire, is united with it, becomes indentical with it, recieves the same appellation (of fire) and does not present any distinction, so when the Yogin, O king, having his sins consumed, becomes unified with the great Brahman, he presents no difference (39—40). As water, when it is thrown into water, is united with it, so the soul of the Yogin becomes at one with the Supreme soul (41).

CHAPTER XLI.

—:0:—

ALARKA said:—"O reverend Sir, I wish to know, in sooth, of the conduct of the Yogin as well as of the ways of Brahman following which he does not meet with deterioration" (1). Dattâtreya said:—"Honour and dishonour are the instruments of success and anxiety to mankind. When they bear opposite meanings they bring on the accomplished state to the Yogin (2). Honour and dishonour are spoken of as poison and ambrosia; of them dishonour is ambrosia and honour is the deadly venom (3). He should not place his footsteps without carefully examining the ground, should not drink water that is not cleansed by cloth, should not speak a word that is not purified by truth, and should not engage in a thought that is not purified by intellect (4). For accomplishing this object a Yogin should not resort to hospitality, the performence of Srâddhas, sacrifices, festivities and singing parties in honour of deities and great men (5). When the house of a householder is freed of smoke and fire and after all of them have taken their meals the Yogin should go out for alms—and this not thrice a day and nor even daily (6). Without desecrating the ways of the good the Yogins should so act that they may be dishonoured and discomfitted by men (7). He should beg alms of the householders and priests—of these the first is spoken of as the best (8). A Yogin should always go to the householders who are modest, reverential, self-controlled, well-read in the Vedas and high-souled, (9) and who again belong to the higher order, are not touched by any sin and are not fallen. To beg alms from persons of inferior orders is considered as the most contemptible life (10). *Yavâgu*, *Takra*, milk, *Yàvaka*, fruits, roots, *Priyangu*, *Karna*, *Pipyâka* and *Sakhis* are the foods (11). These are the pure foods for the Yogins and lead to the accomplishment of their objects. These should be procured by alms and they should live on them with great concentration of mind and devotion (12). Before taking his meals he should observe silence and restrain his self and then saying *Prànàya** (he should sip water)—this has been laid down as the first oblation (13). Then saying *Apànaya*, *Samanaya*, *Udànâya* and *Vyânaya* he should offer the second, third, fourth and fifth oblations (14). Then separating (his body) by Prāṇāyāma (suppression of vital breaths) he should eat according to his desire; then again sipping water he should touch his heart (15). Absence of the desire of stealing, life of celebacy, renunciation, absence of covetousness and harmlessness are the five observances of a mendicant (16). Absence of anger, to minister to the preceptor, purity, the restriction of diet and the daily study of the Vedas—these have been spoken of as the five regulations (to be observed by) them (17). He should seek to acquire that knowledge which is the essence of all and the instrument of the accomplishment of all objects—the variety of knowledge (however) impedes Yoga (18). One who thirsts after knowledge thinking *this should be known! this should be known* does not attain to knowledge even within a thousand Kalpas† (19). Being disassociated, conquering anger, restricting diet and res-

---

* These are the five vital breaths, namely Prana, Apana, Samana, Udana and Vyana.

† The true knowledge according to Patanjali is that of the supreme spirit or the God; from it the knowledge of all other things flows. According to him a man should seek this true knowledge, the essence of all and by and by he will come to know every thing in the world. If however one seeks knowledge of every thing he sees in the world at the sacrifice of supreme knowledge or *Pará Jnána* he will never acquire it even in thousands of years. According to the Arya Rishis this *Pará Jnána* is the only supreme knowledge—the knowledge of the great Brahman which people should strive to acquire if they want to liberate themselves from the three fold pains and the fetters of the knowledge

training senses and forming the gateway by intellect, one should engage his mind in *Dhyâna* or contemplation (20). Resorting to mountain caves, forests or lonely places, a Yogin, intent on practising *Yoga*, should always engage in contemplation (21). He who has been able to control the three *Dandas* or staff namely words, actions and mind, is called *Tridandi* and is a great Yogin (22). O king, who is liked and who again is disliked by him who considers this universe, existent and non-existent, at one with *Gunas* and divorced from them, and identical with himself? (23). He, whose intellect has been purified, who considers a brick bat and gold in the same light, who, concentrating himself in all elements, sees only the eternal and undecaying Brahman, the stay of all, as existing, is never born again (24). The Vedas and all the sacrificial rites are superior to all other things—above it is the recitation (of Mantras) and above, is the road of knowledge and above it, is *Dhyána* or contemplation which is freed from association and attachment. By this one can attain to the eternal Brahman (25). By being self controlled, intent upon meditating upon Brahman, assiduous, pure, whole-mindedly devoted and of restrained senses, one, who acquires this Yoga, attains to the union of the soul with the Supreme Soul and then to liberation proceeding therefrom (26).

CHAPTER XLII.

—:o:—

DATTATREYA said :—Even hundreds of birth cannot dislodge a Yogin from his position, who, intent on practising Yoga, follows such a method (1). Seeing the Great Soul, manifest in the form of the universe, having the universe for his feet, head and neck, the Lord and the Protector of the Universe, he should, for obtaining Him, recite the great and sacred monosyllable *Om*. The study of this (Om) is (nothing but) listening to its great and true form (2—3). A, U, and M, are the three letters—these are the three *Mâtrâs** pertaking of the quality of goodness, passion and darkness (4). There is another half *Mátrá* of this *Om* which is placed high and above the reach of the three qualities; for its dependence on the Musical note *Gàndhára*† it is called *Gândhàri*. Its motion and touch is like that of an ant; it is perceived on the head (5). As, when recited, *Om* goes to the head, so the Yogin, by every letter, becomes identical with *Om* (6). The vital breath is the bow, the soul is the shaft and Brahman is the excellent aim; so by assiduously piercing Brahman like a shaft one becomes at one with Him (7). That Om is the three Vedas, the three worlds and the three fires, Vishnu, Brahmā and Siva, as well as Rik, Saman and Yayush (8). You should know truly that there are three half *Mâtrâs* of *Om*; the Yogin, who is intent upon reciting it, attains to fusion or *laya* into it (9). Again *A* is intended to mean *Bhu* (earth) U Bhuva and M the celestial region (10). The first *Màtrà* is *Vyaktà* (Brahma) the second is called *Avykatà*, the third is the *chit* or thinking principle; and the half *Màtrà* is the Brahman (11). These should be duly known as grounds for practising Yoga; by the recitation of *Om*, all things, existent and non-existent, are realized (12). The first *Màtrà* is *Hrasya* (short), the second *Deergha* (long) and the third *Plutà*‡ and the half *Màtrà* is not within the range of words (13). Thus the person, who thoroughly understands and meditates

* As syllabic foot.

† One of the seven primary notes of Music.

‡ The third sound given to vowel; the protracted or continuous sound being three times the length of the short vowel and occupying three moments in its utterance.

upon the great Brahman designated by the great monosyllable *Om*, renouncing the wheel of the world and being freed from the three fetters, attains to fusion or *Laya* in the Brahman, the Great Soul (14—15). If the fetters of his actions are not snapped, he, knowing death by *Aristha** and having the recollection of the prestine birth, in another, again is born as a Yogin (16). By his accomplished Yoga in another life as well as by that in this life he is always acquainted with *Aristha* and does not sink down at the time of death (17).

CHAPTER XLIII.

DATTATREYA said:—Hear, O great king, I shall enumerate the signs of approaching death; by observing them the Yogin may know when he will die (1). He, who cannot see the road of the celestials, Dhruva, Sukra, the moon, his own shadow and Arundhati, meets with death after the expiration of one year (2). The man, who sees the solar disc without rays and the fire full of the rays of the sun, does not live more than eleven months (3). He, who in a dream sees gold or silver in what is thrown out, urine and excreta, lives only for ten months (4). If one sees ghosts, Pisāchas, the city of the Gandharvas and golden trees, he lives only for nine months (5). If one, who is fat, all on a sudden becomes thin, if one thin built man at once becomes fat, his natural lease of life will surely run out after eight months (6). He, who when he sets his foot on mire or manure, has the mark of

* The sign or symptom of approaching death.

the heel or the fore part half stamped, lives only for seven months (7). He, on whose head, sits a vulture, pigeon, Kākola, crow, other carnivorous (birds) or dark-blue birds, does not live more than six months (8). One, who is assailed by a row of crows, or a downpour of dust or who sees his own shadow in the opposite direction, lives for four or five months (9). He, who, in the absence of clouds, sees lightning in the southern quarter and rainbow in the night, lives only for two or three months (10). He, who does not see his own shadow in clarified butter, oil, mirror or water, or even if he does so sees it without head, does not live more thana month (11). The Yogin, O king, from whose body comes out the smell of a corpse, lives only for half a month (12). He, whose heart and feet are dried up immediately after bathing, whose throat is dried up although he drinks water, lives only for ten days (13). Death is impending to him whose vital parts are pierced by the winds clashing with one another and whose hairs do not stir even by the touch of the water (14). Death is present to him, who, in a dream, proceeds singing to the southern quarter in conveyances of bears and monkeys, (15). He also does not live when in a dream, a female, clad in a dark-blue and crimson cloth, takes him to the southern direction, singing and smiling (16). A learned man, seeing alone a nude, and highly powerful Buddha mendicant in a dream laughing and leaping, knows death to be present (17). The man, who in a dream, sees his own body drowned neck deep in mire, meets with immediate death (18). If a man sees in dream hairs, char-coals, ashes, serpents and rivers void of water, he meets with death on the eleventh day after ten days (19). If a man sees in a dream, a highly terrific, dreadful and dark man, striking with uplifted weapons and stones he meets with immediate death (20). If a jackal passes before a man or behind him or goes round him at sun rise he meets with immediate death (21). Forsooth the lease of a man's life has run out who feels hungry immediately after taking meals and whose teeth gnash against one another (22). He, who does not perceive the smell of a lamp, who becomes afraid either in the day or night, who sees his own reflection in another's eye, does not live (23). The one, knowing his self, should for certain perceive his end who sees the rainbow in the middle of the night and the stars during the day (24). The lease of his life has run out whose nose becomes crooked whose ears are either elevated or depressed and whose left eye sheds tears (15). The wise man should then know his end to be at hand when his face becomes red and tongue yellow (26). Forsooth should he know that his death is imminent who, in a dream, goes to the southern quarter in a conveyance drawn by camels or jackals (27). He, who projecting his ears, does not hear the sound made by himself and the vision of whose eye is lost, does not live (28). There is the end of his life who, falling into a pit in a dream, does not find the entrance and accordingly cannot come out (29). The upward looks, the eyes becoming red, dilated and whirling, the heat of the mouth and the dilation of the navel surely indicate the future birth of a man (30). There is the end of his life, who, entering into fire in a dream, cannot come out nor entering into water can come out of it (31). He, who is assailed by mischevous ghosts either in the day or in the night, forsooth meets with death within seven nights (32). He, who sees his clean white cloth either as crimson or darkblue, has his impending death ascertained (33). It is said that Yama and Antaka are near those who have the perversity of their nature and character (34). The wise designate it as the end of that man who disregards and villifies them before whom he should always be humble and who are worthy of his respect, who does not adore the deities, vilifies the preceptor, the elderly men and Brāhmanas, who does not perform the obsequies of his parents, who does not welcome his son-in-law and who insults the Yogins, the wise and other great men (35—37). O king, the Yogins should with care learn that these fore-bodings bear fruits daily or at the end of the year (38). Observing particularly O king, that these fruits are dreadful they should always think of that time in their mind (39). Knowing full well that time and resorting to a place void of fear the Yogin should practise Yoga so that the time may not be divorced from its fruits (40). Beholding these omens, casting off the fear of death and marking the characteristics of the time when they set in the Yogin should engage in Yoga in whatever division of the day they may appear. In the morning, in the evening, in the noon or in the night or whenever these omens are seen he should engage in Yoga till the proper time comes (41—43). Casting off all fear, controlling the time and restraining his own self he should engage in Yoga with the Great Soul; then conquering the three fold qualities and making his own soul at one with the Supreme Soul he should cast off intellectual faculties (44—45). He will then be able to attain to the great beatitude which is beyond the reach of senses and intellect and is incapable of being described (46). I have described to you all this truly, O Alarka; I shall now relate in brief, how you will attain to Brahman; hear me (47). When the jewel *Chandrakânta* is united with the rays of the moon it discharges water and not when it is not united; this has been described as a simile for the Yogins (48). When the jewel *Suryakânta* is united with the rays of the sun it displays fire and not alone; this is a simile for the Yogins (49). Ants, rats, cats, *Grihagodha* and *Kapinjalas* live in a house where the householder resides; on his death they go elsewhere (50). At the destruction of their master they feel no sorrow. This instance of their dwelling, O emperor, is also a simile for the Yogins (51). An earth-worm, although its mouth is very small, gathers up a heap of earth; this is also an instruction for the Yogins (52). Beasts, birds, mankind and other creatures destroy the trees crested with leaves, flowers and fruits; from this the Yogins should draw a lesson (53). The top of the horn of a young one of a Ruru, although it is like a sessame seed, grows up with it; seeing this the Yogin should attain to the accomplishment of his object (54). Observing the movements of the limbs of a person while ascending an elevation from the surface of the earth with a vessel filled with liquid substance in his hands what does not a Yogin learn (55)? Knowing truly the exertion of mankind that they destroy every thing for their own subsistence the Yogin can attain the accomplishment of his object (59).* Wherever one lives is his house; that by which one's life is sustained is his food and that by which one's object is accomplished is his happiness; so why there should be an attachment (57)? Although solicited as an effect is produced by causes so by intellect and others which are not his own he should strive to accomplish (the union with the) Great Soul (58).

Thereupon saluting him and bending low with humility the king Alarka, filled with delight, said:—(57). O Brahman,

---

* These verses are very terse and an explanation is therefore necessary. The object of the Yogin is to cast off all attachment for the world and to effect an union of his own soul with the Great Soul. For renouncing this attachment he shouid take lessons from the various objects. (48 Sloka) As by the union with the rays of the moon, the jewel, so called, discharges water so the mind, of the Yogin when engaged in the contemplation of the supreme spirit, enjoys a happiness which he cannot otherwise feel. (49)—As when touched by the rays of the sun the jewel, so called, displays fire, so the Yogin, by virtue of Yoga or concentration of the mind, can see the Great Brahman. (59)—From the ants and other creatures, going away to another house after the death of a house-holder and cherishing no attachment for him the Yogin should learn that after the destruction of one body another springs up and therefore he should cherish no attachment for the body. (51)—As an earth worm, though an insigniffcant creature, can collect a heap of earth, so though the attainment of Brahman is a difficult task it can be gradually had by the practices of Yoga. (52)—As a tree, enveloped with blossoms and fruits, is felled by men, so this body, however rich and great a man might be, will fall a prey to death. So the Yogin should cherish no attachment for this body which is frail.

by good luck it is that this dreadful fear of life was engendered by the terror of a defeat from the enemy (60). By good fortune it is that the king of Kashi is gifted with prowess and prosperity for whose ruin I have come hither and been united with you (61). By fortune it is that my strength has been weakened, my servants have been slain, my treasure has been exhausted and I have been possessed by fear (62). By fortune it is that the pair of your feet came within the range of my recollection and by fortune it is that your words have found room in my heart (63). By fortune it is that I have attained to knowledge by seeing you. And by fortune it is, O Brahman, that you showed me this kindness (64). With the advent of good luck to a man even an evil is converted into good; for this calamity, by bringing me to you, has conduced to my well-being (65). Suvāhu is a benefactor of mine, as also, the lord, the king of Kashi, by whom I have been brought to you, the lord of asceticism (66). And that I, having all my sins consumed by the fire of your grace, shall so engage in hard austerities that I may not again come by these miseries (67). Obtaining permission from you who are high-souled and can confer knowledge I shall cast off this condition of a house-holder which is a forest of the trees of ills (68)." Dattātreya said:—"Depart, O king, may you fare well. As related by me, shorn of attachment and egoism, do you so exert as may bring on liberation (69)."

JARA said:—Being thus addressed and saluting him he came speedily where the king of Kashi and his elder brother Suvāhu were (70). Approaching the large-armed and the heroic king of Kashi, Alarka, as if smiling, said to him in the presence of Suvāhu (71). "O lord of Kashi, desiring for kingdom, enjoy this kingdom earned by you as you like or confer it upon Suvāhu (72)." The king of Kashi said:—"Why do you, O Alarka, surrender this kingdom without a battle; such is not the duty of a Kshatriya and you too are converasnt with their duties (73). Having brought under his subjection the host of ministers and cast off the fear of death a king should take arrows aiming at his enemy (74). And having conquered him the king should enjoy all the most desired for objects and celebrate great sacrifices for accomplishing his great object (75)." Alarka said:—"Formerly such was my mind, O hero. But now it is quite the contrary. Hear the cause (76). As the body of a man is but a collection of elements, so all the inner faculties and essential ingredients (Gunas) are composed of elements (77). There exists only one Absolute intelligence and none else; how can then be, O king, the notion of an enemy, friend lord and servant? (78). Afflicted by pain begotten by the fear of you, I have, O king by the grace of Dattātreya, attained to excellent knowledge (79). Having conquered the number of senses and cast off various associations I shall concentrate my mind on *Brahman*. Obtaining Him a man gets every thing (80). A man should set forth every exertion for obtaining Him save whom nothing exists. By controlling the senses one can attain to Him (81). I am not your enemy, nor you are mine. This Suvāhu is not my malefactor. I have learnt all this truly. So do you seek for another enemy (82)." Having been thus addressed the king Suvāhu delightedly rose up and welcomed his brother with saying, "By good luck it is so." He then said to the king of Kashi (83).

CHAPTER LXIV.

—:o:—

SUVAHU said :—"I have obtained in its entirety that for which I sought refuge with you, O foremost of kings. I shall go now ; may you be happy" (1). The king of Kashi said :—"For what did you come to me and what have you obtained? Tell me this, O Suvāhu. I have been stricken with great curiosity (2). Your great ancestral kingdom was occupied by Alarka. You urged me saying "conquering him give me my kingdom" (3). Therefore invading your younger brother's kingdom I have brought it to your control. So do you enjoy it according to the custom of your family" (4).

SUVAHU said:—"O king, of Kashi, hear for what did I make this attempt and make you do it (5). This my brother, although acquainted with the real principles, was attached to ordinary objects of enjoyment. (He thought) "my two brothers, although possessed by stupefaction, were gifted with the knowledge of principles" (6). O king, as our mother, in our fancy, gave milk to us so also did she impart upon us three the knowledge of principles (7). O king, our mother placed, before our minds, the knowledge of all these objects which is worthy of being known by mankind; this is not all (8). As the good feel sorrow at the ruin of the one of many following the same interest so is the case with us, O king (9). O king, possessed by the infatuation of worldliness he was going down. We have a connection with him ; in this body he is our brother (10). Therefore I ascertained that from calamity he would acquire distaste for the world and accordingly I sought refuge with you for making this attempt (11). O king, from this calamity he has acquired true knowledge from which has sprung distaste for the world. My object is accomplished and so I depart. May good betide you (12). Living in Madalasā's womb and sucking in the same way her breast, may, he, O king, wend the way which is not trodden by the sons of other women (13). Ascertaining all this in my mind and seeking refuge with you I made this attempt. My object is accomplished. I shall depart again to accomplish the object of my Yoga (14). O king, I do not consider these men as having their senses in due order but rather deranged who disregard their friends, kinsmen, and relatives when they are assailed by misfortune (15). The friends, relatives, and kinsmen, in the face of whose efficiency a person is assailed by the deterioration of virtue, wordly profit and desire, are censurable; he is not (at all) to blame (16). By your company I have accomplished this great work, O king. May you live in happiness, be the foremost of the pious and participate in knowledge. I depart (17)." The king of Kashi said :—"You have done a great service to the pious Alarka. But why do you not turn your mind towards doing me good? 18. The association of the pious with the pious always bear fruit; it never becomes futile. Therefore it is but proper that I should advance in your company" 19.

SUVAHU said :—Virtue, worldy profit, desire and liberation are the four-fold objects of a man. Of them you have already acquired virtue, wordly profit and desire. But you have the want of the other (*i. e.* liberation) (20). I shall therefore describe them in brief. Do you hear with attention. Hearing them and discussing them properly, O king, you should exert for your well-being (21). You should, O king, never cherish the ideas of 'I and mine'. But you should duly think of virtue for in its absence a man becomes destitute of help (22). Deliberating yourself you should know "To whom do I belong?" Deliberating thus at the end of night you should engage in thinking of external faculties (23). Everything from the invisible (Purusha) to nature is without any metamorphosis and consciousness; you should therefore know what is visible and invisible ; also what else should be known, who should know and who am I?' (24). Knowing this in particular you will know every thing; to consider what is non-soul (body) as soul and what is not own, as own constitutes ignorance (25). According to human practice, O king, I am present everywhere. I have thus described to you everything you asked of me and I shall now go (26). Having thus spoken to the king of Kashi, the intellegent Suvāhu went away. And the king of Kashi too, having worshipped Alarka, repaired to his own city (27). Having installed his eldest son as king, Alarka too, leaving all human associations, entered into woods for attaining the *summumbonum* of his life (28). After a considerable time, being above the influence of opposites, and separated from wife and dependants and acquiring incomparable prosperity of Yoga he attained the most excellent beatitude (29). Beholding this entire universe, with the deities, Asuras and men, bound by nooses composed of the qualities and being perpetually fettered by them (30)—by bonds originating from sons, brothers' sons, one's own relatives and those who are not one's own; and thus appearing as various, and attached by the senses, overcome by miseries ; (31) seeing it hopelessly sunk in the mire of ignorance, and finding himself beyond it, the high-minded Alarka sang this hymn (32) "Alas what pain! We ruled this kingdom before, but I have come to know this afterwards that there is no felicity greater than Yoga" (33).

JADA said :—For liberation, do you resort to this most excellent yoga by which you will get the Brahman, obtaining whom you will not grieve (34) Then I too shall go. O what avail is sacrifice or recitation to me? The blessed always work for ascertaining the true form of Brahman (35) Therefore obtaining your permission, and being above opposites and not wanting anything I shall so exert for liberation that I may find everlasting peace (36)"

THE BIRDS said :—O Brahman, saying this to his sire and

obtaining his permission, the intelligent one, renouncing the company of his followers, went away (37). His father too, in the same way gradually acquiring good understading resorted to the fourth stage of life, namely that of Vānaprashtha. (38) Being united there with his son, casting off the fetters of qualities he attained to the highest state of Yoga by virtue of the noble impulse that arose in him at that time. (39) O Brahmana, we have thus described to you in detail what you asked of us. Tell us, what further more you wish to hear of us? (40)

—oo—

CHAPTER XLV.

JAIMINI said:—O foremost of the twice-born one you should describe to me the two-fold Vaidika rites—*Pravritti* and *Nivritti*. (Or leading to the knowledge of the means of success and the discountinance of the worldly acts.) What a wonder, that by the grace of your sire you have obtained such a knowledge, by which although born as birds you have dispelled ignorance (2). Blessed are you since your minds are in their pristine state and have not been agitated by ignorance begotten by worldly objects (3). Fortunately the revered and intelligent Mārkandeya spoke of you, the dispeller all doubts and ignorance (4). While roving in this greatly perilous world men cannot get the company of asceties like yuorselves (5). If I cannot accomplish my object in the company of such wise persons as yourselves, where can I then meet with success? (6). I do not think any one else has that clear understanding which you have in the two-fold actions of knowledge namely that of the means of success and the discontinance of the worldly acts (7). O foremost of the twice-born one, if your mind is bent upon showing me favour do you describe to me in full all these subjects (8). How has this universe, composed of the mobile and the immobile has originated? And where does it go again at the time of universal dissolution, O great one. (9). How from the various families originate the celestials, the Rishis, the Pitris and other creatures? What are the *Manwantaras* and the accounts of the various families (10). All the various creations, all the various dissolutions, all the various *Manwantaras* (11). The position of the earth, the extent of the earth as well as the situations of oceans, mountains, rivers, and forests (12) The account of the regions of Bhu and celestials, and of Pātala and the movements of the even, the moon, the stars, the planets and other luminous bodies; (13). I wish to hear of them all from the orgin to the dessolution. I wish to know also what will remain after the dissolution of this universe (14).

THE BIRDS said:—O foremost of sages, fearless are the questions you have put to us. Hear, we shall describe them at length, O Jaimini (15). This was formerly described by Mārkandya to the son of the twice-born one Kraushtu, intelligent, of a quiescent soul and who had just completed the period of his studentship (16). O lord, this very question was put by Kraushtuki to the high-souled Mārkandeya when he sat encircled by the leading twice-born ones (17). Hear, O foremost of the twic-born, we shall recount what was said by the son of the Bhrigu (18). Having saluted the lord of the universe, the lotus-sprung Brahmā the orgin of the world, who protects the creation in the form of Vishnu and destroys it in the form of the dreadful Rudra (19) Markandeya said:—As soon as the uncreate Brahmā came into being there came out from his four mouths all these Puranas and Vedas (20). The superior sages compiled many ancient *samhitas*, and made a thousand-fold division of the *Vedas* (21). Righteousness or

Dharma, divine knowledge, renunciation, and power over the elements, these four can never be had except through his (Brahma's) instructions (22). The seven primal *Rishis* (sages), the spiritual offsprings of Brahma, recieved the *Vedas* from him, while his other spiritual sons the primal *Munis* received from him the *Puranas* (23). *Chyabana* had those *Puranas* from Bhrigu, and by him were the twice-born sages instructed in them; by these high-souled *Rishis* again were these communicated to *Daksha* (24). By *Daksha* again they were related to me in those days. I shall relate that to you to-day which destroys the sins peculiar to this *kali-yuga* or dark-age (25). Do you, Oh highly fortunate one, hear all this from me with undivided attention. I shall relate it to you even as I myself heard it, of old, from *Daksha* (26). Having saluted *Brahmâ*, who is himself unborn, and without decay, but from whom has sprung this world, who is the refuge of all the moving and immoveable creat ion, the stay of the universe, the most superior abode (of the spirit), the primal person, from whom is the birth, stay, and final dissolution of the world,—having saluted *Hiranya-garvha* the guide of all beings, and the inspirer of intelligence, I shall duly relate to you the nature of the superior elements (27—29). This creation,—from the unmanifested source of matter and mind—the *Mahat* of the *Sânkhya* philosophy, down to the *Bishesha* of *Kanàd*, with all its changes and properties, that which can only be established by the fivefold forms of testimony, and which is joined with the five avenues of the senses, which though in a state of flux is yet, on account of the presence of the Purusha in it, in the main, beyond change,—hear all about it, O thou highly fortunate one, with superior concentration of the mind (30—31). The unmanifested cause, called the Pradhāna by the *Sànkyas*, which is named by the *Maharshis* or great sages, as *Prakriti*—subtle of nature, composed of both that which is, and that which is not but simply appears to be,—which is everlasting,—which is subtle, is indestructible, not subject to old age, which cannot be measured, which is unrelated, devoid of smell, form, and taste, and is without sound and touch; which is the source of this world, born of the three qualities—*Satva*, *Raja*, and *Tama*; which is above loss or decay; which is not joined to anything else, which is beyond comprehension,—which, in fact, is Brahman and existed from the beginning:—by him is all this endless creation pervaded after each *Pralaya* or elemental dissolution. Afterwards from this harmony of the three qualities owing to the presence in them, of the soul, O *Muni*! at the time of creation again, through the movement of the qualities for purposes of creation, does the essence of the *Pradhana* arise and cover the unmanifested *Mahat* (32—36). Even as the kernel of a seed is encased in its shell, so his *Mahat* enveloped by the unmanifested *Pradhana*. This *Mahat* manifests itself in a three-fold form according as one or other of the three qualities of *Satva*, *Raja*, and *Tama* predominates over the others (37). From this *Mahat*, then, arises the threefold consciousness, named *Baikârika*, *Taijasa* and *Tàmasa*; which is the source of all the elements (38). Even as the *Mahat* is enveloped by the unmanifested *Pradhana* this *Ahankara* or consciousness is enveloped by the *Mahat*; and from this, through the changes wrought upon it by this origin of all elements—the *Mahat*, proceed the primary elements of sound (39). He then created from the primary element of sound, ether or *Akasà*, of which the property is sound; and *Ahankara* then enveloped this *Akasâ*, of which the measure is simple sound (40). There is no doubt of it that from this is born the primary element of touch; then arose air, which is full of force, and it is known that touch is the property of air. *Akasâ* or ether of which the measure is sound, enveloped the air of which the measure is touch (41). Air by undergoing change sent forth the primary element of sight. Air generates light, and of this, form—visibility—is said to be the property (42). Air of which the measure is touch, enveloped that of which the measure is visibility, and light again undergoing change sent forth the primary element of taste (43). From that is born water of which the essential property is taste, and the water of which the measure is taste covered light of which the measure is form (44). Water again undergoing change sent forth the primary element of smell;—from that is born the earth, of which the principal property is known to be smell (45). In this manner by the respective elementals of the primary element, they are said to be measured. There can be no other specification of them, therefore are they called *Abishesha* (46). Owing to this want of any specification, these elementals, thus produced from ignorant consciousness, *Ahankara*, are neither tranquil nor disturbed, nor inert (47). From the *Ahankara* that is moved by the quality of *Satva* and that is of the nature of that quality, and undergoes evolution, all this evolving creation is simultaneously proceeded (48). The five senses and the five organs of action, these senses full of light are called the ten evolved *Devas*, of these the mind is the eleventh;—all these are taken as the evolved *Devas*. (49) The ear, the tactile nerves, the eye, the palate, and the nose, these obtain knowledge of sound and touch &c, therefore are they said to be joined with intelligence (50) The two feet, the arms the generative organ, the two hands and the organ of speech, these are the five organs of action; for by these are the functions of walking, discharging the fœces, generation, manufacturing various articles, and that of speech are performed. (51) *Akasà* of which the measure is sound, entering into that of which the measure is touch, the tri-qualitative air is brought forth; of this air touch is said to be the elemental property. (52) Both the qualities of sound and touch entered in the same way into the elemental of visibility, whence is produced the tri-qualitative fire. It has the three properties of sound, touch, and visibility (53) Sound, touch, and visibility entered into the elemental of taste, from that is produced water, which has four properties, and which is known to be of the nature of taste. (54) Sound, touch, visibility, and taste entered into the elemental of smell and this elemental of smell being condensed composed and covered this earth. (55) That earth possessing the five qualities of sound, touch, visibility, taste, and smell becomes visible among the gross objects; therefore are these specified elements,—the *Bisheshas* are specified as tranquil, disturbed, and inert. (56) These enter into one another, and hold up one another; all this crowded world as far as the region of the sun has this earth as its stay and basis (57). Owing to their persistence the specified elements are declared to be the objects of the senses, and the succeeding elements receive the qualities of the proceedings ones (58). When existing unconnected with one another, and with their energies independent of one another, they cannot bringforth any of the objects of creation, (59). Entering into mutual relation, and being interdependant upon one another, and thus coming into a mysterious union with one another, through the favour of the Unmanifested, these elementals become the seat of the *Purusha*, or soul, and give birth to the egg of this universe, containing all objects from the *Mahat* to the *Bishesha* (60—61.) Like a buble of water is this egg, and produced from the elements, the great egg, Oh highly intelligent one! sleeps in that very water (*i. e.* exists in those elements) (62). The soul, whose consciousness is that of the *Brahman* grows in this Nature's egg; he is called the owner of the body, the First, and the *Purusha* (63). He is the first master of the elements, he is *Brahmà*, who existed before everything else, by him is all this world both that moves and that moves not, pervaded (64). The poles came into existence after him, as also the mountains *Jarayu*; the oceans are as it were the inner waters of that infinitely capacious egg (65). All this world with the gods, the men, and the *Asuras* that inhabit it, the islands, the mountains, the oceans, and all the multitudes of the celestial bodies, are contained in the egg, while water, air, fire, the sky and and the earth cover the outside of this egg by the ten properties. (the five subtle and the five gross properties of sound, touch visibility, taste and smell), severally and jointly (67). It is also covered, along with these, with *Mahat*, which stand as their measure and proof; and with all this, including the *Mahat* itself, it is covered by the unmanifested *Prakriti* (68). This egg is covered by these seven-fold *Prakritis*, and the eight *Prakritis* (including the egg which is the eighth) exist entering into one another (69). This (collectively) is that *Prakriti* which is everlasting, and he is the *Purusha*, who inheres in it; of whom, called *Brahmâ* I have already spoken to you. Hear of him once more from me in greater details (70). Just as a man getting drowned in water throws up while getting out of it, both the things that are born in the water and the water itself, in the same manner is *Brahmà* the author of the *Prakriti* (71). The Unmanifested is designated as the *Kshetra* or the field, and *Brahmà* is called the knower and owner of the field. Know all these to be the specification of the propertios of the *Kshetra* and the *Kshetrajna* (62). This natural creation, presided over by the *Kshetrajna*, first came into being, without any premeditation, like a flash of lightening (73).

CHAPTER XLVI.

KRAUSTUKI said :—The revered one has duly related to me the birth of the egg,and the high-souled one has similarly told me of the birth of the soul in this egg of Brahmā (1). And I desire to know in truth, O thou descendant of the clan of Bhrigu, when, in course of time, all this enter into final dissolution ? At the end of this period of dissolution, what becomes of the elements, and how are they reproduced, or whether do they exist at all (2) ?

MARKANDEYA said :—When this fleeting universe loses itself in *Prakriti* or Primordial nature, the learned call this as dissolution into the *Prakriti* (3). When the Unmanifest, having withdrawn unto himself the course of creation, lives in himself, then both *Prakriti* and *Purusha* remain in their own nature (4). Then the two qualities of *Tamas* and *Satwa* remain in a state of equilibrium, without increase or decrease and in harmony with each other (5). Just as oil exists in the sesamum seed, or butter in milk, so does the third quality of *Rajas* exist in the qualities of *Tamas* and *Satwa* (6). The limit of the life of Brahmā are 200,000,000,000,000,000 years ; the length of the days of the supreme-lord is the same as that of the period of his sleep and night (7). At the commencement of the day, he the un-caused cause of this fleeting world, the source of all, unapproachable by thought, the supreme spirit, who is above all activities,—awakes (8). The soul of the world immediately enters into *Prakriti* and *Purusha*, and the superior lord of all quickens them thus by means of his superior union with them. (9). Just as pubescence quickens the nerves of a young maiden, just as lightning quickens the atmosphere, even so does this lord, entering into

Prakrati and *Purusha*, quicken them (10). And I have already told you that, when *Prakriti* is quickened, that bright one called Brahmā manifests himself through living in the "egg" (11). He is at first the quickener of the *Prakriti*; and having quickened her, he becomes himself her spouse and is moved himself; and thus he resides in the *Prakriti*, holding to the two-fold characters of drawing in and sending out that which inheres in the *Prakriti*. At first he was the cause of the quickening of Primordial Nature, then he, the lord of Primordial Nature, himself became quickened; in this way, through the dual process of dissolution and evolution, it is he who exists even as Nature or Pradhana (12). Having thus come into activity he, the origin of this fleeting universe, though himself beyond the three qualities, took hold of the quality of *Rajas* as Brahmā, and entered upon the work of creation (13). As Brahmā, having created the creatures and coming afterwards into an excess of the quality of *Satwa* in the form of *Vishnu*, he ruled and sustained the world as *Dharma* or Law (14). Then owing to the growth of the quality of *Tamas*, as *Rudra*, he withdraws into himself all this immense universe, and becomes once more inactive. Thus though he is really beyond and without the three qualities of *Rajas*, *Satwa*, and *Tamas*, in the three periods of creation, preservation and dissolution of the world, he takes to these three qualities respectively (15). In as much as he, who exists before creation as occupying by his essence all space, becomes, by turn in creation, its mover and owner, preserver and destroyer, he is designated as *Brakmà*, *Vishnu* and *Maheswara* (16). As Brahmā he creates the worlds, as Rudra he dissolves them; and as Vishnu he preserves them; yet the self-caused one, though he attains these three states, exists equally indifferent to all (17). *Rajas* is *Brahma*, *Tamas* Rudra, and *Satwa* Vishnu; the lord of the universe becomes all these, through the preponderance of the qualities; thus are the three gods manifested through these three qualities. (18). These are however joined in pairs, one with the other, and are related to one another ; there is not even a moment's separation among them ; they never leave one another (19). In this way, before the sending forth of this world, the four-mouthed *Brahmà*, the god of gods, adopting the quality of the *Rajas*, entered upon the work of creation (20). He is *Hiranyagarbha*, the first of the gods ; and in a sense, he is without beginning. This Brahmā, who resides in the sheath of the lotus-seed of the world, (i. e.—who is himself the seed of all that is—) was the first to come to being (21). The age of that high-souled being is a hundred years. The calculation of these years is made on the standard of Brahmic measurement ; hear this from me. (22). Fifteen *Nimesha* (the time taken up in a twinkling of the eye) make one *Kasta*. Thirty *Kastas* make one *Kalá*,—thirty *Kalàs* make one *Muhurta*. Thirty such *Muhurtas* make one human day and night. Thirty such days and nights or two *Pakshas* or fortnights make one month. By six of these months is one *Ayana* or equinox made ; and by two *Ayanas* is made a year—these *Ayanas* or equinoxes are called the southern and the northern *Ayanas*. This year with two *Ayanas* makes one day and night of the gods ; of these *Ayanas* the northern *Ayana* forms the day of the gods (23—25). By twelve thousand years of the gods are the four *Yugas* called *Satya*, *Tretá* &c., *(Satya, Tretá, Dwápara*, and *Kali)* formed. Hear from me their divisions (26). Four thousand years of the gods are called *Satya-yuga* ; the evening and twilight of this *Yuga* are each of four hundred years' duration (27). *Tretá* is formed by three thousand years of the gods, and its evening and twilight contain three hundred years each (28). *Dwápara* contains two thousand years, and its evening and twilight are each of two hundred years (29). O most excellent Brahmana ! *Kali* is one thousand years of the gods, and its evening and twilight are each said to be of one hundred years' duration (30). These twelve thousand years are called, by the learned, *Yugas*, and these multiplied a thousand fold is declared to be a day of Brahmā (31). O Brahmana in such a day of Brahmā twelve *Manus* are generated,—and the period of each *Manu* is again divided into a thousand parts (32). The gods, the seven Rishis with Indra, Manu and the Manu's sons, the kings, are all created with each Manu, and are, as before, dissolved again with him (32). One *Manwantara* takes place in more than seventy such *Yugas*. Hear from me an enumeration of the years contained in a *Manwantara* as measured by human years (34). Full thirty crores sixty seven millions and twenty thousand human years make one *Manwantara*. Hear from me now the measurement of a *Manwantara* according to the year of the gods (35—36). Eight hundred thousand years of the gods, with another twice fifty thousand years, multiplied by fourteen, are said to be a day of Brahmā. At the close of this, it is said by the sages, the periodical dissolution takes place (37-38). The terrestrial, the celestial, and the etherial worlds are all liable to destruction, and therefore they are all then destroyed; only the *Mahalloka* or the fourth world, remains (39). The inhabitants of this world also, are driven to the *Janaloka* by the heat that is generated at the time of the dissolution. The three worlds become one vast ocean, and on this ocean, Brahmā sleepeth during his night (40). The measure of the night of Brahmā is the same as that of his day; at the close of this night, he again creates this world. Measuring by this a year of Brahmā, multiplying it a hundredfold and again multiplying the result by a hundred,—is found the period of time] called *Param*. Fifty such periods of years are declared to be a *Parárdha* (41—42). At the close of such a *Paràrdha*, O most superior Brahmana, occurred that *Mahàkalpa* which is heard of as *Padma* (43). The present is the second *Paràrdha*, O thou twice-born one,—of the *Kalpa* called *Barâha*, which is thought to be the first *Kalpa* (44).

CHAPTER XLVII.

—:o:—

KRAUSTUKI said :—Tell me in detail the manner in which the lord, the lord of creation, the first creator Brahmâ created all creatures (1).

MARKANDEYA said :—I shall relate to you, O Brahmana, how the author of this universe created all the mobile and immobile objects—he, who is possessed of the six qualities or powers,—the *bhagas*, and is everlasting (2). At the close of the *Mahàkalpa* called *Padma*,—when the world existed in a state of dissolution, having awakened from his nightly slumber or inactivity, the lord looked on the universe moved by the quality of *Satwa* and saw it a void (3). Here is mentioned this verse which has been applied to *Narayana* —who is of the nature of Brāhmana and is the cause of the growth and destruction of this world (4). I have heard it said that, *Nárá* is the name of water. And he sleeps on that water, therefore he is called *Nârâyana*,—(he whose shelter is water) (5). On awaking from this sleep, he inferred that the world had gone down into that water, and then he became desirous of recovering the earth (6). As of old, at the commencement of the previous *Kalpas* he had assumed the bodies of fish and tortoise, similarly now he assumed another body—that of the boar (7). The all-prevading deity of whom are made all the sacrifices of the Vedas, the author of all, he who has entered into all,—the lord of the world—the object of meditation of the sacred souls inhabiting the *Janaloka* —having assumed the luminous form composed of Vedic sacrifices,—entered into the waters, and recovering the earth from the nether regions posited it upon the waters (8—9). On that collection of water the earth stood like an immense boat, and owing to the extendedness of its body it did not sink (10). Then having levelled the earth, on the earth he set forth mountains. As the previous creation had been burnt by the heat of dissolution, the mountains all over the world were found shrivelled up by that same heat (11). These mountains had been sunk in the universal deluge, beaten by the wind; and now they came up and became stationary in the very places where they had sunk (12). Having divided the universe, adorned with the seven islands, he thought of the creation of the four worlds as before (13). Meditating on the creation of this universe, as in the previous *Kalpas*, the un-premeditated creation, composed of the quality of *Tamas*, came into existence from it (14). *Tamas*, or inertion, *Moha*, or ignorance, *Mahàmoha*, or infinite ignorance, *Tamisra* or darkness, *Andhatamisra* or blinding darkness and *Avidyà* or nondiscrimination, these five, as before, came into being from the high-souled Brahmã (15). Proceeding from him thus meditating, the unconscious creation, both the internal and external of which were un-illumined, where the spirit lay concealed, and which was composed purely of mountains, became stationed in five different quarters (16). Because the principal mountains came to light in this creation, therefore it is called the main creation. Having seen this creation fruitless, he meditated again on a fresh creation (17). From him thus meditating another creation, that of oblique currents, came forth. Because from this have originated all indirect and oblique movements therefore it is called an oblique current (18). The lower animals are known to belong to this creation; they are almost inert, without reason, followers of evil ways, and though devoid of wisdom yet have the conceit of it (19). They are proud and self-conceited, and are of twenty-eight kinds or classes; they have a little light within themselves, but are covered from one another (20). Finding this creation also as useless, he meditated; and from that meditation another creation came forth. It is the creation of an upward current, the third creation, of the quality of *Satwa*, and it moves upwards (21). The creatures born of this upward current are full of love and happiness; their inner and outer natures are both uncovered and illumined (22). This third creation which gave satisfaction to his soul, he named as the bright creation. Then, on the accomplishment of this creation, Brahmā became pleased (23). After this he, at that time, began to meditate for the creation of another creation that should be useful and good. From him, the Unimanifest one, thus meditating, whose meditation is ever true, came forth the creation of a lower current fitted to serve his purpose. These creatures, though largely enlightened, are yet moved by *Tamas* or ignorance, and have an excess of the quality of *Rajas*; therefore they are largely subject to pain, and are repeatedly born; both their inner and outer natures are illumined; they are men, fitted to serve the purpose of Brahmā (24—27). The fifth is the creation of favour, it is posited in four classes,by division into *Biparyaya*, *Siddha*, *Shànta* and *Tushta* (28). The creatures of this creation know both the past and the present object of all the creatures commencing with the elements. This is called the sixth creation (29). The creatures of this creation are all the recipients of sacrifices, and are also engaged in dividing these; they are the inspirer of all, they are known as the origin of elements (30). Of these creations of Brahmā, the first is to be known as that of *Mahat* or Primordial Nature; the second is the creation of the measures of Primordial elements—it is called the elemental creation (31). The third is the creation of degeneration and is called the sensual creation; this is the natural creation made through premeditation (32). The main-creation is the fourth; the main creatures here are the mountains; that which I have stated as the oblique current, that is the fifth creation,inhabited by birds and insects. (33). The next, higher current, is the sixth, it is called the creation of the bright ones; the next is the seventh, and is composed of human beings. (34). The eighth creation is that called *Anugraha*, it is composed of both the qualities of *Satwa* and *Tamas*. Of these, five are creations of degeneration and three are natural creations. (35). Besides these natural and degenerate creations, the ninth creation is called *Kaumara*. These are the nine creations of the lord of creatures, described here by me (35—36).

CHAPTER XLVIII.

—:o:—

KRAUSTUKI said :—The process of creation in due form has been briefly described to me by the reverend one. But O Brahmana, do thou tell me in detail of the birth of the gods and others (1).

MARKANDEYA said :—O Brahmana! at that time, from Brahmā, engaged in the work of creation, proceeded, from his mind, the four kinds of creatures commencing with the gods ending with the inanimate objects, moulded by their previous actions both good and not good, who notbeing liberate are by him drawn back at the time of the final dissolution (2—3). Being desirous of creating the four classes of beings namely, the *Devas*, the *Asuras*, the *Pitris* and the men, he put himself in relation with that water (4). When he joined himself with that water, the quality of *Tamas* arose in the lord of creatures; he then first of all produced the *Asuras* from his thigh (5). He then gave up that body of his which was composed only of the quality of *Tamas*. From that body thus thrown away by him was night immediately produced (6). He took a second body being desirous of creation, and found pleasure in it. From the mouth of that body, moved by the quality of *Satwa*, the *Devas* came forth (7). This lord, the master of creatures, threw away that body also, and from that thus thrown away was produced day, which is almost full of the quality of *Satwa*, the property of which is light. (8). Then he took another body which was composed only of the quality of *Satwa*, and from this were produced the *Pitris*, the manes (9). Having created the *Pitris*, he, the lord, threw away that body also. That body thus thrown away, became the twilight, existing between the intervals of day and night (10). He, the lord, then took another body composed only of the quality of *Rajas*; from that were produced human beings, born of the quality of *Rajas* (11). Having created the human beings, he, the lord, threw away that body; from that was produced the light of the moon, that which exists in the night, but with its face towards the day (12). These then are the bodies of that god of the gods, the intelligent one, called, O thou twice-born one, night and day, and twilight and moonlight (13). Moonlight and twilight, as also the day are called the three bodies composed only of the quality of *Satwa*, while the night is composed only of the quality of *Tamas*; she is therefore of three parts (14). For this reason are the gods most powerful during the day and the *Asuras* during the night;—the human beings are strongest when the moonlight appears, and similarly the *Pitris* are strongest during twilight (15). They become undoubtedly strong and invincible to their opponents during these periods; and during the opposite periods, they become different (16). Moonlight, night, day, and twilight—these four are the bodies of the lord, *Brahmà*, composed of the three qualities of *Satwa*, *Rajas* and *Tamas* (17). Thus the lord of creatures having produced these four bodies, being overtaken by hunger and thirst, took, at night, another body, composed of the two qualities of *Rajas* and *Tamas* (18). In that darkness the lord who is himself uncaused, having created ugly beings, haggard through hunger, and with overgrown beards, they began to eat that body (19).

Among these, others who said, "we shall keep it," were the *Rakskas*; and those who, O thou twiceborn one, said "we shall eat it," on account of their attempt to eat became *Yakshas* (20).* Seeing them, the hair of this Brahmā became separated from his head through displeasure. They, thus detached from the head of the Brahmā, became moving and living objects. On account of this movement, they became reptiles, and from leanness, snakes are they called (21).† Then seeing the reptiles, the enraged Brahmâ, through anger, made carnivorous creatures of irritable nature,by investing them with brown colour (22). Then came forth from him meditating on words (sounds), the *Gandharvas*; and as they were produced by him while meditating on words sounds (lit.—drinking words) therefore are they called *Gandharvas*. That lord, on these eight classes of bright beings having been produced, then from his own body produced others, birds and beasts. From his mouth he sent forth the goats; from his breasts he created sheep; from the abdomen and from his two sides, the Brahma produced the bovine species; from the two feet were born horses with elephants, asses, hares, deer, camels, colts, and other animals of various forms (24—26). From the hair of his body, he produced herbs bearing fruits and having roots (27). In this way, the lord having created the herbs and the beasts and others (*i.e.*, birds, reptiles &c.) performed sacrifices, in the beginning of the *Kalpa*, in the face of the second or the *Tretà-Yuga* (28). Cows, goats, buffaloes, sheep, horses and colts, and the asses, these are called domestic beasts or animals. Hear from me of those that are wild and live in the jungles (29). The

---

* *N.—B.* 20 There is a reference in this stanza to the two roots from which the two words *Rakshasa* and *Yaksha* are formed—*Rakshasa* has been derived from the root *Raksha*—to keep; *Yakshas* from the root *Yaksha*—to eat.

† Here again, there is a reference to the roots of the two words *Sarpa* and *ahi* meaning both snakes. Their connection being with *Sarpa* and *hina*.

murderous animals with two hoops, the elephant, the monkeys, and fifthly, the birds; the sixth class are the animals that live in water, and the seventh the reptiles (30). The *Gayatri*, the *Thrich*, the *Tribith*, the *Sama*, the *Rathantara*; *Agnistoma* also, these sacrifices he made from his first mouth (31). From his southern mouth, he created the *Yagus*, the versification called *Trishtub*, and likewise the fifteen *Stoma*, the large *Saman* and *Uktha*—a portion of the *Saman* Veda (32). The *Samans*, the versification called *Jagati* and likewise the fifteen *Stobham* or verses in praise of God, the *Bairupa*, the *Atiratram* he made from the western mouth (33). The twenty-one *Bráhmanas*, the infallible *Aryamanas*, *Anustubh* with the *Bairaja*, he created from his northern mouth (34). Lightning, the thunderbolt, as also the clouds, the straight rainbow and the curbed rainbow, and also the birds, the revered lord created these at the commencement of the *Kalpa*—(35). The good and the evil creatures, are produced from his limbs; having first created the four classes of creatures, the gods, the Asuras, the *Pitris* and men, he then created the immoveable and the moveable objects. *Yakshas*, *Pishachas* (goblins) *Gandharvas*, and similarly the classes of *Apsaras* (36—37) men, *Kinnaras*, *Rakshasas*, birds, beasts, reptiles all these that are stationary, and that move, that are perishable and that perish not, the works that they performed in the previous creation, being created again and again, they perform those very functions (38—39). The murderous and the not-murderous, as also the mild and the cruel instincts, as well as righteousness and unrighteousness, truth and untruth, all these enter into the creatures as they are meditated upon, and liked by them (40). The director of all, even the lord himself, did join their senses to their different objects, in the bodies of the creatures (41). He made from the original Vedic-sounds, the designations, the forms, and the multitudinous functions of the gods and other creatures (42). In this way he named the Rishis and those that are created among the gods, as also those that come to being at the close of the night (43). Just as at the time of the various seasons the different signs of that seasons appear, similarly do the signs of creation appear at the commencement of each cycle (44). At the close of the night, on the awakening of Brahmā, of unmanifested origin, at each *Kalpa*, are the creations produced in this wise (45).

—:o:—

CHAPTER XLIX.

—:o:—

KRAUSTUKI said:—O Brahman, that *Arbāk* current of creation whence human beings sprang, which has been related by the revered one, kindly tell me in detail how Brahmā created it. O thou of noble aspirations! tell me all as to how the castes and the qualities and the respective ordained duties and functions of Brahmanas and others, were created (1—2).

MARKANDEYA said:—O Muni! from the mouth of Brahmā meditating on truth and entering upon the functions of creation, were produced a thousand pairs (3). They, thus born, were all moved by the quality of *Satwa*, and were joined to the right understanding. Another thousand pairs he created from his breast (4). They all were moved by the quality of *Rajas*, and were full of strength and invincible. Another thousand pairs he created again from his thigh (5). They were moved by the two qualities of *Rajas* and *Tamas* and were full of energy and enterprize. From his two feet he created another thousand pairs (6). They were all moved by the quality of *Tamas*, and were without beauty, and of little understanding. Then these beings, thus produced in pairs, were moved by delight, and being desirous of one another commenced to come together. Since then, in this *Kalpa*, creatures are born in pairs (7—8). In those days the females did not keep time every month, therefore though the pairs came together, they never pro-created (9). Only once, at the close of their life they would give birth to pairs. Since then in this *Kalpa* creatures are born in pairs (10). Only once, through meditation, were creatures brought into being by the mind, and the pairs were pure and invested with the five functions, of which the objects were sounds, &c., (11). This then is the mental creation of the lord of creatures, as it took place in the beginning, subsequent to that were produced those creatures by whom this world is filled (12). The creatures could then use and enjoy the rivers, the oceans, the lakes and the mountains at their pleasure, and in that cycle both heat and cold were moderate, therefore the creatures could move about everywhere (13). O thou of high aspirations ! having found natural gratification in the objects, they had no obstacles in their way, and no envy, and no anger (14). They were entirely without any habitation, they used to live in mountains or in the oceans, they moved about without any desire, and their minds were constantly full of delight (15). Pishachas, serpents, Rākshasas, as well as envious beings, beasts, birds, alligators, (16) fishes, reptiles all, whether born of mothers or from eggs, were produced by unrighteousness. In those days there were neither roots nor fruits nor flowers of herbs and trees, nor were there the seasons nor the years. (17). All times were pleasant, and there was neither excessive heat nor excessive cold ; in due time their wishes would attain wonderful fulfilment. (18). Then again whether in the forenoon, or at noon, whenever they felt any want, it would be satisfied without any effort, even as they asked. (19.) And similarly, whenever they wished, they could put forth their intellectual efforts. Then again, owing to the subtle powers of the waters in those days, the attainment of their various wishes full of delight would be secured, such as would fulfil all their desires. Those creatures had no need of sacraments for the purification of their bodies, and their youth was permanent (20—21.) Without any determination they would beget creatures in pairs; who were like them in the process of their birth, in their form and beauty, and they would also die like them (22). They were without any conflicts of desires, and without envy or ill-will and in this way they would live, with one another; the term of their life was the same, and they were all without any distinction of superior or inferior among them (23). They would live for four thousand years, measured by human measurement, and were without any misery, and did not come by any harmful accident (24). Now and then they would come into being a second time, always owing to the good fortune of this earth, just as in course of time human beings are reborn (25). Similarly, they, whose objects were attained always, would gradually die; and on all of them being destroyed, men would drop down from the sky (26). Generally they would appear with the heavenly tree that satisfied all wishes, called the house-hold *Kalpa*-tree and from them they would gain the satisfaction of all their desires (27). In those days, at the commencement of the *Tretâ-Yuga*, they lived holding on to these heavenly trees. Afterwards in course of time, of a sudden, attachment grew upon them (28). This caused the repeatition of the monthly courses, which led to repeated child-bearing. Then owing to the birth of attachment in them, those trees, called the household trees, O Brahmana, next began to throw out other branches, and also produce garments and ornaments and fruits;—in those fruits of those trees was produced honey in quantities measured by *putahas* (a sort of cup) and which was full of sweet smell and flavour and of beautiful colour, which was highly strengthening and which was not produced by bees.

(29—31). At the commencement of the *Treta-Yuga*, they lived on this honey. Then, in course of time they were overtaken by greed (32). And on their heart being overcome by the sense of ownership of these trees, they took possession of them, and on account of the wrong thus committed by them, those trees were destroyed (33). Then came conflicts, between cold and heat &c., and to overcome those conflicts they, for the first time, built houses (34). In deserts, passes, mountains, and caves, (*another reading*—rivers) they took shelter, also in fortresses built in trees, mountains, and on water. Similarly they made artificial fortresses having measured (the ground) by the measure of their own fingers; for which purpose they had previously made standards of measurement (34—36). Of those measurements, the first is the most subtle atom, then the *Trasarenu,* which is equal to six atoms, next the *Mahiraja*, next the end of an hair, then the *Nishka*, then the *yuka* then the *yabodar*, of these, eleven *yabodars* make one *anguli* or finger, sixteen *angulis* make one *pada* or foot, and two *padas* make one *bitasti*; similarly two *bitastis* make one cubit; which is the measure of the circumference of a *Brahmya tirtha*; four cubits make one bow-rod,—and also one *nadikayaga*. Two thousand bow-rods make one *Gabyuti*, and four times this is called by the wise a *yujana* which is the highest of all (lineal or spatial) measures (36—40). Of the four kinds of fort, three are self-made, the fourth is artificial, and they (men) always build it (41). O thou twice-born one, house, village, *Khetaka*, and like them, *Dronimookha*, and suburb, and *Karbataka* or small towns,—these three;—and villages without wall, and *Sanghosha*, with dwelling houses built separately in them, with high walls and surrounded on all sides by ditches—these they built themselves (42—43). One-half of a *Yojana* is called a *bishkambha*; and one eighth of a *bishkamba* is the measurement of a *pura*. These *puras* were extended towards either the east or the north and were spacious, eht central beam supporting them was pure and went beyond it (44). By one-half of this (Pura) was made similarly a *Kketaka* and by one-fourth of a *Khetaku* was *Karbataka* made; and that which was less than a *Karbata* by one-eighth, was called a *Dronimookha* (44). The *pura* that was devoid of wall and ditch used to be called a *barma*; and another place the resort of the ministers and the courtiers for purposes of pleasure, was called a *Sukhanagar* or suburb (46). Similarly the place which was inhabited mostly by *sudras*, and of which the wealth consisted in the capacity of the agriculturists, which was situate in the midst of cultivated fields, was called a village or *Srama* (47). When people come from another place and live in a place, for purposes of transacting any business in the city, that is known by men as a residential quarter (*basuti*) (48). The village which is mostly inhabited by bad men, who are powerful, and not owning any fields themselves, live upon the fields of other people, this village, the place of resort of the favourites of the king, is called an *Akrimi*. (49). Having thus made towns &c for their own residence, they made houses for the habitation of the pairs (54). Those creatures, remembering the house-like trees that they inhabited of old, made all their present habitations after the same model (52). Just as the the tree sends forth its branches, the new houses also similarly sent out its branches, one standing below the other, and they similarly made coverings for the house like the barks of trees (53). Those that of old, O thou most exalted of the twice-born, were the branches of the *Kalpa* tree, now they became the branches of the houses, and for that reason, they were invested with the qualifications of dwellings (54). Having thus adopted means to overcome the conflicts between heat and cold, they began to meditate upon the means of protecting their cattle and crops, because of the entire destruction of the *Kalpa* trees with all the honey they produced (55). The creatures became down cast and distracted through being pressed by hunger and thirst. Then at the commencement of the *Treta Yuga* in those days, they attained to miraculous powers in agriculture (59). The cattle and the crops were obtained by them, and for them the rains came down at their will; and on earth those rain-waters began to flow downwards (57). With the obstruction of this down-flowing rain-water rivers, and canals were made. The rain-water that had previously found the level of the earth, afterwards coming in contact with the earth, became faultless. Then fourteen kinds of trees and herbs that had not been cultivated by the plough, that had not been sown, and that put forth flowers and fruits at all seasons were created. At the commencement of the *Treta Yuga* season-flowers and herbs also came into existence, and on those herbs, O Muni! did the creatures live in the *Treta Yuga*. All of a sudden the creatures being moved by attachment and greed, in those days, began to appropriate to themselves rivers and fields, and mountains, and trees and herbs, according to each person's might (58—62). On account of that wrong, O thou twice-born one! the vegetables were destroyed. O thou high-minded one, at that time those herbs were, all of a sudden, eaten up (by the earth) (63). At the destruction of those herbs and vegetables those bewildered beings, driven by hunger sought the protection of Brahmā, of most superior will (64). By virtue of his spiritual insight, he too, having then known of the eating up of the herbs by the earth the lord, the possessor of all the powers and riches,—milched the earth having made a calf of the northern pole (65). By him was this cow thus milched of seed-grains; those seeds, being of two kinds, those that grew near human habitations (cultured) and those that grew in the jungles (wild), were created on the surface of the earth (66). These herbs are destroyed on the ripening of their fruits and are said to be of seventeen kinds, namely paddy wheat, *yaba*, *kanu*, jinjily, *priyangu*, *udára*, *koradosha*, *chinaka*, *nishpaba*, *kulathaka*, *adaka, mash, moong, masoor, chauaká*, these are the seventeen herbs, these were, in the olden times, grown near human habitation (67—69). The herbs used in sacrifices and that grow in villages and jungles are fourteen in number, paddy, *yaba, wheat, anu*, jinjily, and *priyangu*, these are seven, while the eighth is *Kuluthwaká, shamaka*, and *nibara, yattila, sagabedhuka, kurubinda, markataka, benu*, and *gradha*, these are said to be the fourteen herbs that grow both near habitations and in the jungles (70—73). When, though thus fully brought forth, the herbs did not again germinate, then he, the Brahmā, created means for their growth and subsistence (73). The self-created lord Brahmā created the skill of hand born of work, (with reference to the art of agriculture). Since then the herbs began to grow, and became difficult of decomposition (74). In this way after the establishment of the means of subsistence for them, the lord himself, established honour and precedence among them according to their respective rights and qualifications (75). The chief of the upholders of righteousness thus created the castes and the orders, engaged in the due performance of their duties and the attainment of their purposes, as also the law of duty for people of all castes (76). The honor of the Brahmanas devoted to sacrificial works is to be of the station of the lord of creatures. Of the Kshatriyas who do not run away from the field of battle, the honour is that of *Indra* the chief of the gods. The place of the *Baishyas* living by the performance of their own duties is that of *Marutha* and the station of the Gandharba is assigned to the Sudra following the law of service (78). The place of the disciple who lives with his master is that where eighty-eight thousand Rishis, the conquerors of lust, live (79). The station which is said to belong to the seven Primal Rishis is that of the hermits who live in jungles. The station of the lord of creature is the meed of the householders; of those who have relinquished everything for God, the plaec and honour is that of the Brahman himself, while the place of the *Yogis*, is immortal life. These are the statements of the positions of honour among men.

CHAPTER L.

——oo——

MARKANDEYA said :—Afterwards from him thus meditating came forth objects born of his mind, with all the functions and senses produced from his body (1). From the limbs of him—the intelligent one, came out created souls; they, that is, who have already been deseribed by me (2). All creatures beginning with the gods and ending with the inanimate objects, are said to be composed of the three qualities of *Satwa*, *Rajas*, and *Tamas*. Like these are all creatures both animate and inanimate (3). When all these creatures of this Brahmā—the intelligent one, did not increase, he then created others, sons born of his mind, and like his own-self (4). Namely :—Bhrigu, Pulasthya, Pulaha, Kratu, Angira, Maruchi, Daksha, Atri, and Bashishta, all born of his mind (5). These nine have been ascertained by the *Puran* to be the sons of Brahmā. Afterwards Brahmā again created Rudra, born of his angry self; as also *Sankalpa* and *Dharma*, which last was born before even the firs-t born (6—7). Sananda and other who had been of old created by the self-created one, they being absorbed in meditation and listless to everything, did not attach themselves to this world. They were all possessed of the knowledge of that which is yet to come, and were devoid of attachment, and free from envy (8—9). On them, indifferent to the creation of progeny, came down the anger of the high-souled Brahmā. Of this came forth a person of huge size whose body was half-man and half-woman, "Divide thyself into two"—having said this, he disappeared from that place (10). He, being thus addressed, differentiated his female nature from the male, and divided the male portion into eleven parts. The beautiful and the not-beautiful, the peaceful and the not-peaceful, in this way, he, the lord, the god, divided the male and the female into many according to colour and nature (12). Then the lord of creatures, the lord Brahmā having created at first from himself, the self-begotten Manu, who was like himself, and Satarupa; this lord Manu,—the self-begotten one, took unto him as wife that woman whose sins had been washed by penance (14). By that person Satarupa had two sons both distinguished by their own works, Priyabrata and Uthānapada by name (15). Similarly she bore two daughters Riddhi and Prasuti. Then the father gave Prasuti to Daksha, and Riddhi to Ruchi, in those days (16). He, the lord of creatures, produced from them Jajna with Dakshina; and then O, thou highly fortunate one, joined this son and this woman as husband and wife (17). And on Dakshina were produced twelve sons of Jajna—they are the gods Yāma of the age of the self-begotten Manu (18). They were the bright sons of Jajna born of Dakshina, similarly Daksha produced on Prashuti twenty-four daughters. Their names are here given each by each, Sradha, Lakshmi, Dhriti, Tushti, Pushti, Kriyā, Medhā, Budhi, Lajjā, Bapu, Shānti, Shidhi, Keerti, these thirteen of Daksha's daughters were married to Dharma, while the remaining and younger eleven daughters, namely, Khyāti, Satya Sambhuti, Smriti, Preeti, Kshamā,Shannati, Anāshuya, Urjjā, Shwahā, Shwadhā were given in marriage to Bhrigu, Bhaba Mareechi, Angira, Pulastya, Pulaha, Kratu, Bashista, Atri, Banhi and Pitara in order. Sradha gave birth to Kāma, Sree to Darpa, Dhriti, to Niyama, Tushti to Shantasha, Pushti to Lobha, Sruta was born of Medhā, Kanda, Naya and Binya, of Kriyā, Bodha of Budhi, Benoy and Bapu of Lajjā Byeboshaya and Kshema were born of Sānti, Shukha of Shidhi, Yasha of Keerti. These were all sons of Dharma. Kāma game birth to Atimukha and Harsha. These were the grandsons of Dharma (19—28). Hansa was the wife of Adharma and Anrita was born of them Niriti was the daughter of Adharma. Of Niriti were born two sons, namely, Naraka and Bhaya who married Māyā and Bedanā. Māyā bore desolating Mrityu. Of the marriage of Rourab and Bedanā was born Dukha. It is said either Mrityu or Dukha gave birth to Byadhi, Jarā, Shoka, Trishnā, Krodha. All these are ungodly, They have neither wife nor children. Mrityu has got two other wives, namely, Niriti and Alakshmi. By Alakshmi he has fourteen sons who do his biddings and deal with men at the time of death. Hear all about them. They dwell in the ten senses of perception and action and in the mind of men to lead them to to their respective objects. They attack the senses with the help of anger and attachment and lead men to ruin by diverting them from the path of virtue. Some of them live in the *Ahankâra* or egotism and some in the understanding. Hence men are deluded and strive after ruining women. Certain of them live in the houses of men. Amongst them there is one, Dushaha by name, who has a voice much like that of a crow and is so ill-dressed with rags as to be almost naked. He is always hungry and his face is always down caste and his voice is like that of row. And he, the riches of penance, was created by Brahmā to devour everything, and as this hideous and all devouring Dushaha who is fearful to look was about to devour all, Brahmā at the creator the changeless, the pure, all pervaded with Brahman, and the origin of men, said,—devour not this world, withhold thy rage and be calm (39—40).

BRAHMA said :—This world is not fit to be eaten by thee. Forsake thy anger, be calm. Give up this *Tâmasa* desire, and throw away that part of the quality of *Rajas* which is moving thee now (41).

DUSHAHA said:—I am weak through hunger, O lord, of the world, and am thirsty and feeble. How shall I gain satisfaction, how shall I become strong? What is my refuge, tell me, on what may I live in peace (42).

BRAHMA said:—The house of men is thy refuge; the unrighteous man is thy strength; by the default of sacrifice thou shalt grow, my son. Useless words are thy garments, and I am assigning also proper food to thee. The wounded, that on which worms have grown, similarly that which has been bitten by dogs, that which is kept in broken vessels, that which has been subdued by breath of mouth, the remains of food, that which is not ripe, that which has not been cooked, that which is not worshipped by the strong, that which has not been sanctified, that which is eaten by persons sitting on broken seats, and during twilight with their face to the north, that which is eaten by one dancing or playing on any musical instrument or singing, that which has been stirred or polluted by women keeping time or eaten or seen by women keeping time, or whatever food or drink is decomposed, these and others shall I assign to thee for thy growth (43—47). Whatever is offerred to the sacrificial fire without faith, or whatever is given with disrespect to persons whose caste and station are not known, as also whatever is given without due offering of water, or whatever is thrown away without any purpose or whatever shall be exposed simply to be thrown away, or given through excessive surprise, or whatever is given by one overcome by anger, such polluted object, O Jaksha, is thy portion (48—49). Or whatever sacrificial works are performed for purposes of the next world by a person born of a mother who had taken unto her a second husband, or whatever is done similarly by a woman born of a mother who has taken a second husband, that is assigned, O Jaksha, to thee for thy satisfaction (50). Or whatever works are undertaken for the attainment of wealth for paying the price of brides, and whatever sacrifices are performed in accordance with unauthoritative and untrue scriptures, or whatever is satisfied by mere wealth, and whatever is not studied guided by the spirit of truth, (according to a second reading whatever works relating to the next world are performed by men while weeping) all these are thy portion, I give them for thy satisfaction (51—52). Those that approach women in their family way, who do not perform the daily worship in proper time, and whatever is polluted by unscriptural works or words among men, O Dakshaha! always will these be subject to thy influence (53—54). In the division of rows while eating, in the division of cooking in vain-preparation of food, and in family desputes, will be thy permanent abode (55). When cows and horses &c are kept confined but not given proper food, and when the dwelling-house is not besprinkled with water of an evening, then shalt thou be the dread of men (56). Those who when overtaken by evil stars or when seeing the three kinds of omen—such as earth-quake &c, shall not perform any sacrifice for obviating the evils due to them, shalt thou overtake and overthrow (57). Those men who fast without cause, those who are addicted to wine, women, and gambling; those who speak ill of their benefactors, those who adopt the vow of the cat (*i. e.* who are hypocritical), who study the *Vedas* without knowledge (of the rites) and the works of of those who shall live in forests for purposes of penance but shall not be the master of their appetites, and shall seek vulgar enjoyments, and also the works of those Brāhmanas, and Kshettriya's and Vaishyas and Sudras who have fallen from the duties of their station, and those works that have for their object the attainment of good in the world to come, and whatever are the fruits of those works, all these works, all these, Oh Jaksha! shall be thine. I shall tell you of other things also assigned for thy growth hear of them with attention

(58—61). Whatever offerings shall be made to thee, uttering thy name, with the words, these are thine,—at the close of the sacrifice to the *Vaishvya-deva* shall be subject to thee (62).

He who eats food duly sanctified, whose mind and body are pure, who is not greedy or avaricious, who is not subject to his wife, do thou avoid his house (63). Who worships the gods by offerings of *ghee* to the fire, and the manes similarly by offerings of cakes of rice &c—and who worships the sons of Yama, do thou, Oh Yaksha ! avoid his house (64). The house where there is goodwill towards children, old men, women and men, and similarly towards friends and relations, that house too shalt thou avoid (65. The house to which the women are strongly attached and are not anxious to go out, and are full of modesty, always, Oh Yaksha, avoid that house (66). The house where seats and beddings are arranged in accordance to age and relation, that house is to be avoided by thee, O Yaksha, through my command (67). Where people are kind, and constantly engaged in good works, and satisfied with the commonplace necessaries of life, that house is to avoided by thee, Oh Yaksha ! (68) Where at the approah of the spiritual guide, the aged, and the Brāhman those who are seated occupy their seats no longer (*i. e.* receive them with due respect, standing) that house is to be avoided by thee always, Oh Yaksha (69). The house the threshold of which is not overgrown with trees and herbs, or where the heart of men are not pierced with grief, that house is not proper for thee (70). Where the food of the owner of the house consists of what remains after offerings have been made to gods, the manes, the guests, and men (needing food), avoid thou that house (71). Avoid thou, O Yaksha, men who speak the trnth, who are forbearing, not given to injuring others, who are net remorseful, as well as those that are not envious (72). Avoid thou those women also who are devoted to the service of their busbands, who avoid the company of bad women, and who live on the food left after their relations and husband have had their fill (73). Avoid thou also those twice-born persons (Brāhmanas) whose minds are attached to sacrifice and study and religious exercises and charity; and who are engaged in performing sacrifices for others and in teaching others, who live by what comes as gifts unasked and unsought (74). Avoid, Oh Dushaha! that Kshetriya also who is always after works of charity, and study, and sacrifices, and who earns his livelihood by collecting rightful taxes or by receiving pay using his weapons (75). Avoid also that sinless Vaishya who is joined with the three above-named virtues (namely charity, study, and sacrifice), who breeds cattle, and earns his livelihood by agriculture and commerce (76). Avoid, O Yaksha, that Sudra also who makes charity, and sacrifice and the service of the twice-born classes, the chief object of his existence, and who earns his livelihood by the service of the Brāhmanas and others (77). The house where the house-holder earns his livelihood by works that do not go against the injunctions of the *Vedas* and the Law, and where his wife follows him in everything, and where the son worships the spiritual guide, the gods, and similarly his father; and where the wife worships the husband, how can there be any fear of Alakshmi (the goddess of poverty and misfortune) in that house? (78-79) Where early in the morning and in the evening the house is besmeared and besprinkled with water, and where sacrificial offerings are adorned with flowers, that house thou canst not strike (80). Where the beddings are not seen by the sun, and where fire and water exists always, and where lights are presented to the sun, that house is loved by Lakshmi, the goddess of fortune (81). Where there are bull, and sandal-wood, and Vina, and mirror, honey and *Ghee* and the *Kâsha* grass, as also where there are Brāhmanas and vessels made of coper, that house is not be possessed by thee* (82). Where the trees are thorny, where there is

* Bull, sandal, *vina*, *mirror*, &c—are all needed for household sacrifices hence the stanza means where there are sacrificial appliances.

the *Nishpàba* creaper, where the wife is a widow who has taken a second husband, where there is an anthill, that, O Yaksha, is thy temple (83). The house where there are five men, three women, three cows, and where the fire is kindled in darkness, that house is thy abode (84). The house where there are one goat, two *chamari* deer, three cows, five buffaloes, six horses, seven elephants, that house, O Yaksha! do thou destroy soon (85). When shovels, and cutlases, and cooking utensils and plates and other vessels are thrown about everywhere, they shall give thee excellent shelter (86). When women sit on pestle and the grain grinding vessel, and similarly on the wooden bases of the door-frame, or on rubbish, and thus sitting they converse with one and other, these become, O Yaksha ! thy benefactor (87). The house where both ripe and unripe paddies are threshed, and similarly where the scriptures are over-riden,* there, O Dushaha ! mayest thou move about at thy will (88). In the house of endless sin where fire is given on cooking utensils or on the lid thereof, or on spoons or on a cutlass or other weapon, there shalt thou find superior repose (89). The house where there are human-bones, or where the dead body remains for one day and night, there, O Yaksha, is thy abode, as also of other Rākshasas (90). Whoever take their food without first giving cakes and water to friends and relations, as also to those who are partakers of the funereal cakes and water, thou shalt at once possess those men (91). The house where lotus, large lotus, young women desiring conjugal felicity, and bull and white elephant exist avoid thou that house (92). The house where gods without weapons and with weapons but without war are established, do thou avoid that house (93). When the people perform the feasts celebrated of old, in their own house, as they used to be celebrated before, move not thou in that house (94).

* The word *langhyante* in this stanza is used in two different senses viz., that of threshing and over-riding one referring to the paddies and the other to the scriptures.

Those who bathe in currents of air produced by the winnowing fan, or in water contained in a pot, or in water dripping from wet clothes, or in that in which the ends of the nails have been dipped, go to them of evil-nature (95). Thou art not to keep the company of men who follow the ordinances of their class, perform *Japa* and *Homa*, and the auspicious worship of gods, according to the custom of the country, and in due forms prescribed for the particular time or *yuga* to which they belong and who duly follow the rules of purity and tradition (96).

MARKANDEYA said:—Having told all this to Dushaha, Brahmā at once disappeared, and the former also followed these injunctions as they were related by him who is born in the lotus (97).

——oo——

CHAPTER LI.

MARKANDEYA said:—Dushaha had a wife known by the name of Nirmasti, who has born of the wife of Kali, who had seen a *Candala* while keeping time (1). Of these two were born sixteen issues extending over all the world, eight of whom were sons and eight daughters and all of them exceedingly fearful beings (2). Dantakrista, and Ukti, while another was Paribarta, Angadhuk, Shakuni, Gandaprāntarati, Garbhahā, and another Shashyahā,*

* These names are distinctly and palpably allegorical—viz (1)—He who draws by hls teeth, (2) the meaning of *Ukti* speech is not clear, (3) change, (4) He whe burns the limbs; (5) Vulture; (6) He whose love is in the extremities of the chops, (7) The destroyer of fœtus, (8) The destroyer of harvest similarly the names of the daughters also show that they are mere allegories.

—they are the sons of these two (3). There were also others, daughters, similarly eight in number, hear also as their names from me (4). The first is Niyojikā, similarly another is Birodhini, Swayambārikā, as also Bhrāmani, and Rituhārika; Smritiharā and Bijaharā, these are two other daughters of this pair who are very cruel and the eighth is Bidveshini, she who causes dread to men (5—6). I shall relate to you the works of these, and how the evil caused by them may be averted; and also hear, oh thou superior Brāhman the works of the eight sons (of Duhshaha and Nirmasti) (7). Dantākristi living in the teeth of the new born babes, being exultant, tries to open the way for the coming of Dushaha (8). The means of averting his evil is to throw white mustard seed on the bed as also on the teeth of the sleeping child (9). By bathing in the water containing white herbs, similarly by the chanting of right scriptures, by wearing *ushtra-kantaka* and the bone of the rhinocerus, and silk dresses, (is the evil caused by Dantakristi averted) (10). The other son, similarly exists, who says again and again, this is good, and thus impels men to evil, therefore is he called Tathokti there is no doubt about it (11). Therefore to avert the evil caused by him, the unseen good is always to be described by the learned, and the name of Janārdana is to be chanted, or that of Brahmā the preceptor of the whole world both that moves, that moves not; or that of the family god (12). He who changes the fœtus of the womb of one woman into that of another, and changes the speech of the speaker into something contrary to what he means is the son called Paribarthaka (13). The evil caused by him is also to be averted be white mustard; and by repeating mystic formulas, do the learned save themselves from him (14). Angadhuk like fire cause the evil of irruptions on the limbs (of men), he is to be averted with the *Kusa* grass (15). Living in crows and other birds as well as entering into dogs and jackals, the other son, it is said, direct men's good and evil (16). Therefore has the lord of creatures said this that in evil things delay as also an absolute giving up of all endeavours is proper, while in matters that are good men should work with despatch (17). The other son living within men's mouth, O most superior of twice-born persons! in half a second, eats up all the works of men and destroys their good name and good-will (18). By hearing instructions from Brāhmanas, by the adoration of gods, and also by drawing out certain specific herbs by the root, O twice-born one! and by bathing in water containing the urine of the cow and white mustard, by worshipping the natal star of the person, and also by the worship of other stars, as also by seeing weapons which are used for the support of righteousness, and by disregard of this world is the Gandabān propitiated (19-20). Similarly the other, Garbahā by residing in the womb of pregnant women destroy their fruit. The safety of the fœtus against him is always to be secured by perpetual observance of purity (21) by writing wellknown *mantras*, by wearing garlands &c., as are usually used, and by living in purified and clean houses, O thou twice-born one, and by not overexerting one's self—is the evil produced by Garbahā averted (22). Similarly another the Shashyahā who destroys the growth of grains; his evil is to be averted by putting on wornout shoes (23). Likewise is his evil averted by walking southwards, by the entrance of a *candala* into the field, and by offerings given outside the field, and by chanting hymns dedicated to the moon and the clouds (24). The daughter who directs men and other beings to rob other's wife and wealth she is Niyojikā (25). By reading pure scriptures by giving up anger and greed, &c., "she directs me to these" thus thinking and by giving up all conflicts, is the evil caused by her averted (26). When attacked by others or driven by others the wise should not be subject to feelings of retaliation, thinking that it is this

Niyojikā who thus impels me to it (27). "This Niyojikā is leading me, to have connections with other's wives" the wise shall think also this wise (28). She, the other one, Birodhini creates discord among husbands and wives who ought to love each other as also between friends and friends and relations and relations, between father and son, and between people of the same caste; from her, safety should be attained by sacrificial offerings, by forbearance even when abused, and by observing the ordinances of the scriptures (19-30). The daughter (of Dushaha) who eats paddy from the barn or from the house, robs milk from the cows, and similarly robs butter from the curd, and robs the value of things having value, she is called Swayamhārikā, always engaged in spiriting away things. From the cookroom she robs half-boiled rice, as also rice that is preserved in the place where rice is kept (31-32) as also rice that has been put out on the plates, and she eats with those engaged in eating, and this Durhara also robs the food left after eating by men (33) From the place where paddy is stored or boiled, she robs boiled paddy, Oh thou twice born one! and robs milk from the breasts of women and cows, she is therefore always the robber of milk (34). She robs butter from curd, oil from jinjily, and similarly from the place reserved for storing away wines, she robs wine, as also the colour from *kusum* and other flowers, and the tibres from cotton (35). She, this Swayamhārikā, O thou twice born one, incessantly robs things. For protection against her, a pair of peococks or artificial women should be made; and the vessels for milk and *ghee* &c, should be cleansed by the ashes of *homa* performed in honour of the gods, or by those of incense burnt to them. These are said to be charms against her (36-38). Another causes disturbance to men living stationed in one place, and that daughter is called Brāhmani (39). Protection against her is secured by strewing white mustard on the seat, the bed, and on the ground where that man lives (40). And that man shall also meditate thus—"this evil minded (girl) leading me from one place to another," and shall again and again repeat the *Bhu-Sutka* of the Rigveda, with all-absorbing concentration of the mind (41). Another daughter of Dushaha is engaged in robbing the flower (generative power) of the women, she is to be known as Rituhārikā (42). For averting the evils caused by her the woman should be made to bathe in holy places sacred to the gods, in places of worship (or in Maths of the Buddhists), on table-lands, at the junction of two or more rivers, and in canals (43), and should be treated with superior medicine prescribed, by a twice-born person wellversed in the treatment of diseases, and who knows the *Mantras* and the esoteric meaning of actions (44). She is another daughter [of Dushaha] who runs away with the memory of women, she is Smritihārikā; by living in solitude is the evil caused by her averted (45). There is another, a most dreadful girl, who destroys the seed of both women and men. By eating sacrificial food and by bath is the evil caused by her averted (46) The eighth daughter is by name Dbeshini,—the source of dread to men and women, the object of people's malice. For the cure of her evil *homa* should be performed by jinjily soaked in honey and milk and *ghee,* and similarly by performing the sacrifice called Mitrabinda is the evil caused by her averted (47—48). Of those sons and daughters, O thou most superior among the twice-born; there are thirty-eight offsprings, hear their names from me (49). Of Dantakrista there was a daughter Bijalpa as also Kalaha. Bijalpa chatters always disdainful words, and lies, and evil expressions. For her cure the wise shall meditate even on her, and the householder shall exersise self-restraint. Kalaha creates quarrels in the houses of men incessantily (50—51). She is the cause of the destruction of one's own relations. Hear the means of her cure. It consists in making sacrificial offerings of grass-blades soaked in honey, *ghee,* and milk (52). These should be thrown into the fire and thus the *homa* performed as well as the following hymn should be chanted :—For the satisfaction of the boys—with the mothers of creatures, for the satisfaction of all knowledge and penance, and self restraint and discipline, for agriculture and the attainment of commercial prosperity, may they all grant me peace (53—54). May they be worshipped as laid down in the sacred books, and find entire satisfaction the pumpkins, and the *yatu* grain and other vegetables called *ganah* (55). Through pleasure of the Mahādeva or the great god, according to the will of the great god, may all these rest satisfied with men (56). Being satisfied may they dispel all the evil deeds and evil ceremonies as also that give rise to mortal sins, as also that cause other evils (57). Through their favour may all our evils and obstacles be destroyed during marriages and all ceremonies concerning the manes (58). During virtuous rites and during the worship of the *guru* and the gods, as also during the sacrifice called *yapayajna* as also during occasions of leaving the house on journeys (59), may they grant peace and health and enjoyment of my body, as also happiness, and charity and wealth to the old, the young and the infirm,—of my family (60). The moon, the sun, the fire, the wind and the oceans may they all grant me peace. Of Ukti similarly, the son was Kalijibha, whose abode is in the palm-tree. Whose mother he possesses that vicious person he kills. The sons of Paribarta were two, O thou twice-born one! Birupa and Bikrita (61—62). They two lived on the top of trees, on walls and ditches and lakes,—and on the trees etc., change the fœtus of the pregnant women (63). Therefore O Kraustiki, women in the family way shall not walk among trees, or in mountains, on walls or travel on expanses of water nor on ditches. Angadhuk got a son known by the name of Pishuna (64—65). He eats up the strength of the bones and nerves of the men who have not conquered themselves. Shakuni had five sons, the eagle, the crow, the dove, the vulture and the owl,—the Suras and the Asuras took them. The eagle was taken by Death, Time took the crow, Niriti took the dreadful owl. Disease took the vulture, while his lord Yama himself took the dove (66—68). These are said to be their instruments in working evil. Therefore, O thou most superior among the twice-born people! he on whose head, eagles and others alight or in whose dwelling they enter, by them should sufficient sacrifices and propitiatory rites be performed for purposes of self-preservation (69). The house where they breed, similarly where they build their nests, that house shall man forsake, as also that the top of which is attacked by the doves (70). On the entrance of the eagle, the dove, the vulture, the crow, and the owl, O thou twice-born one, into a house, the days of the dwellers of that house are said to be numbered (71). Such a house shall the learned quit, and perform propitiatory rites, the sight of a dove even in dream is not considered as auspicious (72). Similarly of Gandaprāntarati the issues are said to be six. They live in the courses of women, hear from me of their time also (73). Four days and nights before, and another the thirteenth, and similarly another the eleventh day after the courses,—these are his son's (74). These days, as also others, namely, the day when offerings are made to the manes, as also other days when there are any festivals, by the wise are these avoided for that reason (75). Of Garbahā the son was Nighna and daughter Mohini. Entering into the womb of the pregnant woman, one eats up the seed, and another having eaten the flesh of the woman hypnotises her (76). Through her charm frogs and tortoises and reptiles or again mere phœces are born of her (77). In this way they eat the flesh of the pregnant woman for six months without any restraint. The woman who lives in the shade of trees during night, or at the junction of three or four roads; or sleeps on the ground where the dead are cremated, or goes about without a second covering, or cries out at night, this (Mohini) possesses that woman (78—79). Similarly of Shashyahā there was one son known by the name of Kshudraka. He always on finding an opening, destroys the strength and value of the harvests. Hear from me all about him (80). Whoever sows the grain seeds on an inauspicious day, with a dissatisfied heart, into his field, whose end is near, he enters (81). Therefore on a day recognized as fit for the purpose, having worshipped the moon, with a gladdened and satisfied heart, and taking due help from others should the work of sowing the seed be undertaken (82). Of that daughter of Dushahā, of whom I have spoken as going by the name of Niyojikā, was born a daughter by name Prochodikā. Of her there were four daughters (83). They are Mottā, Unmottā, Pramattā, and Nabā. These women always enter into men for their destruction, and move them to most cruel acts (84). They present unrighteousness as righteousness, lust as not lust, evil as good, and bondage as salvation, to men, who are proud and have no purity of mind and body; and driven by these eight maidens men incesantly stray away from the highest object of human existence (85-86). Their entrance into the house is during even-tide, when the offerings are not made in proper time to *Dhâta* and *Bidhâta* (87). Those are contaminated by the entrance of these, among whom men and women eat and drink together (88). Of Birodhini were three sons, Chodaka, Grāhaka and another Tamaprachādaka Hear from me all about their characteristics (89). Where the pestle, the mortar, shoes, seats, and women are polluted by coming in contact with lamp-oil; where the winkowing fan and the cutlass, &c., are drawn by the feet, and sat upon, and where people move about in the house without having adored it by besmearing it with water, &c.; where fire is collected or taken from one place to another on the spoon, the sons of Birodhini, inspired by their mother, spread themselves there (90-92). Of these one given to lies and falsehood, entering into the tongue of men and women, causes malice and ill-will in the house, he is called by the name of Chodaka (93). Another with great attention resides in the ear, he is Grâhaka, of exceedingly evil nature, who runs away with the words of men (94). Another of evil nature, who having drawn people's mind forcibly towards him and having covered it with ignorance, creates anger; he is Tamapraschâdaka (95). Of Shwavamhârikâ were born three sons by Chaurya,—namely Sarbahâri, and Ardhahâri, and similarly Biryahâri (96). In the houses where the inmates do not wash their mouth before and after meals, in the houses where evil ways prevail, where the inmates enter the cook-house with unwashed feet; in the household where, whether in the ground used for threshing corn, or in the field where the cattle graze, there are constant quarrells, in those houses they all move about and enjoy themselves as of right (97—98). Of Bhrâmani there was only one son, known as Kâkajangha, those that are possessed by him find no pleasure whatever in their him (99). Whoever sings while eating; sings and laughs while attending calls of nature, and the man who meets his wife just at the junction of the day and night,in such a man,O thou twice-born one,does he enter (100). The girl called Rituhârini, gave birth to three daughters (101) One girl is Kuchaharâ, another is Byanjanahârikâ, while the third daughter is named Jâtahârini (102). Of the woman whose marriage rites are not duly performed, or performed after the proper period of life, the one, Kuchaharâ, robs the two breasts of such a person (103). The girl who is given in marriage without due offerings have been made to the manes or without due worship of her mother, similarly the other, the Byanjanahârika, robs her of the marks of womanhood (104). Entering into the confinement room which is devoid of fire, and water, and incense, and light and iron, and mortar and mustard seed, and collirium, she robs the baby just born of her mother, of its life and even there, O thou twice-born one, leaves the carcase (105—106). She whose name is Jātahārini is exceedingly cruel, and she eats the meat of the new-born babe, therefore the confinement room should be protected with great care (107). Her son Prachanda by name living in works mischief to the memory of those persons who do not live empty houses according to the law (108). From his grandsons were born a hundred thousand Likās, and the eight kinds born of Chandala women, all exceedingly dreadful through always going about with staves and ropes (109). The Likās then and those begotten of Cāndala women, possessed by hunger, ran after one another, desirous of eating up one another (110). Those Likās and those offsprings of Chandala women being restrained by Prachanda, in time, settled down. The manner in which they did so hear thou that from me (111). Henceforth whoever shall give quarters to the Likās, there is no doubt about it that on him I shall inflict immeasurable punishment (112). And the Likā that will give birth to a child in the house of any offspring of Chandala women, all her children and she herself shall meet with destruction that self-same day (113). The girl Bijahārini, who robs both men and women of their seed, gave birth to two daughters,—Bātarupā and Arupā, these two are her weapons (114). The man and wife on whom the Bātarupā throws her child, get certain diseases of the reproductive organs (115). Similarly by Arupā is the man robbed of his reproductive power, who eats without bathing or has connections with low caste women (116). That girl Bidbeshini by name whose face is made crooked through frowns, has two sons, one, who works men evil, and the other who leads them to trumpets torth their own good deeds (117). The man or woman who disregards the rules of purification, who is given to malice, who is avaricious, and who drinks foul water, lose the reproductive power (118). They two exist attacking the man who is moved by malice. The man who is the object of the ill-will of mother, brother, similarly of friends and relatives and well-wishers and enemies meet with destruction both in his religious and his worldly life. One of these, the worker of iniquity, leads one to publish one's own virtues among men, the other destroys the qualities of friendship among men. Thus, these are all the progeny of Yaksha and Dusaha; they are noted for their iniquities, and by them is the whole world covered (119—121).

CHAPTER LII.

—:o:—

MARKANDEYA said:—This then is the creation of Brahmā, of unmanifested birth, that is composed of the quality of *Tama* or ignorance and sin. I shall presently relate in detail the creation that is called Rudra, listen (1). As also his daughters, as well as his eight wives, and similarly his sons, (all these shall I presently relate to you). On the lord meditating, at the commencement of the Kalpa, on a son, who shall be like him in all respects, a son, called Nilalohita came forth from his limbs, and moving about cried in sweet tones, O thou most superior Brāhmana (2—3). Him thus crying Brahmā asked,—why dost thou cry; and he spoke in reply to the lord of the world,—"Give me a name (4). (He said):—Thou, O Deva or Bright One, shall be of the name of Rudra. Do not cry. Be patient. Thus spoken to, then he cried again and again seven times (5). Then to him the lord gave seven other names, and also the abodes of these eight Rudras, and their wives and sons, O thou, twice-born one, (were duly assigned) (6). The lord, the

Grand-father (Brahmā), spoke and gave these names,—namely Bhaba, Sarba, similarly Eshāna, likewise Pashupati, Bhima, Ugra, Mahādeva and made abodes for these (7—8). The sun, the water, the earth, the fire, the ether, the initiated Brāhman, and the moon, these became respectively their abodes. Subarchalā and similarly Umā, Bikeshi and another, Shwadhā, Shwāhā, and likewise Disha, Dikshā, Rohini these respectively, O thou superior among the twice-born, became with the sun &c., the possession of the holders of the names commencing with Rudra &c., (9—10). Their sons respectively were Shanaishchara, Shukra, Lohitānga, Monajaba, Skandha, Sarga, Santāna, and Budha, (11). In this way. this Rudra welcomed Sati as his wife,—and that Sati through being angry with Daksha gave up her body (12). She became, O thou most superior Brāhman! the daughter of Himavat, and his wife Menā. Her brother is Maināka, than whom the ocean has not a better friend. The lord Bhaba again married that self same Sati (13). Khyāti, the wife of Bhrigoo gave birth to two gods Dhātā and Bidhātā and also to Sri,—she the wife of the god of gods Nārāyana (14). Of the high-souled Meru there were two daughters Ayati, and Niyati, they were given as wives to Dhātā and Bidhātā. Of these two were born two sons (15). They were Prāna, and Mrikandu—he is my father known to fame. I was born of him on Manashbini. My son is Bedashirā, born of my wife Dumrabati. Hear also from me of the sons of Prāna. The son of Prāna is Dyutimān. His son is Utpanna (15-17), and also Ajarā. Of these two were born many sons and grandsons. Sambhuti, the wife of Marichi, gave birth to Paurnamāsa (18). Of him, the high-souled one, were born two sons Birajā and Parbata. At the time of the enumeration of the geneology of any family, O thou twice-born one, the names of their sons should be preserved (19). Smriti, the wife of Angirā, similarly gave birth to daughters, *viz.*, Sinibāli, Kuhu. Rākā, Anumati (20). Anusuya similarly, the wife of Atri, gave birth to sons free from all sins—they are Soma, Durbāsasa and Dattātreya, the *yogi* (21). Of Priti, the wife of Paulasta was born Dattoli; in a previous birth he was known as Agastya, born during the age of the Swāyambhuba Manu (22). Kshamā, the wife of the lord of creatures Pulaha, brought forth three sons namely Kardama, Charbbira and Shahishnu (23). Sannati the wife of Kratu gave birth to the Balkhilyas, who were sixty-thousand Rishis all of whom had completely mastered their sexual instincts (24). Of Urjjā, the wife of Bashishta were born seven sons, namely, Rajogātra, Urdhabāhu, Sabala, Anagha, Sutapā, Shukta,—these all are the well-known seven Rishis (25). He who is the presiding deity in fire,—the eldest among the sons of Brahmā,—from him Shwada had three sons all of them, O thou twice-born one, of most superior powers;—namely Pābaka, Pabamān and Shuchi whose food is water (26—27). Their sons were forty and five in number, these sons and fathers are highly spoken of (28). They are (the father, three sons and the grandsons) thus forty-nine in number, and are spoken of as invincible. The Pitris as created by Brahmā have already been described by me to you (29). They who were the Agnishwatta, the Barhiṣhada the Anagnaya, and the Sāgnaya, from them Shwadhā had two daughters, Mena and Baidhārini (30). They were both, Oh thou twice-born one! teachers of the wisdom of Brahman and were both *Yoginis*, and were possessed of superior wisdom and were adorned with all the virtues (31). These are the sons and the descendents of the daughters of Daksha related by me. When they are remembered with faith and reverence, the descendents of the person so remembering them are extended and increased (32).

CHAPTER LIII.

—:o:—

KRAUSTUKI said:—This Manwantara associated with the Swaymbhuba Manu which has been described by thee, I desire to hear in detail everything about it, Oh thou possessor of the six miraculous powers or Bhagas, tell me all about it. Tell me the measure of that Manwantara, as also of the gods, and the godly Rishis, and of those that were the lords of earth, and the king of the gods—the Indra—tell me all these exactly as they were (1—2).

MARKANDEYA said:—The measure of Manwantaras is made by the figure seventy one; hear from me the measure of a Manwantara calculated by human standards (3). Thirty crores, multiplied twenty thousand times, and sixty seven *nijutas* (of years) are the measurement of a Manwantara, and not more (4). Measured according to the standards of the gods it is said to consist of eight-hundred thousand and another fiftytwo thousand (years) (5). The first was the Swāyambhuba Manwantara, next the Swāruchisha, then Auttama, them Tāmasa, then Raibata, then Chākshusha. These six Manus are gone. The present is the Manwantara of the Bibashwata Mauu. The coming ones will be the five Sābarni Manwantaras,* the Rauchyā, Bhautyā (6—7). I shall tell you in detail who are the gods, at the comig on of each of these Manwantaras and Rishis and Yakshas, and the Indras and the Pitris (8). Oh Brāhmana, the birth and the duration, and the progeny of these Manus, as also they who were their wives, and who also were their high-souled sons,—hear all this from me (9). Of the Swāyambhuba Manu there were ten sons all like himself; by

* The five Sabarni Manus are Brahma-Sabarni, Dharma-Ṣabarni, Rudra-Sabarni, Deba-Saberni, Indra-Sabarni. Some authorities mention another Daksha-Sabarni, and one who is simply Sabarni.

whom this world with all the seven islands and mountains are inhabited (10). They entered into this world, each one into a seperate continent, consisting of oceans and mines. In the *Tretayuga*, at the time of the first or Swāyambhuba Mawantara, was the earth thus occupied by the sons and grandsons of Priyabrata, the son of Swāyambhuba Manu. Of the mighty Priyabrata was a daughter born unto Prajābati (11—12). That girl, endued with the six great virtues of kindness &c, bore two daughters and ten sons to the lord of creatures Kardama,—these two daughters bore princes in their womb (13). Their ten brothers were mighty personages, even like unto the lord of creatures in prowess. They are Agnidhra, Medhātithi, Bapushmān Jyotishmān, Dyutimān, Bhabya, Sabana,—these seven. Priyabrata anointed them in due form as kings of the seven lands. Hear from me also all about these lands. The father made Agnidhra,—king in Jambudwipa (14—16). By him was Medhātithi made the lord of Plakshadwipa, in Shālmali Bapushmanta, and in Kushabhaya Joytishmanta, in the Kraunchadvipa Dyotimanta, and of Shakāhbaya Bhabya was made the lord. While he made his son Sabana the lord of Pushkara (17—18). The two sons of the lord of Pushkara were Mahābita and Dhātaki. Having divided Pushkara into two parts, these two were installed there (19). Of Bhabya the sons were seven, hear fron me of them, by their names. Jalada, and Kumāra, and Sukumāra, and Baniyaka and Kushottara and Medhābi and Mahādruma, who was the seventh. He (*i. e.* Bhabya) made countries called after their names (20—21). Similarly of Dyutimān there were seven sons, hear of them from me. They were Kushala, Manuga Oshna, Prākāra, Arthakāraka Muni, and Dundubhi, who is described as the seventh. And after their own names were countries established similarly in Kraunchadwipa (22—23). In Kushadwipa also the different kingdoms were marked by the names of the sons of Jyotishmān. Hear of their names from me (24). They are

Udbhida, Baishnava, Suratha, Lambana, Dhritimat, Pravākara and Kāpila which was the seventh (25). Of Bapushman, the lord of Shālmaladwipa, there were seven sons, namely Shweta, Harita, Jimuta, Rohita, Baidyuta, Mānasa, and similarly Ketumān, who was the seventh. Similarly in Sālmaladwipa also were seven kingdoms established whose names were equal to those of these princes (26—27). Of Medhātithi, the lord of Plakshadwipa, were there also seven sons, according to whose names kingdoms were marked in Plakshadwipa into seven fold (28). Of these the first is the Shākabhaba continent and next Shishira, then Shukadoya, then Ananda, Shiba, Kshema, and similarly Dhruba (29). The law, according to the division of the castes, of the five islands commencing with Plakshadwipa and ending with the Shakadwipa, should be known as everlasting, devoid of the injunctions regarding the destruction of creatures; and they are common in these five continents (30–31). To Agnidhra did his father, O thou twice-born one, give at first Jambudvipa. He had nine sons, all like the lord of creatures. The eldest was called Nābhi, of him the younger was Kimpurusha; the third was Haribarsha, the fourth was Ilābrita (32—33), the fifth was Ramya, the sixth was called Hiranya; of them the seventh was Kuru and Bhadrashwa is known to have been the eighth (34), the ninth was Ketumāla; by their names were principalities established. Those places names Kimpurusha and others, with the exception of that called Himabhaya gained their objects naturally, and they were full of enjoyments which could be had without any efforts; and in them there were no reverses nor the fear of old-age and death (35—36), nor unrighteousness were there (in those continents) neither righteousness nor even (the distinctions) between good, middling, and bad; nor were there in them, any of the conditions of the four *Yugas*, neither the courses of women nor of the seasons (37). Of Nābhi the son of Agnidhra was born a son, Oh thou twice-born one, by name Rishabha. Of Rishabha was born Bhārata, the brave, and the most superior among a hundred (sons) (38). Rishabha having anointed his son as king took to the order of *Bànaprastha* or final renunciation of the household life, and the highsouled one practiced penances, taking shelter in the hermitage of Pulaha (39). The father gave to Bhārata the southern continent of Himabha (another reading—the continent to the south of the Himalayas); and therefore from the name of that highsouled prince is it called Bhāratabarsha (40). Of Bhārata there was a son, Sumati by name, who was a righteous king,and having placed the kingdom upon him, Bhārata too went to the forests (41). By their sons and grandsons,—as also by the (other)sons of Priyabrata, was the world consisting of the seven islands, enjoyed during the time of the Swāyambhaba Manu (42). This creation is called *Swâyambhuba*,—the first Manwantara, as described to you by me, Oh thou superior among twice-born persons what more shall I tell you? (43).

CHAPTER XLIV.

—:o:—

KRAUSTUKI said :—How many are the islands, the oceans ; how many, O thou twiceborn one, are the mountains, and how many are also the continents, and what are the rivers of these ? What again are the measures of the great elements, and similiarly of the mountain *Lokàloka* and the changes, the measures, and the movements of the moon and the sun. Tell me, O thou great Muni, all this in detail (1—3).

Markandeya said :—This earth, Oh thou twice-born one, is fully a hundred and a half crore (of *yojana*) in extent. I shall describe to you all the places contained therein, hear thou of that (4). Those islands that have been described by me, commencing with the Jambudwipa, O thou twice-born one, and ending with the Puskaradwipa, hear of them again in detail, Oh thou possessor of the eight good qualities of kindness &c. (5). The islands called Jambu, Plaksha, and then, Shamala and ·Kusha, and Craun-cha, similarly Saka and the island Puskara, of these, each succeeding one is double the extent of that which is named before it (6). And they are covered on all sides by the seven oceans, namely the Labana, the Dugdha, the Sarpi, the Dadhi, the Ikshu, and the Jala, of which also each one is twice the extent of the preceding one (7). I shall tell you of the position of the Jambudwipa, listen to me. It is in length and breadth a *lâc* of *yojana* (8). The seven *Kula* mountains in this are Himabān, Himakuta, Rishabha, Meru, Neela, Sweta, similarly Sringi (9). The two great mountains in the middle of it are each a *làc* of *yojana* in extent. Of these two, that which is towards the south and that which is towards the north, of them one is less than the other by ten thousand *yojana*, their hight is two thousand *yojana* and similarly the whole extent of the base is also two thousand *yojana* (10—11). All the six *Kula* mountains enter into the womb of the ocean; and the earth here is sloping towards the south and north, and at the middle it is raised to great heights (12). Know that on the southern side of this are three continents or Barshas and similarly three on the northern side; and between them the Ilābrata-Barsha stands as a crescent (13). Towards the east of it is the Barsha of Bhadrāshwa, and to the west that of Ketu-māla, and in the centre of Ilābrata is the golden mountain, Meru (14). The height of this great mountain is eightyfour thousand *yojana*; and it has entered into the earth to sixteen thousand *yojanas*, and is sixteen thousand *yojanas* in breadth (15). Because it stands in the form of a circular plate therefore its top is thirtytwo *yojanas* in extent, and on the four sides, commencing with the east, of the four colours, white, yellow, black and red,—the four castes reside, according to their respective colours* (16—17). In this mountain are the courts of Indra aud other protectors of the world, and in the centre of them all, is the court of Brahmā, which is fourteen thousand *yojanas* in height (18). Similarly below it is the Biskamba mountain, whose height is ten thousand *yojana*. In the division of sides according to the east &c., are one after another stationed the mountains Mandara, Gandhamādana, Bipula, and similarly Supārsha, adorned with trees peculiar to each. The mount Mandara has got the *Kadamba* tree as peculiar to it; while the distinctive tree of Gandhamādana is the *Jambu* or the *jaman*; similarly the *Aswathwa* tree is peculiar to Bipula, and the immense *Bata* is peculiar to Supārsha; and these mountains are eleven hundred *yojanas* in extent in all (19—21). The mountains on the eastern side are Jathara, and Devakuta, and Anila and Nishadha which two have run into each other (22). Nishadha and Pāripātra are situated on the western side of Meru, as in the eastern mountains similiarly also in these, the extent is the same as that of Anila and Nishadha (23) On the south are the two great mountains Kailāsa and Himabān they two are extented from east to west and stand extended to the limits of the ocean (24). Similarly the mountains to the north are Sringabān and also Jārudhi; as in the south so also in the north these extend to the limits of the ocean (25). Oh thou most excellent Bráhman, these eight are called the Maryādā mountains. Himabat, Himakuta, and other mountains are at the

* The Brahmins being of white colour occupied the white or the eastern side, the Vaishya of yellow colour, the western side, the Sudra of dark colour occupied the northern side, while the Kshettrya of red colour inhabited the southern side.

distance of nine thousand *Yojanas* from each other, from east to west, and south to north; and are situate on all sides of Meru in the Barsha called Ilābrita (26—27). Those Jaman or *Jumbu* fruits that grow in the Gandhamādana mountain, of the size of the body of an elephant, fall on the top of the mountain (28). From the melting of those fruits arise the river known by the name of Jambu, where is produced the gold called Jambunāda (29). She (this river) having encircled the Meru enters again into its own source, and the waters of it are drunk, Oh thou tiger among the twice-born persons, by the people of those regions (30). Vishnu exists in the Bhadrāshwa as Ashwasirā, in Bhārata as the tortoise, in Ketumāla as the boar, and in the next Barsha Ilābrtiha as fish (31). In these four Barshas objects that defeat the evil influences of stars are arranged according to the arrangement of the stars. (32).

——oo——

CHAPTER LV.

—:o:—

MARKANDEYA said:—In the four mountains commencing with Mandāra; Oh thou most excellent among twice-born persons, the gardens that are four in number, and lakes, hear of them with attention (1). On the east is the garden named Chaitraratha, on the south the garden Nandan, on the eastern peak is the garden called Baibhrāja and on the northern mountain is the garden called Sābitra (2). The lake Arunoda is on the east, and the Mānasa on the south, Shitoda, on the west of Meru and similarly Mahābhadra on the north (3).

Sitārta, Chakramunja, Kulira, and then Sukankabān, Mani shaila, then Brishabān, Mahanila, the mountain Bhaba, Sabindu, Mandara, Benu, Támasa, Nishadha likewise Debashaila—the great mountain to the east of Mandara, Trikuta, Shikharādri, Kalinga, and then Patangaka, Ruchaka, Sānumān mountain, then Tāmraka and Bishākhabān, Shetodara, Samula Basudhāra, Ratnabān, Ekasringa Mahāshaila, Rājashaila, Pipātaka, Panchashaila, then Kailàsha, and the most superior among mountains Himabat these mountains are said to be situate on the right (or southern) side of the mountain Meru (4—8). Suraksha, Shishiraskha, Baidurya, similarly Pingala, Pinjara, and then Mahabhadra, Surasa, Kapila, Madhu, Anjana, Kukkuta. Krishna, and the best of mountains Pàndura; and the mount Sahasrashikhara, Pàripatra, with Sringabān, are similarly situate on the west of Meru, and Biskama is similarly situate on the other side of the west *i. e.* the eastern side, of Meru (9—11). Hear of the other mountains to the north, Sankhakuta, then Brishabha likewise the mountain Hansanàbha, similarly the mount Kapilendra, and Sànumān, and Nila, Swarnasringi, Shatasringi, Puspaka, and the Meghaparbata; Birajāksha, the mountain Barāha, Mayura,—these are the mountains to the south of Meru. The valleys of these mountains are exceedingly charming (12—14). They are adorned with gardens, and lakes and pure water; in them are born men of virtuous deeds (15). These are as heaven on earth, more meritorious than even heaven itself. In them there is no acquisition of fresh virtue or sin (16). In them, it is said, that even the gods enjoy the fruits of their righteous deeds. O thou most excellent among the twice-born, towards the close and beginning of the winter, in these mountains, are formed the great and beautiful habitations of Bidyādharas, and Yakshas and Kinnaras, and Nagas, and Rakshasas, and gods, and of the Gandharvas (17—18). They are highly pure, and have pleasuregardens attached to them that are pleasing to the mind,—and similarly there are in them lakes pleasing to the mind, and of which the breeze is pleasant in all seasons (19). In these there never arises any uneasiness or want of satisfaction among men. This is the selfsame mundane lotus, described by me, of four leaves; Bhadrashwa and Bhàrata etc these are its leaves on the four sides. That region towards the south, called Bhàrata which has been described by me, is the place of merit and demerit (*Karmabhumi*) in no other place are the fruits of *Karma*, enjoyed; in it are all laws established. For this reason are heaven, and the fruits of merit, and all births, human or hellish, and those of birds or of any other animals, attained here only by men (20—23).

CHAPTER LVI.

THAT foot of Nārāyana which is the sure refuge of Brahmā, the cause of this fleeting world, the goddess of Ganga, who flows in three currents, proceeded from that (1). Having entered into the source of nectar and the stay of the waters; (the moon) and from there, having been purified, and attaining powers for the purification of others through coming into relation with the rays of the sun, she fell on the back of the mount Meru, and from there flowed in four channels and fell in torrents obstructed by the ends of the mountains Meru and Kuta (2). With her waters spread on all sides without any support, she fell at the feet of the mountains Mandara and others, and her waters were divided equally (4). The waters fell in four currents, on the head of four different mountains, the eastern current well noted for its went to the garden of Chitraratha (5). And having deluged it, it went to the lake Barunoda and from there to the mountain Shitānta, and thence gradually to other mountains (6). And having descended to the earth, from mount Bhadrashwa it went (and fell) into the ocean. Similarly that current, of the name of Alakamandā, having gone to the Gandhamādana in the south, and the garden at the foot of the Meru,—Nandana, that which pleases the gods, and having by great force deluged the lake Mānasa, and having similarly gone to the peak of the Prince of mountains, and from there to all the mountains that rise in the south, and having flooded them, found the great mountain Himagiri. There Shambhu held her, and he whose ensign is the bull (*i.e.*, Shiva) would not release her (7—10). The lord having been worshipped by Bhagiratha, by means of fasts and praises, released her. Released from there by Shiva the flooding great river, in seven channels entered the southern ocean; and also entered the eastern in three channells; and following the car of Bhagiratha in one current flowed towards the south (11—12). Similarly that great river entered the large western foot of mount Meru, and from there under the name of Swarakshu went to the mountain Baibhrāja (13). From there the great river having flooded the lake Shitodā, having found the mountain Swarakshu went to mount Trikuta (14). From there gradually falling on the top of the mountains and finding Ketumāla, entered into the ocean called Lavana (15). Similarly having gone to the Supārshwa, at the foot of the mount Meru, and attaining there the name of Soma, she went to the garden Sabitu. Having purified that she found next the lake Mahābhadra, from there the great river went to Shankhakuta (16—17). From there having one after another found the mountains Brishabha and others, and having flooded the northern Kuru country, she found the great ocean (18). O thou bull among twice-born persons, thus is the story of the Ganges related to you by me, from her entering into the Jambudwipa, as also the Barshas in due form (19). In all those Barshas commencing with that called Kimpurusha live creatures, full of happiness, free from fear, devoid of all inequalities of greater or less (20). In all these nine Barshas there are, in each, seven mountains, called the Kula mountains, and in each there are rivers flowing from these mountains (21). In the eight Barshas, O thou most excellent among the twice-born persons, commencing with that called the Kimpurusha, the waters flow from out of the womb of the earth; in Bhārata, however, water is obtained from the clouds (22). In these eight Barshas the attainment of people's objects are of six kinds, namely, those that are called *Bârkshi*, *Swábhábiki*, *Deshya*, *Toyottha Mânasi*, and *Karmaja* (23). The attainment of objects from divine trees that fulfil people's desires, is called *Bàrkshi*, and that which fulfils itself is called *Swábhábiki*—natural *Siddhi*; and that which is due to the virtue of any peculiar country is *Deshya*; and that which is attained through the subtility of the waters is *Toyottha Siddhi*; and that which arises from meditation is called *Mànasi Siddhi*, while that which results from works of divine worship is the *Karmaja Siddhi* (24—25). Besides, in these Barshas there are neither mental pain nor disease, nor the conditions of the *Yugas*, and no works giving rise to merit and demerit; none of these are in these Barshas, O thou most excellent Brāhmana (26).

CHAPTER LVII.

—:o:—

KRAUSTUKI said:—O Revered One, you have in detail described to me the Jambudwipa. This has been related by the revered one that leaving Bhārata, actions that produce merit, or that lead to vice, do not exist anywhere else, it is from here that men attain heaven and salvation, both temporary and final; and in no other place on earth are works assigned to men; therefore O Brāhman, describe this Bhàrata to me fully :—what are its divisions and what its limits, as also its exact position, and O thou tiger among the twice-born, tell me also what are its mountains (1—4).

MARKANDEYA said :—Of this Bhārata there are nine divisions, of which hear from me with attention. They are to be known as existing between oceans, and unapproachable from one another (5). Indradwipa, Kasherumān, Stāmrabarna. Gabhastiman, Nāgadwipa, likewise Saumya, Gāndharba, Baruna, and of them the ninth is this island surrounded by the ocean. This island is one thousand *yojana* in extent from south to north (6—7). Of that country, to the east are the habitations of the Kirata people, and to the west lie those of the Yabanas; while within it live Brāhmans, Kshetriyas, Baishyas and Shudras, O thou twice-born one! (8). They are purified by the performance of sacrifices and daily worships, and by trade and other works; and their conduct is also regulated by these works (9); and the attainment of heaven or of earthly good, of merit or demerit is also due to these works. The seven Kulāchalas here are the Mahendra, the Malaya, the Sahya, the Suktimān, the mount Riksha, the Vindya and the Pāripatra (10). Near them are another thousand mountains (11). They are of great extention and height, and their tablelands are large and pleasant. Their names are Kolāhala, Baibhrāja, Mandara, the mount Dardura, Bàtaswana, Baidyuta, Maināka, Swarasa, Tungaprastha, Nāgagiri, Rochana, and the mount Pándarā, Puspa, the mount Dujjayanta, Raibata, and Arbuda, Rishyamukkha, Sagomanta, the mount Kuta, Kritasmara, and the mount Sri, and Kora, and hundreds of other mountains; and on them are interspersed habitations divided among the Aryas and the Mlechchas (12—15).

Hear from me also of those excellent rivers, the waters of which are drunk by them—namely the Ganges, the Saraswati, the Indus, and likewise others, the Chandrabhāgā (the Chenāb) and the Jamunā, and the Shatadru, the Bitasta, (the Jhelum), the Irābti, (the Rāvi), the Kuhu, the Gomati, the Dhutapāpā, and the Bāhudā and the Drishadbati, the Bipāshā, (the Bewā), the Debika, the Raukshu, the Nirschira, the Gandaki, the Kaushiki, the Apagā, all these, O Brahman, that have proceeded from the foot of the Himalayas (16—18). The Bedasmriti, the Bedabati, the Britraghni, the Sindhura, the Benwa, the Sānandanī, the Sadānirā, and likewise the Mahi, the Pārā, the Charmanwati, the Tāpi, the Bidishā, and also the Betrabati, and likewise the Shiprā, and the Abarni,—all these are said to be dependents of the mount Pāripātra (19—20). The Sone, the Mahānada, the Narmadā, the Surathā, and the Adrijā, the Mandākini, the Dashārna, and similarly another the Chitrakutā, the Chitrotpalā, with the Tamasā, the Karamodā, the Pishāchikā, similarly others, the Pippali, the Srini, the Bipashā, and the river Bajjulā, the Sumerujā, the Shukīmati, the Shakuli, and the Tridibā, and the Akramu, and likewise many others of strong current have risen from the foot of mount Skandha, (another reading, the mount Riksha) (21—23). The Shiprā, the Payoshni, the Nirbindhyā the Tāpi with the Nishadhābati, the Benwa, the Baitarani, and also the Sinibāli, the Kumudbati, the Korotayā, the Mahagauri, the Durga, and likewise the Antashirā,—all these rivers of pure water, and beautiful have proceeded from the foot of the Vindya mountains (24—25). The Godābari, the Bhimarathā, similarly another the Krishnabenwa, the Tungabhadrā, the Suprayāga, the Bāhyā, the Kāberi, and likewise the Apagā, all these excellent rivers have also their sources at the foot of the Vindhya range. The Kritamālā, the Tāmraparni, the Pushpajā, with the Utpalābati, these rivers of cooling waters have proceeded from the mount Malaya. The Pitrikulyā, Somakulyā, Rishikulyā, the Ikshukā and that which is the Tridibā, the Lāngoolini, the Bansakarā, these are known to have taken their rise from the mountain Mahendra. The Rishikulyā, the Kumāri, the Mandagā, of gentle current, the Kripā, (second reading, the Krisha) the Palāshini are known to have risen from the mountain Shuktimat. They are all sacred rivers like the Ganges, and flow into the ocean; they are all mothers of the world, and are all said to possess the power of taking away sins. And there are, O most excellent among twice-born persons, other thousands of small rivers (26—31), those that flow only during the rainy season, as well as those that flow during all seasons. Matsya, Aswakuta, Kulya, Kuntala, Kāsi, Koshala, and Atharba, and Kalinga, Malaka with Brika, are generally spoken of as the provinces of the Madhyadesha or central division (32—33). That province which is situated on the north of mount Sahya, where the river Godābari flows, that is the most pleasant country in all the earth (34). The pleasant city, Gobardhana, of the high-souled Bhārgaba, and Bālhika, Bātadhāna, Abhira, Kalatoyaka, Aparanta, Sudra, Pallaba, Charmakhandikā, Gāndhar, Yabana, Sindhu, Saubira, Madraka, Satadruja, Kalinga, Pārada, Hārabhushika, Māthara, Bahubhadra, Kaikeya, Dashamālika,—all these the colonies of Kshetriyas, as also of Vaishyas and Sudras;—Kamboja, and Darada, Barbara, Harshabardhana, China, and Khara, Bāhula peopled by men; and Atreya, Bhāradvāja, Pushkala, and Kasheruka, Lampaka, Shulakāra, Chulika, with the Jaguda, Aupadha, Anibhadra, belonging to the tribes of Kiratas;—Tāmasa, Hansabhārga, Kashmira, Tungana, Shulika, Kuhaka, Jarna, and likewise Darba (35—41). These are the provinces of the north, hear from me of the countries to the east. Adhrāraka Mudakara, Antargirya, Bahirgirya, likewise Prabanga, Rangeya, Mānada, Mānabartika, Brahmottarya, Prabijaya, Bhārgaba, Jneyamallaka Prāgjyotisha, Madra, Bideha, Tāmraliptaka, Malla, Magadha-Gomanta,—these are known to be the eastern provinces (42—44). Then there are other provinces inhabited by the people of the Deccan:—Pundra, Kerala, and likewise, Golangula, Shailusha, Mushika, Kusuma, Basaka, Maharāstra, Māhishaka, Kalinga, all these and Avira, with Baishikya, and Adakya, and Shabara, Punlinda, Bindhya. Mauleya, Bidarbha, with Dandaka, Paurika, Maulika, and Ashmaka, Bhogabardhana, Nāshika, Kuntala, Andhra, Udbhida, Banadāraka; these are the provinces of the southern countries. Hear of the western countries from me. They are Suryāraka, Kālibala, Durga, Anikata, Pulinda, Sumina, Rupapa with Swāpada, likewise Kurumina, Katakshara, Naśikyaba, and others that are on the north of the Narmada; Bhirukaccha, Samāheya with Sāraswata, Kashmir, Surastra, Abanti with Arbuda—these are all the western provinces. Hear of the provinces on the Vindyarange (45—52). Sharaja, Karosha, Kerala with Utkala, Uttamarna, Dasharna, Bhojá with Kiskindhaka, Toshala, Koshala, as well as Tripura, and likewise Bidisha, Tumbura and Stumbula, Pataba, with Nishada; Annaja, Tushtikāra, Birohotra, Abanti all these provinces are on the back of the Vindya hills (53—55). I shall next relate to you the mountainous countries; *viz*—Nihāra, Hansamārga Kuraba, Gurguna, Khasha, Kunta, Prābarana, Urna, Darba, Sakritraka, Trigartha, Mālaba, with Kirāta and Tāmasa. In these places the *Yugas*, Treta &c, and the laws of these are well established. This is the Bhāratabarsha, which has countries on all its four quarters (56—58). In the south, the west, and the east of it is the great ocean, while the Himalaya stands to the north of it like the string of a bow (59). This is that Bhāratabarsha, O thou excellent among twiceborn persons, which contains the seed of all that exist. It is here, O Brāhman, that according to the fruits of people's action the state of Brahman, of the lord of the immortals, of the gods, the state of Maruta similarly, and likewise the births of deer, beasts, Apsarās and of all reptiles, and that of the inanimate objects, are attainable. This is the field of *Karma* such as exists nowhere else. Oh thou wise among Brāhmans, it is the heart's desire even of the gods to be deprived of their state as gods to come to earth as men (born in Bhāratabarsha). Man here does that which even the gods and the Asuras are not able to do. People here are bound by the chains of Karma, and are anxious to finish that Karma; they do no works moved by the least happiness (60—64).

CHAPTER LIII.

——oo——

KRAUSTUKI said:—O revered one, by thee has Bhārata been duly described to me; including the lakes, the mountains, the provinces as well as those that inhabit them (1). But I am exceedingly eager to hear of the position of Hari who has been described by thee as living in Bhārata as a tortoise (2). How that bright one, the oppressor of the Asura—*i. e.* Bishnu, exist in the form of tortoise, and from that how are peoples' merits and demerit revealed, tell me all that in detail, from begining to end (3).

MARKANDEYA said:—The Possessor of the six qualities and powers called Bhagas, the bright one, of the form of tortoise, exists with his face towards the east, holding this Bhārata, divided into nine parts (4). On all sides of him are stationed, in nine quarters, nine stars; and the countries that are ruled by them, hear of them, O most superior among twice born persons, with attention from me, in due manner (5). Vedamantra, Bimandabya Shalmanipā, Shaka, Ujjihāna, likewise Batsa, Ghosha, Sankya, similarly Khasha, Sāraswata, Matsya, Shurasena with Mathura, Dharmāranya Jyotishika, Gauragriba, Gudashmaka, Udbehaka with Pānchala, Sanketa,

Kankamaruta, Kalakoti with Pāshanda, and the province of the inhabitants of Pāripatra, Kapingala, Kururbāhya and similarly Udumbara, and Gajabhaya these are situate in the middle of the tortoise that live in the water (6—9). And the three stars Kirtikā, Rohin, and Saumyā, are the workers of good and evil among these inhabitants of the central portion (of the tortoise) (10). Brishadhvaja, Anjana, Jambuākhya, Mānabāchala, Shupakarna, Byaghramukha, Kharmaka, Karbatāshana, and likewise, Chandreswara, Khasha, Magadha, Giri, Mithila, Pundra, Badanadantura, Prāgjyotisha with Lohita Samudra, Purushadaka, Purnatkāti, Bhadragour, likewise Oh thou twiceborn one, Udayagiri, Kashāya, Mekhala, Mushta, Tamralipta, Ekapādapa, Bardhamāna, Koshala, are all situate in the mouth of the tortoise (11—14). And the three stars, Raudra, Punarbashu and Pushya are stationed at this mouth. Oh Kraushtuku, hear me, I shall tell you of the countries that lie on the south feet of the tortoise. Kalinga, Banga, Jatharu, Koshala, Mrishika likewise, Chedi, Urdhakarna, and the inhabitants of Matsya &c., on the Vindyarange, the people of Bidbarbha, Nārikela, Dharmadwipa, similarly Alikā, Byaghragriba, Mahagriba, of Tripura, and Shmasrudhāri, of Kiskindā, Hemkuta, Nishadha and of Katakasthala, Dashārna, Harika and the naked people of Bishāda, and Kakula and Alaka and similarly of Panashabara exist in the south east foot of the tortoise. Ashleshá, likewise the star culled the Pitri, as well as the First Falguni, these three exist holding on to the southeastern foot. Lankā, Kālājina, Shaulika, and likewise the people of Nikata, and those that live in the mountains Mohendra, Malaya, and Durdara, and these that live in the forest Karkotaka, and the people of Bhrigukacca with those of Konkan, all these and similarly the people of Abhira and those living on the banks of the river Benwa, the people of Abanti, Dāsapara, and likewise the inhabitants of Akani, the Maharattas with the people of Karnata, Gonarda, and Chitrakuta, Chola and those of Kolagiri, Krauncbadwipa and of the mounts Shankha, Sukti and Baiduryya, and similarly the people of Bāricharā, and of Kol and Charmapatta, the people of Gandhavāhya, and Para and those that inhabit the islands Krishnà; those people that inhabit the mountains Sarya and Kumada and also those of Aukhavana, with those of Pishika, and those that belong to Karmanayaka,those of southern Kurusha, and those of the hermitage of Rishika, those of Rishabha, and of Singhala (Ceylon) and the inhabitants of Kanchi and of Tilanga, Kunjara and those people that inhabit Darikaccha, and Tamraparni likewise Kukshi, these all live on the southern portion of the tortoise (15—28). The Uttara Falguni, Hasta and Chitra, O thou twice-born one, these three stars reside in the southern belly of the tortoise. Similarly the people of Bapyapāda and Kamboja, of Palhaba, and likewise of Badavāmukha as those of Sindh, and Sauvira with the people of Anarta and Banitamukha. The people of Drabana, those of Sargiga, those of Sudra, and the savage people of Krānapreyadha, the Kiratas, the Paradas, those of Pandru likewise those of Pārashaba and Kala, those of Dhurtaka and Hemagiri, those of Sindh, Kalaka, and Raivata, and those of Surastra, and Darada, and Dravida and of Maharnava, these habitations are situate on the other one of the two southern feet of the tortoise. The stars Sāti Bishākha, and Mactin, these three (are the workers of their good and evil) (29—33). Manimegha, Kshuradri, Khanjana and likewise Astagiri, the western Haihaya, Santika Biprashasthaka, Konkan, Panchanadaka, Baman and likewise Abara,Taraksbara, Angataka, Sarkar, Shabnabeshmaka, Guruswara, Falgunaka Benumabi—those inhabiting these places, likewise those that live in Falguluka, Ghora, Gurubha, and Kala and those of Ekekshana, Bajikesha, Dergagriba, with those of Chuleka, and Aswakesha, all these people live in the tail of the tortoise. Aindra, Mula and likewise Ashada, these are the three stars (that rule over their destinies). The people of Mandabya, and Chandakhara, and Ashmaka, and Lalana, and Kunyata, and similarly those of Ladaha and Stribajya, and Balika and Nrisimha, and Benumati and others likewise of Balabasta and similarly those of Dharmabadha, and Aluka, and the people that live in Urukarma, these people live on the side of the left feet of the tortoise; where the three stars Ashada, Sraban and Ghanishta are stationed. Kailash, Himaban and Dhanushman, and likewise Basuman, and the people of Krauncha, and of Kurubaka, and Kshudrabina and Rasālaya, with those of Kaikeya, and Bhogaprasta, with those of Yāmana and Antardwipa, Trigartta, Agnija with the inhabitants of Ardana, similarly the people of Ashwamukha, Prapta and of Chibida who wear long hairs, those of Dasaraka and Batadhana, and Shabadhana; those of Pushkala, and the inferior Kairata similarly those that live in Takshashila; those of Ambala, Malaba, Madra, Benuka, with those of Badantika, those of Pingala, Mānakalapa, Hana, and Kuhalaka, those of Mandabya, and Bhutiyubaka, Saptaka and Hemataraka; those of Yoshamati with those of Gāndhara with those whose refuge is Svarasagara, those of Yaudeya and Dasameya and Rajanya and those of Shyamaka, as well as those of Kshemadhurta,—all these live in the left belly of the tortoise (34—47). Here the star is Baruna, likewise the two Praustapada. The kingdom of the Kinnaras, Pashupāla, with that of Kichaka, and that of Kashmir, and likewise the people of Abhisāra and those of Dabada and of Angana, and those of Kulata and of Banarashtra, and those of Saurista and Brahmapura and similarly those of Banabahya those of Kirata, and Kakshikānanda, and the people of Palhaba and Lolana and those of Darbada, and of Maraka, and of Kurata and of Anadāraka, and of Ekapāda and those of Khasha, and Ghosha who are as faulters as the people of heaven—similarly those of Hinga with the Yabasas, and those of Chiraprabarana, those that live in Triantra and those of Puru, and the Gandharbas, on most excellent among twice-born persons, these live on the north-eastern foot of the tortoise ; and Rebati, Ashwini, and Yamya, these are the three stars of this region (48—53). In the regions mentioned by me the stars belonging to them cause, good and evil, O thou excellent Muni. In these countries, O thou twice-born one, these stars in the order related by me cause pain to them. While they grow and gain all sorts of good when the stars are in their proper places (54—55). The particular planet which is the lord of the particular star ruling over a country, of that country, O thou superior among Munis, both fear and happiness are caused by that planet (56). In each country, O thou most excellent one among twice-born persons, the evil or good, befall men equally, from these stars and planets (57). When the natal stars of creatures are inauspicious, the evil that befalls them is slight, and similarly by the planets also they are subjected to slight pain (58). Similarly when the star is auspicious by the sages who know all these things, it is said, that by planets in evil stations but little harm is caused to men (59). When the evil sight of the planets falls on the effects of the virtuous men, or on their cattle, or on their servants, or on their friends, or on their sons, or on their wives or their houses there is fear of evil (60). When the sight of the evil planet falls on one's own self, there is cause of great fear to men of little merit or those that are given to sin, while there is no cause of fear to the sinless (61). All the good and evil arising from either the locality or the quarter in which people live, or from their kings or from their own selves, or from the operation of the stars and the planets,—all these men suffer or enjoy (62). Their mutual safety is caused by stars that are not inauspicious, and by them when they are inauspicious is caused loss of good, O thou prince among Brāhmans ! (63). The position, of stars in the particular parts of the tortoise as related by me, is common to all the countries situate in those parts, and so is also the evil or good caused by them (64). Therefore knowing the presiding stars of the country as also the unfavourable influence of one's own (natal) stars, the wise and the good shall propitiate them according to *lokabada* (65). The desires, of the gods and Datyas that fall on the earth from the sky, are called *lokabada* (66). The learned shall duly perform those propitiatory rites nor give up the *lokabada* of those men who perform these ; the coming in of evil is obstructed, and the good arises and evil is utterly destroyed, O most excellent among twice-born persons; while of those who do not observe these, they (the stars) destroy the senses, and also the household properties, &c. Therefore are the wise given to the performance of propitiatory rites, and are devoted to traditions similarly ; the propitiatory rites should be performed and the *lokabada* observed whenever the stars are unpropitious (67—69). Then the wise do not work harm, do not fast, perform auspicious works, and pay homage to places of sacrifice, and perform *japa* and *homa*, and likewise acts of charity, and bathing and give up anger and other passions, and ill will towards all creatures, and practise good will towards them, avoid bad words, and similarly harsh and unpleasant words, and the worship of the stars ; these should men do when suffering from evil stars. In this way, O thou most excellent Brāhman, all evils are fully remedied in men who thus control and discipline themselves. The lord, the possessor of the six high qualities, the *Bhagas*, the spirit who is unapproachable by thought, Nārāyana, who exists as tortoise in Bharata, and in whom all is established, and where the gods are also established,—has all been described by me (70—74). In this (tortoise) the gods exist holding on each to a star. There in the middle exist the carrier of sacrificial offerings—the god Agni, and the earth, and, O thou twice born one, the moon and three stars (of the signs of the zodiac) the lamb &c—exist in its middle, and the pairs &c—exist in the mouth of the tortoise, while the crab and the lion exist in the south-eastern foot; the lion, the maiden, and the balance, these three exist in the belly : the balance and the scorpion exist on the south-eastern foot ; the scorpion exists on the back with the archer; the archer and the three stars commencing with the horse, exist on the north-eastern foot, while the tortoise and the fish, O thou most superior among the twice born persons, similarly exist in the northern belly of this (tortoise), while the fish and the lamb exist on the north-eastern foot (75—78). In this way are the different regions of the earth and in those regions their respective stars, and in those stars their respective signs of the zodiac, and in those signs their respective planets stationed. Therefore the evils arising from the stars and the planets are said to be *Deshapida* or evils pertaining to particular regions. And on these evils arising the injunction is that people shall bathe and perform *hom* and acts of charity. That foot of Vishnu which exists among the planets is Brahmā, called even as the Nārāyana; he is unthinkable and is the cause and lord of the world 79—81.

——oo——

CHAPTER LIX.

OH Muni, the Bharata Barsha is duly described by me. The Satya, the Treta, the Dwapara, and the Kali, these are the four Yugas; and it is here alone that these Yugas and the four castes exist, Oh thou twice-born one! Oh Brāhman, in the four Yugas, Satya, Treta &c here people lived for four, three, two, and likewise one hundred years respectively. The Barsha Bhadrashwa by name that is situate to the east of Debakuta, at the back of the Prince of mouutains, hear of it from me. In this Barsha, Swetaparna, and Nila, and the most excellent among mountains, Shaibāla, Kamanja, Panashālāgra, these five are the Kula mountains ; their offsprings there are many others, small mountains (1—5). In them are a thousand provinces, of various kinds, that appear like flowers, and the table-land of these smaller mountains is clean and auspicious looking (6). Shita, Shankābati, Bhadrā, Chakrabarta, these and others are the rivers in this Barsha,—they are all of great extent, and the carriers of great volumes of cooling waters. The men in this Barsha are possessed of the glamour of pure gold and mother-of-pearl, associates of the gods, righteous, and the length of their life is a thousand years. Among them there is neither good nor bad, all of them look on this creation with an equal eye, and they are endowed with the eight natural virtues of indifference to the conflicts of heat and cold &c—There the four-armed god Janarddana, exists as Aswashira, adorned with three eyes, and having head, breasts, the reproductive organ, the feet and the hands. Of him, the lord of the world is this to be known as the property (6—11). To the west of it is the Ketumala Barsha; hear of it from me. Bishāla, Kambala, Krishna, Jayanta, the mountains Hari, Bishoka, and Bardhamān, these seven are the Kula mountains here. There are a thousand other mountains wherein people live. The Manlaya, the Mahakāyā, the Shakapota, the Karambakā, the Angulā, and others, hundreds of peoples live there, who drink the waters of the Rangkshu, the Shyāma, the Kambalā, the Amoghā, the Kamini, and of a thousand other great rivers (12—15). The duration of human life here is the same as in the previous Barsha, and Hari, the possessor of the six great qualities, the Bhagas, exists in the form of the boar with his feet, breast, back and sides, all like the boar,—in this Barsha, which has three stars attached to it, and all these stars are propitious. Thus then, is the Ketumála Barsha described to you, O most excellent Muni, by me (16—17). Next I shall describe Kuru—hear that from me. There the trees produce fruits of honey and they constantly bear flowers and fruits; and they produce cloth and in their fruits are produced ornaments; those trees are able to fulfil all desires, and bestow the fruits of all sorts of wishes (18—19). The earth is made of precious stones and metals, the air is sweet-scented and pleasant during all seasons. Men, who fall off from the region of the gods, are born there. They are born in pairs of males and females, who live for equal periods, and are attached to each other, even as the Cakrabakas (20—21), The duration of their life is fourteen and a half thousand years. In that Barsha Chandrakānta, and Suryakanta these two princes of mountains are the Kulācalas; and between them the great river Bhadrasomā flows on the earth and the current of its waters is pure and without any unclean things. Similarly in the northern part of this Barsha there flows a thousand other rivers, some of whose currents are of *ghee* and of some of milk. In that Barsha there are likewise many lakes of curd, and many smaller mountains; and many kinds of fruits whose flavour and taste are like those of nectar, are there in the forests of that Barsha, which number hundreds and thousands. And there Vishnu, the possessor of the six great qualities, the *Bhagas*, he whose face is towards the east, is of the form of fish (22—26). O thou most excellent among Munis, there the stars are nine in number arranged in groups of three, and the quarters are also divided into nine parts. In the ocean (of this Barsha). one island is Candradwipa and another likewise Bhadradwipa and these, O thou great Muni, are well-known as sacred among places in the ocean. Thus is the Kurubarsha described by me to you, O Brāhmana. Hear from me now all about the Kimpurusha and other Barshas (27—29).

CHAPTER LX.

I shall presently describe to you, O thou twice-born one, that which is Kimpurusha Barsha, where the duration of the life of men with well-grown bodies is a ten thousand year; where men and likewise the women are without disease and without bereavement. The Plaksha tree there is said to be as big as in the garden of the gods—Nandana. Those men always drink the juice of the fruit of that tree; and the women have permament youth, and are possessed of the sweet scent of the lotus (1—3.) Next by me will be described the Hari Barsha which is situate next to the Kimpurusha Barsha. The men there are born with the glamour of gold,—they have all fallen off from the region of the gods, and are in every respect possessed of the beauty of the gods. In the Haribarsha, all men drink the auspicious juice of the sugar-cane. There old age does not oppress people nor make them lean in any way; as long as they live they live free from disease (4—6). That which has been described by me as Ilabrita, is the Meru Barsha; it stands in the middle—there the sun does not burn, nor do the men there become infirm and decrepit; there the rays of the sun or the moon do not gain their own objects (they do not give light); nor even the rays of the stars and the planets; there the glow of the Meru is the most superior light. There men are born having the colour and brightness of the lotus and eyes like the petals of the lotus and the sweet scent of the lotus, and who live on the juice of the *Jambu* fruit. (7—9.) The duration of life is thirteen thousand years, in Ilāvrita which exists like a saucer in the body of the Meru. There the Meru is the great mountain. Thus is Ilāvrita Varsha described.

From this I shall describe to you the Ramyaka Barsha, hear me. There too the Nyagrodha tree is of exceeding height and of green leaves, and drinking the juice of the fruit of this tree, so they live. There the duration of life is a ten thousand years, and the men enjoy the fruits thereof; they are distinguished for their affections, and are pure, and devoid of old age and bad smell (10—13). From that to the North is the Barsha called Hiranmaya, there the river is the Hiranvati brightened by immense lotuses. Men there are born of exceeding strength and full of vigour, and of the form of Yaksha, and possessing great energy, riches, and pleasant to look at (14—15).

—oo—

CHAPTER LXI.

KRAUSTIKI said:—O Mahāmuni, what I asked thee has been duly described by thee,—namely the positions of the land and the waters and likewise their measurements and the stars; and their position and measure, and also of the three *lokas*, *Bhu* &c., and all the nether worlds,—and likewise has the Manwantara of the Swayambhuba Muni, been described to me—O Muni, I desire to hear now of the other Manwantaras with the masters of those Manwantaras, and the gods, the Rishis, and the sons of the Manus and the kings (1—3).

MARKANDEYA said:—After that Manwantara called the Swayambhuba, which has been described to you by me, there was another Manwantara, called the Sançisha Manwantara, hear of that from me (4). A certain superior person among the twice-born castes lived in the town of Arunāspeda, on the banks of the river Barunā, O Brāhman, who was in beauty even as the twins the Aswinis (5). He was of a mild disposition, living by righteous occupation and learnt the Vedas and the Vedāngas in all their entirety, a lover of guests, and the shelter of persons coming to his house after night fall (6). But he had this idea, "I shall see the whole world, which contains most pleasant forests and gardens, and is adorned with many cities (7)." Then once upon a time came a guest to his house, who knew of the virtues of many herbs, and was an expert in magical formulas (8). This (guest) having been served by him with a mind purified by reverence, told him of many countries, and beautiful cities, and forests, and rivers, sacred and extensive, and mountains. He then being possessed with admiration addressed that most superior among twice-born persons (thus) (9—10). "Thou must be overtaken by extreme fatigue for having seen many places, but thou art not very old, nor hast thou gone very far away from youth, O thou twice-born one, how dost thou in this short period travel all over this world (11)."

THE BRAHMANA said :—O Brahman, by the power of a herb sanctified by magic forumlas with unobstructed movement, I walk a thousand *Yojana* in half a day (12).

MARKANDEYA said :—Then that Brāhman again spoke to him thus with due respect, being possessed by unshaken faith in his words (13). "Grant me this favour, O thou possessor of the six great qualities the Bhagas, of the power born of magic or mystic formulas. I have got a very great desire to see this world (14)." That Brāhman, of a generous mind, gave to him the feet-salve and also influenced the quarters named by him by the power of mystic formulas with great care (15). Then, O thou most superior among twice born persons, that twice born one, having covered his feet with that salve, with a view to see it, went to the Himalays that have many springs,—thinking that while I shall go a thousand *Yojana* in half a day in the other half I shall return (home).

(16—17). Having found the top (lit the back) of the Himalayas without getting any bodily fatigue the twice born one then walked there, the top of the mountain covered by snow (18). Then of him thus walking the feet salve, produced by superior herbs dissolved by the snow, was washed away (19). Then his movement being made slow, he walking here and there saw many most pleasant table-lands of the Himālaya mountain (20). Seeing these table-lands inhabited by Sidhas and Gandharbas, and enjoyed by the Kinnaras, and which was pleasant on account of there being held the play grounds and promenades of the gods—, and crowded by hundreds of heavenly Apsarās, this person, most superior among the twice born, O Muni, though full of delight, was not however satiated (21—22). Some place was pleasant because of the falling of water from some springs; another place was resounded by the sound of the dancing peacocks (23). Some place was full of most pleasant looking Dātyahoka, Yastikā and other birds, and of the notes of the blackbirds that run away with the hearing of people (24). He, full of rapture, saw the great Mountain Himālaya which is fanned by wind scented by the smell of flowering trees (25). Having seen this great Mountain Himalaya, this son of the twice born person, thought "I shall see it again," and turned his mind towards his home (26). Then with his feet salve dropped off, and with his movement gradually becoming slow, he began to think, "what is this that has been done by me through ignorance (27). My salve has been destroyed, having been dissolved by the waters of the snow, and this mountain is also very difficult to walk, and I am come here a great way off from my home (28). I shall, consequently, be subject to loss of the daily sacrificial rites as the keeping up of the fire at the family altar; what shall I do here, in the face of this great difficulty (29). In this snperior mountain, crying this is beautiful, this is beautiful, I shall tnever, with my eye thus attached to it, find satiation or satisfaction in a hundred years (30). From all sides the songs of the Kinnaras attract the ear, and the smell of flowering trees attracts the sense of the smell (31). Similarly the breeze here is pleasant to the skin, and the friuts are full of flavour and the lakes, that are beautiful to the mind, rob the heart per force (32). Under these circumstance if I can see some jewel of a hermit, he will instruct me in the means by which I can go home (33)."

MARKANDEYA said :—That Brāhman, thus thinking, walked about on the Himālayas, having been exceedingly distracted owing to the loss of the power of the mystic feet-salve (34). Baruthini, the daughter of Maulā, a most superior Apsarā, possessed of great beauty, and possessed of the eight qualities, namely, kindness, &c.,' said to that superier *Muni* thus walking on the Himalayas (35). Then seeing that superior twice-born person, Baruthini, immediately being moved by love, her heart drawn by cupid, began to think, "who is this man, with most beautiful features? My birth shall be full of fruit if he does not reject me. O the sweetness of the beauty of this person! O the'graceful movement of this person! I have seen gods and likewise Asuras and Siddhas and Gandharbas, and Pannagās, but there has not been a single one equal in beauty to this great souled one. Should he be as full of love to me as I am to him, then shall I know that I had accumulated a mass of virtue. If he should cast to-day affectionate and loving glance on me, then what woman in the three worlds is more endowed with the fruits of virtue than myself (36—42)."

MARKANDEYA said :—That æthereal woman, stricken by Cupid, thus thinking showed herself of most lovely figure, (to the Brahman). That son of the twice-born person seeing Baruthini of most superior beauty, approaching her with due respect, spoke these words (43). "Who art thou, the glow of whose face is of that of the unfolding lotus,? Whose art thou? What art thou staying here for? I am a Brāhmana who have come here from the city called Arunāspada

(44). Dissolved by the waters of the snow my feet-salve has been destroyed, by virtue of which I had come here, O thou whose eyes are like the rapturous Khanjana bird (45)."

BARUTHINI said :—I am the daughter of Muleya, am the possesser of the eight qualities of kindness &c., known by the name of Baruthini. I always rove about this beautiful great mountain (46). Such am I; now, O Brāhmana, seeing you, I have been stricken by lust. Order whatever you want, that shall be done by me, I am subject to thy will (47).

THE BRAHMANA said :—O thou whose smile is pure, tell me by what means I may get to my home. O thou auspicious one, all my sacrificial works are being neglected; and the non-performance of the daily and the periodical sacrifices is the greatest loss to twice-born persons. Therefore O gentle one, do thou deliver me from the Himālayas (48—49). Living away from their homes is never permitted to the Brāhmanas; neither have I any fault, O thou timid one, except the curiousity to see strange countries (50). Always in the house of superior twice-born persons, there is the performance of all sacrificial works; and there is non-performance (a loss) of both the daily and the periodical sacrifices of the Brāhman who lives away from his home (51). What more shall I say, do, O thou of good name, that by which I may see my own home before the setting of the sun (52).

BARUTHINI said :—Do not say thus, O thou possesser of the good eight qualities of kindness, &c. May that day never be to me when leaving me thou shalt repair to thy own house (53). O thou son of a twice-born person, even heaven itself is not more beautiful than this Himalaya. Therefore, we live here leaving the city of the gods (54). Therefore O my love, by roving about this lovely snow-peaked mountain, with me, thou shalt not recollect thy earthly friends (55). I, who have been subject to thee by cupid and whose heart has been robbed by thee, shall give thee here garlands, and wearing apparel and ornaments, and food, and objects of enjoyment, and scents and annointments (56). The music *Vika* and *Vena*, and songs of the Kinnaras that please the mind, the breeze that delights the limbs, warm rice, and pure water (57); bed after thy mind, and sweet-scented annointments,—all these are to be constantly had here, O thou possesser of the eight good qualities of kindness, &c., what more is there in thy own home (58). Living here, old age shall never be thine, this land of the inhabitants of Tridasha, the country of the gods) is the giver of every thing that keeps up the youth (59). Thus saying she, whose eyes are like lotus,—saying this, "O thou favour me"—intent on enjoying him, all of a sudden, embraced him full of love (60).

THE BRAHMANA said :—O thou vile one, touch me not, go to others who are of thy class and nature. By one art thou sought for one thing, and thou seekest me for another thing. By performing sacrifice with sacrificial offerings morning and evening men go to the eternal abode of bliss. O thou fool, all these three worlds are established on the sacrificial offerings. Therefore tell me of that by which I may swiftly go to my own house (61—62).

BARUTHINI said :—Why, O Brāhmana, am I not dear to thee? Is not this mountain pleasant? Leaving the Gandharbas and Kinnaras, who can be the object of thy desire. There is no doubt of it that thou, O reverend one, shalt go from here. For a little while do thou enjoy that pleasure with me which is difficult of attainment (64).

THE BRAHMANA said :—The three sacrificial fires, Garhapatya and others are the objects of my desires, the place for the sacrificial fires is most pleasant of all places to me, and the goddess Bistarani is my love (65).

BARUTHINI said :—O thou twice-born one, those that are the eight virtues of the spirit, of them the first is mercy; O thou observer of the right law, why dost thou not perform that (mercy) to me (56). I am so full of love for thee that forsaken by thee I shall not live. This what I say is not false, therefore be kind to me, O thou the gladdener of thy clan (67).

THE BRAHMANA said :—If thou art really full of love, and if thou dost not say so to me merely from courtesy, then explain to me the means by which I shall be able to reach my own home (68).

BARUTHINI said :—Thou, O revered one, shalt without doubt go from here to thy own home; only for a little while enjoy with me those pleasures that are difficult of attainment (69).

THE BRAHMANA said :—O Baruthini, nothing is permitted to the Brāhman to be done for the sake of enjoyment. All the works on earth of the Brāhmanas, are for pain, but they bear fruit in the world to come (70).

BARUTHINI said :—By working the salvation of me who is dying the friut of thy meritorious action shall be assured in the next world, as also enjoyment in another birth. In this case, thus these two are causes of thy advancement. By thy rejection I shall find death and thou shalt attain, sin (71—72).

THE BRAHMANA said :—A strange woman shall not be desired, so said my preceptors (gurus, meaning both father, mother, the teacher of the vedas and the spiritual preceptor). Therefore I do not desire thy love, however much thou mayest lament or grieve (73).

MARKANDEYA said :—So saying that possessor of the eight good qualities of kindness &c., having touched water, being calm and subdued in mind, and pure, having saluted the Garhapatya Agni, said this in such a way that none might hear it :—Thou revered Grahapatya Agni ! thou art the root of all sacrifices; from thee have sprung the Ahavanya Agni, and the Dakshina Agni, not from any one else; through thy satisfaction do the gods become the cause of rain and harvest, and from that harvest, the whole exists, not from any thing else. In this way by the power of truth by which from thee all these worlds grow, similarly (by thy power) may I see my own home to-day when the sun is still (on the firmament). As by me the Vedic rites have never been neglected in their due time, by the power ot that truth may I see the sun while stationed in my own house. As I never had a desire for other's riches or other's wives, by virtue of that may the desire of mine find fulfilment ((74—79).

CHAPTER LXII.

MARKANDEYA said:—In the body of the son of the twice-born person, speaking in this wise, the *Agni Gàrhapatya* even then entered (1). Thus possessed by him, he, (the Brāhmana) thus illumined that region even as a second sacrificial fire (2). Necessarily, the love of the æthereal woman (Baruthini) looking on this twice-born person thus glowing with the brightness of the sacred fire) became great towards this Brāhmana (3). Then that son of the twice-born person possessed by the carrier of sacrifices—the *Gârhapatya Agni*—began at once to move as before (4). Thus looked on by that goddess he swiftly went out of her sight, by the sighs of whom of lean figure, the whole forest region began to tremble (5). Then in a moment's time he having got to his own house, the most superior among the twice-born persons, performed all the sacrifices as they all declared (in the law) (6). Then that woman, all whose limbs were beautiful, being attached to him with all her mind and soul, made sighs her chief refuge during both the day and the night. That woman, of unblemished limbs, sighing cried *hâ hâ*—(these exclamations) and cried repeatedly; and she, whose eyes were like the rapturous Khanjana bird, cursed her bad luck (7-8). In those days she did not bind the desires of her heart either to walking, nor to eating, nor to the beautiful forest, nor to valleys pleasant to the mind. Her desires went only to the rolling pass of *Cakravakas*, forsaken by him. That excellent woman only cursed her own youth (9—10). Drawn by the force of evil fate why did I come to this mountain, and who brought such a man before me (11). If that possessor of the eight great qualities does not meet me to-day, then the fire of Cupid, hard to bear, shall surely burn me up (12). That (Himalaya) which was so pleasant to the mind owing to its being resounded with the notes of the black-bird, on account of his absence,—even that seems to be burning me to-day (13).

MARKANDEYA said:—In this way she, possessed by Cupid, went about, O thou most excellent among the *Munis*. And then her love towards him also grew at every moment. (14). A Gandharva, Kali by name, who having loved, had been repulsed by her, previous time, saw her now in that state (15). He thought within himself, "why is this Baruthini, whose movement is like that of the elephant, dried up by the breath of sighs, moving about in this mountain (16)? Is she wounded by the curse of some Muni? or has she been insulted by any one? For which reason she is bearing this face wet by tears (17)." Therefore he, Kali, moved by curiosity, thought over this for a long time; and then by virtue of Samādhi knew everything exactly as it happened (18). O Muni, he, Kali, again thought, having known all this, "this has happend owing to my good fortune earned by meritorious actions performed in a previous existence (19). By me, full of love was she repeatedly prayed and she, who repelled me then, will by me be found to-day (20)

She is full of love for man; therefore I shall assume that form, and she will unsuspectingly enjoy pleasures with me. Why should I delay—I shall do so (21)."

MARKANDEYA said:—Having by the power of his spirit assumed the form of that twice-born person, he began to walk about the place where that Baruthini was lying (22). She, of most superior form, who was charmingly lean, seeing him, with her eyes somewhat opened with delight, came near him and repeatedly cried—"Be kind to me, be kind to me (23). Forsaken by thee there is no doubt of it that I shall give up this life, then that will be a greater sin to thee, and will also lead to loss of thy sacrificial works (24). In the beautiful valley of this mountain that has many great valleys, by coming near me thou shalt surely earn the merit of saving my life. O thou of great understanding! surely the end of my days has approached, therefore hast thou, O gladdener of my heart, abstained from going away from men (25—26)."

KALI said:—What shall I do? Here there will necessarily be loss to any sacrificial work, and O thou, of lean waist,—thou too speakest in this wise—therefore I am now in a painful fix. If thou dost as I bid thee, then there may be my connections with thee, otherwise not (27—28).

BARUTHINI said:—Be kind, whatever thou shalt say that shall I do. This is not untrue—Tell me what thou wantest to have done by me without any doubt or apprehension (29).

KALI said:—This day at the time of the enjoyment, I am not to be seen by thee in this forest. O thou of beautiful brow, thy connection with me shall be with closed eyes (30).

BARUTHINI said:—So be it. That which thou wishest, is well, and be it so; I am now in every way subject to thee (31).

——oo——

CHAPTER LXIII.

Markandeya said:—Then he roved about with her on the table lands of mountains, or heart satisfying gardens with flowering trees, and on lakes that are pleasing to the mind (1); on pleasant valleys and on the banks of rivers that are pleasant to the mind and likewise, O thou twice-born one, in many other regions (2). She with closed eyes began to think of the beauty of the Brāhman as he appeared when possessed by the fire, at the time of living with Kali (3). At that time she, O thou most excellent Muni, became pregnant, through connection with the Gandharva and thinking on the beauty of the twice-born one (4). He (Kali), who had assumed the form of the Brāhmana then having pacified Baruthini bearing his child, and having been given leave by her with love, went away (5). That child was born full of light even as the burning fire; as the sun illumines all the quarters by his own rays (6), glows by the glamour of his own rays, even did that boy; therefore he became known by the name of Sharochi (7). That possesser of the eight good qualities of kindness, &c., grew with his age every day, and with many good qualities, even as the new moon grows disc by disc (8). He then, the possesser of the eight good qualities, kindness, &c., coming to youth, learnt the knowledge of weapons, (military science) and also of the Vedas, in right order, and also other kinds of knowledge (9). Once upon a time walking about the mount Mandara, he, whose works were all lovely, saw a maiden on the mountain pass, stricken with fear (10). Seeing him she at that time uttered the words "save me." He also to her whose eyes were filled with tears from fear, said thus "be not afraid" (11). 'What is the matter,'—being thus addressed in bold words by that high-souled one, she then said with her words broken by sighs (12).

THE MAIDEN said:—I am the daughter of the Vidyadhara Indivaraksha, Manoramā by name, born of the daughter of Marudhanva (13). Vibhavari born of the Vidyādhara Mandāra is my friend; and also another Kalāvati, the daughter of Muni Pāra (14). Going to the excellent tableland of the mount Kailasā, there a certain *Muni*, of an exceedingly lean and hagard figure, was seen by me along with them, whose throat had grown very lean through hunger and whose eye balls were without lustre and sunken deep in the socket (15). Being laughed at by me, and getting enraged he at that uttered a curse on me in very feeble tones and with his lips moving sightly (16). O thou non-Aryan, thou whose penance is for evil, as I have been laughed at by thee, therefore thou shalt without delay be overcome by a Rākshasa" (17). When he had thus cursed me, that Muni also was chidden by my two friends, (who said) " Fie to thy station as a Brahmana, by thee have all these penances been made without practising the virtue of forgiveness. Thou hast grown lean through malice and through the strictness of thy penance. The essence of the quality of a Brāhmana resides in forgiveness,—and his penance is the subjugation of his anger (18-19)." He, of unabated effulgence, hearing this, cursed those two also, namely that on the limbs of one there shall be leprosy, and the other shall get consumption (20). These grew exactly on those two even as uttered by the Muni, even at that very moment, and on me also a great Rākshasa is coming following my foot (21). Dost thou not hear this terrific sound, of him who is roaring near; this is the third day that he has not given up his pursuit of me (22). I shall communicate to thee all the knowledge of weapons and all the knowledge of heart (*Hridayagnanā*) save me, O thou high-minded one, from this Rākshasa (23). This knowledge was at first communicated to Swāyambuba Manu, by Rudra himself, the holder of the bow *Pináka*; Swayambhuva gave it to that most superior among the *Siddhas*; by him was it communicated to Citrāyudha, my mother's father. His father-in-law himself gave it to my father at the time of his marriage as a marriage gift (25). In my early age it was learnt by me, O brave one, from my father—this *Hridaya* of all the weapons, that can punish all foes (26). Do thou accept this soon, which is the refuge of many weapons, and then kill this evil-spirit as soon as it comes near me "(27).

MARKANDEYA said :—On his saying so be it, then by touching water she gave to him that knowledge called the *Hridaya*, with all the secrets regarding its calling back and sending out (28). In the meantime that Rākshasa of fearful features, roaring with a dreadful roar quickly came there (29). He, Swarochi, saw him saying,—"I shall eat thee, without any loss of time," and seeing him approach her, he thought within himself, "let him take her, and let the words of the great Muni be fulfilled;" and that Rākshasa, also coming near her quickly, took her of fine-waist who was crying, 'save me, save me, in most piteous tones (30—32).' Then Swarochi, moved by anger, directed that fierce weapon on the Rākshasa, and looked with fixed eyes. Then being overwhelmed, he, that Rākshasa letting off that girl, cried "be gracious, control the weapon, and hear me (33—34), O thou of great effulgence, by thee am I delivered from a most dreadful curse, uttered against me by the most austere and wise Brahmamitra (35). There is no greater benefactor to me than thou, O possessor of the eight good qualities of kindness &c., by whom I am delivered from a great curse which caused me such immense pain (36)."

SWAROCHI said :—For what reason wast thou cursed by the great-souled Muni Brahmamitra. And of what kind was that curse given of old (37).

RAKSHASA said :—Brahmamitra, having gathered from the *Atharvaveda*, studied the whole of the *Ayurveda* with the

Adikâras (38). I am the father of this (maiden) known by the name of Indivara; and am the son of the lord of Vidyadharas, Nalanābha, the holder of the sword (39). The Muni Brahmamitra had been besought by me (with the words) "O revered one, it is fit that thou shouldst give to me the whole of the *Ayurveda* (40). When though repeatedly besought by me with humility, he, O thou brave one, did not communicate the knowledge of the *Ayurveda* ; the knowledge of the unfailing *Ayurveda* was then obtained by me by eaves dropping, from him when he was communicating it to his disciples (41—42). Eight months after my thus gaining this knowledge, one day I was overwhelmed with joy and began to laugh again and again (43) Knowing the secret of my laughing he, the great Muni possessed with anger, with trembling neck, told me these harsh words (44). 'As like a Rākshasa, O evil-minded one, by thee has this knowledge been got from me, unseen, through stealing and as thou hast been laughing to show thy want of respect for me, therefore in seven nights, O thou evil one, being overtaken by my curse, thou shalt without doubt become a cruel Rākshasa (45—46).' On his saying this, being propitiated by salutation and other means of worship, he again told me, being softened in mind at once (47). "What has been uttered by me, must come to pass, O Gandharva; there can be no violation of that; but having become a Rākshasa thou shalt again find thy own body (48). When with thy recollection destroyed thou shalt, moved by anger, desire to eat thy own offspring, and thou shalt find the character of the prowlers in night (Rākshasa) then burnt by the fire of her weapon, finding back thyself consciousness, thou shalt get thy own body, and likewise find thy own station in the community of the Gandharvas (49—50)." He am I, O thou possessor of the eight good qualities of kindness *etc.*, who has been delivered from this great and fearful state of the Rākshasa, by thee. Therefore, O thou brave one, accept my prayer (51). This daughter I give thee as wife, accept her; and O high-souled one, take then also the whole of the *Ayurveda* with all its eight divisions, which had been gained by me from the Muni (52).

MARKANDEYA said :—So saying he, who had found his old divine lady glowing in heavenly garments and wearing garlands and ornaments, gave him that knowledge (53). Having given him the knowledge (of *Ayurveda*) he began to make ready to give him his daughter; at that time that daughter thus spoke to his father who had attained to his own form (54). "Father, by me too, here, this great souled one my special benefactor, has been loved ever since I saw him (55). But they, my friends, are suffering from the miseries caused by me, therefore I do not wish to enjoy objects of enjoyment with him (56). Such cruel acts even men cannot perform, how then shall I, a woman like me, by nature of a loving disposition, do it (57). Father ! Such am I; as those two maidens are overtaken by miseries caused by me, so shall I also live in that miserable state, burnt by the fire of their grief (58).

SWAROCHI said :—By the grace of the *Ayurveda,* they two shall be made fresh again—thy friends, therefore refrain, Oh thou of beautiful waist, from grieving for them (59).

MARKANDEYA said :—Then he the father himself gave that daughter, according to prescribed forms, and in that mountain Swarochi married her of lovely eyes. Then the Gandharva having consoled that maiden,—his daughter given in marriage, went in ethereal gait from there to his own city (60—61). He also (*i. e.* Swarochi) with the lean one then went to that garden where the two maidens had got diseased through that curse (62). Then he, Swarochi, the unconquerable one, the knower of the inner significance of things, by means of medicine and juice that kill diseases, made them of healthy body (63). Then those two maidens of exceeding beauty, the auspecious ones, being cured from the disease, began to walk on that mountain, having illumined all the four quarters by the glamour of their beauty (64).

CHAPTER LXIV.

MARKANDEYA said :—Thus cured of her disease the maiden, moved by delight, thus spoke to Swarochi,—"Hear my words, O lord" (1) I am the daughter of the Vidyadhara Mandāra known by the name of Vibhāvari. O my benefactor! I give myself to thee, accept me (2). I shall also give thee that knowledge by which the speech of all creatures shall de revealed to thee. Therefore be then gracious to me (3).

MARKANDEYA said :—On this being said by the righteous Swarochi—so be it, the second maiden then spoke this word (4). "My father, Pāra by name,—he who is a Brahmarshi had been a Brahmacāri from his boyhood; he was greatly possessed of the eight good qualities of kindness etc., and had seen the limits of the *Vedas* and the *Vedangas* (5). Then of old, during spring time which is made pleasant by the cooing of blackbirds, came to him an Apsarā known by the name of Punjikastaná (6). Being overtaken by Cupid, he the superior Muni, then met her, and on her was I born in this great mountain (7). Leaving me when I was a mere baby, alone in this forest that is devoid of human-beings, and full of all sorts of murderous animals, my mother also went away (8). Then, O excellent one, I grew from day to day by drinking the growing disc of the moon (9). From that was my name Kalāvati—given me by my high-souled father who took me (10). Then I was asked for in marriage by the Gandharva, Alina, of beautiful face, who was the foe of the gods ; and on my not being given, by him was my father cursed and killed (11). Then owing to excess of grief, I was about to kill myself, and was forbidden by Sati the wife of Shambhu, of unfailing truth—saying,—"grieve not, thou maiden of beautiful brow, great shall be thy fortune on earth ; Swarochi shall be thy husband ; and of him thou shalt have a son who shall be a *Manu* (12—13). The *Nidhis* shall with respect obey thy orders ; and shall give thee wealth as thou desirest, O thou beautiful one (14). By virtue of this, O darling, thou shalt attain all this ; accept from me that knowledge, *Padmini* by name ; this knowledge is worshipped by all the gods (15)." Thus spoke to me the daughter of Daksha, Sati, whose highest refuge is truth. Thou art Swarochi. That goddess would never say a thing which was not true (16). Such am I who today want to give that knowlepge as also my own body to thee ; accept them, being gracious to me (17).

MARKANDEYA said :—'So be it' he said also to that maiden Kalāvati and finding his action approved by the affectionate glance of Vibhāvari, he married them two there, and the place was resounded with the music of divine musicians and dancing of Apsarās (18-19).

CHAPTER LXV.

THEN he (Swarochi) of immortal effulgence, enjoyed life in that prince of mountains adorned with pleasant gardens and springs, with those his wives (1). The *Nidhis*, subject to the knowledge called Padmini, brought to him at will, all sorts of most precious objects of enjoyment, and the sweetest honey; and garlands, and clothes and ornaments and ointments rich in fragrance, and most white seats, and gold, and cups and plates of gold, likewise different kinds of bed, furnished with most bright and beautiful beddings (2—4). Thus he enjoyed life, in that superior mountain scented with heavenly fragrance, and glowing with the effulgence of his (Swarochi's) own rays with them (his wives) (5). They too found most excellent pleasure with him, on that mountain, even as (the goddesses) find pleasure in the enjoyments in heaven (6). A certain *Kâlahansa* (a species of duck), moved by desire, at the loving relations of him (Swarochi) and then (his wives), spoke (thus) to a Chakravāka living in water. "He is blessed, he is endowed with the fruits of most superior merits, who, on attaining to youth, enjoys such desirable pleasures with these his beloved ones (8). There exist many highly qualified youths, but their wives are not very beautiful; there are but few husbands and wives in this world, who are both exceedingly beautiful (9). Of some (husband) the wife is most beloved; of some (wife) again the husband is most desired; but conjugal pairs, who are rich in each other's love, are rare indeed (10). Blessed is this (Swarochi) so much loved by his wives, and these (his wives) also are most dear to him. Of the blessed alone is born such mutual attachment (11)." Hearing these words spoken by the *Kâlahansi*, the Chakravâki told her, with her mind unmoved by any great admiration (12). "This person is not blessed because he is not shy on account of the nearness of his other wives; he enjoys one of the wives, his heart is not on all of them (13). As, O friend! the affection of the heart is placed always on one person only, then how shall this person be full of love to all his wives (14)? They are not the beloved of their husband, nor is the husband their beloved; they are mere pastimes (to him) like any other attendant (15). If he be really the object of the desire of these (women) then why do not they give up their life? Even as he embraces one of his wives, he is meditated upon by others (16). This person is sold, as a slave, for the price of the gift of knowledge. Love does not equally flow to or rest on many objects (17). O *Kálahansi*! blessed is my husband, and blessed also am I whose hearts are for ever fixed in one person only (18).

MARKANDEYA said :—The invincible Swarochi, who was acquainted with the language of all beings, hearing this, felt ashamed (of himself) and thought,—"This is true, and not false (19)." Then after a hundred years had gone (after this) while (one day) walking about with them (his wives) on the great mountain, he saw in front of him a deer, of lovely and fat limbs, and roving about among a herd of deer, and surrounded by sweet-scented female deer like itself (20—21). Then on those female deer drawing the reservoir of his scent—(the musk, supposed to exist in the navel) and beginning to smell him, that deer said;—"O woman, immodest as you are, get you gone. I am not Swarochi, nor am I of his character, O you of beautiful eyes. There are many shameless persons like him, go to them (22—23). As when one woman follows many men she becomes the object of division among men, similarly also when one is looked upon by many with an eye to enjoyment, that one becomes an object of deresion (24). From day to day the sacrificial duties of that man are neglected and lost; he is always attached by lust to another wife, even when enjoying one wife (25). Others who are like these, and of their character, who have turned their face from the next world and the good thereof, do you desire them. I am not like Swarochi (26).

CHAPTER LXV.

Markandeya said:—Hearing those female deer thus repulsed by the deer, Swarochi began to feel himself even as a fallen being (1). He, who was thus spoken of by the Chakravāka and the deer, and who was the subject of the disdainful speech of the deer, resolved, O thou most superior Muni, to forsake them (his wives) (2). But on being met by them again his desire grew, and the instructions for renunciation were thrown away and he enjoyed life with them for six hundred years (3). But the charitable-minded Swarochi enjoyed objects of pleasure with them, while performing all religious duties, and without violating the injunctions of the Law (4). Then were born of him—Swarochi, three sons, Vijaya, Merunanda, and Prabhāva, of great strength (5). Manoramā, the daughter of Indivara, gave birth to Vijaya, and Vibhāvari gave birth to Merunanda and Kalāvati to Prabhava (6). He, their father Swarochi, by power of that knowledge called Padmini which secures all objects of enjoyment, made for them three cities (7). On the east, on the top of the mountain Kāmarupa, the excellent city by name Vijaya, he gave to his son Vijaya (8). On the north he made the city of Merunanda, known by the name of Nandavati, adorned with high table lands, and walls (9). For the son of Kālavati, Prabháva, was built a city, called Tāla situate on the Southern country—(Deccan) (10). That foremost among men, having in this way established the sons in three cities, roved about, O Brāhmana, with them in pleasant lands (11). Once that holder of the bow while walking about in the forest, seeing a boar running fast before him, drew his bow (12). At that time some female deer coming near him said, repeatedly—"On me do thou send thy arrow, be gracious unto me (13). What good wilt thou gain by killing this (boar) today? Soon kill me; the arrow discharged by thee shall deliver me from misery (14)."

SWAROCHI said :—Thy body is not found to be full of disease by us. What then is that cause, for which thou desirest to kill thy life (15).

THE DEER said :—My heart has made one, whose heart is attached to another person, its object. Without him, death is my remedy. What greater medicine is there?

SWARCOHI said :—Who is he who does not desire thee, O thou timid one, and to whom art thou moved by love, by not gaining whom thou art resolved to give up thy own life? (17).

THE DEER said :—May good befall thee, even thee I desire. By thee has my mind been carried away. Therefore I shall embrace death. Do thou discharge the arrow on me (18).

SWAROCHI said :—O thou of lovely glance, we are of the form of men, and thou art a deer, how can there be any connection with thee of persons like ourselves (19).

THE DEER said :—If thy heart is set on me, then do thou embrace me. If thy heart be good, I shall do whatever is desired by thee, and shall be most glorified (20).

MARKANDEYA said :—Then Swarochi embraced that female deer; and embraced by him she at once became invested with a most bright and beautiful body (21). He, then struck with wonder, said "who art thou?" She too told him (this) in accents stricken with loving modesty (22). I am goddess of this forest, honoured by the gods. O thou high-souled one, Manu is to be produced on me by thee (23). I say this to thee according to the instruction of the gods; do thou beget on me, who am full of love for thee, a son who shall be the ruler of this world (24).

MARKANDEYA said :—He then begat even at that moment on her a son, marked by all the auspicious marks, full of energy, and like unto himself (25). As soon as he was born the musicians of the gods struck (pleasant) notes, and the lords of the Gandharvas began to sing, and the Apsarās began to dance (26). The Rishis, and those whose wealth is their penance, and the gods showered flowers from all sides (27). Seeing his effulgence his father himself made his name,—Dyutiman, because by his effulgence even all the quarters illumined (28). That boy, maned Dyutiman, full of great strength and prowess, because he was the son of Swarochi, therefore became Swarochisha (29). He Swarochi, while walking about a pleasant mountain streamlet, saw a duck with his mate (30). That duck said to the female duck who was repeatedly expressing her desire for him :—"Restrain thyself; long hast thou enjoyed with me (31). What is the good of indulging in enjcyments at all periods of life? Thy last days are near. O thou rover on the water, the time has come when both thou and I should renounce (all pleasures) (32).

THE FEMALE DUCK said:—What time is there which is not fit for pleasure. The whole world is for enjoyment. Even the self-restrained Brāhmanas perform sacrifices for the sake of the enjoyment (33). And those, who have attained the power of discrimination, desirous of enjoyments both seen and unseen, porform works of charity and other meritorious works (34). Why then dost thou not desire enjoyment. Enjoyment is the result of human exertions,—as much of those that have gained the power of discrimination and those that are self-restrained. Why then shall it not be good for birds and beasts? (35).

THE DUCK said:—The mind, of those whose heart is attached to pleasure, and who are eager for the association of friends, is rarely moved towards God (36). Attached to sons, friends, wives, people's minds languish, even like the elephant sinking in the slough of the lake (37). Dost thou not see, good lady, that Swarochi, being overcome by attachment even from his boyhood being moved by desire, has sunk in the mire of worldly affection (38). In youth exceedingly attched to his wives, now to his sons and grandsons, the mind of Swarochi is sunk (in the mire of this world)—how shall he find deliverance (39)? O thou who movest in water, I am not like Swarochi, subject to women. Presently I have attained to discrimination, and have withdrawn myself from enjoyments (40).

MARKANDEYA said:—Hearing the speech of the bird, being uneasy and taking his wives he went to another forest for practising penance (41). There the charitable-minded one, having performed most austere penances, and having repelled all sins, went to the most pure region (42).

CHAPTER LXVII.

THEN the possessor of the six Bhagas, (Brahmā) made the son of Swarochi, Dyutiman by name, *Manu*, the lord of creatures. Hear (all about) his *Manwantara* (1). Those that were the gods in that, and those that were their sons, and those that were kings, Oh Kroustiki, I am relating all these, hear (2). O thou twice-born one, the gods in that *Manwantara* of Swarochisa, were *Paravat* and likewise *Tushita*, and the Indra, was called Vipaschita (3). In that Urja, Stāmva, Prāna, Dattoli, Rishabha, Nishchara, and Aurvaviran these became the seven Rishis (4). Chaitra and Kimpurusha etc., were the seven sons of these high-souled ones; they were of great eneregy, and the rulers of the earth (5). As long as his *Manwantara* lasted so long their descendents enjoyed this earth; then was the second *Manwantara* (6). Men, hearing with faith and reverence of the age of Swarochisha, are liberated from all sins (7).

CHAPTER LXVIII.

KRUSTUKI said.—O revered one, by thee has the life of Swarochisha as also the story of the birth of Swarochisha been described in all their details (1). That knowledge, Padmini by name, which brings all objects of desire, as also those *Nidhis* that are attached to it, tell me of them in detail (2). O *Guru*, the eight Nidhis and the objects they live in, and their nature, all these I desire to hear, related by thee (3).

MARKANDEYA said:—The knowledge that is called Padmini, has Lakshmi as its presending goddess; its receptacles are the *Nidhis*; hear of them from me (4); Padma, Mahāpadma, likewise, Makara and Cacchapa, Mukunda, and Nandaka, as also Nila, while Shankha is the eighth *Nidhi* (5). Wherever there is *Riddhi* (good fortune) they exist there, and of them *Siddhi* is born. These eight are called *Nidhis*; they have been described to thee, O Kraushtuki (6). O Muni, through the grace of the gods, and through the service of the society is the property of men illumined by these always (7). Of what nature they are, hear from me speaking to you. The first *Nidhi* Padama by name belongs to Maya, O thou twice-born one (8). It belongs perpetually to his son and his sons, and their grandsons. When possessed by this *Nidhi* men become strong in prowess and skill (9). And, O thou possesser of the eight good qualities of kindness etc, he becomes the receptacle of wealth, for this *Nidhi* is of the quality of wealth (10). He gets gold and silver and copper and all other metals, in very large quantities, and also trades in them (11). He also performs sacrifices and gives the sacrificial fees; with devotion he causes assemblages (of the learned to meet) at the temples of the gods (12). There is another Nidhi, the receptacle of the great of *Satwa*, spoken of as Mahāpadma; possessed by him a man becomes strong in the quality of *Satwa* (13). He gets *padmarâga* and other jewels, and pearls, and corals, and buys and sells them (14). Those who live according to the laws of *Yoga* to them he gives all this wealth as also habitations (for them) and himself becomes of their character, (15). His sons become of that character, with their sons and grand sons. It does not leave his descendants to the seventh generation (16). The *Nidhi*, Makara by name, is of the quality of *Tamas*; looked on by him a person, of most excellent character, becomes overtaken with ignorance and indiscrimination (17). He gains arrows, swords, double-edged swords, bows and shields, prepares binding instruments (Pāshas) and attains friendship with kings (18). He give these to those persons who live by valour, and to kings, and to those who are liked by them; and finds pleasure in the rightful sale and barter of weapons (19). All these happen to one only and it does not follow his descendants; he finds destruction for these objects from soldiers or in battle (20). The man, who is looked on by the *Nidhi* the Kacchapa (tortoise), becomes possessed of the quality of *Tamas* because this *Nidhi* is of the quality of *Tamas* (21. He performs works of various kinds shorn of righteousness, and builds all sorts of places for business; and does not put his trust in any one (22). Even as the tortoise withdraws unto itself all its lines, so having drawn unto him people's hearts, he himself exists with his own mind perfectly restrained (23). He neither gives (his wealth) to others nor does he himself enjoy (it) being always distracted by the fear of its destruction, and puts it in the earth. This *Nidhi* is also enjoyed only by one person—(not by his descendants) (24). The other *Nidhi*, Mukunda by name, is of the quality of *Rajas*. O thou twice-born one, the man, who is looked on by it, becomes of that quality (25). He gets *Vinà*, flute, *Mridanga*, etc., the four kinds of musical instruments, and settles pensions on singers and gives (money) to dancers (26). O thou twice-born one, he gives objects of enjoyments day and night to bards, and ministrels and Māghadhas, and to those addicted to sexual pleasures, and dancing girls, and enjoys these with them (27). The man, whom this *Nidhi* worships, does not move in the company of harlots, and others like them; he always finds the company of one (woman) only (28). The other *Mahànidhi*, Nanda by name, is composed of the qualities of *Rajas* and *Tamas*; the man, looked upon by it, attains these (qualities) very largely (29). He gains all kinds of metals and precious stones and also pure and pleasant food grains etc., and also performs their sale and barter (30). He also gives protection to relations and guests, and travellers, and he does not brook the least indignity, O thou great Muni (31). On being praised he finds great satisfaction, and he gives to people whatever they want and attains to a mildness (of disposition) (32). Many most beautiful and child-bearing (women) become his wives, and this *Nidhi* Nanda follows his descendants to the seventh generation (33). O thou evcellent one, growing in eight divisions (this *Nidhi*) gives the longest term of life to the man (whom it possesses) among all men (34). Nanda feeds the friends as also those who have come from a distance. It is not admired in the next world; nor does the affection grow towards associates; it becomes indifferent to former friends and makes friendship with others (35-36). Similarly the name of the *Mahànidhi*, which maintains the two qualities of *Satwa* and *Rajas*, is Nila; the man, who becomes its companion, attains to its character (*i.e.* the qualities of *Satwa* and *Rajas*) (37). He gains, O *Muni*, cloths and cotton, and foodgrains &c., and fruits and flowers, and also pearls and corals and conches and mother of pearls (38), and also other things that are born in water, and wood &c; as also he sells and barters them, and his heart is not set on any other thing (39). He makes lakes and ponds and likewise gardens, and bunds, and cannals, and plants trees (40); he grows by enjoying scents and flowers, and the *Nidhi* Nila becomes his for three generations (41). The other *Nidhi*, Sankha by name, is composed of the qualities of *Rajas* and *Tamas*, and O Brahmana, by it also is the lord of this *Nidhi* led to attain these qualities (42). It becomes of one man only and does not find any other man (*i.e*, his descendants); hear of, O *Kraustiki*, the characteristics of him whose this Sankha *Nidhi* becomes (43). He, by himself, eats the rice cooked by him, and similarly also wears fine clothes, while the members of his family as also his dependants and servants eat bad rice and do not put on fine clothes (44). He becomes always devoted to his own maintenance, and does not give (proper food and clothes) to friend, wife, brother, son or daughter-in-law and others (45). Thus these are the *Nidhis*, reputed to be the presiding deities of the wealth and riches of men; they are superior on account of their superior look, and are the givers of fruits according to the natures of men (46). Through being looked on by them a man attains that character which belongs to them. O thou twice-born one, the Padmini, which is of the character of the goddess of fortune—Lakshmi, exercises control over all these (47).

CHAPTER LXIX.

KRAUSTUKI said :—O Brāhmana, the Swārochisha *Manwântara* has been related to me by thee in detail, and likewise also the eight *Nidhis* as asked by me (1). And the first *Manwântara*, called the *Swâyambhuvam* has also been described. Now tell me about the third *Mânwântara* called *Auttama* (2).

MARKANDEYA said :—The son of Utthānapāda and Suruchi was known by the name of Uttama—a king reputed to be possessed of great strength and prowess (3); and righteous and high-souled and endowed with the wealth of manliness, who having surpassed all beings became as glorious as the sun (4). O thou great Muni, he was impartial both to friends and foes, and just to son or servants ; to the workers of iniquity he was even as the god Yama, and to the virtuous even as the moon (5). Uttama, that righteous son of Uttānapada, married Vahulā. well-known to fame, the daughter of Babhru, even as Indra did Shachi. His mind was always full of affection (towards her)—and he placed his (heart's) stay on her, even as that of the Moon was towards Rohini (6—7). His mind never was moved by attachment to any other object. The mind of that supporter of the earth rested on her even in dream (8). That king, immediately on seeing her of exceedingly lovely limbs, would embrace her body, and immediately on touching her body would lose his consciousness in her* (9). Her words that caused pain to the ear were also very pleasant to the lord of the earth, and even

* The word *tanmaya* has a significance that is very hard to express in English—*lit.* it means to be full of that,—"That state of the mind, when it loses its individual and personal consciousness in that of the object of its love or thought sees only that object, hears, smells, only that object, is called *tanmaya*."

insults from her he regarded as great honour (10). She would despise the garland and even most lovely ornaments (when) given by him; and would get up (i.e. leave his company (unceremoniously) causing bodily pain to him, when he would be drinking most superior wine (11). In this way she was not favourably disposed towards that high-souled one who was always favourably disposed to her; (and yet the lord of the earth would love her more than ever (12). If held by the hand even for a moment by the lord of men, she, not being sufficiently pleased, would, O thou twice-born one, eat but little food (13). Then, once, the king, while engaged in drinking, with great respect offered her, the intelligent one, a drinking cup filled with wine (14). She, looked upon by the supporters of the earth, (*i. e.* the assembled princes) with the coutezans who were adepts in dancing and singing, and who were singing most sweet tunes, turned her face from it, and did not wish to accept that cup, in the presence of the lords of the earth. Then that king repulsed by that lady so loved by him,—her husband not loved by her,—being angry, said, calling the keeper of the gate, and breathing even like a serpent (15—17). O keeper of the gate, taking this one whose heart is bad, leave her soon in a lonely forest. Thou art not to judge this order of mine. (*i. e.* thou art not permitted to think whether I shall do as the king bids or not &c) (18).

MARKANDEYA said—Then that door-keeper, obeying the order of the king without judging (of its propriety or impropriety) having placed her on a chariot, left her in the forest (19). Thus taken by him, she (the Queen) also regarded that banishment in the forest, being put out of sight of the lord of earth, as even a great favour (done to her) (20). He also, that supporter of the earth, the son of Uttānapāda with his mind burning with the pain of his love for her did not take a second wife (21). And he thought of her, of most lovely limbs, without break day and night, and performed the works of his kingdom according to the law as prescribed for the government of subjects (22). To him governing (his subjects) even as father his self-begotten sons, came a Brāhman, in a painful state of the mind, and said this (23).

THE BRAHMANA said :—O great king, hear me speak, I am in great distress. The distress of men is not remedied by any one else except the king (24). My wife has been stolen by some one when I was asleep at night, with the door of my house not bolted. Thou shouldst bring her back to me) (25).

THE KING said :—O thou twice-born one, thou dost not know by whom she has been stolen, or where she has been taken, then for whose punishment shall I exert myself, or whence shall I bring her (26).

THE BRAHMANA said :—O lord of the earth, if the wife, of a man sleeping with the doors closed, be stolen, by whom and why (has she been stolen) should be found out by thee (27). Thou, O lord of men,—who takest the sixth part of our produce) as thy remuneration, art the protector of the law, therefore the sons of Manu (*i. e.* men) sleep fearlessly at night (28).

THE KING said :—Thy wife has not been seen by me; of what form is she physically, what also is her age, tell me, as also what is the character of thy Brāhmani (29).

BRAHMANA :—Of hard eyes is she, and exceedingly tall, and of short arm, and shrunken face; she is very ugly, O lord of the earth, I don't speak ill of her, she is really such (30). In words she is, O king, exceedingly harsh, and by character she is not amiable. Thus is my wife described by me, she is in form exceedingly unpleasing to the sight (31). O king, her first youth has jused passed,—of such a description is my wife; this is the truth spoken by me (32).

THE KING said :—No need hast thou, O Brāhman, of her. I shall give thee another wife. A lovely wife becomes a cause of happiness, one like her is only a cause of pain (33). Beauty and good character becomes a cause, O Brāhman, of happiness; for that reason she, who is without character, is to be forsaken (34).

THE BRAHMANA said :—Is it not, Oh king, a good injunction of the scriptures, that the wife is to be protected, for on the wife of being protected the children are protected (35). On her is the self begotten, therefore, O lord of men, she is to be protected; on the children being protected self is protected (36). If she is not protected intercaste connections arise, and that brings down, O lord of the earth, the ancient forefathers from heaven to hell (37). Of me deprived of my wife, there will be daily violation of the sacrifical rites, and owing to the violation of daily sacrificial duties it will be for my fall (38). Of her, O preserver of the earth, will be born my children; and she will thus become the giver of the sixth part of the produce, and the cause of the maintenance of the Law (39). Therefore has my wife, who has been taken away, been thus described by me to thee, O Lord. Bring her, for by right art thou our protector (40).

MARKANDEYA said :—Hearing these words of his the lord of men, being somewhat displeased—ascended his great chariot supplied with all the necassaries (41). By him, wandering here and there about the earth, was seen in the great forest an excellent hermitage (42). This (king), getting down there (from the car) and entering (the hermitage), saw there the Muni sitting on the seat made of the *kusha* grass, which imparts vigour and energy, and as if burning by his effulgence (43). He, on seeing the king's approach, getting up with alacrity, and having honored him by saying—*Swagata* (welcome), asked his disciple to bring the offerings (due to a prince by visitors) (44). To him the disciple said in a low tone, "what offering is to be given him, O Muni! order me that after due deliberation; I shall do thy bidding (45)."

Then having known the story of that king the twice-born one, who has been established in his self, honoured him by a seat and words of welcome (46).

THE RISHI said:—For what object hast thou come? what is thy purpose? I know thee, king Uttama, the son of Uttānapāda (47).

THE KING said:—From a Brāhman's house his wife has been stolen by some one, O Muni, whose identification is unknown; looking for him have I come here (48). Therefore whatever I shall ask thee, O possesser of the six great virtues, (the *Bhagas*), that thou shouldst moved by mercy tell me, who am a guest in thy house, and am adoring thee (49).

THE RISHI said:—Ask what thou desirest to ask, O protector of the world, without any reserve or delicacy; if that may be spoken to you by me, I shall relate it truly to thee (50).

THE KING said:—That offering, O Muni, which on seeing me at first approach thy house, thou wert on the point of making me, why is that offering withheld (51)?

THE RISHI said:—When, O king, on seeing thee out of eagernesss and delight was this disciple ordered by me, then I was by him called back to my own consciousness (52). This disciple knows, through my favour even as I know myself, whatever is past or is present or has not come to pass in this world (53). On his saying "consider and oder" by me was also then every thing known, therefore I did not give you offerings according to the injunctions of the scriptures (54). Thou art, O king, truly deserving of offering being born in the race of Swāyambhuva; inspite of that we did not consider you as deserving of superior offerings (55).

THE KING said:—O Brāhman! what has been done by me either consciously or unconsciously, for which although coming here after a long time, I am not thought deserving of receiving due offerings from thee (56)?*

---

* The highest offering, that is fit to be given to a spiritual guide,

THE RISHI said:—Has it been forgotten by thee that thy wife has been sent by thee to the forest? With her, O king, have also all the sacrificial rites been forsaken by thee (57). Man becomes unworthy of being touched, by violation or neglect of the sacrificial rites for a fortnight, and the violation of thy daily sacrificial duties has extended over a year (58). As the wife must be favourably disposed towards the hasband if he be of bad character, similarly is the wife of bad character to be supported (by the husband), O lord of men (59). That wife of that Brāhmana who has been stolen, is against her husband, still that (Brāhmana), O king, desirous of merit, is anxious to regain her (60). O lord of the world, thou dost re-establish those that are fallen from their duties, in their respective functions, who else shall establish thee when thou art shaken from the law (61),

MARKANDEYA said:—That lord of the earth thus spoken to by that wise one, being ashamed, and saying "it is as thou sayest," asked of that twice-born one, about the stolen wife (62). O thou the possessor of the six great qualities, the *Bhagas*, by whom has that wife of the Brāhmana been taken, and where. The revered one knows truly that which has occurred and that which is yet to come in this world (63).

THE RISHI said;—The Rākshasa,, Valāka by name, the son of Adri has stolen her. O king, thou mayest see him this day in the forest of Utpalāvatam (64). Go, and do thou, with despatch, join that most excellent person among the twice-born with his wife; let him not go to the place of the sinners from day to day like their own self (65).

---

to the king, to the son-in-law, &c., consists of calf or cow, but the ancient authorities say that this offering is due to those guests who come at least after a year. Hence the king here mentions the length of time.

CHAPTER LXX.

MARKANDEYA said:—Then having saluted the great Muni, he got upon his own chariot, and by it he went to that forest known as Utpalāvatam (1). The lord of men then saw that wife of the twice-born one of the same description "as related by her husband, eating bael fruits (2). He asked, "Why, O good one, hast thou come to this forest, tell me distinctly; art thou the wife of Susharmā the son of Bishāla (3).

THE BRAHMANI said:—I am the daughter of the twice-born one, Atirātra, who lives in the forest; and the wife of the son of Bishāla whose name has been mentioned by thee (4). That am I who has been brought away by the Rākshasa Valāka of evil spirit, when I was asleep in my house, and have thus been separated from my brother and mother (5). May that Rākshasa be reduced to ashes by whom I am separated from mother, brother and others and am placed here in great misery (6). Brought by him I have been left in this dense forest; I do not know the reason, why he neither enjoys nor eats me up (7)?

THE KING said:—Dost thou know where the Rākshasa has gone after leaving thee here? O thou daughter of twice-born parents, I have been sent here by thy husband (8).

THE BRAHMANI said:—That rover in the night exists even in the borders of this forest: enter and see him, if thou art not afraid of him (9).

MARKANDEYA said:—Then he entered from there, by the road pointed out by her, and saw the Rākshasa surrounded by his family (10). Then immediately on seeing him that Rākshasa made haste to touch the ground with his head from a distance, and went near his feet (11).

THE RAKSHASA said:—By thee coming here to my house

has great favour been done to me. Be gracious, tell me what may I do for thee, I live in thy kingdom (12). Accept this offering, take this seat, we are servants, thou the lord, order me firmly (13).

THE KING said:—By thee have all the rites due to a guest been fully performed. Why has the wife of the Brahman been brought by thee, O thou rover in the night? This one is not beautiful, of excellent limbs, that she has been stoten by thee for making her thy wife. If brought for eating why has not she been eaten by thee, tell me this (14—15).

THE RAKSHASA said:—We are not cannibals, O king, they are other Rákshasas. We eat that, O king, which is the fruit of our merit (16). We eat the character of men and women when insulted or honoured (by them), but are not eaters of animals (17). Therefore when men's power of forbearance is eaten by us they become subject to anger; and on their bad disposition being eaten up, they become full of good qualities (18). We have females who please us, O king, equal in beauty to Apsarās, and when these Rāksasis exist what cause is there for our becoming attached to women? (19).

THE KING said:—If this woman, O thou night-walker, is is not meant for enjoyment nor for food then why has she been stolen by thee, entering into the Brāhman's house? (20).

THE RAKSHASA said:—O king, that superior person, among the twice-born, is well versed in spells; and by reading spells for the destruction of Rākshasas he expels me from every sacrifice where I go (21). We suffer from hunger by his reading the spells for the expulsion (of the Rākshasas); where shall we go, that twice-born one becomes the priest in all the sacrifices (22). Therefore has this disqualification of him been worked by us; in the absence of their wives, men become unfitted for the performance of sacrificial rites (23).

MARKANDEYA said:—Then that king, on the fact of the disqualification of the high-souled Brahman, being related (to him) became exceedingly sad (24). By speaking of the disqualification of the Brāhmana, he is condemning even me; that most superior Muni also said that I was not competent to receive offering due to a guest (of my position) (25). The disqualification of that Brahmana, as also of mine, is spoken of by the Rākshasa. Such am I, who owing to want of wife, have come to this great difficulty (26),

MARKANDEYA Said:—O Muni! to the king thus meditating, the Rākshasa, saluting low, and with his hands joined said once more (27).

THE RAKSHASA said:—O lord of men, by ordering me as to what I should do, favour me, who am thy servant, and obedient to thee, and who live in thy kingdom (28).

THE KING said:—This which has been spoken by thee, O thou night-walker,—that we eat the characters of men,—even that do we desire (of thee), hear from me of the work by which thou mayst (fulfil my wishes) (29). By thee to-day is the bad character of this Brāhmani to be eaten; so that with her bad character eaten up by thee, she may become mild of disposition; (30). And by thee, should she be taken to his house, O thou night-walker, whose wife she is. On thy doing this, every thing (needful) will be done to me who have come (as a guest) to thy house (31).

MARKANDEYA said:—Then that Rākshasa, by force of his own occult powers having entered into that woman, ate up her evil disposition by his own powers, in accordance with the command of the king (32). That wife, of that twice-born one thus relieved of her exceedingly fierce evil disposition, told that lord of the world (33). "By virtue of my own works have I been separated from that great-souled one, my lord, this Rākshasa was only an instrument (in the hands of Providence) (34). This is not the fault of this one (*i.e.* the Rākshasa; nor of him, my high-souled husband; it is my fault, not of others. People always enjoy the fruits of their actions (35). In a privious birth separation of some woman (from her husband) had been worked by me. That has come to me also. What fault is there (for this) of this high-souled one (36).

THE RAKSHASA said :—Lord, I shall, in accordance with thy command, take this (woman) to the house of her lord. Command me, O king, what also is to be done by me (37).

THE KING said :—O thou rover in the night, on thy doing this everything will be done to me. Thou, O brave one, wilt come to me, whenever, I may remember thee, for the performance of any work (38).

MARKANDEYA said :—Then, "So be it"—saying this, that Rākshasa taking that twice-born woman, who had become pure through removal of her evil disposition, conveyed her to her husband's house (39).

—oo—

CHAPTER LXXI.

MARKANDEYA said —Having sent that woman to the house of her husband, the king also began to think, sighing, "what shall be good for me under these circumstances (1). That high-minded (Rishi) spoke to me of my pain for my unworthiness to receive the offerings meet for a guest (of my position); and this night-walker spoke of my disqualification, referring to the case of the Brāhmana (2). Such am I, what shall I do? That wife of mine has been forsaken by me. Or shall I ask that most superior Muni possessed with an illumined vision (3)? Thus meditating, that lord, of the earth getting into that chariot of his, went there where the righteous great Muni who knows the three periods of time (*i.e.* the past, the present, and the future) lived (4). Getting down from the chariot, he then approaching him and making due obeisance, related his interview with the Rākshasa exactly as it happened (5), and similarly his interview with the wife of the Brāhmana, and her cure of her evil disposition, and also her despatch to her husband's house, and that which was the object of his visit (6).

THE RISHI said :—That which has been done by thee, O Lord of men, as also the object of thy coming to me, all this was already known by me (7). Ask me now,—what is to be done by me, I am anxious in mind, on thy coming to me. Hear that which is to be done by thee, O lord of earth (8). The wife is the most powerful incentive of men to the observance of the law and the attainment of merit; especially is the law forsaken on her being forsaken (9). The wifeless man, O king, is not entitled to perform his sacrificial duties, be he, O king, a Brāhmana, Kshatriya or Vaishya. In forsaking thy wife thou hast not done a graceful act; for even as wives cannot desert their husbands, so too men cannot forsake their wives (11).

THE KING said :—O thou possesser of six great qualities the *Bhagas*, what shall I do? This is the result of my actions. Because she was not favourably disposed towards me who was always lovingly inclined towards her, therefore, has she been forsaken by me (12). Whatever she did I forbore all that with a burning heart, O possesser of the six great qualities, with my mind always afraid of the pain of her separation (13). Now that she has been left in the forest I know not where she has gone, or whether she has been eaten in the jungle by lions or tigers or Rakshasas (14).

THE RISHI said :—She has not been eaten, O lord of the earth, by the lion or tiger or Rākshasa, she is now living in the lower region with her character unsullied (15).

THE RISHI said:—The king of serpents, known as Kapotaka, lives in the nether regions; that beautiful young lady, forsaken by thee, and roving about in that great forest was seen by him, who knew her story, and was moved by love towards her,—and taken to the nether regions (16—18). His daughter with beautiful eye-brows was Nanda by name, O lord of the world, and the wife of this king of the serpents, possessed of intelligence, was Manoramā, by name (19). This beautiful (lady) will become the co-wife of my mother,—(she thought), and seen by her, she was taken to her own house and artfully concealed in the female appartment (20). When besought, Nandā did not reply to the king; then the father told that daughter "thou shalt be dumb" (21). Thus was his daughter cursed by him, and she, the chaste one, (thy wife) O lord of the earth! captured and taken by that lord of the serpents, lives there (now) (22).

MARKANDEYA said:—Then the king overcome with great joy asked him the most superior among the twice-born the cause of his misfortune so far as his wife was concerned (23).

THE KING said:—O thou possessor of the six great qualities, the *Bhagas*, the affection of the whole world towards me is very great. What then is the cause, for which my own wife is not overhanging towards me (24). O thou great Muni, my love towards her is very great, even more than that towards my own life, but she is ill-disposed towards me, tell me the cause of it, O thou twice-born one (25).

THE RISHI said:—At the time of taking her hand (*i.e.* thy marriage) thou wert looked upon by the Sun, the Venus, and the Saturn, and thy wife by the Mercury, and the Jupiter (26). At that moment the moon became hers, while similarly the son of the moon became yours, these two are mutually opposed; therefore, O king, is thy misfortune (27) Therefore go and govern the earth according to the injunctions of thy order and class; taking thy wife as thy helpmate perform all sacrificial and other religious duties (28).

MARKANDEYA said:—Being thus spoken to, Uttama, the governor of the earth, having saluted this (Brāhman) and then getting upon his chariot, went to his own city (29).

CHAPTER LXXII.

MARKANDEYA said:—Then having found his own city the king saw that twice-born one with his wife who had attained an excellent disposition, and was full of delight (1).

THE BRAHMANA said:—O thou most superior king, I am gratified, for the law is maintained unto me by thee who knowest the law and who brought my wife to me (2).

THE KING said:—Thou art gratified, O most superior among twice-born persons, owing to the due observance of the law of my order, but we, O Brāhmana, whose wife is not in the house, are in a most painful situation (3).

THE BRAHMANA said:—If she has been, O Lord of men, eaten up by wild animals in the woods, what can be done by her. Why there is not the hand of some other (maiden) taken by thee (in marriage). Owing to thy subjection to anger the law is not being observed by thee (4).

THE KING said:—My love has not been devoured by wild animals: she lives, in truth, with unblemished character. What shall I do now (5)?

THE BRAHMANA said:—If thy wife lives and is not attached to any other person then why is the sin, caused by the absence of the wife, committed by thee (6).

THE KING said:—Even if brought she will always, O Brahmana, be opposed to me, she is only for my sorrow and not for my happiness—she has no love for me. Do thou so try that she may be subject to me (7).

THE BRAHMANA said :—For her love towards thee, I shall perform that sacrifice, called ***Mitravinda,*** which great and beneficial sacrifice is performed by those who desire love (8). That sacrifice is the worker of superior love among husband and wife who are not loved by each other. For thy benefit I shall perform that sacrifice (9). O Lord of the earth, bring her, thy wife, of beautiful eye-brows, from where she exists; she will give thee most superior happiness (10).

MARKANDEYA said :—Being thus spoken to, he, the lord of the world, brought the endless objects (needful for the sacrifice) and he, that most superior Bráhmin also performed that sacrifice—(*yajna*) (11). With a view to work up the wife of that king, that superior person among the twice-born, again and again performed that sacrifice seven times (12). When that great Muni felt that the love of her (the queen) had been fully established on her own husband, then that Brāhmana told the lord of men (13). "O thou most superior among men, bring her, who is the object of thy love, near thee; and enjoy the objects of pleasure with her, and perform sacrifices likewise being honoured (by her) (14).

MARKANDEYA said :—Being thus spoken to, by that Brāhmana, the ruler of the world, at that time, overcome with wonder, then remembered that Rakshasa of great energy and steadfast resolution (15). O great Muni, remembered by him at that time, that (Rakshasa), immediately approaching the lord of men, after salutation said,—"What may I do" (16)? Then having been informed in detail by that lord of men, going to the nether regions and securing the wife of the king, he came back to him (17). Thus brought she beheld then her lord with great love, and said again and again, being full of delight—"Be gracious" (18). Then that king embracing that honoured one with great eagerness exclaimed—"I am always gracious to thee, my love, why then dost thou say so again" (19).

THE WIFE said.—If thy mind is exceedingly gracious towards me, O lord of men, then I beg this of thee, "do thou do this which is the object of my worship" (20).

THE KING said:—Tell me without fear, whatever is desired by thee of me,—that will not be unattainable, O thou timid one; there is no doubt of it, that I am under thy control (21).

THE WIFE said:—For my sake by that serpent has his daughter, my friend, been cursed—saying,—"thou shalt be dumb," and she too has come by dumbness (22). If thou canst effect a remedy of her, for the removal of her dumbness, moved by thy love for me, what great good wilt thou then do unto me (23).

MARKANDEYA said:—Then that king asked that Brāhmana "under the circumstance what kind of work (sacrifice) is to be performed for the remedy of that dumbness," and he also said that to the king (24).

THE BRAHMANA said:—In obedience to thy order, O lord of the earth, I shall perform the *Saraswati* sacrifice and owing to the setting in of the power of speech of Nandā this thy wife shall be released of her debt (of gratitude (25).

MARKANDEYA said:—That most superior, among twice-born persons for that object, performed the sacrifice called *Saraswati* and with concentrated mind repeated the *Saraswati Suktas* (26). Then Garga told her, whose power of speech had began to work, in the nether world, "this good, very hard to work, has been done thee, by the husband of thy friend" (27). Coming by this knowledge, Nandā, the self begotten daughter of the serpent, having quickly found that city and then having embraced her friend the queen, and having also done honour to that ruler of the earth, and having repeatedly uttered benedictions (on them),—the serpent woman taking her seat spoke (thus) sweetly (28—29). "By the good that has just been done to me by thee, O brave one! my heart has been drawn to thee. Hear what I speak (30). O thou lord of men, thou shalt have a son endowed with great energy, on this earth; his arms shall be invincible (31). He shall know the meaning and significance of all scriptures and shall be devoted to the law and the sacrifices; that intelligent one shall be a Manu, the lord of *Manwantara*" (32). Thus having uttered this blessing on him, the daughter of the king of serpents, O Muni, after embracing her friend duly went away to the nether regions (33). There a long period passed of that king enjoying life with her (the queen) and governing his subjects (34). Then a son was born of that high-souled king unto her, just as the full-diced and beautiful moon appears on the full moon night (35). On the birth of that high-souled one all the people found great delight and the flutes of the Gods were played and flowers fell in a shower (36). Munis, having come (to see him) and seeing the loveliness of his limbs, and his future character, gave him the name—Auttama (37). 'This one is born in a good family, similarly in a good time, and unto Uttama, and is of a good form, therefore he shall be Auttama' (38).

MARKANDEYA said:—Then this one, the son of Uttama, and similarly known by the name of Auttama, became Manu; hear of his prowess from me (39). Whoever, that hears daily the whole of the story of Uttama,and that of birth of Auttama, shall never become the object of men's ill-will (40). Of him who shall hear or read these, there shall never be any separation with objects of his desires or wives, or sons, or friends (41). Hear, O Brāhman, of his *Manwantara*, from me as also of him who is the Indra (in that *Manwantara*) and who are the Gods and who are Rishis (42).

CHAPTER LXXIII.

MARKANDEYA said :—Listen to me who am relating (to you) the gods, the lord of the gods, the Rishis, and the kings in this *Manwantara*, the third one, of the Auttama (*Manu*) (1). The gods were *Swadhámás*, they whose works imitated their names; (*i.e.*, whose conduct bore testimony to the truth of their names) and a second class named *Satyas* were similarly of the species of the celestials; and also a third class, similarly of the species of the gods, were O most superior Muni, called *Shivas*; they were of the nature of Shiva himself, and were reputed to have been the destroyers of sin (2—3). And a fourth class of the species of the gods, O thou superior Muni, named *Pratardaas*, are also spoken of in connection with the *Manwantara* of the Manu Auttama (4). A fifth class there was also in that (*Manwantara*), O thou twice-born one, of the species of the gods, (called) the *Bashabartinas*; and all these, O great Muni! were of the nature indicated by their names (5). These are known to have been the five classes of gods, all eaters of sacrifices, in this *Manwantara*, O thou most superior among men; all these were the twelve species of gods (6). Their lord, the possessor of the eight good qualities of kindness and known by the name of Sushānti, having gathered together the hundred sacrifices, became the lord in the three worlds (7). Hymns adorned with the letters of their name are sung by men in this earth, even to this day, for the cure of diseases (8). The lovely lord of the gods was Sushānti, with the gods *Shivas, Satyas* and others and similarly *Bashabartins* (9). Of that Manu there were sons, strong and powerful and famous like the gods,—namely, Aja, Parashuchi, and Divya (10). As long as the *Manwantara* of that most energetic Manu lasted his offsprings, being lords of men, governed the whole world (11). The seven sons of that great souled one, who was the most superior person among men by their own energy born of penance, became, in that *Manwantara* the seven principal Rishis (12), This is the third *Manwantara*, now related to you by me; the Tamasā is said to be the fourth *Manwantara* (13). O Brāhman, hear from we who will relate to you (presently) the birth of that Manu, by whose fame, though he was born of a low caste mother, the whole world was illumined (14). The character of the others as well as of his, and likewise his birth, and the influence of these high-souled ones should be known as beyond the comprehension of the senses (15).

CHAPTER LXXIV.

MARKANDEYA said :—There was on earth a king Swarastra by name, famous, and full of energy, the performer of many sacrifices, wise, and unconquerable in battle (1). Worshipped by his councillor the sun-god gave him long life, and O thou twice-born one, his wives were a hundred in number (2). Of him, the long-lived one, the wives were not long-lived, O Muni! and in time the servants and the councillors similarly all were dead (3). In this way separated from his wives as also from his attendants who were born with him, being restless in mind he began to lose his energy day by day (4). Then at that time, (a king) by name Bimardda deposed him from his kingdom,—who had lost his vigour and was sad, having been forsaken by most intimate attendants (5). He, the possesser of the eight good qualities, deposed from his kingdom, with his mind bowed down by sorrow and bereavement, going to the forest, and living on the banks of the river Vitastā, practised penances (6). He practised the penance of the five fires in summer, and got himself wetted in the waters of the clouds during the rains, and lying in water during winter, he lived without food, taking the vow of self-control (7). Then while he was thus practising the penances, during one rainy season, there was a great deluge owing to an incessant down-pour from the clouds (8). The quarters could not be distinguished, neither the east, nor the south nor the west, nor the north; everything seemed to be covered with darkness (9). Then owing to the great deluge that king was carried away by the extremely rapid current of the river, and though praying for rescue he did not find its banks (10). Next the lord of the earth, carried to a long distance by the current of water, came across a deer in that water; and he caught her by the tail (11). By that craft (of a tail) was he conducted here and there, in that darkness, on this earth, and at last he found land (12). Having crossed extensive and deep sloughs, pulled by that deer, that king found another pleasant forest (13). In that darkness did the deer draw the lord of the world attached to her tail, and grown lean (and weak) by cruel austerities (14). Walking about again and again in that darkness, his mind being moved by passion, he found great pleasure in her touch (15). In that forest knowing that lord of men full of love (towards her) and engaged in touching her back, that deer (thus) spoke to him (16). "Why dost thou touch my back with trembling hands, O lord of men? This action has taken a contrary course (17). Thy mind, O lord, is not set on an unworthy object; thy connection with me is not forbidden—but this Lola stands in the way of my union with thee (18).

MARKANDEYA said:—Hearing this speech of that deer the lord of the world, moved by curiosity, spoke this word to the deer (19).

THE KING said:—Tell me who thou art, O deer, and how dost thou speak like a human being and who again is this Lola who stands as an obstacle to thy connection with me (20).

THE DEER said:—I am, O king, thy wife, known before as Utpalāvati, the chief queen among a hundred wives, and the daughter of Dridadhana (21),

THE KING said:—But what didst thou do by which thou hast found this birth. Why has she, who was devoted to her husband, and assiduous in the observance of the law, come by such a state (22).

THE DEER said:—In my fathers's house, as a maiden, I went with my friends and companious to the forest for a pleasure-walk, and there saw a he-deer united with a female-deer (23). Then by me, who went near, was the female deer driven away and through fear of me she went to another place; then the male deer being angry said (24). "Thou fool, why hast thou become so mad; fie to thy evil disposition, by which is this my union frustrated i (25)." Hearing his word, who was speaking like a human being over-taken with with fear I told him this—"who art thou that hast attained this birth (26). Then he said:—" I am the son of the Rishi Nribrittichakshu, Sutapā by name; being moved by desire for this female deer, I have become a deer; (27). And become subject to her through love, I was also desired by her in this forest; but O evil one, we are separated by thee; therefore shall I curse thee (28)." By me was also spoken this:—"O Muni, through ignoronce I have offended thee; be gracious to me, it is not meet, O respected one, that thou shouldst curse me (29)." Thus being spoken to, O lord of the earth, that Muni also told me this:—"I will not curse thee, if I may give myself to thee (30)." By me was also spoken (this) —"I am not a female deer, thou who art of the form of a deer shalt find another female deer in the forest; therefore control thy passion for me (31)." Being thus spoken to, he said, with his eyes becoming blood shot through anger, and his lips trembling, "I am not a female deer," by thee has this been spoken; thou, fool, shalt become a female deer (32). Then being extremely pained I told the Muni, who, though he had been exceedingly angry, was now fully composed, again and again after salutation,—"be gracious to me! (33). I am a mere girl, inexperienced in (the use of) words, therefore has this been spoken by me; in the absence of the father alone is the husband accepted by the maidens themselves (34). O most excellent Muni, when my father exists, how can I accept (thee); or even if I am guilty, be gracious to me, O lord, I salute thee (35)." O thou high-souled one! to her who was saying—be gracious, be gracious, after salulation, that most superior Muni said this (36). "The word spoken by me shall never be otherwise; thou, being dead, shalt surely become a female deer even in this forest, in the next birth (37). In thy state as deer will the son of the Muni Siddhabirya, O thou lovely one! Lola by name, mighty of arm, find thy womb (*i.e.*, will be born of thee) (38). Thou shalt regain thy memory of thy former birth, on that pregnancy occurring to thee, and finding thy lost memory, thou shalt speak in the tongue of men (39). At his birth, being liberated from the state of the deer, and honoured by thy husband, thou shalt gain those *lokas* which are not attainable by the workers of iniquity (40). That Lola also, mighty of energy, having killed his father's enemies and conquered the entire world, shall at last become *Manu* (41)." Being thus cursed, and attaining the state of the beast after death, by thy touch is this fætus born in my womb (42). Therefore I say that thy mind, set on me, has not been misplaced, nor am I beyond the range of thy lawful love, but this Lola in my womb has created an obstacle (43).

MARKANDEYA said:—Then being thus spoken to that king also found supreme delight (in the thought) that my son having conquered my enemies shall be a *Manu* on earth (44). Then that female deer brought forth that son endowed with all good signs, and at his birth all beings found delight (45). More particularly this king, on the birth of this son, mighty of strength, found great delight, and that female deer, released from the curse, found most excellent *lokas* (46). Then, O most excellent Muni! all the Rishis coming to him, and seeing his future glory, gave a name to that high-souled one (47). He is born of a mother who found a *Tamasa* birth, and the world also is covered by *Tama* therefore this one will be (known as) *Tamasa* (48). Then that Tamasa, nursed by that father in the forest, when his intelligence grew, spoke this to the father, O most excellent Muni! (49). "Who art thou father, and how am I thy son, who is also my mother, and why hast thou come (here) tell me this in truth (50)."

MARKANDEYA said:—Then the father, the lord of the world, mighty of arm, related to that son all that happened commencing with his deprivation of his own kingdom (51). Having heard all this, he, also after worshipping the sun, found in all fullness divine and fatal arms (52). Thus being an adept in arms, having conquered the enemies and brought them to the father, by him, established in the observance of the duties of his station, were they released, according to the order of the father (53.) His father also, having found the happiness caused by the sight of the son's face, separated from the body found the *lokas* earned by penances and sacrifices (54). Having conquered all the world that king, called Tamasa, became the *Manu* called Tamasa; hear of his *Manwantara* from me (55), of all those who were the gods, and who was the lord—the king of the gods, as also who were the Rishis, and those who were the sons of that *Manu*,—the rulers of the earth (56). O Muni, the Satyas and similarly others the Siddhis, the Surupās, and likewise the Haris, these were the twenty-seven classes of gods in that (*Manwantara*) (57). Similarly the lord of those gods was the Lord Shikhi, mighty of strength and energy, and joined to a hundred sacrifices (58). O Brâhman, Jyotirdhâma, Pritha, Kâvya, Chaitra, Agni, Balaka and Pivara, these seven were the seven leading Rishis (59). The kings exceedingly powerful,—Nara, Kshânti, Skanda, Dânta, Jangha &c., were likewise the sons, of Tamasa (60).

CHAPTER LXXV.

MARKANDEYA said:—The Fifth Manu is spoken of as Raivata, O Brâhman: hear of his birth in detail, I shall relate it to you (1). O thou possesser of the eight good qualities of kindness, &c., there was a Rishi known as Ritâvak; of him the high-souled one, who was sonless, was born a son in the (sign of the) star Revati (2). He performed according to the law all his sacraments commencing with that of *Jatakarma* (or the birth ceremony) and likewise *Upanayana*, and he too, O Muni became a bad character (3). From the time when this one was born that Rishi, the most superior among Munis, was overtaken by a lingering and enduring disease (4). His mother, laid up with leprosy and other diseases, was subjected to extreme suffering, and his father being sad thus thought (within himself) (5). "What is this?" And then that exceedingly evil-minded son of his took away the wife of another Muni's son who was attached to him (6). Then Ritavâka uttered with a heavy mind:—"Sonlessness of men is better than the possesson of bad sons (7). A bad son always causes pain to the heart of the father and of the mother, and brings down (to the lower regions) his ancestors stationed in heaven (8). He is of no good to friends, nor of any satisfaction to the manes; he is a source of misery to his father; the birth of such an evil-doer is to be lamented (9). Blessed are they whose sons are after the mind of all the world, the workers of good unto men and of a quiet disposition, and devoted to virtuous works (10). Our life is unhappy, and bad, and not tending towards the next world, but tending towards hell, and not heaven, owing to its connection with an evil son (11). He causes humiliation to friends, and glorification to those who wish us ill, and also brings on old age and infirmity on the father before his time; a bad son surely does all this (12)."

MARKANDEYA said:—That Muni, with his heart burnt by the conduct of this bad son, asked Garga the cause of all this) (13).

RITAVAK said:—By me were the Vedas of old duly learnt from Subrata; having finished (the study of) the Vedas, I took unto me a wife in accordance with the injunctions of the law (14). And by me have all sacrificial works, works, that are ordained in the *Sranta Sutras*, as also those by the *Smritis*, as also the sacrifices to fire,—been performed with my wife (as help mate); O great Muni! none of my works has been imperfectly done till now (15). According to the law of producing progeny, not under the influence of lust but for the sake of a son, has this one been begotten by me, who was afraid of (the hell) called Put (16). Such is this one (my son); O Muni, is it for his own fault, or through any guilt of mine, that he has become the source of misery to us and the giver of pain to my friends by his bad character (17).

GARGA said:—O most superior Muni, this thy son is born within the sphere of the star Revati; therefore has he become a source of thy misery, for he is born in an evil time (18). There is no wrong due to thee, or to his mother, or to thy family; the cause of his evil disposition is his coming to this world within the sphere of the star Revati (19)

RITAVAK said :—As this evil disposition of my only son is due to the influence of the star Revati, may that Revati therefore even fall (from her orbit) (20).

MARKANDEYA said :—In this way on the curse being uttered by him, the star Revati fell (from her orbit) in the presence of all the world whose hearts were over-powered by wonder (21). The Revati star also fell on all sides of the mountain Kumuda, all of a sudden illumined the forests, the caves and the streamlets (22). On account of that fall the mountain Kumuda also became known as Raivataka, the most pleasant mountain on all the earth (23). The loveliness that was of that star became the lake Pankajini :—from it was born then a maiden most charming on account of her beauty (24). O Bhagura! seeing that maiden, born of the loveliness of Revati, the Muni Pramucha gave her the name of Revati (25). That possesser of the eight good qualities of kindness, &c., Pramucha, even in this great mountain, brought up this girl born in the vicinity of his own hermitage (26). That Muni, seeing that maiden endowed with great beauty, come to youth, thought (within himself) who shall be the lord of this (girl)? (27). O Muni! Thinking in this way a long time elapsed, and yet the great Muni did not come across a bridegroom worthy of her (28). Then to enquire of the god of fire about her bridegroom that Muni Pramucha entered the place of sacrificial fire, and to him thus questioning the eater of sacrificial offerings (*i. e.*, the god of fire) said (29). 'The lord, of the earth, Durgama by name, mighty of strength and energy, of pleasant speech and devoted to the law, shall become the husband of this one" (30).

MARKANDEYA said :—Afterwards, O Muni, that lord of men, the wise Durgama, born of the race of Priyavrata, and mighty of strength and valour, the son of Vikramashila, born in the womb of Kâlindi, came, in course of a hunting expedition, to his hermitage (31—32). That lord of the earth, entering the hermitage and seeing her of slender limbs, calling her as his dear one, asked about that Rishi (33).

THE KING said:—Where has the most superior Mun the possessor of the six great qualities, the *Bhagas*, gone from this hermitage; I desire to salute him here, therefore tell me this, O thou graceful one (34).

MARKANDEYA said:—The Brahmin, who had gone to the place of the sacrificial fires, hearing those his words, as also his addressing her as the dear one, came out in haste (35). That Muni saw the great-souled king, possessed of all the signs of the lord of men, and bending before him in reverence (36). One seeing him then he addressed his disciple Gautama thus—"Gautama, bring soon due offerings for this lord of the world (37). On the one hand this one is a king come after a long time, on the other hand he is my son-in-law, therefore it is my opinion that he is worthy of especial offerings (38).

MARKANDEYA said:—Then that king began to think upon the cause of his being (spoken of as) the son-in-law, and could not decide it; therefore the king accepted that offering in silence (39). The great Muni welcomed that lord of kings, who had taken his seat and had accepted the offering and said:—"Is everything well with thy home, (40), O lord of men, with thy treasury, with thy army, with thy friends and feudatories, thy servants and courtiers and likewise with thy ownself on which are all these established (41). Thy wife also is well; I do not ask therefore of her, who lives here; are thy other wives well (42)?

THE KING said:—O thou of good vows! through thy mercy there is no bad news concerning any one belonging to me. But I am curious, O Muni, to know who is here my wife (43).

THE RISHI said:—That excellent woman Revati, the possessor of the six good qualities, and who is most beautiful in all the three worlds, is thy wife ; dost thou not know her, O king? (44).

THE KING said:—Subhadrā, the daughter of Shāntā, the daughter of Kaberi, O lord, and also Sujāta the daughter of Surashtra, and Kadamva the daughter of Barutha, Bipāthā, and also Nandini, I know as my wives living in my home, O thou twice-born one. O thou possessor of the six great qualities, the *Bhagas*, I do not know who this Revati is (45—46).

THE RISHI said:—That one of superior colour who has just been spoken to by thee as the dear ene, O lord of earth, has this wife of thine, worthy of all praise, been forgotten by thee? (47).

THE KING said:—Truly has this been spoken by me, but O Muni, my motive was not bad. In this case it is not meet that thou, O revered one, should be angry with me—I beseech thee for it (48).

THE RISHI said:—Thou sayest truly, O lord of earth, thy meaning is not evil ; O lord of men, thou didst say this moved by the god of fire (49). The great god of fire (lit, the carrier of the sacrificial offerings) having been asked by me as—who shall be the husband of this one, by him was it said even this day that thou, O revered one, shalt be (her husband) (50). Therefore accept, O lord of men, this maiden given unto thee by me. She has also been addressed by thee as the dear one, then why dost thou hesitate? (lit think of it in thy mind) (51).

MARKANDEYA said:—Then this lord of the earth, being thus spoken to by him, became speechless ; the Rishi also made himself ready to perform her marriage rites (52). That maiden, with her face cast down by modesty, spoke a few words to him, her father, who was making preparations for the marrfage (53). "Father if thou art full of love for me then it is meet that thou shouldst show me this favour that being gracious towards me thou shalt perform my marriage at the time of the star Revati (54).

THE RISHI said:—The star Revati, existing in conjunction with the moon; exists not, O thou good one! There are other stars, O thou whose eye brows are excellent, fit (to preside over) thy marriage (55).

THE MAIDEN said:—"It seems to me, father, that without him, the time of my marriage shall be fruitless. How shall the marriage of one like myself be performed at a fruitless time" (56). The performer of penances, well known by the name of Ritavāk, became angry with Revati, and by him thus angry was the star destroyed (57). And by me also has it been promised to this one that this one, with intoxicating glance, shall be thy wife. If thou dost not desire marriage, a great difficulty has presented itself to me (58).

THE MAIDEN said:—What penances have been practised by that Muni Ritavak, such as have not been practised by thee, my father? Am I then the daughter of an inferior Brāhmana? (59).

THE RISHI said:—Thou art not, my girl, the daughter of an inferior Brāhmana, nor even of the performers of penances; thou art my daughter, who is capable of creating other gods (60).

The MAIDEN said:—If my father be one who has attained the virtues of penance, then why is not marriage performed in that star, having previously set it in the bright firmament (61).

THE RISHI said:—So be it then for thy good, O thou good one—Be pleased, for thy sake I shall again establish the star Revati on the orbit of the moon (62).

MARKANDEYA said:—Then O thou superior Brāhmana, by the power of his penances the great Muni made the star Revati, as before, joined with the moon (63). And having performed the marriage of the daughter, according to the law, and to the accompaniment of sacred formulas, being filled with delight he again thus spoke to the son-in-law (64). "O governor of the earth, say, what shall I give thee as thy marriage present; I shall give thee even things that are most hard to get; the power of my penances is invincible" (65).

THE KING said:—I am born of the descendants of the Swayambhuva Manu, O Muni; I pray that I may have, by thy favour, a son who shall be the lord of the *Manwantara* (66).

THE RISHI said:—This thy desire shall come to pass. Thy son, O ruler of the world, shall be Manu and shall enjoy all the earth, and shall also be righteous.

MARKANDEYA said:—Then taking her the king went to his own city; and from her, Revati, was born a son, the Manu Revati (68). He was invested with all the virtues, and was unconquerable by men, and knew all the sciences, and was versed in the knowledge of the meaning of the Vedas and other scriptures (69). Hear with undivided attention, O Brāhman, O Muni, from me relating the gods, the lord of the gods, the earthly kings, &c., (70). O thou twice-born one, in that (*Manwantara*) the Sumedhas, the Bhupatis, the Vaikuntas, the Amitābhas, were the gods, each divided into fourteen classes (71). The lord of these four classes, Bibhu, by name, was the enjoyer of a hundred sacrifice (72). In the *Manwantara* of the Manu Revata Hiranyaromā, Vedasri, Urdhavāhu, similarly others,—Vedavāhu, Sudhāmā, and also Parjjanya, the great Muni Vashista, the possesser of the six good qualities of kindness, &c., and who had gone to the utmost limits of the Vedas and the Vedantas these were the seven primal Rishis (74). Balabandhu, Mahabirya, Suyastavya, and likewise others, Satyaka, &c., were the sons of the Manu Revata (75). The Manus, ending with Revata, who have been related to you by me, are all, with the exception of the Manu Swarochisha, the descendants of Swayambhuva Manu (76).

CHAPTER LXXVI.

MARKANDEYA :—Thus have the five *Manwantaras* been described to you by me. Hear next of the sixth, belonging to Chākshusha (1). In the previous birth this one was born of the eye of Paramesti, therefore, O thou twice-born one, even in this birth his name became Chākshusha (2). The wife of the high-souled *Rajarshi* (the princely Rishi) *Anamitra* bore a son, learned, and pure, and possessed of the recollections of all former births, and powerful (3). At his birth his mother embraced him with love, lying on her lap, loudly expressing her joy, and again and again did she so (4). He was born endowed with the knowledge of former births, therefore lying on the mother's lap he laughed; at this the mother becoming angry spoke these words (5). "I am overtaken by fear. What is this my child? There is smile on thy face—thy intelligence is born prematurely. Dost thou see any happy augury? (6)."

THE SON said:—Dost thou not see that this female cat before thee is willing to eat me; and the secend one (wishing to eat me) is this Jātahārini, who is out of thy sight (7). Because moved by the love of thy son, thou, O revered one, art beholding me with affection, and by crying aloud art embracing me many times, from which arises rapture (in thee) and thy sight is filled with tears born of love,—therefore has this smile come to (my lips); hear also its reason (8—9). Drawn by selfishness this female cat is longingly looking at me; and similarly the other one the Jātaharini, who is out of sight (10). Just as these two are devoted to me with tender hearts from selfishness similarly thou too also art moved by selfishness, so it seems to me (11). But while the female cat and Jātahārini are bent upon enjoying me (immediately) thou desirest such fruits of me as thou mayst enjoy gradully in time (12). Thou dost not know me,—who this one is; nor hast thou been benefitted by me, our association is not of long, only of five or seven days (13). Still thou lovest me, embracest me with tears, and dost address me with such words as father, son, the good one, &c.

THE MOTHER said:—Not for any benefit, O beloved one, do I embrace thee with love. If this be not pleasant to thee, and I be deserted by thee, whatever selfish objects may be gained from thee, they are given up by me (15).

MARKANDEYA said:—Thus saying, she, leaving him, got out of the confinement house, with her external senses be numbed and unfit for work, but her inner spirit pure (16). Then Játāharini took that (child); and she, having stolen their boy, placed him on the bed of king Vikrānta, and took his son (17). And taking him also to another house, and taking up the son of that house, gradually Jatāharini ate up that third one (18). This exceedingly cruel one, thus continually stealing (peoples' children) and exchanging one after another, always eats up the third one (19). Then the lord of earth Vikrānta performed all the sacramental ceremonies which are performed by the kings (20). The father, that lord of men, Vikrānta, moved by supreme delight, according to law, gave him the name Ananda (21). To him, and the boy after his *Upanayana* sacrament had been performed, the *Guru* said, "at first go and make obeisance to thy mother" (22). Hearing that word of the *Guru* he said laughing:—"Which mother is to be adored by me, whether she who gave me birth or she who nursed me (23)."

THE GURU said:—This, O thou possesser of the eight great qualities, is she who gave thee birth, she the daughter of Jārutha, and the chief queen of Vikrānta, known by the name of *Haimini* (24).

ANANDA said:—She is the mother of Chaitra, resident of Vishālagrāma and son of the Brāhman Agravadha, who is born of her; we are born of another (25).

THE GURU said :—Whence art thou, say Ananda? who again is Chāitra spoken of by thee? where art thou born, and why art thou here; tell me, I apprehend a great difficulty (29).

ANANDA said :—The universe being thus stationed where is the opportunity for stupifaction? O Brāhmana saint, who is whose son and who is whose friend? (52). All such relations originate with the birth of mankind and they are all snapped by death, O Brāhmana (33). The relation, with the friends that springs up with the birth, ceases with the dissolution of the body; such is the law of the universe (34). Therefore do I say that there is no friend while living in the world. Who is else is an eternal friend? Why then is thy understanding bewildered? (35). Even in this birth I have got two fathers and two mothers. What wonder is there if this happens again in the next birth? (36). I shall (now) engage in devout penances. Do thou therefore bring him from Vishālagrāma who is the son of the king (37).

MARKANDEYA said :—Thereupon the king, along with his wife and friends, was stricken with wonderment. Then withdrawing all attachment he orderd him to retire into woods (38). Then bringing his son Chaitra and reverencing the Brāhmana by whom he was brought up in the light of a son he trained him up for the kingdom (39). Then Ananda, a mere boy, engaged in rigid austerities in the forest for exhausting his actions that stand in the way of salvation (40). Whilst thus engaged in rigid austerities the deity Brahmā said to him "O son, tell me why hast thou engaged in such rigid austerities" (41).

ANANDA said :—"O Reverend Sir, with a view to purify my own soul, and exhaust those actions that have fettered me I have engaged in this devout penance" (42).

BRAHMA said :—"One, engaged in actions, has no right (to practise devout penances) and is unworthy of salvation.

How canst thou, possessed of energy, attain to salvation? (43). Thou must be born as the sixth Manu; do thou therefore go and become so. There is no need of asceticism unto thee; by doing this (*i. e.*, becoming a Manu) thou shalt attain to salvation (44)."

MARKANDEYA said:—Having been thus addressed by Brāhma and acquiesed in it the magnanimous (Ananda), bent on becoming (a Manu), desisted from carrying on devout penances and repaired therefrom (45). Having taken him away from his ascetic observances Brāhma addressed him as Chākshusha Manu (46). He espoused Vidarbhā the daughter of the king Ugra and begat on her a number of sons of well-known prowess (47). Hearken, O twice-born one, who during this *Manwantara* were the gods and the Rishis, who was the Indra and who were his sons (48). In it the gods were called Aryas and they were divided into nine classes. O Vipra, they were all of illustrious deeds, used to feed upon Havya in a sacrifice, were of well-known prowess and energy and were difficult of being eyed for their effulgence. There was another class of deities called Prasuta who were divided into eight sects (49—50). Another class of deities came into being called Vavyas who also were divided into eight sects and then came the fourth class of deities who were also divided into eightfold divisions (51) O twice born one, in this *Manwantara* the fifth class of deities, who appeared, were called Lekhas and used to feed on ambrosia (52). He, who having celebrated a hundred sacrifices became their lord, was called Manojava and was a partaker of sacrificial offerings (53). Sumedhā, Virajās, Havishmān, Unnata, Madhu, Atināma and Sahishnu, these seven were the Rishis (54). Uru, Puru, Shatadyumna and others were the highly powerful sons of Manu Chākshusha and they all became the lords of the earth (55). I have thus described to you, O you twice-born one, the sixth *Manwantara*, the birth and the character of the high-souled Chākshusha (56). The one, who has now appeared, is called Manu Vaivaswata. Hear, I shall now describe the deities and others of this seventh *Manwantara* (57).

——oo——

CHAPTER LXXVII.

MARKANDEYA said:—O great one, the daughter of Vishwakarman was the wife of the sun, by name Sajnā who begat on her a son, by name Manu, who, illustrious as he was, was equally a master of various branches of learning. He was the son of Vivaswat and was therefore called Vaivaswata (1—2). As soon as she was espied by the sun Sajnā used to close her eyes and therefore he, in anger, addressed to her cruel words (3) "Since, O stupid one, you close yours eyes as soon as I cast my looks on you therefore will you give birth to Yama, the destroyer of creatures (4)." Thereupon the goddess, stricken with fear, assumed trembling looks, at which the sun again said to her (5). "Since beholding me, you have assumed trembling looks you will give birth, as your daughter, to the fickle river (6)." Thus by the imprecation of her husband she gave birth to Yama and the great river celebrated under the name of Yamunā (7). Henceforth she, with great difficulty, began to suffer the effulgence of the sun. And unable to bear it she began to think (8). "What shall I do? Where shall I go? Repairing where can I get respite and be not subject to the ire of my husband?" (9). Thus meditating in many ways the great daughter of the Patriarch thought well of the protection of her father (10). Thereupon bent on going to her father's house the illustrious (goddess) converted her own body into the favourite shadow of the sun and said to her. " Do thou, like me, live in the abode of the sun and like wise shouldst thou behave thyself towards the sun and his offspring (11—12). Even when accosted thou shouldst not tell him of my departure. On the other hand thou shouldst always tell him. "I am Sajnā." (13). The illusory Sajnā said :—"O goddess, I shall carry out thy mandate so long the sun does not pull me by the hair or imprecate a curse on me; I shall relate the story when he will pull me by the hair or curse me" (14).

Having been thus addressed the goddess repaired to her father's abode and saw there Twastri who had all his sins washed away by ascetic observances (15). She was received with great honour by Vishwakarman and that blameless lady too lived for some time in her father's house (16). Thereupon having greeted his daughter of beautiful limbs who had not lived there for a long time with great love and honor (he said) (17) :—"When I behold thee, my girl, even many live-long years appear as the half of a moment. But virtue is disappearing (18). It is not praiseworthy for females to live long in the house of her relations; and it is the desire of their kinsmen that the women may live in the house of their husbands (12). Thou hast been wedded to the Sun the lord of the three worlds. It does not behove thee, O my girl, to live for ever in the house of thy husband (20). Do thou therefore repair to the house of thy father. I have been pleased with thee and do adore thee. Come again, O auspicious girl, to see me (21).

MARKANDEYA said :—Having been thus addressed by her sire, O ascetic, she said "So be it;" and then having worshipped her father she repaired to Uttarakuru (22). Thereupon reluctant to bear the effulgence of the Sun and afraid of his rays, she, having assumed the form of a mare, engaged in ascetic observances (33). Thereupon regarding her as Sajnā the Sun begat on his second wife two sons and a highly beautiful daughter (24) The illusory Sajnā did not manifest that excessive affection towards the sons and daughter of Sajnā as she did towards her own offspring (25). She daily looked after their own comforts. Manu forgave her for this but Yama could not do so (26). Then to strike her he raised up his foot in anger—and then immediately stricken with mercy he did not let it fall on her person (27). Thereupon, O twice-born one, the illusory Sajnā, with her palms trembling and lips expanded in anger, imprecated a curse on Yama (28), "Since, out of irreverence thou hast raised a foot against me who am thy father's wife thy that very foot shall drop off to-day" (29). Having thus heard of the curse thus imprecated by his mother and been stricken with fear Yama approached his sire and having saluted him said (30):—"It is a great wonder, O father, never witnessed by any that a mother, relinquishing all affection, imprecates a curse on her son (31). Methinks, as does Manu hold, that she is not our mother, for even when a son grows unnatural a mother does not become so" (32).

Hearing Yama's words the Divine Sun sent for the illusory Sajnā and asked her where Sajnā had gone" (33). Whereto she replied :—"O Sun, I am the daughter of Twastri, Sajnā, thy wife and the mother of all these children" (34). Although accosted by the Sun in many ways she did not communicate any thing else. Then the Sun in anger-addressed himself to imprecate a curse (35). Thereat she communicated everything truly to the Sun. Informed of all the Sun repaired to the abode of the divine Twastri (36). Thereupon he worshipped the Sun with great reverence, adored of the three worlds who had come to his house (37). Then when questioned about Sajnā, Vishwakarmā told him :—"Despatched by thee she came to my house" (38). Then having concentrated his mind the Sun saw her, carrying on ascetic observances in the form of a mare in the province of Uttarakuru (39). The Sun then came to know of the object of her penances namely, "May my husband become of a mild form and the performer of auspicious deeds" (40). The Sun then, O twice-born one, said to Vishwakarmā, the father of Sajnā, "do thou to-day losen the fierceness of my rays (41). Vishwakarmā then reduced the effulgence of the Sun who travels over a year and the deities then began to hymn him (42).

CHAPTER LXXVIII.

MARKANDEYA said :—Thereupon having assembled together the celestials and the Rishis began to hymn the glories of the sun, worshipped of the three worlds in the following words (1).

THE CELESTIALS said :—Salutation unto thee who art in the form of *Rik, Saman, Yayur*, salutation unto thee, who art the refuge of all and dost light all (2). Salutation unto thee who art the only stay of knowledge, identical with pure effulgence, who art pure, whose soul is purified and who hast not the tinge of the quality of ignorance (3). Salutation unto thee who art the greatest and the most excellent of all, the great soul and whose manifestation is the whole universe and whose form is Atman (4). Salutation unto thee, the primary cause of all, the stay of all who have their intellects illumined by knowledge, who art identical with the light and the soul that manifests itself (5). Salutation unto thee who art Bhāskara and who dost make the day; salutation unto thee who art the instrument of the making of the night, eve and moon-light (6). O lord, thou art all this (universe); by thy motion forward and backward thou art sustaining the whole universe, mobile and immobile (7). Touched by thy rays all this becomes purified; touched by thy rays even the water becomes purified (8). As long as this universe is not connected with thy rays so long the performance, of *Homa*, charities and other ceremonies, does not lead to the well-being (of the performers) (9). From thy one limb has emanated the *Rik*, the *Sâman* from the other and *Yayur* from the third (10). O lord of the universe, thou art identical with *Rik*, *Yayur* and *Sâman* and therefore, O lord, thou art identical with three (11). Thou are the subtle and gross form of Brāhman; thou art with form and without it; thou dost exist both in thy gross and subtle forms (12). Thou art identical with Nimesha, Kashtha and other (divisions of time) as well as with *Kàla* the destroyer of all. Be thou pleased of thy own accord and make an end of thy own effulgence (13).

MARKANDEYA said:—Having been thus eulogised by the deities and the saints the undecaying bundle of effulgence (the Sun) renounced his own lustre (14). The earth was engendered by that portion of his effulgence which was identical with *Rik*—the etherial region was created by what was identical with *Yayur* and heaven by what was identical with *Sâman* (15), The Divine Architect, made with those fifteen divisions of his eflulgence that had been exhausted, the trident of Siva, the discus of Vishnu, the dreadful maces of Vasus, Sankara and the fire god, the conveyance of the god of riches and other shnining weapons of Yakshas, Vidyadharas and other celestials (16—18). Thenceforward the Divine Sun bears only the sixteenth portion of his effulgence, which was thus distributed into fifteen divisions by the celestial Architect Viswakarman (19). Thereupon, having assumed the guise of a horse the Sun repaired to the province of Uttarakuru and espied Sajnā in the form of a mare (20). Seeing him thus approach and taking him in fear to be another person, she went in front of him (21). Then united with each other, they smelt each other's nose; then on the seminal fluid being discharged there came out of the two nostrils Açwinis and Revanta seated on horseback with swords, daggers, armour, arrows and quiver (22—23). Thereupon the Sun displayed his own matchless form. Beholding this form Sajnā assumed her own and was delighted (24). Then the Sun, the stealer of water, brought her own loving wife Sajnā, who had assumed her own form, to his house (25). Then was born his first son the Manu Vaivaswata; his second son Yama, on account of the imprecation of his mother, became of virtuous looks (26). His father brought about an end of his imprecation saying,—"The worms, taking the flesh of his feet, shall fall down on the earth (27). Because he was of virtuous looks and impartial both towards his friends and enemies his father appointed him in the office of the Regent of the Dead (28). Yamunā became the tributary of Kālindi, the two Açwinis were appointed by their divine father as the physicians and Revanta became the king of Guhyakas. Hear now, from me, of the mandate issued by the illusory Sajnā towards her sons (29—30). The first of the first born sons of illusory Sajnā was like Manu. This son of the Sun obtained the appellation of Sāvarniki (91). He will become Manu in that *Manwântara* when Bali will attain to the dignity of Manu. Sani was appointed one of the planets by his father (32). Kuru, the king of men, was begotten on her third daughter by name Tapati by Samvarana (32). I shall now relate to thee the seventh *Manwântara* of that Manu Vaivaswata, the king of the period, the Rishis, Indra and his sons (34).

CHAPTER LXXIX.

MARKANDEYA said :—Adityas, Vasus, Rudras, Sādhyas, Vishwadevas, Maruts, Vrigus and Angiras were the gods of that period (1). Adityas, Vayus and Rudras should be known as Kashyapa's sons—Sādhyas, Vasus and Vishwadevas were sons of Dharma (2). The Bhrigus were the sons of Angiras; they should all now be known as the sons of Marichi, O twice-born one (3). The king of all these gods was the high-souled Urjāshwi, who was the partaker of sacrificial offerings. All these kings of the gods past, present, and future were endowed with equal marks—thousand-eyed and holders of thunder-bolt; they were all subduers of foes (4—5). They were all performers of sacrifices, were like bulls, with horns and were performers of hundred sacrifices and were all capable of over-powering creatures (6). They were all, by virtue and other pious rites, endowed with governing qualities and were ordainers of past, present and future. Hear, O twice-born one, of the three worlds (7). The earth is called the region of Bhu, the etherial region Div and heaven Divya—these are called the three regions (8). Atri, Vashshtha, the great saint Gautama, Bharadwāja, Viswamitra Koushika, and Jāmadgni, the son of the high-souled Richika, these were the seven Rishis of that *Manwantara* (9—10). Ikshwāku, Nābhaga, Dhrista, Sharyāti, Narishwanta, Dishta,—Karusha, Prishadra, and Vasuman, well-known in the world, these nine were the sons of Manu Vaivaswata (11—12). O Brahman, I have thus related to you, Vaivaswata Manwantara; men, hearing of it, O great one, are released from all sins and attain to great piety (13).

CHAPTER LXXX.

KROUSHTI said:—You have described all Manus beginning with Syambhuva as well as the gods, kings, and Rishis of those periods (1). Do thou describe in detail the seven Manus and the various gods of those *Manwantaras* that will rise in the present Kalpa (2).

MARKANDEYA said:—I have spoken to you about Sāvarni the son of the illusory Sajnā. He is equal to the previous Manus and will be the eighth (3). Rāma, Vyasa, Gālava, Diptimān, Kripa, Rishyashringa, and Drouni will be the seven Rishis in that period (4). Ara, Sutapa and Amitabha, were the gods—divided into sixty classes (5). Tapa, Tapas, Shatru, Dyuti, Jyoti, Prabhākara, Prābhasa, Dayita, Dharma, Teja, Rashmi, Vakratu and others were the twenty deities called Sutapa. Prabhu, Vibhu, Vibhasa and others were the twenty of the class of deities called Amitābha. Hear, I shall describe the third class; Dama, Dānta, Rita, Soma, Vintā and others were the twenty of the class of gods called Mukhya, they were all the lords of *Manwantaras*; they were the descendants of the Patriarch, Maricha the son of Kashyapa; they will be gods in the *Manwantara* of Manu Savarni (6—9). O Muni, Virochana's son Bali is their future Indra. He is still now, by virtue of a contract, living in the nether region (10). Virajācharvavira, Nirmoha, Satyavak, Kriti, Vishnu and others will be the sons of Manu Sāvarni (11).

CHANDI.

CHAPTER LXXXI.

MARKANDEYA said :—"The Savurni (son of the sun) was said to have been the eighth Manu. Hear ! I will copiously relate his birth.

Manus, possessors of great shares, were the founders of Manwantaras, by the favour of Mahāmāya, among them was Savurni.

In the Manwantara of Swāro-chisha in former times Suradha, who was born of the race of Chytra, became a monarch of the whole earth.

He ruled this subjects paternally; the kings who were hunters of wild boars then became hostile to him.

A valiant and mighty king, among the hunters of wild boars, conquered him in battle, and reduced his power.

Thence the holder of extensive portions returned to his city, and ruled over only his own tract of country; that king then became encompassed by the greatest enemies.

The counsellors and evil disposed possesssed the wealth of the humble king, who lost all the treasures in his city.

He lost his royalty. Under the pretext of hunting, he retired to a dreary forest alone, mounted on his horse.

He saw the hermitage of an excellent Dwija, thronged around with wild beasts and adorned by the presence of his disciples and sages.

He lived there some time, revered by the Muni, and wandered about here and there.

He ruminated there on the love that agitated his mind thus ; what my predecessors ruled, I afterwards lost.

I wonder whether my subjects are governed with equity or not, I know not the fate of my counsellors, and my trained elephant Surahusti.

They are now in the possession of my enemies; what pleasure can they now enjoy, who were formerly pampered with food and riches.

Now they are certainly maltreated by the foreign kings; lavished on vain purposes is the treasure that was assumed.

The king was sorrowful that his treasury was expended. On these and other things he was perpetually meditating.

He saw a Vysa near the cell of a Vipra, "O who art thou" said he "what is the cause of thy coming here?"

Why dost thou appear pensive and melancholy, O wealthy man? why are your eyes red with sorrow?

Mārkandeya said, "hearing the humble speech of the king, the Vysa obsequiously replied to him."

My name is Samadhi, a Vysa. I am born of a wealthy tribe, I am banished through my sons and wife's covetousness, and wickedness.

My sons are possessed of my fortune, and I have become destitute of wealth, a consort, and children; in sorrow I took refuge in the forest, leaving behind me my friends and relations.

I live here unacquainted with the happiness or misery of my sons, the welfare of my people, or wife.

Whether their house is in safety or danger, at present? how my sons are, whether they are engaged in moral or evil deeds?

The Rajah asked, " why do you love those sons and that wife, through whose avarice you are banished?"

The Vysa replied, " knowing my sentiments, why do you interrogate me, I cannot harden my heart, what can I do."

Covetousness has extinguished their filial affection, yet I feel for my people.

O mighty wise man, I am simple, for my heart is attached to my treacherous kinsmen though I know them.

How can I hate them, or bear malice in my heart.

Markandeya said, "the Vysa by name Samadhi, and the noble king went to the Muni."

They were duly respected by him as prescribed in the ordinances: they both conversed on history.

The Rajah raid, "O divine personage! I am desirous to ask one thing from thee, explain it to me, my mind has lost its function, I am troubled with anxiety?

O excellent Muni! what is this? though conscious of transitoriness, yet like an ignorant person I love my kingdom, and all my retinue.*

He was banished by his son, wife, attendants, and his relations, yet he feels pity for them.

In this manner we both excessively grieve, love draws us unto reprehensible actions.†

What is this, O magnificient sage, though we are ingenious, yet our affection produces cecity in action.

The Rishi said, "O great sharer, wisdom exists in all living creatures that are desirous of life, love predominates in each individually.

Some animals are blind in the day, others at night, and others again that appear equally blind both day and night.

It is true, that kings appear prudent, but are not really so; all the beasts, birds, animals have knowledge.

What knowledge mankind is possessed of, the others are equally endowed with.

See the birds being wise, though oppressed with hunger themselves, yet lovingly pick up the crumbs with their beaks and feed their young ones?

---

* Though conscious, &c., that is, though I have sufficient knowledge to know the instability of human transactions, yet like an ignorant person I am subservient to the emotions of my soul.

† Reprehensible action; *viz.*, mundane affections and the neglect of abstracted religious devotion.

O chief of kings! do you not see men lovingly support their offspring for the benefit of others.*

By attraction they fall in the vortex of love. By the power of Mahāmayā, the world was originally created.

Mahāmayā seized the lord of the world when at his slumber yoga; the great illusion enveloped Hari, she shackles the world.†

The divine goddess possesses irresistibly the heart of even the wisest, and forcibly leads into great deception,

By her the universe consisting of animates and inanimates was created, her blessings procure emancipation.‡

The knowledge of her is the means of supreme salvation; she is eternal and links mortality; she is the supreme goddess over all goddesses.

The Rajah said, "O divine personage! who is that goddess? O twice-born! whom you mentioned just now, how was she born? what miracles did she do?"

What stupendous action did she, whose form is admirable, perform? I am desirous of hearing about those things, O excellent among those who know the almighty, tell me?

The Rishi said, "the form of the world is eternal, all things were created by her, I was frequently told her birth."

She is eternal and only took form for the benefit of the gods.§

When the world was deluged, Vishnu the Divine Superior Lord was reclining on the serpent bed at the end of Kalpa.

Then two horrible Asuras: named Madhu and Kitabha, was born from the wax of Vishnu's ear and endeavoured to slay Brāhma.

Prajapati residing in the lotus naval of Vishnu, saw the two wrathful Asuras and the sleeping Janarddana, who was

---

* Of others viz., posterity.

† Shackles the world, being the great attractive power,

‡ Procures emancipation from secular concerns.

§ Benefit of the Gods, that is, to destroy demons.

(in Yoganidra), he thus prayed with strict faith to her, who made Hari's eye to be her abode.

O goddess of the universe; mother of the earth! creator of matter and destroyer of it. Goddess of the slumber of Vishnu, who has extreme brilliancy, is surpassing and superior.

Brāhma continued, "thou art Swaha, thou art Swad'ha, thou art Vash-ut-kara, thou art Sudha, thou art Akchara, thou art eternal, and of three powers; Mātra.

Ardha-matra, constant, perpetual, thou art she who is moreover inexpressible, thou art Savitri, thou art the light, and a superior matron.

Thou art the sustainer of all things, thou hast created all things, thou governest all things,* thou existest to the end constantly.

Thou art the principle of creation, thou art plastic, thou art the preserver, thou art the destroyer in the end, thou pervadest through the universe.

Thou art the supreme knowledge, thou art the great illusion, the supreme intellect, the supreme memory, the great love, the ample light, the mighty goddess.

Who contemplates all matter by three kind of powers, Kālaratri, Mahārātri, and Moharātri, dreadful.

Thou art prosperity, thou art the goddess, thou art Hari, thou art the wisdom that creates understanding, thou art modesty, strength, and gratification; thou art mildness and forgiveness.

Thou art Khudgini, Sulini, the frightful Gadini, Chakrīni, Sankhini, Chāpini Bāna, Brusundi, Parigha.

Thou art placid, the greatest among the meek; beautiful, excellent, supreme among the excellent; thou art the great goddess.

Thou existest in all that is little, and all that is great; in

---

* Three powers.—Creation, preservation, and destruction.

gay and sad things, and thou powerful by the acquirement of their strength, who is left to praise thee?

Thou makest the world, thou destroyest the world, who can praise thee?

Thou possessest the body of Vishnu, and also Mahā Esāna, both of whom were made by thee, and who is able to praise thee?

He plauds the goddesses' eminent actions, that she may link the wicked giants Madhu and Kitabha.

And that she might awake the supreme lord, who was to slay both the great wicked demons.

The Rishi said, the creator thus praised, that the enraged goddess might awake Vishnu to kill Madhu and Kitabha.

She liberated Vishnu's eyes, nose, arms, bosom, and breast, and appeared to Brahmā, whose birth is pure.

Janarddana was delivered by her; the lord of the earth arose from his serpent bed in the ocean and beheld them.

Madhu and Kitabha, ill disposed heroes; warlike, with red vision, endeavoured to extirpate Brahmā.

Rising afterwards, they both wrestled with the divine Hari for five thousand years.

They were intoxicated by the great deception; the elate with pride desired Keshava to mention his wish.

Bhagavān relied, "You shall both die by me! what other desire have I, know this is my only wish."

The Rishi said, that they looked at the universe overflowed with water and deemed themselves deceived, they looked at the divine lotus-eyed, and spoke thus—

"We are satisfied with the combat and praise thee; O vanquish and conquer us in a spot not moistened by water!

The Rishi said to the holder of the Sanka and Chakra, the divine said, I will do so. He then cut off their heads with the Chakra on his thigh.

Brahmā himself applauded the deed. I will tell thee copiously of the miracles of the goddess, hear them.

Thus far extends the first chaper, mentioning the destruction of Madhu and Kitabha.

——oo——

CHAPTER LXXXII.

In former times war was waged between the deities and demons for the full space of one hundred years; also between Mahisha-sura, the greatest of demons, and Poorunder (the greatest of deities).

The Asura of ample heroism repulsed the army of the Devas; Mahishasura vanquished all the angels and became as Indra.

After this, the conquered deities went with Prajapati whose abode was the lotus to Garuda-dhwaja (or the eagle bannered.

The Tridasas laid before him the distress of the gods with an account of Mahish-asura's actions.

That he had usurped the authorities of Surya, Indra Anila, Indu, Yama, and Varuna; and others himself.

They said, the gods are oppressed by the ill disposed Mahisha; the whole multitude of Devas have left heaven and wander on the earth like mortals.

Those are the deeds of the enemies of the immortals, we humbly bow to thy asylum to meditate on their death.

Madhusudana hearkened to the words of the deities; Sambhu was wroth contracting his brows with furious ire.

Afterwards, Chakrini's face was transported with rage, abundance of light issued from Bramhā and Sankara.

An immense mass of light proceeded from the bodies of Sakra and all the other Devas, and conglomerated.

This effulgent lustre appeared as a flaming mountain: the Suras having seen the flame receded to the extremities of regions.

The peerless light issued from the bodies of all the Devas and the phenomenon was transfigured as a woman extending through the three worlds.

The energy of Siva created her face; the brightness of Yama made her hair; her arms were formed by the light of Vishnu.

Her two breasts were made by the moon; the space between them by Indra; her thighs and the calves of her legs by Varuna; her loins by the light of Bhuvi.

Her feet by the energy of Brahmā; her toes by the rays of the sun; her fingers by Vasus her nose by Cubára.

Her teeth were created by the brightness of Prajāpati; her three eyes by the energy of Pāvaka.

Her forehead by the light of Sundhia; her ears by Anila; the brightness of other deities formed her body.

From the glory of the light of all the Devas, Siva sprang; the Amaras perceived the destroyer of Mahisha and exulted.

The holder of the Pināka took out his Sula and conferred it on her; Vishnu gave her a Chakra drawn from his own Chakra.

Varuna gave her the sank; Hutasana the Sacti; Maruta spread a bow with arrows, and quiver complete.

Indra took the Vajra from his Culisa, the one thousand eyed god took the bell from the elephant Iravata, and gave it to her.

Varuna gave her a Cala-dunda; and Yama the Pasa; Prajāpati, lord of the subjects, bestowed an Akchamāla and Comundala on her.

The maker of day filled his rays in the roots of her hair; Cāla granted a transparent sword and shield.

A necklace pure as milk, immaculate Panoply, a Chudāmani, and divine Cundala and Cataca.

A crescent; a beautiful Keyura over her arms; shoulder ornaments and beautiful neck jewels.

Rings of precious stones, on all her fingers. Viswa Karma afforded her the limpid Parasu.

Implements of different forms: likewise an invulnerable coat of arms; a never fading garland of lotus for her head and neck.

Jaladhi conferred on her a prosperous Chaplet of lotus; Himavunt gave her lion vehicle and various gems.

Dhanadhipa gave her a golden vase with imperishable wine to drink; Sesha gave her a necklace of serpent's ornaments and magnificient gems.

Prudhwi granted a neckless of snakes, and the other Suras geve her jewels and arms.

She shouted frequently with a terrible voice, the sound of which filled the sky.

The eternal vault echoed with the terrific sound of "O Mayah," all the world was alarmed, the ocean trembled.

The earth quaked, all the mountains were moved, the Devas joyously exclaimed, "victory be to the rider of the lion."

Munies were delighted and faithfully made obeisance to her; she beheld the whole of the three Lokas grieved by the enemies of the Amaras.

All the nearest armies were amply provided with implements, Mahisha-asura furiously said, "O what is this?"

The sound of his voice reached the surrounding multitude of Asuras; he saw the goddess pervade the three Lokas.

She indented the earth, occupied by her foot, her crown struck the sky: the sound of her bow-string terrified the whole subterraneous world.

She grasped all the space of the regions by her one thousand arms; fierce war was waged between the goddess and the enemies of the Suras.

They shot many powerful arrows; her arms extended towards all the cardinal points; the leader of the army of Mahisha-sura was a great Asura, by name Chickchura.

He fought at the head of an Ayuta of great cheeked Asuras. The mighty Asura Asiloma, advanced with 50,000 *Neyutas*.

Bhaskala conducted one hundred and sixty thousand *Ayutas* to the battle, accompanied by one hundred elephants, and many steeds.

Bidāla led one *Koti* of *ruths* in that war, and fifty thousand *Ayutas*.

The other leaders were attended by one *Ayuta* of elephants, *ruths* and horses.

The great Asuras encountered the goddess with *Koti-Koti* thousands chariots, and elephants.

And with the same number horses, Mahisha-asura wielded the Tomara, Bindivala, sacti and Musala.

He fought the goddess with his Khudga, Parasa, and Puttisa; some of the Asuras threw the sacti, and some the Pāsa.

Devi began to destroy them with her sword Chundica afterwards threw arrows and *astras*.

She sportively cut them in pieces by the shower of her powerful shafts and arrows, Devi, the imperishable was greeted by the excellent Suras and sages.

The goddess shot the powerful shafts and arrows, and severed the bodies of the Asuras; the lion of the goddess being enraged, swiftly shook his mane and marched against the hostile army, like fire against a forest.

During her achievments in war, the goddess sighed thereby instantly were produced hundreds and thousands of Ganās (or Amazons).

Who fought with the demons, with Parasa, Bindivala, and Puttisa; the powerful voice of Devi, destroyed the hosts of Asuras.

The Amazons sounded the Pataha, likewise the conches, kettle-drums, and other instruments in the festival of war.

Afterwards Devi, by the trident, by the mace, by the sactivrusti, by the sword, and so forth, killed immense number of Asuras, and made others to fall by the ringing of the bell.

She tied the Asuras with the Paśa on the earth; and some were cut down into pieces by the keen cut sword.

She afterwards crushed the troops with her mace on the earth: some vommited blood, having been struck by the *Musala.*

She cast some on the earth, breaking their bosom with the trident, she destroyed some by the keen shaft, in the field of battle.

The commander of forces, the oppressors of Tridasas, forfeited their lives: some had their arms, others their throats cut.

The heads of some of the vigorous Asuras were cut off, and the calves of the legs of others were severed and thrown down to the earth.

Devi had maimed each of the Asuras of an arm, an eye, and a foot; and though their heads were severed from their bodies, the trunks rose again.

The trunks, holding the excellent arms, fought with Devi; the Apsaras danced during the battle, accompanied by great shouts.

The trunks of the Asuras, whose heads were cut off, still held the sacti, Khudga, Vrusti, and spoke aloud: stand! stand.

The fallen chariots, elephants, and steeds of the Asuras were innumerable; where the great battle was fought, instantly rivers of blood were streaming.

The centre of the army of Asuras, the chariots and horses of Asuras were annahilated by Ambikā.

In a moment the forces of the Asuras were destroyed in abundance by fire, like grass and wood.

The Kesari (or lion) made an excessive roar, it produced a concussion among the bodies of the foes of the Suras.

By the Amazons of the Devi, victory over the Asuras was achieved, the gods were gratified and poured down Amaranthine flowers from heaven.

CHAPTER LXXXIII.

THE RISHI said:—The mighty Asura, by name Chickchura, general of the army, on beholding the destruction of his force proceeded to fight against Ambikā.

That goddess poured a shower of arrows on the Asur, as the clouds rain on the peak of Meru mountain.

The goddess sportively cut his mighty weapon, and killed the steeds, and driver by her arrows.

She instantly broke his bow and his highest flag-staff: she wounded him in the body.

Having lost his bow, he was deprived of his chariot, his horses, and drives were killed: the Asura, holding a shield and sword, ran against Devi.

He struck the head of her lion fiercely with the keen blade of his sword: he struck the right arm of the goddess.

O prince! when the sword reached her arm, it broke: the Asura then took a Sula, his eyes being red with wrath.

And discharged it at Bhadra-Kāli, flaming with a brightness equal to the orbit of the sun in heaven.

The goddess receiving the Sula, discharged by the demon, threw a trident which cut the mighty Asura's weapon into a hundred pieces and killed him.

When the great valiant demon was dead, Chāmara, the general of Mahisha's army, oppressor of Tridasas, mounted on an elephant.

Firmly discharged a Sacti on the Devi, but by her shout she made it to fall on the earth innoxious.

With anger he beheld the Sacti broken and fallen, and discharged a Sula, she then cut it with her arrows.

She leapt from the lion to the globular forehead of the elephant, and direly wrestled with the foes of Tridasas.

During the combat, they both dismounted and began furiously to beat one another.

Afterwards the enemy of the beasts,* swiftly attacked and separated the head of Chāmara, from his body, by the strokes of his paws.

Devi killed Vudagra, by hurling stones, trees, &c. upon him, she made Carāla to fall by her teeth and feet.

Devi being enraged by the blows of her mace, ground him into powder; Bhāscala by Pindivala; Tomara and likewise Andhaca by her arrows.

The supreme goddess killed Vugramsa, Vugra-Virya likewise Maha-Hanu and Trinatra, by her trident.

She made the head of Bidala to fall by her sword; destroyed Durdhara and Durmukha by her arrows.

While she was thus destroying his army, Mahishāsura impeded those Ganās in the form of Mahisha.

Some by biting with his mouth, and others by kicking with his hoofs, some by the lashes of his tail and by the goring of his horns.

Some of them by the loudness of his bellow, by his burning breath he made them to fall to the ground.

* Enemy of the beasts—lion.

The Asura having caused Pramadas to fall, angrily ran to kill the lion of the goddess.

The great hero enraged, tore up the earth with his hoofs and cast down the highest hills.

He speedily turned about, cracked the earth, lashed the ocean with his tail, and made it to overflow everywhere.

The clouds were dispersed by his long horns, the mountains and sky were blown into hundred pieces by his breath and sighs.

The great Asura wrathfully bellowed! Chandikā looked, highly enraged and endeavoured to lay hold on him.

She threw out a Pāsa to bind him, he was tied, and relinquished his buffaloe's form in this great combat.

He instantly turned into a lion, within the time that Ambikā cut of this head; he then converted himself into a man, held a sword and disappeared.

Afterwards the goddess pierced him with her arrows, he with his sword and shield turned into a mighty elephant.

The elephant pulled the lion with his trunk, and made a terrific noise, the goddess cut his proboscis with her sword.

Afterwards the great Asura assumed the form of a buffaloe, and terrified the three Lokas of animates and inanimates.

The passionate Chandikā, matron of the world, frequently drank excellent liquor, bearing wrathful redness in her eyes.

The Asura being highly endowed with bravery and lust, furiously hurled mountains with his horns on Chundikā.

She pulverized them with her strong arrows, and with increased intoxication and angry looking face.

Devi cried, Oh! vain noise! noise! wait a moment until I perfectly drink this liquor; when you are slain by me here, all the gods will exclaim.

The Rishi said, she laid hold on the great Asura, (who advanced towards her conveyance), with her feet, she struck him with her Sula.

When he was caught hold on by her feet, his half real form

from his face became manifest; the goddess was surrounded by a blaze of glory.

The great Asura being half issued and fighting with her, the goddess cut off his head with her ample sword.

Afterwards every one exclaimed, that the army of the Daitya was annihilated; then a multitude of deities were highly delighted.

The band of deities, with the magnificient sages applauded the goddess, the kings of Gandharvas sung, Apçarās danced.

Thus far is related in the third Chapter, containing the destruction of Mahishāsura.

CHAPTER LXXXIV.

THE eloquent Indra, and the crowd of Suras, after the death of the demons bowing their heads were delighted, and the hair of their beautiful bodies became erect. O Goddess! by thy power this world was created with spirits and gods of different and numerous forms. O Ambikā! thou art revered by all the deities; the magnificent sages faithfully prostrate themselves to thee: mayest thou give us prosperity.

Thy miracles are unparalleled, Bhagavān, Ananta, Brahmā, and Hara are unable to express it. Mayest thou, O Chandikā! endeavour to preserve the world, and dispel the fears of the giants.

Thou residest in the mansion of the virtuous as a goddess of riches, and as an unfortunate deity in the abode of the vicious, as sense in the heart of the wise, as faith in mankind, and modesty in the superior castes: to thee, O Goddess! I make obeisance and implore thee to rule the universe.

How can I describe thy form which is inconceivable? thou art great, heroic, ample: destroyer of the giants. Thy deeds in war are admirable, O Goddess! and superior to the hosts of giants and gods.

Thou art the instigating cause of the universal earth, of three powers; incomprehensible to sinners, and even to Hari-Hara, and so forth; thou art attended by all, and art the proprietress of this world: thou art undefinable, inscrutable, and the excellent principle of matter.

Thou art Swāhā in all the sacrifices. By the devout expression of thy name all the deities are gratified: people pronounce thee by the name of Swadhā for the expiatory oblation for deceased ancestors.

Thy stability confers inconceivable salvation, which is obtained by those votaries, who subdue their organs, thou art a goddess, thou art the supreme knowledge to edify the searcher after beatitude, sages, and those that are free from different offences.

Thou art the word, source of the purest *Rig*, *Yaju*, and *Sáman*, of eloquent florid phrases. O divine Goddess! thou art of three powers: for the augmentation of the world; thou art the destroyer of the universe and remover of severe evils.

O Goddesss! thou art intelligence; essence of the substance of various sciences; impenetrable; a vessel on the difficult sea of secularity; unassociated; chiefly resident in the heart of the enemy of Khytābha.* Gouri, thou art worn by the crescent crowned god.

With a soft smile, thou art the purest representative of the perfect orbit of the moon; thou hast a beautiful golden hued body. It is an entire wonder that Mahishāsura, with self-created anger could look on the enraged, and brow-contract-

---

* Vishnu.

ed countenance of the goddess glowing as Sasadhara,* and not instantly quit his soul; who can live in the sight of the enraged Untaka?

O Goddess! we now entreat thy countenance for the ample increase of generations; we implore thee to destroy in thy wrath the extensive posterity of the force of Mahishāsura, and to bestow the desired wealth, fame, inexhaustible virtues, offsprings, attendants, consorts, and promotion on the people of the countries thou favourest,mayest thou countenance them.

O Goddess! the virtuous by faithfully performing every day the different divine services, and consecration depart to heaven, and thereby reap the fruit of their labour in the three worlds.

O Durga! all creatures lose their fear by praying to thee; thou dost grant abundance of prosperities; thou dost release from pain and grievous distress; who is more watchful to oblige in every respect; and who more compassionate than thee.

All the universe was made happy by the death of the giants, and though they have committed transgressions a long time which are deserving hell, yet by slaying them in battle you have sent them to heaven.

Why did not all the adversaries of the deities turn to abundant ashes, when they saw the dire implements cast forth by thy hand? thou deeming it meet, that they should approach to heaven, hast purified them by thy weapons.

The Asuras looking at thy fine large face, resembling the crescent of the moon, became insensible to the vivid flashes of the trident.

O Goddess! thy fortitude will cause to cease the practice of all profligate acts, thy unequalled from is inconcievable, thy heroism will absorb other's valour, and even thy foes acknowledge thy merits.

---

* Sasadhara—literally, hare-holder, the moon.

Thy prowess is without equal, thy form will create fear in the enemy : in peace thou art complacent, and in war thou art implacable. O goddess! thou givest benedictions in the three worlds.

Thou hast killed the foes at the head of the battle, and saved the whole of the three worlds; multitude of enemies proceeded to heaven. We are exempt from fear, and prostrate ourselves to thee, who art a foe to the intoxicated enemies of Suras.

O Ambikā! preserve us by thy trident and sword; preserve us by the ringing of thy bell, and by the sound of thy bow-string. O Chandikā! guard the East and the West, and the South. Oh Brahmani! defend the North with thy trident.

Mayest thou support the saints and good spirits that wander in three *lokas*; mayest thou retain a number of tremendous forms on the earth, that wield the sword, trident, club, and other instruments in their hand, to defend us at all times and places.

The Rishi said, the Suras thus praised and joyfully worshipped her with the divine flowers of the garden of Nandana, rubbing sandal on the universal Dhātri.

All the Tridasas faithfully offered her sweet smelling incense, the mild faced goddess said to the humble Suras.

Devi said, O Tridasas! I am pleased with your worship I will affectionately give you whatever you desire. The Devas replied, O divine goddess! we have every thing that we require.

Thou hast slain our adversary Mahishāsura, all our desires have been obtained through thy favour, we have only one thing more to request of thee.

Secure from harm whatever mortal recollects to call upon thee, repeatedly, in the time of danger.

O beautiful Face! deign to give them augmentation of

riches, spouses, and properties. Mayest thou eternally promote us.

The Rishi said, the supreme goddess, supporter of the world granted the request, and blessed Bhadra-Kali; and then, O King! she vanished away.

He related to the king the history of the conformation of the goddess from the emanation of the deities who were anxious for the weal of these three worlds.

Again she was born from the body of Gouri, in order to destroy the evil Daitayas, together with Sumbha, and Nisumbha

To preserve the universe and to gratify the deties. Listen I will perfectly, detail it to you.

Thus far is related in the fourth Chapter containing the praise of Sakra or Indra, and so forth.

CHAPTER LXXXV.

THE RISHI said, formerly the Asuras, Sumbha, and Nisumbha, by the strength of inebriation possessed the whole portion of the sacrifices of the three worlds. They likewise usurped the powers of Indra, Surya, Kubera, Yama, Varuna, Sakra, likewise Pavana, Vunhi; the deities were beaten by them and deprived of their realms and fled.

He assumed the authority of Tirdasas, expelled them all; the mighty Suras being deserted recollected the goddess.

"Thou hast bestowed this favour on all of us, that if we shall remember thee in the hour of danger, that thou shalt remove the peril from us."

Thus they meditated on the goldess in their hearts and repaired to Himavant, (king of mountains) there they greeted the goddess of the illusion of Vishnu.

The Devas said, we salute the great goddess, maker of joy, and continually prostrate ourselves and pay homage to the auspicious matter; we humbly bow to the pious.

Salutation be for ever to Radri, reverence be to the Dhātri, eternal prostration to the light, to the form of the moon and beatitude; twice obeisance to the prosperous, to the prolonger, maturer, and Kurme.

Twice salutation to the Niruta supporter of the earth, and the goddess of riches, Sarvāni.

Twice salutation to Durgā, remover of difficult limits; constant salutations to the renowned one, likewise to the sable and dusky.

Twice salutation to the ample, the mild and the austere; prostration to the establisher of the world and to the goddess.

Five times salutation to the goddess, who is called an illusion of Vishnu in all creatures.

Five times salutation to the goddess, who is the mind in all creatures.

Five times salutation to the goddess, who is the intellect in all ceatures.

Five times salutation to the goddess, who is repose in all creatures.

Five times prostration to the goddess, who is the appetite in all creatures.

Five times salutation to the goddess, who is the shadow in all creatures.

Five times salutation to the goddess, who is a power in all creatures.

Five times salutation to the goddess, who is gratification in all creatures.

Five times salutation to the goddess, who is mercy in all creatures.

Five times salutation to the goddess, who is a caste in all creatures.

Five times salutation to the goddess, who is modesty in all creatures.

Five times salutation to the goddess, who is pity in all creatures.

Five times salutation to the goddess, who is the faith in all creatures.

Five time salutation to the goddesss who is splendour in all creatures.

Five times salutation to the goddess, who is the form of prosperity in all creatures.

Five times salutation to the goddess, who is the intellect in all creatures.

Five times salutation to the goddess, who is the memory in all creatures.

Five times salutation to the goddess, who lives as favour in all creatures.

Five times salutation to the goddess who lives as joy in all creatures.

Five times salutation to the goddess who exists as a mother in all creatures.

Five times salutation to the goddess, who lives as a form of delusion in all creatures.

Five times salutation to the goddess, who exists as wisdom in all creatures.

Five times salutation to the goddess, who is above the organs and eternally pervades through all creatures.

We salute the goddess who resides in all the world as a form of effulgence.

Suras, Indras, Dinesa assembled together and prayed to her according to their former request. O goddess! causer of happiness; bestow prosperous blessings on us; dispel the danger that encompasseth us.

We and the Suras salute thee. Destroy the proud Daityas

whoever contemplates thee with obeisance, their misfortunes shall be instantly removed.

The Rishi said, when the deities applauded Pārvati, O prince! she went to perform ablution in the water of Jānhavi.

She asked them, "Whom did you greet there." The resplendant Siva emanated from her body, and spoke thus to her.

"They recited my praises, because they were expelled by the giant Sumbha, all the deities retreated before Nisumbha in the war."

From the body of Pārvati, Amvikā issued, and was denominated Kouçiki throughout the universe.

When she had emanated from Pārvati, (who turned black), she was called Kouçiki and resorted about Himāchala.

Her transcendent form beautiful, and creating admiration was seen by Chanda and Munda, who were attendants of Sumbha and Nisumbha.

They mentioned to Sumbha, O great sovereign! there is a beautiful female, exalted on the Himāchala mountain, she charms the heart of all beholders.

There is no shape resembling her yet seen by any body. Find out who she is and pass that angelic female.

That charming body is a gem among the damsels, glowding in all directions; O Indra of the giants! it remains for thee to behold her.

O Lord! you have already stored in your mansion, all the precious gems of these three worlds; steeds and elephants. The elephant Airāvata, you have brought from Purandara, or Indra, the tree Pārijāta, likewise the steed Ucchaisravā.

The car with divine swans remains in your mansion, which was made of precious stones to the astonishment of Vedā, you have brought the Nidhi and Mahā-Padma from the god of riches.

The ocean has conferred on you the lotus and a garland of unfading lotus.

The gold shedding umbrella of Varuna is in your house, and so is the excellent vehicle of Prajāpati, who passed it formerly.

You took the Sakti, by name Utcrānta, the cord of the king of waters, was occupied by your brother.

Vanhi has bestowed on Nisumbha, all sorts of gems found in the sea at the time of his performing his holy rites.

O sovereign of the demons! you have acquired all the precious articles; why do you not take this auspicious female gem.

The Rishi said, Sumbha was constantly listening to the speech of Chanda and Munda; the mighty giant sent a messenger Sugriva, to the goddess.

Said he, "go and tell her that I want her; convey my errand swiftly, effect the mandate you are sent upon, pleasing her in any manner."

He proceeded to the mountain, where the auspicious was stationed, and delivered the message to the goddess, endeavouring to move her with mellifluous accents.

The Duta said, O Goddess! Sumbha is the lord of the Daityas, he is a mighty sovereign of the three worlds, I am hi s messenger sent by him hither.

He has perpetual and unbounded authority over all the deities, he has conquered all the foes of Daityas, hear what he says.

I possess all the deities of the three worlds, and receive solely all the sacrificial oblations.

I have gained the excellent gems of the three worlds; the precious elephant of Indra, he humbly delivered to me. I am lord also of the horse, named Ucchaisravā, which was producted from the milky ocean, when the mighty Suras churned it.

All the precious things found among the deities, Gandharvas and Uragas are mine.

The world esteems thee, O Goddess ! as a female gem come to us and we will wear thee.

O thou of the darting glance ! choose either me or my valarous younger brother Nisumbha, who are the possessors of the gems.

You shall gain abundant and unmeasured wealth by taking me ; consider and be wise, and forthwith possess me.

" The Rishi said," the goddess with a disdainful smile, replied to him.

"Devi said," what you have declared is true, there is no falsehood in your speech. Sumbha is lord of the three worlds, and so is Nisumbha.

But how can I repeal my determined vow, hear what I formerly swore to without consideration.

That whoever can vanquish me in combat, whoever can oppress my pride, whoever is equal to me in vigour in this world : he shall be my husband.

Whether Sumbha, or the mighty demon Nisumbha, call them here to conquer me, I will seize their hands without delay.

The messenger said, how do you arrogantly say this in my presence, is there any individual in the three worlds able to cope with Sumbha and Nishumbha.

All the deities united were unable to withstand the giants in the war, then how canst thou, a single woman, resist them.

Indra and all the other deities could not cope with him ; how could it be possible for Sumbha to enter into the presence of a woman ? You will be obliged at last to go, disgracefully dragged by the hair, to Sumbha and Nishumbha.

Devi said, "is such the vigour of Sumbha, and is such the great valor of Nisumbha ! I have formerly resolved and vowed without deliberation, what can I do now?

Go directly and reveal to your master all that I spoke,

and appeal to the Indra of demons; and let them do what is expedient.

Thus far is related in the fifth Chapter, containing the conversation of the goddess and messenger.

——oo——

CHAPTER LXXXVI.

THE RISHI said, hear the word of goddess! the messenger transported with rage went to the king of Daityas, and addressed him thus—

O sovereign of Asuras, hearken to the speech of your messenger, he then related the whole circumstances to Nisumbha, who furiously told Dhumralochana, (who is a superior of the giants).

O Dhumralochana,* surround with your force and bring that wreth to me, forcibly drag her into my presence by her hair.

If there is one remaining to protect her, bring him also whether he be immortal, Yaksha, or Gandharva.

The Rishi said, the giant Dhumralochana, as directed, marched accompanied by sixty thousand Asuras.

To the goddess, resident on Tuhināchala,† he beheld her and spoke loudly, "come to Sumbha and Nishumbha.

If you go not cheerfully, I shall convey you by force to my King, dragging you by your hair."

Devi said, "the Lord of the Daityas has sent a valiant demon with an army, if you carry me away what can I do?"

---

* Dhumralochana—liberally smoky-eyed.

† Tuhinachala—snowy mountain.

The Rishi said, the giant Dhumralochana expeditiously proceeded to Ambikā, who reduced him to calx by her breath Humkāra.

She became mightily enraged, and raised the keenest arrows and Sakti and Parasu.

She furiously rose and made a frightful shout, and destroyed the force of Asuras by her lion.

Grasping some of the demons she dashed them against each other and killed the great Asuras, she demolished some by the blows of her hand.

The lion tore some with his claws, and some by the strokes of his paws, separating their heads.

Having their hands and heads broken by the beatings of the lion, they vomitted hot blood.

In a moment all that army was destroyed by the magnanimous and enraged lion of the goddess.

The Asura heard of the death of Dhumralochana by the goddess, and that the whole of his army was defeated by the lion of the goddess.

Sumbha, king of the Daityas, with agitated lips thus commanded the great Asuras Chanda and Munda.

'O Chanda and Munda proceed attended by a large body of forces, go and swiftly bring her here.

Either lay hold on her hair, or hand, if you suspect the issue of the battle, with the various arms and the giants

Kill the wicked lion quickly, seize Amvikā, bind and bring her to me.'

Thus far is related in the sixth Chapter, mentioning the death of Dhumralochana, general of Sumbha and Nisumbha.

CHAPTER LXXXVII.

SUMBHA having directed those giants. Chanda and Munda attended by four sorts of armies and arms, they marched the foremost to the fight.

The goddess being on the lion over the peak of the stupendous golden mountain, saw them with a smile.

The demons beheld her and higly exerted themselves to accomplish their designs, and the holder of the sword, and bow drew near to her.

Amvikā then became terribly angry at her enemies; rage changed her face into a hideous black.

Her contracting brows overshadowed her forehead, the terrific faced Kāli slung her Pāça.

She wore a wonderful Khutwanga, adorned by a string of human skulls, she wore a tiger's hide, her flesh became dried.

Her mouth expanded, she had a lolling tongue, a horrible red-tinged eye, her front filled the regions.

She furiously fell upon the Asuras, and destroyed the foes of deities and devoured their forces.

She took Parswagrāhi with one hand and Kusagrāhī, Yadha-Ghumta, with the other, and put them into her mouth.

Likewise the troopers' chariots with their drivers, she threw them in her mouth, and chewed them with her teeth horribly.

She laid hold of some by their hair, others by the throat, or by the hand, she crushed some with her foot, broke the bosoms of others.

She wrathfully swallowed up her enemies she discharged powerful arrows, and the arms of the Asuras she furiously chewed with her teeth.

The magnanimous goddess devoured or crushed all the forces of the valiant Asuras.

She killed some with the sword, and struck some with the Khutwanga weapon; the giants died with the pressure of her teeth.

In a moment all the forces of the Asuras fell; Chanda beheld it and ran to the frightful Kāli.

The mighty Asura, with a shower of numerous and tremendous arrows, and thousands of Chakras speedily enveloped the dreadful eyed goddess.

Abundance of the discuses she swallowed, her face became as the orbit of the sun enveloped by the clouds.

Then Kāli, angrily shouted: her voice was horrible, her mouth became distended and frightful, and she gnashed her tremendous teeth.

The goddess made her lion to rise, ran at Chanda, and laying hold on him by his hair, she cut off his head with her sword,

After this Munda seeing the fall of Chanda, marched against her, she made him to fall on the earth and instantaneously killed him with her sword.

The surviving forces perceived the fall of Chanda, and the valiant Munda, and through fear retreated in all directions.

Kāli took the heads of Chanda, likewise of Munda, and shoutingly exclaimed to Chandikā.

I have killed the great beasts Chanda and Munda, you will slay Sumbha and Nisumbha, in the sacrifice of battle.

The Rishi said, she gently replied to the prosperous Kāli, "as thou hast brought the heads of the great demons

Chanda and Munda, you shall be renowed in the world by the name of Chāmundā."

Thus far is related in the seventh Chapter, comprising the death of Chanda and Munda.

CHAPTER LXXXVIII.

THE RISHI said, Chanda was killed and Munda fell, their abundant forces were diminished.

The bravest lord of the Asuras, Sumbha was moved to anger,and directed all the forces of the demons to be prepared.

Then the giants of various forces with eighty-six sorts of arms, eighty-four kinds of cumboos, set out in legions.

One *koti* of heroes, fifty thousand of the giant race, the tribes of Dhoumra marched by his order.

Kālikas, great Mowryas, and likewise Kālakeya, directly prepared for battle by his order.

The lord of the Asuras, the frightful leader Sumbha, advanced, attended by myriads of cohorts.

Chandikā viewing the approach of this dreadful army, filled the extremeties of the regions, and sky with the sound of her bow-string.

The lion roared tremendously ; the goddess rung the bell ; Ambikā shouted.

The sound of the roar penetrated to the extremeties of the regions, the mouth of Devi expanded hideously.

The army of the giants having heard the sound in the four points, furiously surrounded the goddess, the lion, and likewise Kāli.

O king ! previous to the time, that the enemies of the Suras met their dissolution, for the benefit of the heroic brave immortals.

The powers of Brahmā, Eça, Guha, Vishnu, likewise of Indra, issued from their bodies and proceeded on their respective forms towards Chandikā.

The similar forms with their vehicles, ornaments, and valour of the deities went to fight with the giants.

She who rode in front in a car, drawn by divine swans, with a string of beads, and a pitcher of water in her hand, she was called Brāhmani.

Maheswari rode on the ox, she held an excellent trident, great serpents were coiled round her, she was adorned by the signal crescent.

Koumāri held a Sakti in her hand, she was mounted on an excellent Mayura, and proceeded in the form of Guha to fight with the giants.

Vaishnavi sitting on the Garuda, held the conch, discus, mace, Sārana, and a sword in her hand and marched out.

Hari assumed the peerless form of Yagna-Varāha, took the form of the boar and attended there in a terrific shape.

Narasimha assumed the dreadful body of Narasimhi, and with her mane extinguished the constellation.

Indri, holder of Vajra, was mounted on a mighty elephant having one thousand eyes like Sakra.

Eçāna was surrounded by the Sakti,* of the deities, and said to Chandikā, "kill directly the Asuras for my satisfaction."

The implacable power of Chandikā proceeded from the body of the goddess in a dreadful form, named Siva, whose voice increased an hundredfold.

She said to Eçāna, (who was smoky-hued, unattainable, and a divine messenger), "go to Sumbha and Nisumbna.

Tell those proud giants to prepare for war, together with the other demons.

Indra shall resume the three worlds, and gods will devour the sacrificial oblations: if they wish to live, let them go to Pātāla.

If they presume to wage war with me, the jackals shall be glutted with their flesh.

---

* Sakti—powers.

As Siva sent the message by the goddess to the giants she was called a Siva-Dutā, or Siva's messenger in this world.

The great Asura having hearkened to the message of the goddess sent by Siva, was transported with rage and repaired to the place where Kāttyāni lived.

First the enemies of the immortals furiously rained showers of arrows and Saktis on the goddess.

She in turn discharged the great arrows from her bow and sportively cut off their arrows by her trident, Chakra and Parusu.

In their front Kāli struck them with her trident, and with the Khutwanga and achieved mighty deeds.

Brāhmani destroyed wherever she went, the heroic and valliant enemies, by pouring water from her Kamandalu on them.

Maheswari, by her trident, likewise Vaishnavi with her discus, Kaumāri with her wrathful Sakti killed the giants.

Indri pierced one hundred demons, and evil genies with her Kuliça, and threw them on the earth, their blood gushed out.

Brāhmamurti broke their breasts with the discus.

By her nails, she tore and devoured many of the great Asuras; Narasimhi talked in the battle; her voice filled the directions and sky.

The goddess shouted; she struck the domons to the ground and devoured them.

The chief amazons detested the mighty Asuras, and the various demons were ineffectual, and having overcome their measures and stratagems, the warriors, adversaries of god, fled away.

Seeing the retreat of the Daityas, the great demon Rackta-Bija, (whose blood is a seed), became enraged and proceeded to fight.

When a drop of the blood from his body fell on the earth: it produced the same sized giants from the ground.

The great demon holding a mace in his hand, fought with Indri, who held the Sakti Vajra.

He was struck by the Kuliça, the blood gushed out: other demons immediately arose of similar form and valour.

Equal in number to the drops of blood that fell from his body, demons of the same heroism, vigour and fortitude, were produced.

By the severe beating of the weapons of the chief amazons as also by the cut of the Vajra, his head fell off.

When the blood was streaming, thousands of demons were produced by it; Vaishnavi beat him in the battle with her discus.

Indri smote the lord of giants with her mace; Vaishnavi struck him with her discus, and the blood was spilt.

Thousands of the giants of the same feature abounded in this world; Kaumāri beat him with her Sakti; likewise Varāhi with her sword.

Brāhmani, with a cudgel of Brāhmani, and Narasimhi tore him with her claws,

Maheswari beat on the bosom of the great giant Rackta-Bija with her trident for he did not move.

He being surrounded by the enraged chief amazons, severely beat them with his clubs.

He cut off abundant of the Sakties, tridents, and so forth and made a hundred to fall on the earth.

The giants produced by the blood thronged over all the world; the gods afterwards were overwhelmed by fear.

Chandikā looked at the discomfitted Suras, and speedily said to Kāli, "O Chāmundā open your mouth widely.

Great Asuras are produced by the drops of the blood of Rackta-Bija, you must instantaneously lick up the lood before it falls to the ground.

Devour the blood before the demons are produced; the Daityas will be diminished and become void of blood.

If you do this they never can spring up again," saying thus—the goddess pierced them with her trident.

Kāli sucked up the blood of Rackta-Bija; Chandikā beat him violently with her mace.

By the vehement beatings of the clubs, a profusion of blood gushed out all over his body.

Chandikā licked it up; Chāmundā drank his blood.

Devi by her trident, arrows, sword, and fists killed Rackta-Bija, and drank his blood.

He being overwhelmed by a number of arrows, O Ruler of the earth! the mighty demon Rackta-Bija, fell on the earth, and became void of blood.

Afterward the deities felt the highest degree of pleasure, the chief amazons proudly danced.

Thus extends the eighth Chapter, mentioning the death of the Rackta-Bija.

CHAPTER LXXX X.

THE RAJAH said, "O divine one! you have disclosed to me the wonderful story, and the sacred action of the goddess, which exterminated Rackta-Bija.

I am now desirous of hearing the actions of Sumbha, and the excessive anger of Nisumbha.

The Rishi said, at the death of Rackta-Bija, and others in battle. Sumbha and Nisumbha were uncommonly enraged.

Seeing their immense army destroyed, the demons were filled with ire. Nisumbha ran to their succour with considerable reinforcement.

In the front, rear, and flanks, he was attended by mighty giants, who were wrathfully biting their lips, and meditating the death of the goddess.

The mighty Asura Sumbha, surrounded by his force, fought with the chief amazons, and furiously proceeded towards Chandikā.

Sumbha and Nisumbha then commenced a dreadful combat with the goddess, and shot powerful showers of arrows, thick as clouds of rain.

Chandikā cut them to pieces with her own parts, and pierced both the chief Asuras with several arrows.

Nisumbha then took his keen sword and resplendent shield, and struck on the head of the lion, the noble conveyance of the goddess.

When her excellent animal was beaten, Chichura took a sharp sword and cut in two pieces, the shield of Nisumbha, called Asta-Chandra.*

That Asura after his shield was destroyed, shot a Sakti, but as it was whizzing towards her, the goddess cleft it in twain with her discus.

Then Nisumbha made a furious charge with his Sula; the goddess pulverized the hostile weapon with her fist.

The demon then swung his mace at Chandikā, but the goddess by her trident reduced it to calx instantaneously.

After this disappointment, the chief of the Daitayas seized a battle axe and approached Devi, she levelled the warrior to the earth with her arrows.

When the dreadful Nisumbha fell to the ground, his brother burning with fire repaired to kill Amvikā.

Being mounted on his chariot, he grasped his missiles,

---

* Asta-Chandra—literally eight moons.

and potent implement, and with unequalled voice penetrated over all the sky.

The goddess perceived his coming and sounded her conch and her bow-string, the noise of which was insupportable,

The sound of her bell filled the etherial space; the different detachments of the Daityas were dismayed.

The lion lustily roared, the sound penetrated the sky earth and the ten directions.

Afterwards Kāli leaped up towards heaven and kicked the ground, at the piercing sound of her voice the giants vanished.

Siva-Duti, shouted at the misfortune of the Asura, the noise reached the giant Sumbha who furiously proceeded towards the goddess.

Amvikā said to him, O impious wretch! stand! stand! the gods immortal inhabitants of the sky have cried "victory to be thee!"

Sumbha discharged a Sakti, which issuing in a terrific flame, became a mass of fire, she opposed him with a Maholka.

The lion like voice of Sumbha, overspread the three world (Oh lord of the earth)! by the appalling sound of it, he hoped to conquer.

The goddess cut off the arrows of Sumbha, by her own shafts, into hundreds and thousands of pieces.

Chandikā, was enraged, and struck him with her trident: the giant thereon fainted and fell on the earth.

Nisumbha having revived, took his bow and beat the goddess Kāli, and the lion with his arrows.

The king of giants, with ten thousand arms, enveloped Chandikā, with numerous weapons, discuses, and arrows.

Then the goddess, the inaccessible, the subduer of various ills, being enraged cut off those direful weapons with her arrows into hundred pieces.

Nisumbha swiftly took the club, (and attended by his giant's forces), ran to kill Chandikā.

The goddess destroyed his club and threw her keen sword the demon took a trident.

Nisumbha, the oppressor of immortals, was going to Chandikā, she broke his bosom with a Sula, with a mace fixed to it.

His bosom being broke, another demon came out of him, the goddess smiled and cut off his head with her sword, and he fell on the earth.

By the teeth of the lion, by Kāli and Siva-Duti, other giants were decapitated.

Koumāri destroyed some giants by her Sakti; Brāhmani with her enchanted water slew others.

Maheswari demolished some by her trident Varāhi by beating reduced them to powder on the earth.

Vaishnavi, with her discus, crushed the giants to pieces; Indri with her weapon Vajra killed others.

Many of the giants retreated, many were annihilated in that horrible war, Kāli, Siva-Duti and the great lion devoured others.

Thus far is related in ninth Chapter, comprising the destruction of Nisumbha.

——oo——

CHAPTER XC.

THE RISHI said, Sumbha perceived the discomfiture of his forces, and the death of his brother Nisumbha, who was dear to him as his own soul), and furiously said.

"O wicked Durgā! do not be proud," "O immodest one! you prevail by the aid of others."

Devi said, "I am alone, who is there besides me in this world. "O profligate one! behold, it is my essence alone that is created into many forms."

As she spoke Brāhmani and the other goddesses dominations, and powers coalesced to her spirit; the goddess then became alone and sole.

Devi said, "I can assume at will several forms, but now shall retain one form only, meet me therefore in battle."

The Rishi said, after this challenge Sumbha and the goddess began a fierce combat; the gods and demons stood spectators of this dreadful encounter.

With showers of arrows, powerful weapons, and cruel arms, they both desperately fought for the dominion of the universe.

Amvikā discharged hundreds of divine shafts, the chief of the Daityas opposed them by others.

Parameswari sportively destroyed his holy arrows by the sound of her voice Humcāra.

The Asura covered the goddess with hundreds of arrows she growing enraged, destroyed his bow with her arrows.

The chief of the giants, having lost this weapon, speedily grasped a Sakti, but the goddess cut it in pieces while it was yet in his hand.

The king of the Daityas took his sword and the shield Sata-Chandra, blazing like the sun, he ran furiously towards the goddess.

Chandikā cut through his sword and discharged her keen arrows, pure as the beams of the sun.

The giant having lost his steeds, chariot, and bow, seized a tremendous Mudgara, intending to kill Amvikā.

She again cut it by her keenest arrows, he ran at her with his fist.

He hastily shot a musti, she made it to fall; and struck the bosom of the chief of the Daityas.

The severity of the blow felled him to the earth; the king of giants speedily rose up again, and flew up to heaven with the desire of laying hold on the goddess; though he was incumbent in the skies, he fought with Chandikā.

They mutually fought in the sky, and performed wondrous feats in battle, to the astonishment of the sages and angels

By leaping, turning, and casting each other on the earth; they fought a long while.

The ill disposed descended to the earth, directly closing his fist with an intention of killing Chandikā.

The goddess saw the lord of giants, coming and pierced his bosom with her trident, and made him to fall on the ground.

He yielded his life, being transfixed by the trident of the goddess; as he fell on the earth, the seven islands and mountains moved.

Every one was delighted at the death of the miscreant, the world was in peace; the sky became serene.

The clouds dissolved in air; inauspicious omens, henceforth ceased; while the sun beams converged as usual; and the rivers flowed in the beds assigned them.

All the gods were filled with joy; Gandharvas, on his death pleasantly sang.

Others shouted, Apsarās danced; hallowing breezes began to blow; the sun became resplendent.

The inflaming fire moderated; the noise of the elephants of the regions was hushed; the planets revolved in peace; the moon enlightened the whole firmament.

Thus far is related in the tenth Chapter, containing the death of Sumbha.

CHAPTER XCI.

THE RISHI said, when the chief of the Asuras was killed by the goddess, Indra, Suras, and Vanhi appeared before her, and with joyful countenances advanced to greet Kātyāni for the favor she had conferred on them.

O goddess ! thy countenance removes the grievances of thy people, thou art the beneficent mother of the whole universe. O sovereign of the world ! save the earth.

Mayest thou preserve the world ; thou art the goddess of animates and inanimates.

Thou dost sustain alone the world in the form of the earth, O parragon of heroism ! thou as water refreshest all the people.

Thou art the power of Vaishnavi, thy valour is endless, thou art the element of the universe, thou art the supreme illusion, O goddess ! thou bindest all things in love, thou art the great first cause, thou art the bestower of salvation on the earth, thou art the essence of all sciences, thou art the rich one, thou fillest all things,—who can praise thy holy eloquence ?

Thou art the bestower of heaven, and salvation on all creatures ; what expression can sufficiently applaud thee?

I salute thee, O goddess ! Nārāyani, who liveth in the hearts of thy subjects, as a form of intellect, and giveth to paradise a local and unperishable abode.

I salute Nārāyani, who protects all things in a spiritual and material form, she is the over-ruling power of the universe.

I salute Nārāyani, who is the auspicious bestower of prosperity, happiness, and every desire ; who is the conferer of obligations, who is three eyed and brown.

I salute Nārāyani, who has power to create, preserve, and destroy; who is the reservoir of virtue from all ages.

I salute the goddess Nārāyani who saveth those that seek her protection, who comforteth the wretched and grieved; who is the dispeller of all sorrows.

I salute Nārāyani, who sits mounted on a car, drawn by divine swans, who asumes the form of Brāhmani, and eats vegetables.

I salute Nārāyani, holder of the Suras, Chundra, Jyuda, who rides on the ample ox in the form of Maheswari.

I salute Nārāyani, attended by the peacock, and holder of the mighty mountain on her nails who acquired the form of Kaumāri.

I salute Nārāyani, the possessor of the Sanka, Chakra, Gadā, and Sarna; who favors all in the form of Vaishnavi.

I salute Nārāyani, who took the ample Chakra, and sustained the earth on her proboscis, in the form of Varāha and Siva.

I salute Nārāyani, who assumed the wrathful form of Nrisimhi, and slew the giants to preserve the three worlds.

I salute Nārāyani, who is crowned Indra, the holder of the Vajra, who glowes with one thousand eyes, the drawer of the soul of Vritra.

I salute Nārāyani, who destroyed the valiant giants, in the form of Siva Duti, whose form was dreadful in the great battle.

I salute Nārāyani, whose teeth and mouth are frightful like the lions; and who is adorned by a necklace of skulls; the crusher of the head of Chāmundā; the modest; the omniscient; the faithful; and strong Swadha; the steady; the mighty; and the skilled in abundant arts.

I salute Nārāyani, who is intelligence and excellence; Sarawati; the bestower of prosperity; the wrathful; the austere; and the giver of all benefits.

I salute the goddess Durgā, who has mainfold forms; who

is the lord of all things : abounding with different powers ; the saviour of the fearful.

I salute Kātyāni, whose face is mild ; who is adorned with three eyes ; who preserves all creatures.

I salute Bhadra-Kāli, whose face is terrific ; who destroyed the whole race of giants ; may such a trident guard the fearful.

May the bell of the goddess, the sound of which has appalled the energy of the giants, and penetrated through all the worlds : preserve us as its childern.

We prostrate ourselves to Chandikā, whose exquisitely bright sword was stained by the blood and flesh of the giants ; and became the instrument of the death of Sumbha.

Thou healing from all kind of disorders, givest pleasure and strength to all people ; those that desire to follow thee, shall not feel distress, but will be restored.

Thou hast destroyed the great Asuras, who are the enemies of virtue, by thy actions and transfigurations.

Thou art supremely exalted in the sciences ; in knowledge ; in wisdom ; in eloquence ; in virtuous practice ; the world is overwhelmed in the excess of thy love.

Thou dwellest even among venomous serpents ; amongst hardened and depraved robbers ; ane where there are combustibles and fire ; thou art in the sea, and thou supportest the world.

O Goddess of the universe ! thou shouldest preserve the world, thou pervadest through the world holding it. The world prostrates itself to thee ; thou art followed by the world ; thou art faithfully loved by the world.

O Goddess ! protect and preserve the people from the fear of enemies, by destroying always the giants, as thou didst of late : extinguish the sins of the world, which proceed from accidental causes.

O Goddess ! thou shouldest favour him, who humbly bows ; O dispeller of universal alarm ! the inhabitants of the three worlds, shall prostrate themselves to thee; O bless the people!

Devi said, "O band of Suras! I will bless you; ask, and I will bestow what you desire, for the benefit of the gods."

The Devas replied, "O supreme goddess of the three worlds! we solicit thee to expel all danger and destroy our enemies; this is thy task."

Devi said, on the twenty-eighth age of Vibhaswatta, Sumbha, and Nisumbha, shall be regenerated.

I shall reside on the mountain of Vindhya, I shall be born in the race of cowherds in the womb of Yasoda, and destroy them.

I shall be incarnate on the earth, and shall slay the great giant Viprochitta,

I shall have my teeth red, like pomegranate flowers, then all the gods and mankind shall give me applause and call me constantly Racta-Danticā.

A famine shall happen for one hundred years without rain; being greteed by the sages I shall be self-born.

Then shall I look at the sages with one hundred eyes, therefore mortals will call me Satākshi, (or hundred eyes.)

The whole world shall subsist by the divine vegetable, which shall be produced from my body until the rain shall fall.

I shall be esteemed in the earth by the name of Sacumbhari, the preserver by vegetables, I shall be denominated Durga Devi.

I again shall assume a dreadful form on the mountain Himāchala, and devour the giants to protect the sages: all the ascetics will bow and applaud me.

I shall be called Bhimā-Devi, when Aruna shall disturb the three world; then I shall turn a roving beettle.

I will destroy the great giant for the advantage of these three worlds: all will applaud me by the name of Bramhāni in the world.

Whenever disturbances shall arise from the giants, then I shall incarnate and destroy the enemies.

Thus far is related in the eleventh Chapter, mentioning the death of Sumbha and Nisumbha.

——oo——

CHAPTER XCII.

DEVI said, he who for ever joyfully applauds me, him I will undoubtedly shield from all kinds of danger.

Whoever recites the dissolution of Madhu and Kaitabha, and the destruction of Mahishasura ; likewise the death of Sumbha and Nisumbha,

On the Astami or eighth, Navami or ninth, Chaturdasi or fourteenth, with an intent and pure heart and faithfully praise of my noble actions,

They shall incur no manner of sin, shall never be exposed to distress, and never suffer any trouble, or feel any pain.

Nor shall he be in fear of foes, or thieves, or fire, sword, or water, at any period.

Therefore my actions should at all times be chaunted in peace voluntarily ; and always be heard with joy.

All the dangers of evil and the three different plagues,* shall be counteracted by my meritorious deeds.

Whoever daily attentively reads my words in his house I shall not leave, but dwell in his presence.

During the offering of food to Bali worship, fire oblation,

* Three different plagues, *viz.*, Adhi-Infirmity, Viadhi-disease, and Itibadha—annoyance by animals.

or festival, mankind should completely read and hear my actions.

Whoever either knowingly or ignorantly gives the offering, food, or fire oblation ;

Whoever yearly performs the adoration in the Sarat (or sultry season), and hears willingly my action recited, they will undoubtedly obtain my favour.

Whoever hears my consecration, prosperity will attend him, and he shall be brave in combat.

Their enemies shall be destroyed ; the rich will attend, and listen to my miracles the race of mankind will be pleased.

Every where, when the preliminary ceremonies are performed, evil dreams, the inauspicious aspect of the planets shall cease during the recital of my actions.

The disturbances, the malignant influence of the planets will discontinue, unlucky dreams shall turn out prosperous.

Evils to which children are liable from demons, I will remove, and heal the breach of friendship in my people.

By reading it with strict faith, the strength of all ill-disposed-persons, the giants, demons, and evil spirits, shall be destroyed !

Whoever brings me an offering of noble beasts, of flowers, Arghya incense, sandal and tapers ;

Whoever feeds, the Vipras, performs the various rites of the Homa, every day and night ;

Pleases me throught a year, and hearkens to my actions, shall have their sins remitted and shall obtain the blessings of earth.

I will preserve all creatures, who read of my birth and deeds in words comprising the dissolution of the wicked giants.

They shall not be in fear of foes and shall obtain the praise of sacred sages.

This is ordained by Brahmā who provides for the prosperous wise. If in the skirts of the wilderness parched by devouring fire;

While surrounded by robbers in the plain, attacked by the lion, tigers, or wild elephants ;

If a king be enraged and give order to bind or execute a person accused of any crime, if any one fail in the wide ocean ;

When in danger of the sword, when fallen in a well or in battle, when in imminent risk and tormented by pain;

Should any one chaunt my actions, I will remove from him his afflictions though they be as fierce as the lion.

By repeating my action, all dangers will be dispelled.

The Rishi said, the warlike goddess Chandikā, while saying this, and as the deities were gazing on her, suddenly vanished, and the gods regained their former authorities without any obstruction.

Their enemies being destroyed, they enjoyed the sacrificial oblations, after the demons and Sumbha were slain by the goddess in battle.

The disturber of the universe, the brave peerless and mighty Nisumbha being dead, the surviving giants retreated to Pātāla.

O King ! the divine goddess was repeatedly incarnated to preserve the world, she shakles and creates the universe.

She gives knowledge, pleasure, intellect. O sovereign of mortals, she pervades throughout the globe of Brahmā.

Mahā-Kāli in the form of a great goddess, the high illusion, the ancient, creates the world occasionally.

And promotes wealth in the lives of the people in future period ; where she is not present their misfortunes cause ruin.

Whoever praises and worships her with flowers, sandal, incense, and so forth, she gives them prosperity, offspring, virtues, &c.

Thus far extends the twelfth Chapter, mentioning the advantages of praying to the goddess.

CHAPTER XCIII.

O KING, these are the excellent actions of the Devi I mentioned now, such is this glorious goddess, the holder of the universe.

The illusion of the divine Vishnu constructed this vast machine; by her, you, the Vysa, and others are being bound in love.

O chief sovereign, go to the assylum of the goddess, whoever adores her, will enjoy both heaven and earth.

Mārkandeya said, Surdha, hearkened to his words; the chief of mankind, the possessor of great shares, prostrated himself before him and made a vow.

Being puzzled by love, and deprived of his kingdom, he instantly repaired to perform devotion.

The Vysa remained on the shoal of the river to have an interview with goddess.

He performed the devotion praying, repeating the Devi-Sukti, he made a clay form of the goddess on the shoal, and invoked her with flowers, incense, Arghya, Tarpana, and other offerings.

He mortified his body, and in this manner he worshipped for three years.

Chandikā, the matron of the world, being pleased, appeared to him, and said, "O King, Prince of a goodly tribe! I have heard you pray, and cheerfully bestow on you all you request.

Mārkandeya said, the monarch being distressed, entreated her to restore his realm, vanquished by the arms of his enemies.

He Vysa, having a susceptible heart, implored from her wisdom, and abstraction from social and secular concerns.

Devi said to the king, O lord of men ! you will destroy your enemies and resume your kingdom ; you shall afterwards die and be regenerated as Vibhaswata, by the name of Savarnika Manu of the earth.

O excellent Vysa, according to your desires you shall obtain wisdom, the goddess thus blessed them and granted their desires ; she then vanished. Suradha, the chief Chatreyah, having thus obtained her blessings, became Savurni Manu in his next birth.

Thus far is related in the thirteenth Chapter, containing the plaudits of Chandikā, and ends Chandipāt Parvas.

CHAPTER XCIV.

MARKANDEYA said:—I have thus related to you in full the *Manwantara* of Manu Sāvarni, the glories of the goddess and the destruction of the buffalloe-faced demon (1); the origin of the goddess and other mothers in the great encounter as well as the origin of the goddess Chāmunda (2). Besides I have described to you the glories of Shivadyuti, the destruction of Sumbha and Nishumbha and as well as that of Rakta-Vija (3). Hear, O foremost of Munis, of another Sāvarni. This Sāvarni is the son of Daksha and is the future ninth Manu (4). O Muni, I shall describe now who will be the gods, sages, and kings. Pārā, Marichibharga and Sudharmā—these will be the three classes of deities (5). These three classes will again severally be divided into twelve each. Their future king will be highly powerful and thousand-eyed (6). The six-faced deity, who is now living as Kārtikeya, the son of the fire, will be the king, by name Advuta, of the *Manwântara* of this Manu (7). Medhathiti, Vasu, Satya, Yotishman, Dyutiman, Savala, Havyavāhana—these will be the seven Rishis (8). Dhrishtaketu, Varhaketu, Panchahasta, Nirāmaya, Prithushravā, Archishman, Bhidyurimna, Vrihadvaya—will be the sons of that Daksha's son and kings. Listen, O twice-born one, I shall now describe the *Manwântara* of the tenth Manu (9—10). During this tenth *Manwântara* of the intelligent son of Brahmā Sukhasenas and Nirudhas will be the gods (11). During (the regime) of this future Manu the gods will be a hundred in number—as the gods will be a hundred in number so will be the creatures (12). Sānti will be the king of all these gods and endowed with all the accomplishments of Indra. Hear now from me, who will be the seven Rishis at that period (13). Apomurti, Havishman, Sukrita, Satya, Nābhāga, Apratishtha add Vashishtha will be the seven Rishis (14). And Sukshetra, Uttamonjā, Bhurisena, Viryayāna, Shatānika, Vrishabha, Anamitra, Jayadratha, Bhuridyumna, and Suparvā—these will be born as the sons of that Manu. Hear now of the *Manwântara* of Sāvarni, thh son of Dharma (15—16). (At that period) there will spring into existence three classes of gods each severally divided into thirty (17). Amongst them, months, seasons and days will be the lords of creations and birds, nights and moments will be able to move on at their will (18). Their lord will be known by the name of Vrisha of well-known prowess. Havishmān, Varishtha, Rishthi, Aruni, Nishchara, Vrishthi and Agni will be the seven Rishis at that *Manwàntara* (19—20). Sarvaga, Susharmān, Devānika, Purudvaha, Hemadhanvā, Drirāyu will be his sons and kings (21). Hear, who will be the gods and Munis during the *Manwântara* of the Manu, by name Sāvarni, the son of Rudra (22). Sudharmanas, Sumanas, Haritās, Rohitās and Suvarnās will be the five classes of deities each severally divided into ten (23). Know of the highly powerful Ritadhāma as their lord endued with all the qualities of Indra, hear, now, from me of the seven Rishis (24). Dyuti, Tapashvi, Sutapās, Tapomurti, Taponidhi, Taporati, and Tapodhriti will be the seven Rishis (25). Devavân, Upadeva, Devashrestha, Viduratha, Mitravan, and Mitravinda—will be the sons of that Manu and kings (26). Hear, I shall now relate to you the sons of the thirteenth Manu Rochya, the seven Rishis, kings and gods (27). O foremost of Munis, Sudharmās, Sukarmās, and Susharmās, will be the gods of that period (28). Their king will be Divashpati of great strength and prowess. Hear, I shall now describe the seven Rishis that will be (29). Dhritmān, Avya, Tatwadarshi, Niratsuka, Nirmoha, Sutapās and Nishprakampa will be the seven Rishis (30) Chitaasena, Vichitra, Nayati, Nirbhaya, Drida, Sunetra, Kshatravuddhi, and Suvrata will be the sons of that Manu (31).

CHAPTER XCV.

MARKANDEYA said :—In the days of yore, the Patriarch Ruchi, being shorn of attachments, pride and fear and restraining his sleep, travelled all over the earth (1). Seeing him divorced from fire, home, hermitage and company and living on one meal his departed manes said to that ascetic (2) :—" O child, why dost thou not go through the most sacered marriage which is the source of heaven and emancipation and the absence of which brings on fetters (3). Having worshipped the gods, the manes, the Rishis and the guests a householder enjoys the various *lokas* (4). (By not taking a (wife) you are being daily fettered by the debts due to the gods, manes, humanity and other creatures (5). He should worship the deities with the exclamations of *Swahá* the manes with those of *Swadhà* and the guests with food (6). Without having engendered progeny and brought about the satisfaction of the gods and manes how dost thou, out of foolishness, aspire to a better state ? (7). We perceive the various miseries that will befall you for leaving a single life. You will attain to hell after death and suffer miseries even in your next birth (8)."

RUCHI said :—Marriage leads to excessive misery, hell and wretched existence ; it is for this I did not marry before (9). The control of the self by various good processes is the instrument of emancipation and not marriage (10). To wash daily the soul that is sullied with the mire of egotism, with the water of eternal consciousness shorn of attachment is the most excellent course (11). Therefore having controlled the senses the wise should wash their souls sullied with the mire of actions begotten in various births with the water of good desire (12)."

THE MANES said :—"Of course it is proper that one, having controlled his senses, should wash his soul. But, O child will the path in which you are now stationed, lead to liberation? (13). As ones' sin is destroyed by making gifts divorced from the desire of fruits so the pristine actions are destroyed by going through the result, good or bad (14). He, who thus engages in chraitable works, is not fettered (by actions); one, by thus engaging in action without desire, is freed from all bonds (5). Thus pristine actions are destroyed by day and night going through happiness and misery; the ways of mankind are thus identical with virtue and vice (16). In this way the wise wash their souls and guard them against bonds for which the soul is not deprived of conscience and accordingly is not sunk in the mire of sin (17)."

RUCHI said :—O ancestors, the road of action, has been mentioned in the Vedas as ignorance then how do you engage me in that action? (18).

THE MANES said :—True it is ignorance, but that ignorace is engendered by action is false; on the other hand without doubt action produces knowledge (19). The self-restraint, that is undergone by the wicked for emancipation without having made arrangements for the satisfaction of their duties, brings on, on] the contrary, a worse state (20). O child, you have made up your mind to wash thy soul but (on the contrary) you are being consumed by sins begotten by the negligence of duties (21). If administered by proper means ignorance conduces to the well-being of mankind like poison; it never brings on bonds for them (22). Therefore O child, marry porperly; let not your life prove futile by wending the way not approved of by mankind (23).

RUCHI said :—O ancestors, I am now an old man, who will confer a wife on me? Besides I am a poor man so it is very difficult for me to take a wife (24).

THE MANES said :—O child, if you do not hear us, we

shall fall down and along with us you will be subjected to a wretched state (25).

MARKANDEYA said:—O foremost of Munis, having said this, the manes disappeared before the very eyes of Ruchi, like a light put out by the wind (26).

CHAPTER XCVI.

HEARIG the words of the ancestral manes his mind was greatly agitated and that Brāhmana saint, desirous of having a bride, wandered over the earth (1). But being unable to secure a bride and burnt by the fire of the words of the manes he was stricken with great anxiety and his mind was agitated (2). (He thought) "Where shall I go? What shall I do? How can I secure a bride by which immediate prosperity may be secured unto my ancestors" (3). Thus thinking the high-souled one arrived at the determination:—"By ascetic observances I shall worship the lotus-sprung deity Brahmā" (4). Thereupon he carried on devout penances dedicated to Brahmā for a hundred celestial years. And observing proper regulations he worshipped him (5). Thereat the Great Patriarch Brahmā appeared before him and said, "I am pleased with thee, tell me what thou desirest" (6). Thereupon saluting Brahmā, the lord of the universe, he communicated unto him what he sought for in accordance with the words of the ancestral manes. And hearing of his wished for object Brahmā said to the Vipra Ruchi (7). "Thou shalt be a patriarch and create progeny. Having created progeny and begotten sons and performed all the ceremonies, thou shalt, at the expiration of thy time, attain to Siddhi. Therefore as commanded by thy manes do thou take a wife (9). Having thus determined do thou worship thy ancestral manes. They, being pleased, will confer upon thee, thy wished for spouse and offspring; when gratified what cannot the ancestral manes give" (10)?

MARKANDEYA said :—Hearing those words of the unborn Brahmâ he began to offer oblations to the manes on the banks of the river Vivikti (11). With whole mindedness, care and with his shoulders bending low with humility that Vipra began to propitiate them with the following hymns (12).

RUCHI said:—Salutation unto those ancestral manes who appear as presiding deities on the occasion of the *Sraddhas* and whom even tbe celestials gratify with the recitation of Swadhâs (14). Salutation unto those ancestral manes in heaven whom even the great saints, desirous of emancipation, gratify at *Sraddhas* with great devotion (14). Salutation unto those ancestral manes whom in heaven even the Siddhas, on the occasion of *Sraddhas* propitiate with the present of diverse most excellent celestial articles (15). Salutation unto the manes, whom even the Guhyakas, desirous of great Riddhi, propitiate with whole-minded devotion (16). Salutation unto those manes whom the mortals on earth propiate by performing *Sraddhas* with reverence and who confer on them wished for regions (17). Salutation unto those ancestrat manes whom the Brâhmanas worship on earth for the attainment of desired for objects and on whom they confer the dignity of patriarchs (18). Salutation unto those ancestral manes who are worshipped by the dwellers of the forest who have their sins washed off by devout penances and with regulations laid down in the Aranyakas accompanied by the restriction of diet (19). Salutation unto those manes who are propitiated duly by the Brâhmanas, observant of pure rites, who engage in meditation by controlling themselves (20). Salutation unto those ancestral manes capable of conferring the fruits of the three worlds whom the Kshatryas worship with *Swadhàs* and with various Kavyas (21). Salutation unto those manes who are daily worshipped by the Vaisyas on this earth, intent upon the performance of the duties of their own order with flowers, incense, food and water (22). Salutation unto those manes who are celebrated under the name of Sukalin, to whom on this earth Sudras offer oblations on the occasion of the *Sraddhas* (23). Salutation unto those manes whom the Asuras, renouncing pride and haughtiness, worship in the nether region on the occasion of the *Sraddhas* and whose food is Swadhā (24). Salutation unto those manes whom the Nāgas in Rasātala duly worship in view of many desired for objects by performing *Sraddhas* accompanied by various objects of enjoyment (25). Salutation unto those manes, whom even the serpents in Rasātala gratify by reciting duly Mantras and dedicating objects of enjoyment on the occasion of a *Sraddha* (26).

Salutation unto those manes who reside in the region of the celestials, in etherial atmosphere and on the earth and whom even the deities worship. May they accept what I dedicate unto them (27). Salutation unto those ancestral manes who are the great souls, and who, assuming forms, drive the chariots, with whom the ascetics of pure souls seek refuge and who are the instruments of the cessation of miseries (28). Salutation unto those ancestral manes who live in heaven with forms, who live on Swadhā, who are capable of fulfilling all desires, who confer emancipation on those shorn of desire, who grant the fulfillment of the desires of those who seek them, who confer the degnity of gods, that of Indra, or even that superior to it, and who give offspring, animals, wealth, strength, home and other things. May they be gratified with my humility (29—30). May those ancestral manes find gratification in the water, food and scents and attain to nourishment therefrom, and who reside in the rays of the moon, rays of the sun and white cars (31). May those ancestral manes here be propitiated with the water and food offered by me, who are satisfied with Havi offered in the fire, who take their food in the guise of the Brāhmanas and who are delighted with the offerings of *pinda* (32), May they attain to gratification here who are propitiated by the celestials and leading saints with the meat of rhinoceros, beautiful celestial black sesame and black vegetables (33). I dedicate those scents, food and edibles unto them, who find delight in various Kavyas and who are adored by the immortals; may they come nearer (34). May those ancestral manes find gratification here who accept worship every day, at the end of every month, at Ashtaka and are worshipped at the end of every year (35). I always bow unto those ancestral manes who, invested with the lustre of lillies and the moon, are worshipped by the Brāhmanas, by the Kshatriyas in their hue of the rising sun, by the Vaisyas in the hue of pure gold and by the Sudras in that of dark-blue. May they find gratification from the incense, food, water etc., which I dedicate as well as from the *Homa* ceremony (36—37). I bow unto them who feed, with great satisfaction, on Kavyas that are offered to the deities in the holy fire, and delighted thereat who bestow various prosperity; may they be propiated here (38). I bow unto them who extirpate the Rākshasas, the fierce Asuras and the ghosts and destroy the inauspiciousness of creatures, who are the precursors of the celestials, and who are worshipped by the leading immortals. May they find gratification here (39). I offer oblations to the ancestral manes called Agnishvātwa, Vahirshada, Ajyapa and Somapa; may they find gratification in this *sraddha* (40). May the ancestral manes called Agnishvātwa protect my western side and may the ancestral manes called Vahirshada protect my south (41). May the manes called Ajyapa protect the east and the ancestral manes called Somapa the north. May their king Yama protect me against the Rākshasas, ghosts, Piçāchas and Asuras. Vishwa, Vishwabhuk, Aradhya, Dharma, Dhanya, Shubhānana, Bhutida, Bhutikrit and Bhuti these are the nine classes of the ancestral manes (42—43). Again Kalyāna, Kālyata, Kartā, Kalya, Kalyatarashraya, Kalyatāpetu and Avadha—these are the six classes (44) Vara, Varenya, Varada, Pushtida, Tushtida, Vishwapātā and Dhāta these are the seven classes (45). Mahān, Māhātmā, Mahita, Mahimāvān, Mahāvala—these five constitute the class that destroys sins (46). Sukhada, Dhanada, Dharmada, Bhutida, these are the the four classes of the ancestral manes mentioned (47). These are the thirty-one classes of the ancestral manes who reside all over the entire universe. May they obtain satisfactiou and nourishment at my *sraddha* and always encompass my well-being (48).

—oo—

CHAPTER XCVII.

MARKANDEYA said:—While he was thus chanting the glories (of the manes) a bundle of effulgence came within his perception and was spread all over the sky (1). Beholding that great stationary effulgence enveloping the universe, Ruchi, kneeling down, chanted the following hymn (2).

RUCHI said:—I bow always unto the manes who are worshipped of all, who have no forms, who have burning effulgence, who are always engaged in meditation and who have celestial vision (3). I salute them, who are the leaders of Indra and others, as well as of Daksha, Marichi and the seven Rishis and who bestow all desired for objects (4). I always bow unto those manes who are the leaders of Manu and other principal saints as well as those of the sun, moon, and the ocean (5). I salute them with folded palms who guide the stars, planets, the air, the fire, sky, heaven and earth (6). I always salute them with folded hands who are the progenitors of the celestial saints, who are saluted by all the world, who always bestow everlasting fruits (7). I bow unto Prajāpati, Kashyapa, Soma, Varuna, and the other Yogins (8). Salutation uno the seven Ganas who live in the seven regions ; I bow unto the Self-sprung Brahmā, who has yoga for his eyes (9). I bow unto the manes of whom Soma is the stay and who have yoga for their forms and unto Soma (himself) who is the father of the world (10). I bow unto those other ancestral manes who have the fire for their forms and from whom this endless universe, full of Agnishtoma, has emanated (11). With a controlled mind I bow again and again unto all those ancestral manes, effulgence is whose support, fire and the sun are whose forms, the universe and Brahman are whose real nature and who always carry on yoga. May they, who feed on Swadhā, be propitiated with me (12—13).

MARKANDEYA said :—O foremost of Munis, having been thus eulogised the manes, lighting the ten quarters with their effulgence, came out (14). He beheld them before him, adorned with flowers, perfumeries and pastes, that he had dedicated unto them (15). Then again bending low with reverence he again honored them severally exclaiming "I bow unto you! I bow unto you!" (16). Thereupon the ancestral manes, delighted, said to that foremost of ascetics: "Pray for a boon." He too hanging his head said (17) :— "O lord, I have been commanded by Brahmā to engender progeny ; therefore I wish to take a wife who may be of a heavenly and glorious life and may give birth to children (18).

THE ANCESTRAL MANES said :—Immediately at this very moment there shall spring up a charming wife for thee, thou shalt beget on her a son, who shall be a Manu (19). O Ruchi, that intelligent lord of a *Manwantara* shall be designated by thy name and he will acquire reputation all over the three worlds under the appellation of Rouchya (20). He will be the father of many highly powerful and high-souled sons who will be all the protectors of the world (21). Thou, too, conversant with virtue as thou art, and a patriarch having created four classes of progeny, shalt, on the expiration of thy regime, attain to Siddhi (22). We will be pleased with that man who will reverentially chant our glories with this hymn and shall confer upon him various objects of enjoyments, the most excellent knowledge of self, good health, children and grand children. Therefore those, who will seek these, must eulogise us with the hymn first instituted by thee (22—24). Whoever, that shall on the occasion of a Srāddha, chant this hymn, so pleasing to us, with reverence before the leading Brāhmanas while taking their meals, when we, delighted with hearing this hymn, shall approach there, shall have Srāddha done without any obstacle. There is no doubt in this (25—26). If that Srāddha be without any Shrotrya, if it be sullied in any way, either with the spending of ill-gotten wealth or otherwise, when carried on by unfair means, or at a bad time, bad place or in an irregular process or if that Srāddha be instituted with haughtiness or irreverence still if this hymn be sung that shall conduce to our gratification (27—29). If this hymn, conducing to our satisfaction, be chanted at a Srāddha we shall obtain gratification extending over twelve years (30). If it is chanted in Hemantā (season of dews) it shall give us gratification for twelve years, if in winter this excellent hymn shall give us satisfaction for twice the period (31). If it is chanted on the occasion of a Srāddha in spring it shall give us gratification for sixteen years and when performed in summer it shall also afford us gratification for sixteen years (32). O Ruchi, if a Srāddha be performed imperfectly during rains, this hymn, if chanted then, shall afford us everlasting gratification (33). If it is chanted on the occasion of a Srāddha during autumn it confers upon us gratification extending over fifteen years (34). In a house where this is daily kept written if a Srāddha is performed it at once draws us near (35). Therefore when the Brāhmaṇas are engaged in taking their meals at a Srāddha, you should, O great one, make them listen to it, and we shall then be satisfied (36). By listening to his hymn, or reciting it in mind one reaps the same fruit as is reaped by the performance of a Srāddha at Gyā, Pushkara, Kurukshetra or Naimishā. Having conferred this boon on Ruchi the ancestral manes attained to Siddhi (37).

CHAPTER XCVIII.

MARKANDEYA said:—Thereupon from the middle of the river there arose before him a most beautiful and charming Apsarā of slender make by name Premlochā (1). That excellent Apsarā Premlochā, of fair eye-brows, bending low with humility, addressed the high-souled Ruchi with sweet accents (2), "Do thou accept as thy wife, O foremost of the ascetics, the most beautiful daughter of mine, begotten on me by the high-souled Pushkara, the son of Varuna. She will give birth to thy son, the highly intelligent Manu (3—4).

He having given his consent she took up from the water her daughter of a fair body by name Mālini (5). Thereupon having brought together all the leading ascetics that foremost of ascetics Ruchi espoused her duly on the banks of the river

(6). He begot on her a highly energetic and intelligent son who was celebrated on earth as Rouchya after the name of his father (7). I have already related to you in detail the gods, Rishis, the king and his sons of that *Manwántara* (8). Forsooth, a man, hearing of this *Manwàntara*, secures an acquisition of wealth, freedom from diseases, prosperity, corns and offspring (9). O great Muni, hearing of the above mentioned hymn of the manes, and of their number, one, by their grace, has all his desires accomplished (10).

CHAPTER XCIX.

MARKANDEYA said :—Hear now of origin of Bhoutya, of the gods, Rishis, his sons and the kings (1). Angiras had a highly wrathful disciple by name Bhuti. For a trifle he used to imprecate a dreadful curse and he never knew what a sweet word was (2). In his hermitage the wind could not blow high, the sun could not pour fierce rays and the clouds could not discharge rain in such a way as to create much mud (3). Even the moon, when full, used to pour not very cold rays. Afraid of that fierce and wrathful (Rishi) the seasons, renouncing their natural order, used to cover, at his command, all the trees of his hermitage with the fruits and flowers of all seasons (4—5). Afraid of the powers of that high-souled one the waters, near his hermitage, used always to enter into his *kamandalu* at his pleasure (6), O Vipra, he was highly wrathful and could not bear the least inconvenience. That great man had no issue and therefore made up his mind to carry on devout penances (7). He thought,

"Desirous of having a son and accordingly restraining my diet and being exposed to cold, wind and fire I shall carry on devout penances" and accordingly he made up his mind so (8). Then the moon began to pour not very cold rays, the sun not very warm rays and the wind blew not very roughly, O great Muni (9). When not assailed by contraries that foremost of Munis, Bhuti did not attain his wished for object he desisted from his penances (10). His brother Suvarcha undertook a sacrifice and invited him to perform it. Desirous of goining there he said to his highly intelligent disciple, Shānti by name, who was of a quiescent mind, humble, ever ready for his preceptor's work, of good conduct, generous and the foremost of Munis (11—12).

BHUTI said :—O Sānti, I shall be present at the sacrifice of my brother Suvarchās. Hear, what thou salt have to do (13). Always awake thou shalt, with every care, so keep the fire in my hermitage that it may not be extinguished (14).

MARKANDEYA said :—Having thus commanded him and his disciple Santi saying 'so be it' the preceptor, invited by his elder brother, proceeded to be present at his Yajna (15). And Santi too collected, from the forest, twigs, flowers and fruits for the maintenance of his high-souled preceptor (16). When filled with devotion to his preceptor he engaged in other actions the fire, that was kept up by Bhuti, was extinguished (17). Beholding that fire extinguished Santi was greatly sorry and afraid of Bhuti the highly intelligent one began to think in many ways (18). "What shall I do? How will the preceptor come here? What shall I do to-day? By doing what shall I reap good? (19). If by my luck the preceptor beholds his fire extinguished he will throw me to-day into dreadful misery (20). If I place another fire here in the room of this fire he will surely reduce me to ashes for he sees everything (21). Sinful as I am I have thus become the subject of both the anger and curse of my preceptor. I do not grieve so mcuh for myself as do I for the iniquity committed towards the preceptor (22). Forsooth, beholding the fire extinguished the preceptor will imprecate a curse on me or even the fire worked up with anger for that twice-born one is equally powerfnl (23). He, terrified by whose prowess even the celestials carry on his behest for what reason will he not curse me who have committed a sin (24)?

MARKANDEYA said:—Thinking thus in many way, he, the foremost of the intelligent and always afraid of his preceptor, sought refuge with the fire (25). Then controlling his mind and kneeling down he, with whole-mindedness and folded hands, began to recite the following hymn (26).

SANTI said:—Om! Salutation unto the high-souled (Agni) who is the stay of all creatures, who residest at the Rajshyua sacrifice in sixfold forms (27). Salutation unto fire who gives maintenance to all the deities, who is highly effulgent, who is in the form of Shukra and who is the supporter of the endless world (28). Thou art the mouth of all the gods, through thee the Lord taketh sacrificial offerings and pleaseth the entire host of the celestials; thou art the life of all the gods (29). The Havi, that is offered unto thee, becomes highly pure and is then converted into air (30). By it are created all the plants. O thou the charioteer of the wind, all the creatures live happily on all these endless plants (31). With the plants created by thee men perform sacrifices. And by these sacrifices O fire, the gods, Daityas and Rakshasas are pleased. O fire, thou art the supporter of all these sacrifices. O fire, thou art the source of all and identical with all (22—33). The gods Danavas, Yakshas, men, beasts, trees, wild animals, birds, reptiles are all satisfied and nourished by thee, O fire. They all originate from thee and meet with dissolution in thee (34—35). O God, thou dost create the water and thou dost drink it up; and all the (plants) when rotten by thee conduce to the nourishment of creatures (36). Thou dost reside as effulgence in the midst of the gods, as physical grace in the midst of the Siddhas, as poison with the serpents and as air in the midst of the birds (27). Thou art anger amongst men, stupidity in the beasts and birds. Thou art the stay in trees and hardness in the earth (38). O lord, thou art the liquid element in water, the velocity in the air, the space in the sky and as the soul every where (39). Thou dost travel in the hearts of all creatures and protect them. O fire, the poets sometimes describe thee as one and again as three (40). And again designating thee as eight the Prime Purusha undertook the sacrifice. The great Rishis say that this universe has been created by thee (41). O fire, without thee, this whole universe at once; meets with dissolution. By adoring thee with Havya and Kavya and with the recitation of Swahā and Swadhā a twice-born one attains to a position ascertained by his own actions. Thou art also worshiped by the immortals. Having emanated from thee, the scintillations, the end, soul and energy of creatures, burn down the entire elemental creation. Thou art Jātaveda, thou art highly effulgent.—thou hast created this universe (42—44). Thou art the author of Vedic rites and the universe, identical with all the elements. Salutation unto thee, O Anala, O Pingāksha, O Hutasana (45). Salutation unto thee, O Pāvaka, who art the beginning of all; Salutation unto thee, O Havyavāhana (the carrier of sacrificial offerings). Thou dost cook what is eaten or drunk; thou dost purify the entire universe (46). Thou dost make the corns ripe—thou art the nourisher of the universe—the cloud, the air,the seed of the corns (47). Thou dost nourish all creatures and thou art the past, present and future; thou art the light in all the elements—and art Aditya and Vibhavasu (41) Thou art the day and the night and two Sandhyās. O Vanhi, thou art Hiranyaretas and thou art the cause of the origin of Hiranya (49). Thou art Hiranyagarbha—thou art bright like gold—art the moment and Khana (lesser division of the time); thou art *Truti* and *Lava* (50). O lord of the universe, thou dost exist in the shape of

Kata, Kashtha, Nimesha and other divisions of time. Thou art the entire universe and Kāla identical with the dissolution of all (51). O lord, do thou protect us from all fear, sin and the great dread of this world as well as of the next with thy tongue called Kāli which is the support of Kāla (52). Do thou save us from all sins and the great terror of this world with thy tongue called Karāla which is the instrument of the great dissolution (53). Do thou save us from all sins and the great dread of this life with thy that tongue which is called Manojava gifted with the quality of Laghimā (54). Do thou save us from all sorts of sins and the great fear of this life with thy that tongue which is called Sulohita and grants the desires of all creatures (55). Do thou save us from all sorts of sins and the great fear of this world with thy that tonge which is called Dhrumravarna and which is the cause of the diseases of all creatures (56). Do thou save us from all sins and the great fear of this world with that thy tongue which is called Sphulaga and is the root of the well-being of all (57). Do thou save us from all sins and the great fear of this life with thy that tongue which is called Vishwa and which gives peace to all creatures (58). Thou art Pingāksha (yellow-eyed) Lohitagriva (dark-nhcked) of black hue and Hutāshana- Do thou save me from all sins and the great danger of this world (59). O Vahni, O Saptarchi, O Krishanu, O Havyavāhan, be thou pleased. I recite thy eight names as Agni, Pāvaka, Sukra etc (60). Be thou propitiated, O Agni, O the first born of all the elements, O Vibhāvasu, O Habyavāha, O eternal and O thou identical with hymns (68). Thou art eternal, incomprehensible Vahni, prosperous, greatly fierce and hard to bear. Thou art undecaying, dreadful and dost destroy all the worlds. Thou art highly powerful and hast a form (62). Thou art most excellent, the heart of all energies, art endless and worshipped of all. From thee has emanated this universe, mobile and immobile. O Hutāshana, thou art one and many (63). Thou art undecaying, art this earth with mountains and forests, art the sky with the sun and the moon, art the time with the day and night and art the forest-fire lying in the womb of the great ocean. By thy great lustre thou dost reside in the rays (64). The great saints, observant of regulations, always worship thee as Hutāsana in the great sacrifice. Invited at the sacrifice thou dost drink the *soma* Juice and Havi after reciting Vasatkāra for the posperity (of the creatures) (65). For reaping fruits the Brāhmanas always worship thee on this earth. Thou art being chanted in all the Vedas and their branches. With a view to worship thee all the leading twice-born ones always master the Vedas (66). Thou art Brahmā ever intent on performing sacrifices; thou art Vishnu, Siva, Indra, Arjamā and Varuna. Being pleased with Havyas the sun, the moon, the celestials and Asuras all obtain their desired for fruits (67). Objects, however impure they may be, are at once purified by the touch of thy rays. Even when bathed with thy ashes one attains to highest purification. For this the Munis adore thee in the evening (68). Be thou, who art Vahni Sachi, propitiated. Thou art Pāvaka Vaidyuta and Prime—be propitiated and save me, O thou the eater of Havya (69). Like unto a father protecting his own begotten son, do thou, O Vahni, protect us with thy all auspicious form and seven tongues. I do chant thy glories (70).

CHAPTER C.

MARKANDEYA said:—He having thus chanted his glories, O Muni, the divine Havyavāhana, enveloped with his rays, appeared before him (1). O twice-born one, the the lord Vibhavasu was delighted with the above hymn and said to Santi, who was bowing, in words deep as the muttering of clouds (2). " O Vipra, I have been delighted with the hymn that thou hast reverentially sung; I shall therefore confer upon thee a boon; pray for what thou likest (5)."

SANTI said:—O lord, blessed am I, since, I have beheld thee in thy form. Still hear what I communicate unto thee bending low with humility (4). O god, my preceptor, leaving his own hermitage, has gone to be present at his brother's sacrifice. May he, on his return to the hermitage, behold thee stationed as before (5). O Vibhāvasu, may that twice-born one behold thee as before, stationed there which thou didst leave before for my folly (6). If thou dost show me another favour, O lord, then let there be an excellent son born unto my preceptor who has no issue (7). And may my preceptor grow equally mild towards all other creatures as he will be towards his own son (8). O eternal, as thou hast been pleased with me, O thou conferrer of boons, for my chanting thy glories, may he likewise be propitiated with me (9).

MARKANDEYA said:—Hearing his words and being again adored with hymns on account of the devotion unto preceptor Pāvaka (Fire) said to that foremost of the twice-born (10).

AGNI said:—O Brāhmana, thou hast prayed for two boons for thy preceptor and not for thy own self. For this I have been greatly delighted with thee, O great Muni (11). Therefore what thou hast prayed for thy preceptor shall all be fulfilled. He will be friendly towards all creatures and will have a son (12). He will be the lord of a *Manwantara* and be known by the name of Bhoutya; and your preceptor too will be highly powerful, highly energetic and wise (13). Whoever, that, being self-controlled, shall chant my glories with his hymn, shall have all his desires fulfilled and piety (14). This most excellent hymn, conducing to my nourishment, when chanted at the sacrifices at Parvas, at sacred places and Homas, will lead to the acquisition of virtue (15). One, by listening to this most excellent hymn which is so delightful to me, will have for sooth his sins committed day and night, dissipated (16). The defects that originate from the performance of a Homa at an improper season and by an improper person, are immediately removed by merely listening to this (17). This, when listened to properly, either at *Purnima, Amavasya* or any other Parva, leads to the destruction of all sins (18).

MARKANDEYA said :—Having said this the divine Agni, O Muni, disappeared immediately in his own presecnce, like unto a light put out by the wind (19). After Vahni had departed Shanti, with a delighted heart and his hairs standing erect in joy, entered the hermitage of his preceptor (20). He saw there fire ablaze as before at the very place where it had been kept by his preceptor. Thereat he attained to an excess of delight (21). In the interval the preceptor returned to his own hermitage from the sacrifice of his high-souled elder brother (22). His disciple at first touched his feet. Then after accepting seat and adoration the preceptor said to him (23). "O child, I find in me a growing love towards thee as well as other creatures; I do not understand what is this. Tell me speedily if you know anything of it (24).

Thereupon, O great Muni, that Brăhmana Santi related truly everything unto his preceptor beginning with the destruction of the fire (25). Hearing this, O great Muni, and embracing him, the preceptor, having his eyes bathed with tears of love, delivered unto his disciple all the Vedas with their divisions and sub-divisions (26) Then there was born to Bhuti a son by name Bhoutya who became a Manu. Hear from me of the gods, rishis and kings of his *Manwantara* (27). I shall describe at length who will be all such in the *Manwantara* of this would-be Manu, as well as who will be king of gods of illustrious actions (28). Chăkshusha,

Kanishtha, Pavitra, Bhrājira and Dhārāvika—these will be the five classes of gods (29). Suchi will be the lord of all these gods—highly powerful, highly energetic and endowed with all the accomplishments of a king of gods (30). Agnidhra Agnivāhu, Shuchi, Muktā, Mādhava, Shatru and Ajita—these will be the seven Rishis (31). Guru, Gabhira, Vradhna, Bharatā, Anugraha, Strikhāni, Pratira, Vishnu, Sankrandana, Tejaswi and Suvala will be the sons of Manu Bhoutya. I have thus described to you the fourteenth *Manwantara* (32—33).

O foremost of Munis, hearing of these *Manwantaras* in order a man acquires virtue and endless offspring (34). Hearing of the first *Manwantara* a man acquires virtue and hearing of that of Swarochisha he acquires the fulfillment of all his desires (35). In Auttoma one acquires wealth, in Tāmasa knowledge, in Raivata the faculty of understanding Srutis and a beautlful wife (36). In Chākshusha people acquire freedom from diseases and in Vaivaswata strength, and in Surya Sāvarniki accomplished sons and grand sons (37). In Brahmā Sāvarni one acquires glory and in Dharma Sāvarni auspiciousness. In Rudra Sāvarniki a man acquires intellect and victory (38). In Daksha Sāvarniki one becomes the foremost amongst his kinsmen and is endowed with accomplishments. O foremost of men, hearing of Rouchya, one has all his enemies destroyed (39). Hearing of Bhoutya *Manwantara* one acquires the grace of gods, Agnihotra and accomplished sons (40). O foremost of Munis, hear what an excellent fruit does a man reap when in order he hears of all the *Manwantaras* (41). O Vipra, hearing of the gods, Rishis, Indras, Manus and their sons of the respective periods one is released from all the sins (42). Indras, gods, Rishis, kings and Manus of the various periods become greatly delighted and bestow excellent inclination (43). Thereupon acquiring good inclination and performing good actions one attains to a better slation as long as the fourteen

Indras exist (44). If one hears in order of all the *Manwantaras* all the seasons do him good and all the planets, without doubt, become propitious towards him (45).

---oo---

CHAPTER CI.

KROUSHTI said:—Reverend sir, you have described in detail and order all the *Manwantaras* and I have heard of them all (1). O foremost of the twice-born, I wish to hear of the progeny of all the kings beginning with Brahmā. Do thou describe them in full (2).

MARKANDEYA said:—O child, hear of the origin and life of all those kings beginning with Prajāpati who is the origin of the universe (3). This family was adorned with hundreds of pious kings who had performed many sacrifices and been victorious in war (4). He, who listens to the origin and story of all these high-souled kings, is released from all sins (5). Hearing of the family in which were born such heroic kings as Manu, Ikshawku, Anaraya, Bhagiratha who were intent on performing sacrifices and conversant with the knowledge of Brahman and who all ruled over this earth a man is freed from all sins (6—7). Hear of this family from which descended thousands of the families of kings like the branches of a fig-tree (8). O foremost of the twice-born, in the days of yore, the patriarch Brahmā, with a view to create various creatures, procreated from his right thumb the patriarch Daksha and from his left thumb his wife. In this wise, the father of the universe the divine lord Brahmā created the great cause of the world (9—10). The beautiful

Aditi was born as the daughter of Daksha. Kashyapa begat on her the divine sun (11). He is identical with Brahman the conferrer of boons in this endless universe, the beginning, the middle and the end and the ordainer of the creation, preservation and destruction (12). O twice-born one, from him has emanated this entire universe and in him it is stationed; he is the entire universe with the celestials, Asuras and mankind (13). He is identical with all the elements with the soul and is the great soul and is eternal. Aditi had prayed for it before and therefore the Divine sun was born in her womb (14).

KROUSTHI said:—O Reverend Sir, I wish to hear of the true form of the sun and why was he born as the own begotten son of the prime deity Kashyapa (15). O foremost of Munis, I wish to hear in detail, as narrated by you in detail, how he was worshipped by the goddess Aditi and Kashyapa and what did the sun say on being adored by them as well as of his prowess when incarnated (16—17.)

MARKANDEYA said:—Vishtapa, the great learning, Jyotisbhā, Shwashwati, Shphuta, Kaivalya, knowledge, Avibhu, Prākamya, Samrit, Bodha, Avagati, Smriti, discriminative knowledge, these were the forms of the sun who is the form of the universe (18—19.) Hear, O great one, in detail as narrated by me, of the incarnation of the sun of which you have asked (20). When this universe was shorn of lustre and light and was enveloped in darkness a huge egg which is the great cause came into being (21). Living inside it the Divine Grand Father Brahmā rent it asunder; that lotus-sprung deity is the creator and the lord of the universe (22). O great Muni, from his mouth came out the great sound *Om*; then originated therefrom *Bhu*, *Bhavas* and *Swara* (23). These three words are the true form of the sun; and from *Om* has come out the great subtle form of the sun (24). From *Om* have proceeded in due order the seven forms, gross and grosser, such as Mahas, Janas,

Tapas, Satya etc., (25). These forms appear and disappear simultaneously for undoubtedly the presence and absence of all these are brought about by this (26). O Vipra, the great subtle form *Om*, which I have described to you, is the beginning and end of all. That great form has no (material form) that is the real great Brahman and his body (27).

CHAPTER CII.

MARKANDEYA said:—O Muni, when that egg was rent asunder, the *Riks* first originated from the mouth of the unborn Brahmā (1). They were of the hue of Javā flowers and were endowed with energy and form. They were invested with darkness and were separate form each other (2). From his that mouth that was towards the south came out without any obstruction *Yayus*—they were of the hue of gold and unconnected with each other (3). Then from the western mouth of Parameshth Brahmā came out the *Samans* accompanied by their respective metres (4). Then from the northern mouth of the creator came out the endless *Atharvans* that were dark like the black-bees and collyrium. They were divided into *Abhicharika* and *Shantikas*, permeated by joy, goodness and ignorance and were of the forms both gentle and otherwise (5—6). O Muni, *Riks* were permeated by the quality of darkness, the *Samanas* by that of ignorance and *Atharvanas* by both goodness and ignorance (7). They, all burning in unparalleled effulgence, continued to exist separately as before (8). Then the effulgence, which emanated from the nature of the prime effulgence that is designated as *Om*, covering it wholly, existed (9). O great Muni, the effulgence of *Yayush*, being united with that of *Saman*, began to exist in the great effulgence (10). Thus O Brahman, Shāntika, Peshthika and Abhichārika these three ended in *Rik*, *Yayush* and *Saman* (11). By it as soon as the darkness was dispelled the whole universe became clear and accordingly the down, up and oblique sides were distinctly perceived (12). Then the best effulgence, of the metres forming a circle, was united with the great effulgence, O Brahman (13). Because it emanated from Aditya it was called so. O great one, that undecaying energy is the cause of this universe (14). *Rik, Yayush* and *Saman* these three shed effulgence in the morning, noon and afternoon (15). *Riks* give it in the morning, *Yayush* in the noon and Saman in the afternoon, O foremost of Munis (16). Santika enters into *Rik* in the morning, Pounchika into *Yayush* in the noon and Abhicharika into Samàn in the afternoon (17). The ceremonies for the manes should be performed in the noon and morning by the Abhicharika and in the afternoon by Saman (18). At the time of creation Brahmā is identical with *Rik*, at the time of preservation Vishnu is identical with *Yayush* and at the time of dissolution Rudra is identical with Saman, and therefore he (Rudra) is considered impure for a sacrifice (19). Therefore the Divine sun is identical with the Vedas, is the stay of the Vedas and is mentioned as the Great Purusha having the knowledge of the Vedas (10). Therefore he is the cause of the creation, preservation and destruction and passes under the appellation of Brahmā, Vishnu and others by resorting to the qualities of darkness, goodness, etc., (21). He has the Vedas, as his form, the entire host of mortals for his forms and is without it. He is the Prime and the support of the universe. He is light and comprehended by Vedanta and is the greatest of the great and the gods always chant his glories (22).

CHAPTER CIII.

MARKANDEYA said :—When the sky and the earth were heated by the rays of the sun the lotus sprung grandfather, with a desire to create progeny, began to think (1). "As soon as I will create it everything will be destroyed by the heat of the divine sun, the cause of the creation, preservation and destruction (2). All the creatures will be deprived of their lives, the water will be dried up by his heat and without water it will be impossible to carry on the creation of the universe (3)." Thinking thus the Divine Brahmā, the grandfather of the world, with his mind fixed on him, began to chant the glories of the Divine Sun (4).

BRAHMA said :—Salutation unto him who is identical with this whole universe, who is identical with all who has the universe for his form, who is the great light which is meditated on by the Yogins; (5). who is identical with *Rik*, who is the root of *Yayush*, who is the origin of *Saman*, who is of inconceivable energy, who, for his grossness, is identical with three, the half *mâtra* is whose great form and who is beyond all qualities (6); who is the cause of all, who is worthy of being eulogised greatly and being known, who is the great light *Avanhi* in the beginning, who is gross being identical with the gross—I bow unto that greatest of the great, the Sun, the first of all (7). Urged on by this prime energy I create water, earth, air, fire, gods and various other endless objects beginning with Om; and in due order preserve and destroy them. I can never do so of my own accord (8). Thou art fire. By thy prowess I dry up the water and create the world and perform the first cooking process of the world. Thou art, O lord, manifest over the universe and identical with Akāsa (space). Thou art protecting this universe in fivefold ways (9). By undertaking sacrifices, persons conversant with great soul, worship thee; thou art Vivaswan—thou art Vishnu—thou art the lord of all and the greatest of the great. Desirous of emancipation and controlling their mind and soul, even the ascetics meditate on thee (10). Salutation unto thee who art in the form of sacrifice, art the great Brahman and being meditated upon by the Yogins (11). O lord, I am engaged in creation—this bundle of effulgence has stood in my way—do thou withdraw it (12).

MARKANDEYA said:—Having been thus eulogised in a most excellent manner by Brahmā, the creator of the universe, the Divine Sun withdrew his own great effulgence and held a little (13). Then the lotus-sprung great Brāhmā, O great Muni, created, as in the previous Kalpa, the similar gods, Asuras, men, beasts and others, trees, creepers and hells (14—15).

CHAPTER CIV.

MARKANDEYA said:—Having created this universe Brahmā, as before, made the proper divisions of Varna, Asrama, seas, mountains and islands (1). And the Divine Lotus sprung Deity made arrangements for the position and form of the gods, demons and Uragas (2). The son, that was born to Brahmā, was known as Marichi—his son was Kashyapa—his son was Kāshyapa (3). The thirteenth daughter of Daksha was his wife. He had many sons amongst the gods, Daityas and Uragas (4). Aditi gave birth to the gods the lords of the three worlds and Diti to fierce Dānavas of dreadful prowess (5). Virata gave birth to Garuda and Aruna to Yakshas, Rākshasas and various other birds. Kadru gave birth to Nagas and Muni to Gandharvas (6). Krodhā gave birth to the river and Rishthā to Apsaras. O twice-born one, Irā gave birth to Airavata and other elephants (7). O twice-born one, Tāmrā gave birth to girls Sweni and others, who (in turn) gave birth to birds such as Swany, Bhāsa and Suka (8). Of Ilā were born the trees and of Pradhā the birds. By the off-spring of Kashyapa who was born of Aditi, by his sons and daughters, grandsons and by their sons and daughters, O Muni, this world was covered (9—10). Amongst the sons of Kashyapa, the gods were the foremost; they were divided into three classes namely those pessessed of the quality of goodness, those of darkness and those of ignorance (11.) The great Patriarch Parameshithi Brahmā, the foremost of those conversant with Brahman, made the gods the partakers of sacrificial offerings and the lords of the three worlds (12). Their step-brothers, the Daityas and Dānavas being united together, began to throw obstacles in their way. The Rākshasas too joined them. Accordingly there was waged a highly dreadful war (13). After a thousand celestial years the gods were defeated and being victorious the Daityas and Dānavas grew powerful (14). Thereupon having beheld her own sons, the gods defeated and ousted from the sovereignty of the three worlds and deprived of the sacrificial offerings by the Daityas and Dānavas Aditi, O foremost of Munis, was overwhelmed with grief. She then set forth mighty exertion for worshipping Savitri (15—16). Then abstaining from food and observing regulation she, with whole mindedness, began to please the Sun, the collection of light stationed in the sky (17).

ADITI said:—Salutation unto thee who hast assumed a subtle golden form. Thou art energy, the lord of the energetic and the eternal support of energy (18) Thou art the ordainer of heat, I bow unto thine that form which thou dost assume at the time of drawing it for the benefit of the world (19). I bow unto thine that dreadful form which thou dost assume for taking in eight months the juice of the moon (20). O Bhāshman, I bow unto thine that most delightful cloud form which thou dost assume at the time of pouring that water (29). I do also bow unto thine that Bhāskara form which thou dost assume for ripening those plants that spring up from the showers discharged by thee (22). I do bow unto thine that cold form of dews that thou dost assume for nourishing the corns at that time (23). I bow again and again, O God, O Ravi, unto that thy gentle form, which is neither very fierce nor very cold which thou dost assume in spring (24). I bow unto thine that form which is delightful unto the numberless gods and the ancestral manes and is the instrument of the ripening of fruits (25). I bow unto thy that form which gives life to the creepers, which is identical with Soma and which is the source of ambrosia which is drunk by the gods and ancestral manes (26). Salutation unto that form dientical with Gana, O Arka, which, being united with twofold forms of Agnistoma, has created this universal form (27. O Bibhāvasu, salutation unto that form which has been created by *Rik*, *Yajush* and *Sàman* united, which is this universe and which is called Trayi (28). Salutation unto that form which is superior to that which is called Om, which is subtle, which has no end, which is eternal and which is not sullied by any shortcoming (29).

MARKANDEYA said :—O Muni, thus observing vows and abstaining from food, that goddess, for worshipping the sun, began to recite this hymn day and night (30). O foremost of the twice-born, thus after a long time the Divine Sun came within the view of the daughter of Daksha in the sky (31). She saw a bundle of light spreading simultaneously over the earth and sky, and growing fierce to look at for being united with highly effulgent rays (32). Seeing this the goddess was possessed by great fear. She then said "Be pleased, O Sun I cannot see thee (33). Abstaining from food, I at first saw thee in the sky, hard to look at, shedding heat and lustre at the same time (34). I again behold the same bundle of thy effulgence on the earth. Therefore O Sun, be propitiated; I wish to see thee. Thou dost show compassion towards thy votaries, O lord, I am thy votary—save my sons (35). Thou art the protcctor; thou hast created this universe: being engaged in the work of preservation thou dost protect it; the whole universe ends in thee at the time of dissolution. Save thee there is no other refuge unto the creatures (36). Thou art Brahmā, Hari, Mahadeva, Kuvera, Yama, the regent of the Dead and Varuna, the king of water, the air, the moon, the fire, the sky, the mountain and the ocean. Thou art the soul and the form of all. How can I eulogise thee (37). Thou art the lord of sacrifices. Following their own actions the twice-born every day worship and eulogise thee with various hymns. Controlling their minds and being engaged in Yoga, they, meditating on thee and assuming the form of Yoga, attain to excellent stations (38). Thou dost heat, ripe, preserve and consume the universe. Thou dost, by spreading and drawing thy rays, display it and benefit it by extending thy rays surcharged with water. The gods and men salute thee. The enemies never obtain thee (39).

CHAPTER CV.

MARKANDEYA said:—Thereupon coming out of the bundle of his rays the Lord Sun appeared before Aditi in the form of burning copper (1). O Muni, beholding the goddess bending low her head as soon as he came in view, the sun said to her:—"Pray for thy desired for boon whatever thou seekest from me (2)." Kneeling down on earth and bending low her head Aditi said to the Sun, the conferror of boons who was before her (3). "O god, be pleased, the Daityas and Danavas growing powerful have deprived my sons of the three worlds and sacrificial offerings (4). O lord of rays, therefore confer upon me this favour, that descending as their brother in a portion of thy rays do thou destroy their enemies (5). O Ravi, being pleased with me do thou show them this mercy, O lord, that my sons may again partake of the sacrificial offerings and be lords of the three worlds. Thou dost remove the misery of the afflicted and thou art spoken of as the lord of creation (6—7)."

Thereupon, O Vipra, the Divine Bhāskara, the pilferrer of water, being prepared to show his favour said to Aditi who had prostrated herself (8). "O Aditi, being born in thy womb in my endless thousand rays I shall speedily make an end of the enemies of thy sons (9)." Having said this the Divine Bhāskara disappeared. She too, having secured all her wishes, desisted from carrying on her penances (10) Thereupon, of the thousand rays of the Sun the one called Soushamna took the incarnation of Vipra in the womb of the mother of the gods (11). She too, being attentive, performed the vows of Krishnachāndrāyana etc and being purified held the conception, O twice-born one (12). Thereupon Kashyapa addressed to her angry words:—"Fasting every day will you kill this embryo (13)?" She too said to him:—"O thou wrathful one, I have not killed the embryo that thou dost see—he is for the destruction of the enemies" (14). Saying this, she, wroth at the words of her husband, at once discharged the conception which began to shine in effulgence (15). Beholding that embryo effulgent as the rising Sun, Kashyapa, bending low, began to hymn its glory with the recitation of the prime Riks (16). Being thus eulogised by him the Divine Bhāshkara, assuming a lotus-hued body, came out of the egg and filled all the quarters with his effulgence (17). Then were heard divine words deep as the muttering of the clouds surcharged with water from the sky, addressing Kashyapa, the foremost of Munis (18). "O Muni, since thou didst ask me to kill (Marita) this egg, so my son will be called Mārtanda. This son will perform, on earth, the functions of the sun and destroy the Asuras who are pilferring the sacrificial offerings" (19—20). Perceiving that the words came out of the sky the gods attained to great delight and the Dānavas were dispirited (21). Thereupon when the performer of a hundred sacrifices invited them to battle the Dānavas delightedly confronted the gods (22). Then there arose a great encounter between the gods and Dānavas (in which) all the corners of the world were illumined with the lustre of the arms of both the parties (23). In that encounter all the leading Asuras, as soon as they were looked upon by the Divine Mārtanda, were burnt down to ashes (24). Thereat all the gods attained to great delight and began to hymn both Aditi and Mārtanda, born of effulgence (25). After they had been stationed as before in their positions and entitled to sacrificial offerings the Divine Mārtanda began to spread his own dominion (26). Then displaying his lustre like that of Kadamva flowers he began to pour his rays both in the sky and on the earth. He became like a buring bundle of fire and assumed a body of great effulgence (27).

CHAPTER C.VI.

MARKANDEYA said:—Thereupon propitiating and saluting him the Patriarch Viswakarmā conferred on Vivaswān his daughter Sajnā (1). Vivaswān begat on her Manu Vaivāswata. I have already described to you in full his true form etc., (2). The lord of rays begat on her three children—two great sons and the daughter Jamunā, O Muni (3). Srāddhadeva—the Patriarch Manu Vaivaswata was the eldest—there were born the twins Yama and Yami (4). The effulgent Mārtanda, with his growing lustre, greatly distressed the three worlds, mobile and immobile (5). Beholding the circular form of Vivāswān and unable to bear his rays, Sajnā, addressing her own Shadow, said:—(6). "May good betide thee. I am going to my father's house. O auspicious dame, at my command, thou shouldst live near the sun without being agitated (7). Thou shouldst with care bring up these my two sons and the most beautiful daughter. Thou shouldst never communicate this unto the Divine Sun (8)."

THE SHADOW said:—O goddess, as long as the sun will not take me by the hair or imprecate a curse on me so long I shall not communicate any thing unto him. Go wherever thou wishest (9)." Thus addressed by her Shadow Sajnā repaird to her father's house; and that one, of auspicious eyes, lived there for some time (10). And thereafter when she was repeatedly requested by her father to go to her husband she assumed the form of a mare and repaired to Uttarakuru (11). O great Muni, that chaste damsel, abstaining from food, began to carry on devout penances (12). After she had gone to her father's abode, she, the Shadow, assuming the form of Sajnā and intent on carrying on her words, appeared before Bhāskara (13). Taking her as Sajnā the Divine Sun too begat on her two sons and a daughter (14). O foremost of the twice-born, the first born of the two, Sāvarni (by name) was equal to the preceeding Manus (in prowess) (15). The second one became the planet Shani ; and the daughter was named Tapati whom the king Samvarana espoused (16). The shadow of Sajnā did not show that affection towards the first born children as she did towards her own (17). Manu forgave her for this but Yama could not do so, and therefore he was repeatedly solicited by his father's wife (18). Thereupon out of anger, childishness and the force of future incidents Yama raised up his foot, O Muni, to strike her ; she too, greatly revengeful, imprecated a curse an Yama (19).

SAJNA said :—"I am thy father's wife and therefore thy superior ; and since thou hast threatened me with that foot, undoubtedly it shall fall off" (20). Having his mind greatly agitated by that curse the high-souled Yama, along with Manu, communicated all unto their sire (21),

YAMA said :—"O lord, our mother does not treat us all equally. Leaving us who are elders she always seeks to rear up the younger ones (22). I raised up my foot against her but it did not fall on her body. If it be either out of childishness or ignorance it behoves thee to forgive me (23). O father, I am her son and still I have been imprecated by the mother. Therefore, O foremost of the ascetics, I do not consider her as our mother (24). O father, a mother does never become hostile towards the sons even when they become so. Then how can she say to her son, "your leg shall fall off" (25). O lord, O divine sun, do thou think of a measure by which, by thy grace, my foot may not fall off on account of the imprecation of the mother (26)."

THE SUN said :—Since thou, O son, truthful and pious as thou art, didst come by anger, undoubtedly there is some cause of it (27). There is a remedy for every curse but there is none such for the imprecation of a mother (28). Therefore

I am unable to undo the words of thy mother but I shall show thee some favour out of my fatherly love (29). Taking flesh from thy foot the worms shall fall down on the earth. By this her words will be verified and thou shalt be saved (30).

MARKANDEYA said :—Then the Sun said to the shadow of Sajnā :—"All the sons are equal, therefore, why dost thou show partiality towards one (31)? How can a mother curse her sons even when they grow disobedient? Forsooth thou art not their mother—but some body else come to me (32). To evade (an answer) she did not say anything to the Sun. Then concentrating his own self he saw every thing in its true form (33). Observing him on the point of uttering a curse, O Brāhmana, the shadow of Sajnā, trembling, communicated every thing truly to the Sun (34). Hearing all and getting angry the Sun went to his father-in-law. Then consoling and adoring him who was desirous of consuming all in anger (Vishwakarmā) of good vows said (35) :—

"The whole universe has been overspread by thy great effulgence. Unable to bear thy form which is so greatly hard to bear Sajnā is carrying on devout penances in the forest (36). Thou shalt behold to-day thy own pious wife carrying on hard penances in the forest for thy form* (37). I remember the words of Brahmā ; O god, O lord of the day, if it pleases thee I shall make thy form charming" (38).

Formerly the form of the Sun was circular ; therefore the Divine Sun said to the (celestial Architect) Tastri "So be it" (39). Having obtained the command and engaged the Sun to travel in the insular continent of Shāka Vishwakarmā set himself to chiselling his effulgence (40). When the Sun, the navel of the endless world, began to roam, the earth, with its seas, mountains and forest, got up to the sky (41). O Brāhmana, along with it the sky, with the moon, planets and stars, came down, O great one, and became greatly agitated

* *i.e.*, The fierceness of the Sun may be lessened and he may assume a milder form.

(42). The waters of the oceans became all agitated—the great mountains were rent assunder and their summits were shattered (43). The huge clouds, driven hither and thither by the velocity of the sun's motion, moving with great sounds, were all dispersed (45). O foremost of Munis, agitated by the motion of the sun, the earth, sky, Rasātala and universe were sent out of their places (46). All the three worlds, O Vipra, thus revolving, the celestial saints and the gods along with Brahmā eulogised the Sun (47). "Thou art the Prime Deity; this is truly known to the gods. Thou dost exist in thy threefold forms at the time of creation, preservation and destruction (48). May good betide thee, O lord of the universe. O thou the mine of heat, rains and dews, O god of gods, O maker of the day, do thou bring peace unto mankind (49)." Indra too, coming there, chanted the glories of the revolving Sun:—"Salutation unto the god who is manifest all over the universe. May thou be victorious, O lord of the universe (50)." The seven Rishis too, headed by Vashistha and Atri, saying, "May good betide thee! may good betide thee!!" pleased him with the chanting of various hymns (51). The Bālakhilyas too, filled with delight, pleased the revolving Sun, by reciting the prime and most excellent *Riks* recorded in the Vedas (52), "Thou art, O lord, the beautitude of those who have obtained it, thou art the object of the meditation of those who engage in it. Thou art the refuge of all creatures engaged in action (53). Thou art the lord of the gods, may good betide the creatures through thy mercy; thou art the lord of the universe; mayst thou encompass our happiness, peace and well-being. May good betide us all always who are two-legged as well as all those that are quadrupeds (54)." Thereupon the Vidyadharas, Rākshasas, Yakshas and Pannagas, with folded hands and heads bending low, began to address the Sun with the following words delightful to the mind and the ears: "Thou art the protector of creatures, may they bear thy effulgence (55—56)." Thereupon Hāhāhuhu, Nārada, and Tumvura, versed in Sharaja, Madhyama, Grāndhāra and the three Tālas as well as the other arts of Gandharvas, began to sing delightful tunes with the accompaniment of Murchanā, Prayoga and time (57—58). Vishwachi, Ghritachi, Urvashi, Tilottamā, Menakā, Sahajanayā, Rambhā and orther leading Apsarās, displaying gestures and various other charming gaits, began to dance at the time of the revolving of the sun (59—60). At that time hundreds and thousands of flutes, Vinās, Darduras, Panavas, Pushkaras, Mridangas, Patahas, Anakas, celestial bugles and conches were sounded (61). When the Gandharvas sang, Apsaras danced and cymbals and other musical instruments were struck all was filled with noise (62). Thereupon with folded hands and with heads bending down with reverence all the deities bowed unto the revolving sun of a thousand rays (63). When there arose a great tumult on account of the gathering of all the clestials Vishwakarma gradually cut off his effulgence (64). Thus the Divine Sun is the source of summer, rains, and dews. Hari, Hara, and Brahmā too chant his glories. One, by listening to the story of lessening his effulgence, attains to the solar region after his death (65).

CHAPTER CVII.

MARKANDEYA said:—Thereupon while thus chiselling his body Patriarch Vishwakarmā, filled with growing delight, chanted the following hymn of the Vivaswat (1).

Salutation unto thee who art the mine of rays, who dost encompass the well-being of and show mercy unto those who bow unto thee, who art the great soul, who hast seven horses all gifted with equal speed, who art of good effulgence and dost give life to the lotuses and who art clever enough to dispell darkness (2). Thou dost purify others, art of pious deeds, dost confer diverse wished-for objects, art the source of the highly effulgent fire, art rays and art the benefactor unto all. I bow unto thee (3). Thou hast no birth, art the cause of the three worlds, art identical with all the elements, the lord of the universe and righteousness,* the foremost of the merciful and the sun who gives vision unto all ; I bow unto thee (4). Thou art the source of rays and the innermost soul of the learned ; in thee the world is stationed and thou art the benefactor of the universe, art self-sprung, the vision of all and the foremost of the gods. Thou hast incomparable effulgence, I bow unto thee (5). Thou dost adorn, for a moment, the hill whence thou risest like a garland of jems and encompass the well-being of the world along with the celestials. The thousand rays are thy body ; to dispell darkness thou dost spread them over the universe (6). Drinking the wine of worldly darkness and under its influence thy body becomes red ; from that arise thy rays that display the three worlds and accordingly dost thou appear in great effulgence (7). O lord, ascending thine highly beautiful chariot of equal proportions moving mildly, thou dost, through the help of numberless horses, always wander about unobstructed for encompassing the well-being of the world (8). By bestowing simultaneously ambrosia and the rays of the moon thou dost bring about the gratification of the gods and manes and the destruction of the enemies. Therefore do I, saluting thee, chisell thine effulgence for the benefit of the world (9). O thou fond of thy votaries, O thou the purifier of the three worlds, O Ravi, do thou save me, who have touched with

* The word in the text is *Vrisha i. e.* bull. In Puranas a bull with four legs is the emblem of righteousnes.

my head the earth, purified with the dust of thy feet and trampled down by golden-hued horses (10). Thou art like the mother of the universe and the highly sacred abode of the three worlds. Thou art the lamp of the entire universe and what more, thou art Vishwakarmā; I bow unto thee (11).

CHAPTER CVIII.

MARKANDEYA said:—Having thus chanted the glories of the sun Vishwakarmā put the sixteenth part of the effulgence of the creator of the day into his circular disc (1). Fifteen portions of his rays being chiselled out of his body the sun assumed a highly charming form (2). With the effulgence that was chiselled out of his body he made the discus of Vishnu, the mace of Siva, the vehicle of the god of riches, the rod of the Regent of the dead and Sakti of (Kārtikeya) the commander of the celestial army (3). With the rays of the sun Vishwakarmā made many other shinning weapons for other gods for the pacification of their enemies (4). With his effulgence thus chiselled as soon as the Divine sun appeared with not very warm rays his body became exceedingly charming (5). Then concentrating his mind he saw his own wife carrying on penances and observing regulation in the shape of a mare never thought of by any creature (6). Thereupon repairing to Uttarakuru and assuming the form of a horse the sun approached her. Beholding him thus approach and taking him for a stranger she turned her face towards him. Thereupon they touched each other's nose

(7—8), The energy of the sun entered into the mare through her nostril and therefrom originated the two gods Açwinis, the foremost of the physicians (9). They both came out of the mouth of the horse and are the sons of Mārtanda assuming the form of a horse (10). From the seminal fluid came out Revantā who had in his hands dagger, bow, arrow and quiver and a coat of mail on his body and was seated on horseback (11).

Then the sun displayed his own improved form; and seeing his mild form she attained to great delight (12). Thereupon the sun, the pilferer of water, took to his own house his loving wife Sajnā who had assumed her own form (13). Then his first son became Manu Vaivaswata and the second Yama, on account of the imprecation and favour, followed only righteousness (14). Having his mind greatly assailed by the curse Yama liked only virtue and therefore he was called *Dharmaraja* or the king of virtue (15). His father brought about an end of his imprecation by saying "Taking the flesh of thy feet the worms shall fall down on earth" (16). Since he had always his eye on righteousness and was impartial both towards friends and foes, the dispeller of darkness appointed him as the Regent of the dead (17). O Vipra, being propitiated with him the Divine Sun conferred on him the dignity of a Patriarch and the sovereignty over the ancestral manes (18). Thereupon he converted Yamunā into a tributary of Kālindi and the two Açwinis were appointed by their high-souled sire as the the physicians of the celestials (19). Revanta was appointed as the king of Guhyakas. Then the Divine Sun, worshipped of all the worlds, said to him. "O child, do thou become adorable by all the worlds (20). Those mortals, who shall, in fear of the forest fire, enemies and robbers, remember thee, will be freed from all those great dangers (21). Adored by them and delighted accordingly thou shalt confer on mankind peace, intellect, happiness, kingdom, recovery from diseases and advancement (22). The highly illustrious Savarni too, the son of the immitation Sajnā, shall also become the eighth Manu by name Savarni at some future period (23). That lord Sāvarni, still now, is carrying on hard penances on the summit of the mount Meru. His brother, Sani, at the command of the sun, has become a planet (24). O foremost of the twice-born, the youngest daughter, that was begotten by Aditya, has become the foremost of rivers Yamunā purifying the world (25). I shall now relate in full the account of Manu Vaivaswata, who is high-souled and the eldest of all and whose reign is now going on (26). He, who listens to or reads the birth and glorious account of the gods, Vaivaswata Manu, his sons and the divine sun, is released from the impending danger and attains to great fame. Hearing of the glorious account of the Prime Deity the high-souled Mārtanda one has all his sins committed day and night destroyed (27—28).

CHAPTER CIX.

KROUSHTHI said :—O Reverend Sir, you have related in full, the birth of the children of the Sun, the Prime Deity, his glory and his true form (1). O foremost of Munis, I wish to hear again fully of the glories of the Prime Deity Bhaskara ; do thou delightedly describe them (2).

MARKANDEYA said :—Hear, I shall recount the glories of the Prime Deity Vivaswān and what he did do in the days of yore when he was adored by people (3). The illustrious Rājyavarddhana, the son of Dama, became the king ; that lord of the earth, governed her well (4). That kingdom being righteously governed by that high-souled one, it grew, O Vipra, daily in men and riches (5). During his administration both the citizens and villagers became hale and hearty and equally rich like the king (6). There was no impediment, no disease and no fear from dangerous animals; (what more) even there was no fear from the scarcity of water when Dama's son became the king (7). He undertook great sacrifices and gave away presents to those who sought for them; and without interfering with real virtue, he engaged in the enjoyment of worldly objects (8). Thus governing his kingdom and ruling well his subjects, seven thousand years passed away like a day (9). The respectful daughter of Viduratha, the king of Deccan, by name Mānini, became his wife (10). Once on a time that one, of fair eye-brows, Mānini, while engaged in picking up the grey hairs of the king, began to shed tears in the presence of all the assembled kings (11). When those drops of tears fell on the body of the king he saw her face bathed in tears and asked her (12). Beholding her weeping and shedding tears in silence Rājyavarddhana said to Mānini "What is this?" (13). Although thus accosted by her husband that great lady did not say anything; thereat the king asked her again (14). Thereupon repeatedly asked by the king the youthful (queen) showed to the king a grey hair growing in the midst of the tuft of hairs (15). (She said) "Behold this, O king; what is this? This is the cause of my grief, unfortunate as I am." Thereat the king laughed (16). Smiling he said to his wife in the presence of all the kings and citizens who had assembled there (17). "O thou of expansive eyes, no more with sorrow; O auspicious dame, do not weep; all creatures are subject to birth, development and decay (18). O fair damsel, I have studied all the Vedas, I have performed a thousand sacrifices, I have made gifts unto the twice-born and procreated progeny (19). I have with you enjoyed many objects of enjoyment which are dear to the mortals. I have governed well the earth and fought many fair battles (20). I have enjoyed much in the forest and elsewhere in the company of chosen friends. What is there, O auspicious dame, which I have not done? Wherefore art thou afraid of my decaying hairs (21)? Let my hairs grow grey, my skin folded and my body slackened—I achieved all my objects O Mānini (22). Repairing to the forest I shall treat all those grey hairs which thou hast seen on my head, O auspicious damsel (23). O fair one, my fore-fathers behaved like infants in their infancy, like boys in their boyhood, like young men in their youth and in the old age they entered into the woods. I shall also act like them. Therefore do I see no reason for thy sheeding tears (23—25). Do not grieve therefore. The grey hair, that thou hast seen, is the instrument of my prosperity; therefore do not weep (26).

MARKANDEYA said:—Thereupon, O great saint, all the assembled kings and citizens, who had come here, saluting him, said to Rājyavarddhana (27). "O king, there is no reason for thy wife to weep, but ourselves and all the creatures shall have to weep (28). O lord, hearing thy words of repairing to woods, the minds of us all, O king, who have been maintained by you, have become dejected (29). Therefore, O king, we shall all go to the forest if you go there. Thyself repairing to the forest, O lord, the works of all the inhabitants of the world shall undoubtedly be stopped. If this leads to the obstruction of virtue do thou give up this idea (30—31). Thou hast ruled this earth for seven thousand years. Observe therefore, O king, the virtue, that has arisen therefrom (32). The devout penance, O king, that thou shalt carry on by living in the forest, is not equal to the sixteenth part of thy governing the world (33).

THE KING said:—I have governed this earth for seven thousand years,—now the time for repairing to woods has arrived (34). I have begotten children and have seen them begetting such. I have seen all this within a short time. So death shall not see it any longer (35). The grey hairs you see on my head, O citizens, consider them as the emissary of the non-aryan Death of greatly fierce temper (36). Therefore, placing my son on the throne and abstaining from all objects of enjoyment I shall repair to woods and shall carry on devout penances so long the soldiers of Yama do not come (37).

MARKANDEYA said :—Thereupon desirous of repairing to woods that great king enquired of the astrologers about the proper day and time for the installation of his son (38). Hearing the king's words their minds were agitated and so they, although conversant with Shastras, could not find out the proper day and hour (39). The astrologers said to the king in suppressed accents—" O king, hearing your words, all our knowledge has been destroyed" (40). Thereupon from other cities, dependant states and from that city came many leading Brāhmanas and approaching that king, O Muni, who was bent upon repairing to woods and bending low their heads, said (41—42), " Be pleased, O king, and govern us all as before. O king, thyself repairing to woods all the worlds will go to ruin (43). Therefore, O king, do thou so act that the world may not go to ruin. O heroe, O lord, as long as we shall live, we shall not like, even for a moment, to see this throne without you (44).

MARKANDEYA said :—Although these Brāhmanas, other twice-born ones, the citizens, the kings, servants, councillors, and others said this repeatedly yet he did not give up his resolution of repairing to woods; on the other hand, he said "death will not let me alone" (45—46). Thereupon the councillors, the servants, elderly citizens and the twice-born ones, assembling together, began to consult what they should do (47). They were all attached to the highly victorious king, O Vipra, and therefore after consultation arrived at the conclusion (48). " Concentrating our minds and controlling ourselves we shall, with penances, worship the divine Sun for a longer lease of life for this king (49)." When they had all arrived at this determination some, in their own houses, engaged in worshipping the sun by duly offering him Arghya and other articles (50). Some with the silent recitation of *Riks* and others with *Yayus* and *Saman* pleased the sun (51). Some Brâhmanas, abstaining from food, lying down on the bank of a river and carrying on devout penances, worshipped the sun (52). Others, engaged in the performance of Agnihotra, recited day and night *Ravisukta* whereas others remained with their eyes fixed on the sun (53). Thus resorting to their respective modes, they all, in various ways, made up their minds for worshipping the sun (54). When they all thus perseveringly carried on the worship of the Sun a Gandharva, by name Sudāmā, coming, there said :— (55). "O ye Vipras, if ye are determined upon worshipping the sun do ye so act as may please him (56). On the huge mountain in Kāmrupa there is a forest called Vishala resorted to by Siddhas. Do ye all speedily go there (57). And with controlled minds do ye worship the sun there where every one gets Siddhi and auspiciousness and attains all his wished for objects (58).

MARKANDEYA said :—Hearing his words and repairing to that forest the twice-born ones saw the holy and auspicious form of the sun (59). There abstemious of food and diligent all the Brahmanas and other castes began to worship him with incense, flowers and other presents (60). Worshipping him with flowers, sandal pastes, incense, scents and other things, recitations, Homa, food, lamp, etc., the twice-born ones, O Brāhmana, with controlled minds, there eulogised the sun (61).

THE BRAHMANAS said :—We seek refuge with the God Ravi who excels in effulgence the gods, Danavas, Yakshas, planets and luminous bodies; (62). He who is the lord of the gods, who stationed in the sky lights up all the quarters, who fills the sky and earth, with his rays; (63) who is Aditya, Bhāskara, Savitā and the maker of the day; who is *Pushà, Aryama, Bhànu, Sharvànu* and the source of light (64); who is the fire of dissolution at the end of four *yugas*, who goes even to the end of dissolution and is hard to look at, who is the lord of yoga, endless, red, yellow, blue, and dark-blue (65). He is stationed in the Agnihotra of the Rishis in all the sacrifices and in gods and is the great word, mystic and the most excellent door of emancipation (66). He wanders in the sky on horses in the shape of metres, and always rises and sets after circumambulating the mount Meru (67). He is ambrosia, truth, all the sacred shrines, the support of the universe and is beyond comprehension; we seek refuge with that sun (68). He is Brahmā, Siva, Vishnu, Prajāpati; he is air, ether, water, and the earth, with mountains and oceans; (69). He is planet, star, the moon, and others, is the plant, trees, and creepers, and is the ordainer of virtue and vice in both, what is manifest or not (70). He has three-fold forms of Brahmā, Vishnu and Siva; may that sun be propitiated with us (71). He is the lord of the universe and is without birth; his limb is this universe and he is the life of the world; may he be propitiated with us (72). May that sun be propitiated with us whose Bhāskara form, enveloped with rays, is hard to look at and whose form is the gentle moon (73). May that Divine Sun be propitiated with us with whose these two forms the world has been created and filled with fire (74).

MARKANDEYA said:—O foremost of the twice-born, having been thus eulogised by them with reverence and worshipped for three months the Divine Sun was pleased (75). Thereupon although hard to work at, he, assuming the effulgence of the rising sun, came down from his disc and appeared before them (76). Thereat trembling in joy and bending low with reverence all the people there bowed unto the unborn sun, who came there in his clean form (77). (They said):—"Salutation unto thee, O thou of thousand rays, thou art the cause of all and the guide. Thou art worthy of being eulogised and worshipped by all. Do thou protect us all. Thou art the refuge of all sacrifices; the Yogins meditate on thee; be thou propitiated with us (78).

CHAPTER CX.

MARKANDEYA said:—Thereupon delighted the Divine Sun said to all the people "O ye twice-born ones and others, tell me what do ye seek from me" (1). Beholding the Sun stationed before them all the Brāhmanas and others, saluting him with reverence, said to that lord of the universe (2).

THE SUBJECTS said:—O Lord, O thou the dispeller of darkness, if thou art pleased with our devotion may our king live for ten thousand years (3). May he be always freed from diseases, may he defeat his enemies, may his treasury remain always full, and may he be ever youthful. May Rājyavarddhana live for ten thousand years (4).

MARKANDEYA said:—O great Muni, having said 'so be it' the sun assumed his own form. They too, having attained their boons, and been delighted, approached that king of men (5). O twice-born one, they communicated every thing fully unto the king how they had obtained the boon from the sun (6). O twice-born one, hearing this his wife Mānini was delighted. But the king thought for some time and did not say any thing to the people (7). Therefore Mānini, having her heart fillled with delight, said to her husband "O king, by luck, you have got a longer lease of life" (8). O twice-born one, although her husband was thus congratulated by Mānini in delight the king did not say any thing and his mind was stupified by pensiveness (9). He began to think with his head cast downwards. She again said to her husband "king, why art thou not pleased with the accession of such a good fortune (10). From to-day thou shalt live a healthy and youthful life for ten thousand years; why art thou not pleased then? (11). O king, tell me the cause of the anxiety that has possessed thy heart even at the advent of such a good fortune" (12).

THE KING said:—O auspicious damsel, what is that good fortune to me? Why art thou congratulating me? A thousand miseries have come for me? Why do you please me? (13). I shall alone live for ten thousand years. Thou shalt meet with death. Will not that cause grief unto me? (14). Beholding my sons, grandsons, their sons and other relations passing away before me shall I experience a small grief? (15). When servants, greatly attached to me, as well as the friends shall pass away, there shall be no end of grief unto me? (16). Even they, who by carrying on penances have reduced their bodies to skeletons for me, will meet with death. Shall I alone live and enjoy? O fie on me (17). Therefore, O fair one, this is no prosperity to me but a great calamity. Why do you not consider this? And why do you congratulate me? (18).

MANINI said:—Undoubtedly what thou hast said, O great king, is true. In our joy, neither myself nor the citizens could observe this defect (19). Therefore, think, O king, what should now be done. What the Divine Sun has said in propitiation shall never be otherwise (20).

THE KING said:—Without repaying the benefit which has been done me by citizens and servants delightedly how shall I enjoy various objects of enjoyment? (21). I too to-day shall go to the mountain and with controlled mind and abstaining from food shall worship the sun and carry on penances (22). As I shall, by his favour, live for ten thousand years, being yonthful and freed from diseases, likewise if my subjects, servants, sons, grandsons, their sons, friends and others live by the favour of the sun, then with delight I shall be their king and enjoy the objects of enjoyment (23—25). If the sun does not encompass this, O Mānini, I shall, abstaining from food, carry on, in this mountain, devout penances so long my life does not run out (26).

MARKANDEYA said:—Having been thus addressed by him she said 'so be it' to the king and with him repaired to that mountain (27). Having reached that valley, O twice-born one, the king, engaged in his service along with his wife, began to worship the sun (28). The king grew lean with fasting and so did she. Bearing cold and heat she carried on hard austerities (29). He thus worshipping the sun and carrying on hard penances for a little over a year the sun was delighted (30). O foremost of the twice-born ones, he then conferred the boon, as desired by the king, with regard to all his servants, citizens and sons (31). Having obtained the boon and returned to his own city the king delightedly governed his kingdom and piously ruled his subjects (32). He performend many *Yajnas* and made charities day and night. And that one conversant with virtue enjoyed many objects of desire in the company of Mānini (33). He lived a youthful and happy life for ten thousand years along with the servants, sons, and grandsons (34). Seeing his life, Pramati, of Bhrigus' race, filled with surprise, composed the following theme (35). 'O what is the power of devotion to the sun, since Rājyavarddhana has gained a long life both for himself and his own men (36.)" O Vipra, as asked by you I have thus recounted to you the glories of the Prime Deity, the effulgent Aditya (37). By listening to or reading in full this most excellent glorious theme the Brāhmanas are released from sins committed for seven nights so also are other men (38). The intelligent man, who meditates on this theme, becomes freed from diseases, rich, prosperous, is born in the family of the intelligent and becomes highly wise (39). O foremost of Munis, those, who are unfortunate and beset with calamities, if they recite this theme of the Sun, three times a day, are freed from sins (40). The sun lives always near the house, where this his glorious theme is chanted and he never leaves it (41). Therefore, O Brahman, you should, desirous of acquiring great piety, meditate over and chant this glorious theme of the sun (42). O foremost of the twice-born, by listening for three days to this glorious theme of the sun one reaps the same fruit which he does by making a gift of a beautiful milch cow having golden horns (43).

CHAPTER CXI.

MARKANDEYA said:—O Kraustbika, the eternal Divine Sun, about whose glories you did reverentially accost me, is thus gifted with rays (1). He is the (*Paramatman* (great soul) of all those Yogins who have concentrated their minds in Yoga. He is *Kshetrajna* of the Sankhya philosophers and the lord of sacrifices of those who perform them (2). The Manu of the seventh *Manwantara* took his birth as his son. He had all his doubts dissipated. Ikshwāku, Nābhaga, Rishtha, Narishyanta, Nābhāga, Prishadra and Dhrista were his sons. They were all very highly powerful, of illustrious renown, were well read in scriptures and became the rulers of the earth (3—5). With a view to have a more accomplished son, that Manu, the foremost of successful men, again undertook the performanee of a sacrifice in honour of Mitra and Varuna (6). O great Muni, on account of the bad conduct of Hotā in that sacrifice Manu got a highly youthful daughter by name Ilā (7). Thereupon beholding that daughter born Manu, pleasing Mitra and Vāruna, said (8):—"Expecting that a most accomplished son would be born to me by your favour, I undertook this sacrifice—but a daughter is born (9). If you are pleased with me and are ready to grant a boon may this daughter, by your favour, become a highly accomplished son" (10). The gods having said, 'so be it' that daughter Ilā immediately became a son known by the name of Sudyumna (11). While going about a-hunting in the forest that highly intelligent son of Manu, again by the curse of the Providence, assumed her female form (12). There she gave birth to a son by name Pururava who became in time Lord Paramount (13). After the birth of the son he performed a great horse-sacrifice. Sudyumna then regained his manhood and became the king (14). Sudyumna, in his manhood, begat three sons, Utkala, Vinaya and Gaya—they were all very powerful and energetic and were intent upon performing sacrifices (15). All his sons, born in his manhood, had their minds devoted to virtue and governed this earth (16). Pururava was born in his womanhood. He did not obtain a portion of the earth since he was the son of Budha (17). According to the words of Vishistha, a best of cities, Pratishthāna, was conferred upon him. He became king in that highly charming city (18).

CHAPTER CXII.

MARKANDEYA said :—Manu's son, Prishadhra, by name, went out a-hunting into the forest. Going about there in that lonely wood he did not find any deer. He was assailed by the rays of the sun and was possessed by hunger and thirst while moving about hither and thither (1—2). There he saw a highly beautiful sacrificial cow belonging to an Agnihotra Brâhmana (3). Taking it for a Gavaya he discharged a shaft at her. Having her heart pierced by the arrow she fell down on earth (4). Beholding the sacrificial cow of his father thus fallen the Brahmachari son of that Agnihotri, ever engaged in Tapas, imprecated a curse on him (5). His name was Bābhraya and was sent by his father to look after the kine. O Muni, he was by nature angry and wrathful. So he was worked up with anger; he began to perspire and her eyes were agitated (6). Beholding the Muni's son angry the king Prishadra said "Be pleased; why are you being possessed by anger like a Sudra (7)? Such an anger can never possess a Kshatrya or a Vaisya even, as has possessed you who are born in an eminent Brāhmana's family (8).

Being thus remonstrated with by the king that Rishi's son imprecated a curse on that vicious-souled one, saying "Be a Sudra (9). Since thou hast killed the sacrificial cow of my preceptor, the Vedas shall not come out (of thy mouth) which thou didst learn from thy preceptor (10)." Being thus imprecated and possessed by anger the king took water in his hand to curse him (11). That foremost of the twice-born became angry for the destruction of the king. But approaching him speedily his father prevented him (12), saying "O child, away with anger which is the great enemy of advancement. Forgiveness only encompasses the well-being of the twice-born both in this world and the next (13) Anger destroys asceticism and longivity. An angry man loses knowledge and riches (14). The angry do not acquire virtue nor riches. Persons, who have their minds possessed by anger, do not attain objects leading to happiness. Even if knowing it full well the king has killed the sacrificial cow still, (actuated by) good sense you should show forgiveness towards him (16). And if unconsciously he has killed this cow how does he then deserve an imprecation since he is not wickedly bent (17). A person, who seeks his own good and at the same kills others, has his good sense destroyed. Such a man is an object of commisseration (18). If the learned punish an innocent man, me-thinks the illeterate are superior to such learned men (19). Therefore, O my son, you should not have cursed the king to-day. By her own *Karma* this cow has met with a painful death (20).

Then saluting the Muni's son with his head down Prishadra said:—"Be pleased, I have unknowingly killed her (21). O Muni, taking her for a *Gavaya* I have, out of ignorance, killed your sacrificial cow (22).

THE RISHI'S SON said :—O king, I have never spoken an untruth since my birth. O great one, to-day my anger shall never be otherwise (23). Therefore, O king, I shall not be able to undo this curse. But I refrain from imprecating the second curse which I was about to do (23)."

On his saying this the father taking his son with him repaired to his own hermitage. Prishadhra too became a Sudra (25).

——:o:——

CHAPTER CXIII.

MARKANDEYA said :—Karusha had seven sons who were all called Kārushas; they were heroic and brave, from them sprang seven hundred heroes and thousands of others (1). Nābhaga was Dishthi's son. When he set his foot on his first youth he saw a highly beautiful daughter of a Vaisya (2). As soon as he saw her his mind was agitated by desire. The prince then began to sigh (3). He, then approaching the father of the girl, prayed for her. The father then, with folded hands, said to the prince whose mind was possessed by desire and whose father he used to fear, words, bending low with humility (4—5) :—"You are kings, we are your servants and ryots. Why do you wish to have an alliance with us" (6)?

THE PRINCE said :—The equality of human bodies is rendered by desires, stupefaction etc. The human body is united with them in time (7). They also lend to their benefaction. The pious, though they belong to different castes, depend on each other (8). By the influence of time even the unworthy objects become worthy and worthy objects become unworthy—the worthiness is thus dependant on time (9). The body is nourished by desirable edibles—thus it is nourished when food is taken in proper time (10). Thus I have come to like your girl. Do you confer her on me or else my body will be destroyed (11).

THE VAISHYA said :—Both of us are equally dependants; obtaining the permission of your father the king, do you take her and I shall give her away (12).

THE PRINCE said :—True, at all times, the people should obtain the permission of their elders; but in such unworthy actions the elders should not be consulted (13). The talking of love affairs and the hearing of the elders are opposed to each other; the elders should be consulted by men in other matters (14).

VAISHYA said :—Of course, this will be a conversation of love for you to ask your father. I shall ask him, this is no love affair to me (15).

MARKANDEYA said :—Having been thus addressed the prince remained silent. He (the Vaishya) then communicated every thing duly unto the prince's father (16). Thereupon having sent for leading twice-born ones, the Richikas and others, as well as the prince he said every thing of what had been communicated (by the Vaisya) (17). Thereupon communicating all he said "I have been placed in this condition, tell me, O ye leading twice-born ones, what should be done in this (18)."

THE RISHI said :—O prince, if you have cherished attachment for this Vaisya girl it will be considered as morality; but this must be observed duly (19). You must first espouse the daughter of the king Murdhâbhishikta and then you must marry her (20). If you enjoy her in this way there will be no sin, but if you carry her away stealthily you will be degraded from your most eminent caste (21).

MARKANDEYA said :—Having been thus addressed and disregarding the words of those high-souled ones, coming out therefrom, taking her away and uplifting his weapons he said :—(22). "I have taken the Vaisya girl under the Rākshasa form of marriage; whoever has the power let him come and release her (23)." Thereupon beholding his daughter thus carried away, the Vaisya, O twice-born one, speedily sought refuge with his father, saying "Save me" (24). Thereupon being worked up with anger the king ordered his huge army saying, "kill, kill this wicked and sinful Nābhāga (25)." Then the soldiers began to fight with the prince. By him too, who was an expert in the use of arms, many of them were killed (26). Hearing of the destruction of the army by the prince, the king, encircled by his own soldiers, himself went out to fight with him (27). Then there arose a great encounter between the king and his own son. The father was excelled by the prince in the use of arms (28). Thereupon all on a sudden coming from the sky the ascetic Paribrata said to the king "Desist from the fight (29). O great one, your son, high-souled as you are, has lost his caste. O king, it is not proper for you to fight with a Vaisya (30). A Brāhmana does not lose his caste, if after marrying first in the house of Brāhmana, he takes wives from other castes (31). Similarly O king, a Kshatriya does not lose his caste, if after first taking the hand of a Kshatriya girl he marries other caste girls (32). So a Vaisya is not excluded from his caste if he marries a Sudra girl after first taking a Vaisya wife. This is the due order (33). O king, the Brāhmanas, Kshatriyas, and Vaisyas lose their caste if they marry the girls of other castes before taking wives from their respective orders (34). If persons, before taking wives from their own castes, marry in inferior races, they cannot enjoy their objects there (35). This your sinful son has become a Vaisya. But you are a Kshatriya. He has no right to fight with you. O king, we do not know the cause which may sanction such an encounter; therefore desist from fight" (36).

——:o:——

CHAPTER CXIV.

MARKANDEYA said :—Thereupon the king desisted from fighting with his own son. His son too espoused the daughter of the Vaisya (1). Thereupon attaining Vaisyahood and approaching the king, he said "O king, order me, what am

I to do," (2). The king said:—The ascetics Bābhravya and others are engaged in looking after the morals; let them say what you should do and act accordingly (3)." Thereupon the ascetics and courtiers all said, "His duty is to look after cattle, agriculture and trade" (4). The prince had deviated from his own order and so he acted according to what had been suggested by the pious sages (5). He begat a son, known by the name of Bhanandana. His mother said to him "go, O my child, and be a protector of the world" (16). Having been thus ordered by his mother and saluted her he approached the royal saint Neepa who was living on the Himalaya mountain (7). Approaching him and saluting his feet duly, Bhanandana said to that royal saint (8). "O reverend sir, my mother has ordered me to be a protector of the earth. So I must protect the earth; but how can I obtain her permission? (9). I can rule over the subjects if she agrees. But my earth has been invaded by my powerful kinsmen (10). I am thy servant. Do thou so order, O lord, that I may, by thy favour, obtain the earth; I shall carry out thy order" (11).

MARKANDEYA said:—Thereupon, O Brahman, the royal saint Neepa conferred upon the high-souled Bhanandana all the arms (12). Having obtained the knowledge of arms and being ordered by that high-souled one he went to his cousins Vasurāt and others (13). He then wanted the half of his ancestral kingdom. They said, "you are a son of a Vaisya, how can you enjoy the earth? (14)." Then Bhanandana began to fight with Vasurāt and others born in his own family who in anger began to make a downpour of weapons (15). Having wounded all their soldiers with weapons and vanquished them all in fair fight that one, conversant with virtue, took the earth from them (16). Having defeated all his enemies he dedicated the entire earth and kingdom to his father, but he did not accept it. He then said to his son in the presence of his wife (17).

NABHAGA said :—O Bhanandana, this kingdom was created by your fore-fathers. This belongs to you. I did not make this kingdom. This was not owing to my inability (18). I have attained to Vaisyahood and did not carry out the order of my father. Having displeased my father I married the daughter of a Vaisya (19). A king is not entitled to the enjoyment of sacred regions till the time of dissolution (20). And then again disregarding the order of my father if I govern the earth I shall not attain emancipation even in a hundred Kalpas (21). I am a respectable person ; it does not behove me to enjoy a kingdom earned by your arms ; (then again) I am weak (22). Therefore do you yourself govern the kingdom or give it over to your kinsmen. I am your father ; it is not so much becomng for you to govern the earth as it is for you to carry out my order (23).

MARKANDEYA said :—Thereupon his graceful wife Suprabhā laughing said to her husband :—"O king, accept this prosperous kingdom (25). You are not a Vaiysa nor am I born in a Vaisya family, O king. You are a Kshatriya and I am also born in a Kshatriya race (25). In the days of yore there flourished a king by name Sudeva. Dumrāshya's son Nala was his friend (26). In the month of Madhu, O king, he, along with his friend and wives, went to a forest of mangoes on a pleasure trip (27). There accompanied by his friend and wives he enjoyed diverse drinks and edibles (28). Thereupon on the bank of the tank he saw the highly beautiful royal wife of Pramati, the son of Chyavana (29). His vicious-minded friend Nala, under the influence of drink, caught hold of her, who was crying out 'Save me, save me' in the very presence of the king (30). Hearing her cries her husband Pramati came there speedily saying "What is this" (31.)? There he saw the king Sudeva and his wife in the grasp of the vicious-minded Nala (32). Thereat Pramati said to Sudeva :—"Desist him. Thou art the governor and king. O king, (in your presence) this Nala has committed such a violence (33)." Hearing his distressful words and on account of his great love for Nala, Sudeva said to him:—"I am a Vaisya: seek refuge with a Kshatriya for her safety (34)." Thereupon when the king said that he was a Vaisya, Pramati, worked up with anger and as if burning all with his energy, said to him (35):—"True it is, that you are a Vaisya. He, who saves one from injury, is a Kshatriya. They take up their arms lest any one sets out a doleful cry. You are not a Kshatriya but the wretch of a Kshatriya" (36).

CHAPTER CXV.

MARKANDEYA said:—O twice-born one, thereupon having imprecated that curse on him and as if burning down the three worlds in anger, Pramati, of Bhrigu's race, said to Nala (1):—"Since you, in my own hermitage, have shown violence to my wife under the influence of desire, you will be consumed at once" (2). As soon as those words were uttered he was immediately reduced to ashes by the fire originating from his own body (3). Beholding his prowess Sudeva, divested of haughtiness and saluting him said:—"Forgive me, forgive me (4). O revernd Sir, I was under the influence of liquor. Therefore forgive me, be pleased and withdraw your curse" (5). Having been thus pleased by him and on Nala being consumed, Pramati, of Bhrigue's race, said with a dried heart (6). "The words, that have been given vent to by me, shall never he falsified. Still being propitiated with you I will show you some excellent favour (7). You will be born in the race of the Vaisyas, there is no doubt about that.

But immediately, in this very birth you will be a Kshatriya (8). When a Kshatriya will take away your daughter by force you will become a Kshatriya" (9). In this way, O king, my father Sudeva became a Vaisya. What I am, O great one, hear all in detail (10). There was a royal saint by name, Suratha in the mount Gandhamādana. Repairing to the forest, abstaining from food and forsaking all attachment he became an ascetic (11). Thereupon as soon as he saw there a Sārikā dropped from the beaks of a Swena his mind was possessed by mercy; and immediately stupefaction came over him (12). When he came to his senses I sprang from his body. Beholding me he took me up with an affectionate heart (13). The lord said, "Since this daughter is born when my mind is possessed by mercy she will be called Kripāvati (14). Then I daily drew up in his hermitage and began to wander about in the forest with my mates of equal age (15). Agastya's brother was equally well-known like his brother. When he came to the forest for gathering the produces thereof his anger was excited by my female companions and he imprecated a curse (16). 'Since you have called me a Vaishya, you will be born as the daughter of a Vaishya. I give you this curse.' After he had said this I said (17), "O foremost of the twice-born, I have committed no offence by thee, why dost thou curse me for another's offence" (18)?

THE ASCETIC said :—Even a good man becomes wicked when he associates with them. Even good things, made of milk, are spoiled with a single drop of wine (19). Still as you are innocent and have pleased me with salutation, hear, O girl, what favour I shall extend to you (20), "When after being born in the race of a Vaisya you will despatch your son for governing the kingdom, you will come to recollect your pristine birth (21). Then again attaining to Kshatriya-hood along with your husband you will enjoy many heavenly objects. Go, you have no fear (22). O king, I was thus formerly cursed by that great saint. My father was also thus crused by Pramati (23). Therefore, O king, you are not a Vaisya nor is my father. So neither yourself nor I am fallen. Why will you be then fallen (in my company) (24)?

CHAPTER CXVI.

MARKANDEYA said:—Hearing the words of his wife and son that pious king again said to them (1). "I shall never accept the kingdom that I relinquished at the behest of my father. What is the use of speaking in vain? Why do you attract my mind (2). I have taken to this Vaisya mode of life. I shall pay you the revenue. Do you enjoy this kingdom as you like or give it up" (3).

Having been thus addressed by his father the prince Bhanandana took a wife and began to govern the kingdom piously (4). O twice-born one, the wheel (of his car) became unobstructed all over the earth. No one had his mind in vice and all the kings became his tributaries (5). He duly celebrated *Yajnas* and properly ruled the earth. He alone became the ruler of the earth and his administration extended all over (6). To him was born a son by name Vatsapri, who, high souled (as he was), excelled, by his accomplishments, even his sire (7). Viduratha's daughter Sounandā became his wife. She was equally great and chaste. Having slain Kujrimbha, the king of demons and the enemy of Indra, the king of gods, he obtained her by his own prowess (8).

KROUSHTHIK said:—"O reverend sir, do you delightedly describe to me how Vatsapri killed Kujrimbha and got her as his wife (9)."

MARKANDEYA said:—There was an illustrious king on earth by name Viduratha. He had two sons, Suniti and Sumati (10). Once on a time, going out to the forest a-hunting he saw a huge, widening pit like the mouth of the earth (11). Seeing it he thought. "What is this dreadful thing? Methinks this is the door to Pātala. This is not of the earth" (12). While thus thinking he saw in that lonely forest a Brāhmana ascetic by name Savrata (13). The king then wonderingly asked him:—"What it this. The very bottom of the earth is being seen through this deep pit (14.)"

THE RISHI said:—O king, methinks, you do not know this; there should be nothing on earth which a king should not know (15). There lives a highly powerful and fierce Dānava in Rasātala. He makes the earth yawn and therefore he is called Kujrimbha (16). Whatever wonder is there on earth or in heaven that is his work. How is it that you do not know him (17). That vicious-minded one stole away the mace Sunanda which was formerly made by the celestial Architect. He kills his enemies in battle with it (18). Living in Pātala he rives the earth with it and accordingly creates a door for all the Asuras (19). Now he has riven the earth with that mace Sunanda. How will you enjoy this earth without having killed him? (20). This dreadful and powerful (demon) spoils sacrifices, distresses the gods and welcomes the demons. He has this mace for his weapon (21). If you can slay that enemy living at the furtherest end of Pātāla then will you be the lord of the entire earth and the great god (22). The mace of that powerful one is spoken of by people as Sounanda; O king, intelligent men call it Balāvala (23.) O king, when touched by a female that mace grows powerless. On the second day it again grows powerful (24.) The vicious one does not know the prowess of his mace and the fact that it becomes powerless as soon as it is touched by a female (25). O king, I have thus described to you the power of his mace (26). Do you now act accordingly. O king, he has made this hole near your city. How are you then at rest? (27)" Having said this he went away. The king too, repairing to his city, began to consult there with his experienced counsellors (28). He duly described, to his ministers as he had heard, the power of the mace and how it is destroyed (29). Living by his side his daughter Mudāvati heard all the counsels of the king with his ministers (30). Thereupon after the expiration of a few days the youthful Mudāvati, accompanied by her friends, went to a garden. Thence Kujrimbha slole her away (31). Hearing that and having his eyes agitated by anger the king said to his two sons who were acquainted with that forest:—"Go ye speedily (32). There is a hole on the bank of the river Nirvindya. Entering through that to Rasātala kill there the wicked one who has taken away Mudāvati (33).

MARKANDEYA SAID:—Thereupon those two sons reached that hole and following his foot steps (they went to Rasātala); and accompanied by their army, they in anger, began to fight with Kujrimbha (34). They set up a highly dreadful encounter with (the discharge of a) number of Parighas, Nishtringsas, darts, Saktis, Parashwadhas and shafts (35). Thereupon having slain in battle their innumerable army that Daitya, powerful of illusion, enchained those two princes (36). O foremost of Munis, hearing of his sons being fettered and worked up with great agony the king said to all his soldiers (37). "I shall confer upon him, this my daughter of expansive eyes who, after having slain the demon, will release my two sons (38). O Muni, giving up all hopes of the release of his son and daughter the king made this proclamation in his own city (39). Thereupon Bhanandana's son Vatsapri heard of this proclamation. He was an expert in the use of weapons and was gifted with heroism (40). Then approaching that best friend of his father's, the foremost of kings and saluting him with all humility he said (41):—"Please command me immediately; slaying that demon by my own energy I shall release now both your son and daughter (42)."

MARKANDEYA SAID:—Having embraced in joy, the son of his most beloved friend, the king said, "Go my child and achieve your object (43). You will really do the work of a friend's son if you encompass this. Do this immediately, my child, if you are worked up with energy" (44).

Thereupon taking up his dagger and bow and putting on finger protectors that heroe speedily went to the nether region through that hole (45). There that prince set up a terrible twang with which the whole of the nether region was filled up (46). Thereupon hearing that twang of the bow, Kujrimbha, the king of Dānavas, encircled by his own army, came there in great anger (47). These arose an encounter between demon and the prince who had not the same strength and army as he had (48). Having fought with him for three days the Dānava, his mind filled with anger, ran forward to bring the mace (49). O great one, that mace, made by the celestial Architect was in the inner appartment and was adored there with incense, garland and scents (50). Mudāvati knew the prowess of that mace. Therefore bending low her neck she touched the mace (51). Then the great demon again took up the mace, and with a view to adore it touched it again and again (52). Then that lord of Asuras went there and began to fight with the mace, but the strokes thereof became fruitless on the enemies (53). O Muni, after his mace Sounanda had lost all its power that demon fought with his enemy in battle with various other weapons (54). That Asura could not equal the prince in weapons. The mace was his strength—but it was made useless by the force of intellect (55).

Thereupon discomfitting all the weapons of the demon the prince immediately brought him down from the chariot. Then taking up daggers and leathern fences he ran forward (56). When displaying greatly his prowess Kujrimbha, the enemy of Indra, came there in great anger and with fury;

the prince, with his fiery weapon, effulgent like the fire of dessolution, killed him (57). Having his heart wounded by the fiery weapon, that enemy of gods gave up his ghost. Then there arose a great festivity of the leading serpents in Rasātala (58). Thereupon flowers were showered upon the prince, the Gandharvas sang and the celestial instruments were sounded (59). Having slain him the prince too released the two sons of the king and his daughter Mudāvati of slender make (60).

After the death of Kujrimbha, the king of the serpents, Ananta, designated Sesha, took up that mace (61). O ascetic, that king of serpents, Sesha, was greatly pleased with Mudāvati (62). That highly beautiful damsel knew of the power of the touch of a woman's hand and so she repeatedly touched the mace Sounanda (63). O twice-born one, therefore Mudāvati was named Sunandā by the king of serpents in great delight. This was on account of the virtue of Sounanda (64). He then speedily brought her along with her two brothers before the king and saluting him said :—(65). "O father, by your command, I have brought your sons and daughter"; command me what more shall I have to do now (66). Thereupon the heart of the king was filled with delight. He then exclaimed in sweet words, "well-done, my boy (67). By three-fold causes I have to-day become a courtier of the gods; you have become my son-in-law, the enemy has been killed and my children have returned unscathed. I command, to-day is an auspicious day, do you accept the hand of my daughter Mudāvati, fair of all limbs and ever delightful, O prince and make my words true" (68—70). The prince said :—"O father, it is my duty that I should carry out your order. But you know whether we have any right in this (71)." Thereupon the king celebrated the marriage of his daughter Mudāvati, with Bhanandana's son (72). Vatsapri was in his youth; he spent his days delightedly in their company in pleasant country and on the terraces of the palaces (73). In time, his father Bhanandana became old and repaird to woods. Vatsāpri became the king (74). He always performed Yajnas and governed his subjects righteously. That high-souled one being engaged in ruling over his subjects like their father his prosperity began to increase. In his time there was no misalliance and no fear of the people from wild animals, robbers and wicked people; that king governing the earth there was no impediment whatsoever (75—76).

CHAPTER CXVII.

Makandeya said:—He begat on Sunandā twelve sons. They were Prangshu, Pravira, Shoora, Suchakra, Vikrama, Krama, Vala, Vataka, Chanda, Prachanda, Suvikrama and Swarupa. They were all great and ever victorious in battle (1—2). The eldest of them, the highly powerful Prāngshu, became the king. The other brothers were submissive to him like servants (3). His sacrifices, in which various articles were given over by the twice-born and other inferior castes, made good the name of Vasundharā (4). He used to govern his subjects well like his own begotten sons. With his wealth, that was in his treasury, thousands of sacrifices were celebrated. There was no number of them—(even it could not be numbered) by Ajuta, Koti, Padma, etc., (5—6). His son was Prajāti in whose sacrifice partaking of the offering, even the porformer of hundred sacrifices, along with other celestials, attained to great delight (7). That foremo st of the powerful killed ninety-nine highly powerful and leading Dānavas and their king Jambha, as well as other highly powerful enemies of the immortals (8). O Muni, Prajāti had five sons headed by Khanitra. Amongst them Khanitra, well-known by his own prowess, became the king (9). He was of quiet nature, truthful, heroic and ever engaged in the well-being of creatures. He was ever observant of the duties of his own order, used always to attend upon the aged and was well read in various scriptures (10). He was a good speaker, humble, an expert in fighting and freed from haughtiness. He was beloved of all and used to say, day and night (11). "Let all creatures be happy always and find delight even in a solitary forest. May they all live happily and be freed from fear (12). May they not suffer from diseases and mental affliction. May all people cherish friendship towards each other (13). May good betide the twice-born and may they love each other. May all other Varnas grow prosperous and may all attain their ends (14). O ye people, may you all wish well of creatures as you do seek that of yourselves and your sons (15). Such a good feeling should be cherished towards all. If no one offends the other there will be a great good (unto all) (16.) Forsooth does a man reap the friut of an evil committed by him foolishly towards another. For the fruit precedes the doer (17). O ye people, considering this, do ye cherish good feeling towards all. Do not commit the worldly sins and then you will attain good regions (18). Good will betide him always on earth who will love me to-day; may he even meet with auspiciousness after auspiciousness who will injure me" (19).

Such was Khanitra, the son of that king. He was gifted with all accomplishments and the goddess of riches embraced him (20). Having placed with delight his brothers in various kingdoms he himself ruled this earth abounding in oceans (21). He placed Shouri in the western portion, Udāvasu in the southern, Sunaya in the eastern and Mahāratha in the northern (23). He and they were of separate *gotras* and had separate priests and ascetics. And their ministers were also heriditary (23). Suhotra, of Atri's race, was the priest of Shouri ; the priest of Udāvasu, Kushāvarta was born in the race of Goutama (24). Pramati, born in the race of Kashyapa, was Sunaya's priest. And Vāshishtha was the priest of the king Mahārath (25). Those kings respectively ruled over their own kingdoms. Khanitra was the king of the whole earth and their emperor (26). That king Khanitra always sought the well-being of his brothers as well as that of his subjects like unto that of his own sons (27).

Once on a time, Shouri's minister Vishwavedin said to him, "O king, I have something to speak to you in private (28). He alone is the king to whom belongs this entire earth and to whom all these kings are dependants. He is succeeded in order by his son and grandson (29). As his brothers are entitled to small properties before so their sons inherit smaller states than theirs, and their grandsons still smaller (30). Thus getting in time poorer from generation to generation, his descendants, O king, become cultivators (in the long run) (31). A brother does not save his brother out of affection. So, O king, the relation, between their sons, becomes more estranged (32). O king, their sons become more and more distant. Why therefore will his son love (the son of his brother) (33)? And if again a king is pleased some how or other, what is the use of his appointing ministers (34)? If you consult with me you will be able to enjoy the whole kingdom. If you are contented with it why do you keep (uselessly) a small kingdom (35)? A kingdom, which does so many things, requires both an actor and an agent. To wish for a kingdom is your work. You are a doer and we are your agents. Therefore govern your ancestral kingdom through our instrumentality. This will give you and not us fruits in the next world" (36—37).

THE KING said :—Our eldest brother has become the

emperor. Since we are his younger brothers he has been ruling over the entire earth and we are ruling over small territories (38). O highly intelligent one, we are five brothers and the earth is one; for this reason we have been ruling over separate portions. How can we all rule over the whole earth (39)?

VISHWADEVI said:—True it is, O king; if the earth is one, why dost thou not, being the eldest, take it and rule over it (40)? Be thou the head of all the brothers and the emperor of the earth. As I am trying for thee so their ministers are also working for them (41).

THE KING said:—Our elderst brother is a king and loves us all like his sons. How can I covet his kingdom then (42)?

VISHWADEVI said:—Becoming their eldest and securing the kingdom you may also please them, O king. Amongst men seeking kingdom there is none who is the eldest and none who is the youngest (43).

MARKANDEYA said:—The king having agreed to this the minister Vishwadevi brought all the brothers to his side (44). He then engaged their priests in the work of their own benediction and the destruction of Khanitra (45). He sowed dissension amongst his followers by the various means of conciliation, charity and others. And he set forth continued exertions for continuing his own power (46). The four priests, having carried on dreadful magicial operations day and night, produced four Krityas (female deities) (47). They were greatly fierce, of dreadful faces and of mighty terrific looks. They had uplifted huge darts in their hands and were highly dreadful to look at (48). They then came where the king Khanitra was. He was not polluted by any sin and so they were obstructed by the collection of his virtue (49). Those female deities then simultaneously fell upon the priests of the kings and Vishwadevi (50). Thereupon the female deity, by name Nihanti, completely consumed the wicked minister of the king Showri, Vishwadevi, together with the priests (51).

CHAPTER CXVIII.

MARKANDEYA said :—They all used to live in separate cities ; so when they were all killed at once all the worlds were filled with great surprise (1). Thereupon the great king Khanítra too heard of the destruction of the priests of his brothers as well as that of his minister Vishwadevi. O foremost of Munis, he was filled with great surprise thinking "what is this?" for he did not know the cause (2—3) Thereupon when Vashishtha came to his house the king asked him why the minister and the priests of his brother had met with death (4). Accosted by him the great ascetic told him all fully—what was spoken to him by his minister, what he did say ; how he (the minister) attempted to bring about dissension amongst the brothers and what the priests did, on being urged on by the wicked minister (5—6) ; why the priests of the king, even compassionate towards the enemies, met with death, on account of their attempt to injure an innocent person (7). Hearing this and exclaiming 'Alas I am done!" the King blamed himself much, O twice-born one, before Vashistha (8).

THE KING said :—" O fie on me, I have no piety—I am unfortunate—every thing is vicious in me. Destiny is adverse to me—I am sinful and the most wretched of all (9). For me, the four Bráhmanas have been killed ; who else there is on earth that is more sinful than I am (10). If I had not been born in this earth as a man then the priests of my brother would not have met with destruction (11). O fie on my kingdom, fie on my birth in the race of the kings, for I have been the instrument of the destruction of the twice-born (12). They were the priests of my brothers ; working for their client they met with death. They were not wicked.

I am sinful for I am the cause of their death (13). What shall I do? Where shall I go? There is no one else more sinful than I am on this earth who have been the instrument of the death of the twice-born (14)." Having his mind thus agitated and with a view to retire into the forest the Emperor Khanitra installed his son (15). Having installed on the throne his son by name Kshupa, the king, along with his three wives, retired into woods for carrying on penances (16). He was conversant with the duties of a Vānaprastha's life. Going into wood he carried on hard austerities for three hundred and fifty years (17). O foremost of the twice-born, having his body reduced by hard austerities and obstructed all the currents, that foremost of kings, living in the forest, renounced his body (18). He attained to highly sacred eternal regions conferring all wished-for objects that are gained by the kings by the performance of horse sacrifices (19). Having given up their lives with him his three wives also attained to the same region with that fortunate king (20). By listening to and reading the story of Khanitra one has all his sins destroyed. Hear now of the story of Kshupa (21).

—:o:—

CHAPTER CXIX.

MARKANDEYA said:—Having obtained the kingdom Kshanitra's son Kshupa pleased and righteously governed all the subjects like a father (1). As that king was charitable and the performer of sacrifices, so was he, in the conduct of men, impartial towards his friends and foes (2). O Muni, one day while he was in his own room, the panegyrists said that he was like the king Kshupa of the days of yore (3).

Brahma's son Kshupa was formerly the king of the earth; the conduct of the present (king) was like his (4). The king said:—"I wish to hear of the life of the great Kshupa. I shall try to lead a life like his" (5). The panegyrists said:— "O king, formerly the king Kshupa freed the kine and the Brāhmanas from taxes. And that high-souled one used to celebrate sacrifices with the sixth portion of his revenue" (6).

THE KING said:—"What man like myself can immitate those high-souled kings. How can one like myself endeavour to follow their best conduct? (7). Hear what promise I have recently made. I shall immitate the conduct of that great king Kshupa (8). I make this promise on this earth of four Varnas that I shall celebrate three sacrifices each with one corn (9). I shall return the taxes to the Brāhmanas and the kine which they had paid before to the king (10)."

MARKANDEYA said:—Having promised this Kshupa satisfied it. That foremost, of those who celebrate sacrifices, performed three sacrifices with one corn (11). He made gifts to other Brāhmanas and kine equivalent to the value of the rents paid to him by the Brāhmanas and the kine (12). That king begat on his queen Pramathā a highly heroic and praiseworthy son by whose prowess and bravery all the kings were brought to subjection (13). Nandini, of Vidharbha, became his wife; that lord begat on her a son by name Vivingsha (14). While the highly powerful Vivingsha governed the earth, its whole surface was continually filled to the brim with people (15). The clouds discharged showers in proper time and the earth yielded harvest. The corns were ripe and the fruits were juicy (16). All the juices conduced to the nourishment—and this nourishment was not converted into the instrument of madness for any one. Although coming by immense riches people were not inflated with pride (17). O great Muni, the enemies were terrified by his prowess and the friends, attaining health, were filled with delight (18). Having celebrated many sacrifices, governed the earth well and been killed in a battle he attained to the region of Shakra (19).

CHAPTER CXX.

MARKANDEYA said :—His son was Khaninetra, endued with great strength and prowess. In his *Yajna*, the Gandharvas, filled with surprise, sang (1). There was none equal to Khaninetra on this earth in the performance of sacrifices. He celebrated an Ayuta of sacrifices and made a gift of the earth with oceans (2). Having made a gift of the entire earth unto the high-souled Brāhmanas, and having acquired articles by asceticism he released it (3). The riches, of that highly charitable king, being multiplied the Brāhmanas had to accept gifts from no other king (4). He collected profuse gifts for sixty-seven thousand, sixty-seven hundred and sixty-seven sacrifices (5). O great Muni, he had no son. Therefore to collect meat for the performance of sacrifices in honor of the Pitris for having a son he went out a-hunting (6). Without any soldiers, he, alone on horse back, with leathern finger protectors, arrows, bow and swords, entered into a huge forest (7). As soon as he urged on his steed for going elsewhere, a deer, issuing out of the dense forest, said to him : "Having slain me do you accomplish your object" (8). The king said :—"Seeing me the other deer have fled away in great fear ; why are you, sacrificing yourself, anxious for death" (9)? The deer said :—"O great king, I have no issue and therefore useless is my birth. O king, thus I see no necessity of living" (10).

Thereupon coming there another deer said to him in the presence of the other deer "O king, there is no use of killing him (11). Slaying me, accomplish your work with my meat. Then only I shall achieve my object and be greatly benefitted (12). O great king, you are willing to celebrate a sacrifice in honour of your manes for having a son. How will you thus accomplish your end with the meat of that deer which has no issue (13). You should procure things befitting the work undertaken. By a bad smell, that of sweetscented articles is not determined (14).

THE KING said :—The deer has just mentioned to me the fact of his having no issue as the cause of his disgust for the world. Relate now why you, out of disgust, wish to renounce your life (15).

THE DEER said :—I have many sons and many daughters. I always live in the midst of the forest fire of sorrow consequent upon anxiety for them (16). O king, the deer are always very weak and are therefore brought under the control of all. I have a great attachment for my children and accordingly I am very sorry (17). For I live in a perpetual dread of men, lions, tigers, wolves, and others, even of the dogs and jackals, O lord, who are inferior to all creatures (18). Therefore, for those children of mine, I always wish that the earth may be freed from the fear of men, lions, etc (19). Even for bringing them up I wish that the kine and horses, that graze on grass may meet with death (20). When my young ones go out into different directions, hundreds of thoughts possess me whose mind is full of attachment (21). (Methinks) my son, while roaming in the forest, is either ensnared in a net, or assailed by a thunderbolt or has been belaboured by men or lions (22). If one amongst them comes home (I always think) "one has come perhaps others have wandered away into the great forest; what may be their state (23)." O king, when all my sons come to me, I feel a little delighted and then begin to think of their well-being for the night (24). When the dawn sets in I pray for their well-being for all the day and when the sun sets I pray for the night. I always wish that they may meet with well-being for all the hours of the day (25).

I have thus related to you, O king, the cause of my anxiety; therefore show me the favour and discharge the shaft at me (26). I have thus described and you have heard O king, why being afflicted with a hundred miseries, I wish to renounce my life (27). Those, who lay violent hands on themselves, repair to the regions void of the sun. But O lord, the beasts, of sacrifices, attain to better regions (28). Formerly the fire became a beast and even Varna, the lord of waters, became so. And then the sun too, meeting with death in the shape of a beast of sacrifice, attained to the region of *Uchriti* (29). Therefore, O lord, confer upon me this *Uchriti*. And then obtaining a son, you will achieve your object (30).

THE FIRST DEER said :—O king, do not slay him; he has may sons and blessed and fortunate is he therefore. Therefore, kill me, for I have no issue (31).

THE SECOND DEER said :—Blessed are you, for you have the misery for one body—I have many bodies and therefore innumerable are my sorrows (32). When I was single I had one single misery on account of my attachment for my body. When I took a wife that misery became two-fold (33). When the children were born the miseries multiplied themselves proportionate to the number of their bodies (34). Are you not blessed as you have not taken your birth for this excessive misery? My birth in this world is for misery—and this will bring in impediments in the next world (35). And as I always think and try for the protection and maintenance of my children I shall forsooth be born in hell (36).

THE KING said :—O deer, I cannot discern, whether a man, with sons, is blessed or one who has no issue. I have undertaken this sacrifice for children, therefore my mind is full of doubts (37). True, a son brings on miseries in this world and the next, but I have heard that a man, who, has no son, is involved in debts (38). Therefore, O deer, without slaying any animal I shall engage in hard austerities for a son like the former king (39).

CHAPTER CXXI.

MARKANDEYA said :—Thereupon repairing to the sin-destroying Gomati, the king, observing regulation, pleased the god Purandara (1). Having restrained the functions of the body, mind and speech and concentrating his mind, he, with hard penances, began to chant the glories of Indra for a son (2). O great Muni, being propitiated by his asceticism, devotion and the recitation of hymns the god Indra said to him (3). "O king, I have been pleased with thee for thy ascetic observances, devotion and the recitation of the hymns. Tell me, what boon you do pray for" (4).

THE KING said .—I am sonless, may a son be born to me and may he be the foremost of heroes, pious, religious and successful and may his prosperity never decrease (5).

MARKANDEYA said :—Sakra having said 'so be it' the king, obtaining the accomplishment of his object, returned to his own city for governing his subjects (6), There he engaged in celebrating sacrifices and governing his subjects well. By the favour of Sakra a son was born to him (7). His father, the king, gave him the name of Balāshwa and trained him in the use of diverse arms (8). After the demise of his father he sat on the throne and became the king. Balāshwa brought all the kings of the earth under his subjection (9). Having taken the principal portion that king made them all pay revenues and governed all his subjects (10). Thereupon all those kings and his powerful kinsmen rose up and stopped the payment of revenue (11). They all, setting themselves up as independent kings in their respective kingdoms and growing discontented, occupied the earth of the king (12). O Muni, he, then growing weak, began to live in his own city. All other kings made dissensions with him (10). Approaching him all those kings, who were highly powerful and gifted with riches and various means, imprisoned the Emperor (14). When his city was beseized he grew angry. But having impoverished treasury and arms he became very much poorly (15). O foremost of the twice-born, then finding no means for the protection of his army, he, with his mind aggrieved, put his hand on his mouth and began to sigh (16) Then invoked by his breath there came out through the cavity of his hand hundreds of chariots, serpents, horses and soldiers (17). That highly powerful and excellent army soon covered the city of the king, O great Muni (19). Then being encircled by that huge and highly powerful army and issuing out of his city the king vanquished them all (19). Having defeated them, brought them under subjection and made them pay tributes, that great king was again crowned with prosperity (20). And because from the shaking of his hands originated that army which destroyed the enemies, Balāshwa was called *Karandhama* by the people (21). He was virtuous, great and friendly towards all animals. The king Karandhama became famous in the three worlds (22). Having obtained this army from virtue he destroyed the enemies of all terror-striken people (23).

CHAPTER CXXII

MARKANDEYA said :—Viryachandra's daughter Veerā, of beautiful eye-brows and observant of vows, married in Sayamvara the great king Karandhama (1). On her the powerful king begat a son by name Avikshita who gained renown on the surface of the earth (2). On his birth the king consulted the astrologers, "Is my son born in good time and under auspicious stars (3)? Have the auspicious stars cast their looks on the birth of my sons Have not the evil stars looked on him" (4)? Having been thus accosted by the king the astrologers said to him :—"This your highly powerful, energetic and great son is born in good conjunction and under auspicious stars. O king, your son will be emperor (5—6). Residing in the seventh house Guru and Sukra have cast their looks on him. Soma, living in the fourth house, has cast his look on him (7). Residing at a corner Soma's son too has cast his look on him. But the Sun, Bhowma and Shani have not cast their looks on him (8). O great king, your son will be fortunate and will be endowed with all auspiciousness and prosperity (9)."

Having heard the words of the astrologers and having his mind filled with delight, the king, in his own house, said to them (10) :—"Amongst the gods, Vrihaspati, Sukra, Soma and his son have cast their looks on him and the Sun, Mangala and Sani have not cast their looks on the boy (11). Since you have repeatedly used the word *Avekshata* (seen) my son will be celebrated on earth by the name of Avikshita" (12).

MARKANDEYA said :—His son Avikshita was well read in the Vedas and their divisions. He received the knowledge of weapons from Kanwa's son (13). That prince excelled in beauty the two Açwinis, in intellect Vrihaspati, in grace, the moon, in effulgence the sun, in gravity the ocean and in patience the earth. In heroism there was none equal to that high-souled one (14—15). Him did accept in Swyamvara, Himadharma's daughter Vara, Sudiva's daughter Gouri, Vali's daughter, Lilāvati, Veerabhadra's daughter Anibhā, Bhima's daughter Mânyavati and Dambhā's daughter Kumudvati (16—17). They all welcomed him in Swayamvara. Having vanquished all the princes as well as the members of their paternal family and resorting to his own strength, that powerful and heroic prince too, elated with his own strength, took them all by force (18—19). Once on a time, Vaishālini, of fine teeth, the daughter of Vishāla, the king of Videsha, held her Swayamvara. He was not selected by her. Therefore that (prince), proud of the strengh, having vanquished all the kings, O saint, carried her away by force (20—21). Thereupon having been insulted and defeated by that proud prince all those numberless kings spoke to each other (22), "Do ye allow this damsel to be carried away by one against so many powerful kings of one caste. Oh! fie on ye, O kings (23). He alone is a Kshatriya who saves one when assailed by powerful man. Others take this name for nothing (24). How is your consideration, that you,born in a Kshatriya race,do not save yourselves from this wicked one (25). O false is the eulogy that is chanted by the poets, panegyrits and prisoners. Make it good, O heroes, by destroying your enemy (26). You are all born in eminent families. Resorting to your manliness do not make an idle sound of the word, king, in all the quarters (27). Who does not fear death? Who becomes immortal without fighting? Thinking of this, manliness should not be destroyed by those who trade in arms" (28). Hearing this and filled with revenge the kings spoke to each other and took up their weapons (29). Some got upon the chariots, some rode the elephants, some horses and others, the infantry, filled with revenge, followed them (30).

CHAPTER CXXIII.

MARKANDEYA SAID:—Thus the kings and princes, arranged in order of battle, vanquished a good many of them, waiting for that time (1). Then there arose a dreadful encounter between him and them—one with many kings and mighty princes, O Muni (2). All those greatly powerful (kings) with swords, Saktis, club and arrows in their hands, fought with him; he too fought with them all (3). That highly powerful son of a king, an adept in the use of arms, pierced them with a hundred fierce arrows. They too struck him with sharpened shafts (4). Some had their arms torn, some had their heads sundered, some were wounded to the very vitals and others were struck on the breast (5). They sundered the trunks of the elephants and the heads of the horses and then again the horses of the other party's cars as well as their charioteers (6). The arrows, falling down, sundered twain the shafts of the enemies. He cut off the sword of the enemies as well as their heads by virtue of light-handedness Their armours being shattered the prince killed the enemies. And seeing others wounded the infantry left the battle-field (8). The entire host of kings being thus agitated seven hundred heroes stood there determined upon meeting with death (9). They were all of respectable pedigree, elderly, heroic and modest. After all the solders had been defeated and taken to their heels, that son of the king, greatly worked up with anger, fought righteously with all those kings, approaching them one by one (11—12). That highly powerful one attempted there to shatter their weapons and coats of mail; they too, O great Muni, worked up with rage, renouncing righteousness, began to fight with him who was combating righteously. All the princes began to perspire like a forest filled with water (13—14). Some he wouned with a collection of arrows; and the armours of others were shattered by him and again he struck down on earth the standards of others (15). Others killed the horses and broke down the chariots and drove the charioteer with the strokes of clubs and arrows (16). On his bow being shattered, the prince, in anger, took up his sword and shield and that even was struck down by another (17). Having his sword and shield shattered that one, the foremost of those holding maces, took up his mace. And that too, one cut off with a horse-shoe headed arrow like one of a sure aim (18). All those kings, ever averse to a fair fight, forming a trough, sundered them, some with a thousand shafts, some with a hundred shafts (19). When assailed by many, he, being over-powered, fell down on earth; thereupon those great princes bound him (20). Then having over-powered that prince by unfair means they all, along with the king Vishāla, entered the city of Vidisha (21). Having brought that prince bound, they all rejoiced and delightedly placed him before the maiden who had arranged for the Swayamvara (22). She was again urged on by her father and the priest, saying "choose any one amongst the kings as your husband" (23). When that honoured damsel did not choose any one as her husband O Muni, the king asked the astrologer, for the marriage (saying) (24):—"Tell me of a day which is best suited for her marriage; to-day has been sullied by a battle which has presented many obstacles (25)."

MARKANDEYA said:—Having been thus addressed by the king the astrologer, Durmanās, imformed of best things, thinking said to him (26), "O king, there shall soon be other days that will be greatly aspicious for the marriage (27). O conferror of honors, you may celebrate the marriage when that comes. There is no need of celebrating this on this day when a huge obstacle has presented itself (28).

CHAPTER CXXIV.

MARKANDEYA said :—Thereupon Karandhama heard of his son being fettered as well as his wife and other heroes of his party (1). Then hearing of his son being taken away by unfair means by all the kings of the earth, O great Muni, the king engaged in meditation (2). Some of the kings said that all those kings, by whom he had been fettered by unfair means in battle, should be slain (3). "Arrange soon the army" said others "what is the use of waiting. The wicked Vishala should be slain as well as others who have assembled there" (4). Others said that the morality was not observed here by Avikshata, for she, not wishing him, was taken away by unfair force (5). In that Swayamvara where numberless kings (were present) that princess was imposed upon by him and he was overpowered by them all collectively" (6).

Hearing those words that heroic (queen) the mother of a heroic son, the wife of a heroic husband, and who had descended from a heroic family, was pleased; and she said before her husband and other kings:—"The kings were treated well by my son who (always) does good. Taking away that girl by force and vanquishing all the kings, he fought for her. To fight with one alone is not fair. Besides, I do not see any blame on the part of my son that may lead to the destruction of his glory (7—9). This constitutes manliness for him who does not observe morality. Even a lion, who kills creatures, does not consider it fair (10). That maiden, who was present at the Swayamvara, was taken away by my son in the presence of many respectable kings (11). Who, born in the race of a Kshatriya, begs—a practice resorted to by the mean. A Kshatriya takes (a thing) by force in the presence of the powerful (12). They (even), when fettered with iron chains, and assailed, do not seek protection; even the pious kings do (things) by force (13). Therefore, useless it is to be sorry; praiseworthy is his being fettered and as well as the fall of weapons on your heads (14). Even if taken stealthily the earth, sons, wealth, wife and preceptors of the kings become sources of their glory (15). Therefore proceed quickly to the battle; get up on your chariots and arrange without delay horses, elephants and charioteers (16). Are you thinking of the fight with many kings? Does a little fight lead to the satisfaction of a heroe (17). Who is not capable of fighting with a small number of kings, whom even the afflicted amongst the enemies does not fear (18)? He is the heroe who discomfits all the worlds like the sun dispelling darkness" (19).

MARKANDEYA said:—O Muni, having been thus urged on by his wife, the king Karandhama made military arrangements for the destruction of his son's enemies (20). O great saint, then there took place an encounter between the king Vishāla whose son had been imprisoned and those innumerable kings (21). There continued for three days the battle between the king Karandhama and all those kings following Vishāla (22). After all the kings had been defeated, Vishāla with Arghya in his hand, arrived before Karandhama (23). Being worshipped by that king and pleased with him and on his son being released Karandhama spent the night happily (24). When Vishāla, with the daughter, arrived there, Avikshita, O sage, spoke before his father, for marriage (25), "O king, I shall not take her or any other damsel who had been seen by others. I had been also defeated in battle (26). I shall confer her upon some body else. Let some one, whose fame is unsullied, who is powerful and who has not been insulted by his enemies, pray for her (27). I was defeated by my enemies and belaboured by them like a poor woman. Where is manliness for me? My heart does not belong to her (28). Men are always independant, only the females are dependant. Where is manliness,for him who is dependant (29)? How can he,who had been before her very eyes thrown on the ground by other kings, see her again. How can I see her" (30)? Having been thus addressed by his son the king said to him:—"I have heard your word, O my son, high-souled as you are (31), O auspicious damsel, select any other husband whom you like. O you of beautiful looks, I shall confer upon you a habitation wherever you like under the Sun" (32).

THE GIRL said:—O king, he has been defeated by many in a battle destructive of his fame and prowess. But they did not act fairly (33). Having confronted many in battle like a lion he displayed his most excellent heroism (34). He not only stood in battle. And although defeated by so many in battle he displayed his prowess (35). He is endowed with bravery and prowess. He fought with all the kings in fair battle but they vanquished him unfairly. Where is the shame then (36)? O father, it is not by his beauty only that I have come to love him,but my mind has been attracted by his heroism, prowess and patience (37). What is the use of speaking more. Beg him for me, O king. Save this high-minded one, no one else shall be my husband (39).

VISHALA said:—O prince, really my daughter has given vent to most excellent words. There is no other prince like thee on the surface of the earth (39). Incomparable is thy heroism and great is thy prowess. By taking this daughter of mine, do thou purify my race (40).

THE PRINCE said:—O king, I shall not take her nor any other damsel. The thought of a woman shall be concentrated on me only, O king (14).

MARKANDEYA said:—Thereupon Karandhama said:—"O my son, take her; the fair daughter of Vishāla has been firmly attached to thee" (42). The prince said:—"O lord, I had never before violated thy command. Therefore order me, my father, I shall carry out thy mandate" (34). (Beholding) the prince firmly made up aginst his daughter Vishāla, having his mind agitated, said to her (44):—"Take away your mind, O daughter, from him. Select any other husband. There are many other princes" (45).

THE GIRL said :—"O father, if he does wish to take me, I shall, after carrying on penances, pray for this boon that even in other births, I may not have any other husband" (46).

Thereupon having spent there in delight three days, the king Karandhama repaired to his own city (47). Having been consoled by his father, other kings and the citizens, with various tokens Avikshita too repaired to his own city (48). Repairing to woods, divorced from her own relations, abstaining from food and cherishing most excellent disgust for the world that maiden too carried on penances (49). Abstaining from food for three months and suffering from great affliction she was reduced and her veins were weakened (50). Having lost all energy and desirous of dying that maiden princess, of a slender body, made up her mind to forsake her life (51). Thereupon coming to know that she had made up her mind to put an end to herself the celestials sent their emissary to her (52). Approaching the princess the emissary said to her :—"Hear, for what I have been sent to you by the gods (53). You should not renounce the body which it is so difficult to get ; you will be the mother of a Lord Paramount (55). O great lady, having slain all his enemies, and with his commands never baffled he will enjoy for long this earth consisting of seven insular continents (55). He will kill first Tarujit, the enemy of the gods as well as the dreadful Ayas-Shanku. And he will establish his subjects in morality (56). By him will be slain the robbers, Mlechas as well as other wicked people (57). O lady, he will perform various sacrifices, sixty-thousand in number, such as horse-sacrifice and others, finished with profuse gifts (68).

Beholding him stationed in the sky and adorned with celestial garlands and pastes the princess said gently to the emissary of the gods (59), "True it is, O emissary of the gods, that thou hast come here from the celestial region. There is no doubt in this. But how without a husband a son will be born to me (60)? I have taken this vow in the presence of my sire that save Avikshita no one else will be my husband even in another birth (61). He does not (however) want me. He was requested by my father, by Karandhama, as well as by myself" (62).

THE EMISSARY OF THE GODS said :—What is the use of of speaking more, O great lady? A son will be born to thee. Do not commit the sin of renouncing thy own life (63). Live in this forest and nourish thy weak body. By virtue of asceticism thou shalt fare well (64).

Having said this the emissary of the gods repaired where he came from. That lady of beautiful eye-brows daily nourished her own body (65).

—:o:—

CHAPTER CXXV.

MARKANDEYA said :—Thereupon the heroic mother of Avikshita, a mother of heroic sons, summoning him on an auspicious day, said (1), "O my son, I shall fast for observing the vow of *Kimichaka*. I have been ordered by your high-souled sire (2). This is within the power of yourself and myself. If you promise, my son, I shall take the vow (3). I shall confer upon you the half of your father's treasure. The wealth is your father's (no doubt) but I have obtained permission from him (4). The vow, although a very hard one, is in my power and will produce well-being. Even if you can accomplish it by putting forth your power and energy, even if it be beyond your power, or you can accomplish it with difficulty, still if you promise it, O my son, I shall get it; speak out your mind" (5—6).

AVIKSHITA said:—"Wealth is in my father's possession. I am not its master. Whatever can be accomplished by my body, I shall do it at your command (7). You will accomplish your *Kimichaka* vow, O mother, if you have obtained the permission of my father, the king, who is the master of riches. Remove your anxiety and sorrow" (8). Thereupon the queen began to observe the vow. With words, body and mind restrained she began to worship the king of kings, the numberless Nidhis, the protectors thereof and as well as Lakshmi, (the goddess of riches) with great devotion (9—10). The king Karandhama, while he was seated in his house, was thus addressed by his ministers well-versed in the science of Polity (11).

THE MINISTERS said:—O king, governing the earth you have grown old. You have only one son Avikshita who has made up his mind not to take a wife (12). While that sonless (prince) shall engage in religious practices, O king, the earth shall forsooth pass into the hands of your enemies (13). You race will be exterminated and the ancestral manes will be deprived of water and Pinda. This great fear of the enemies will put obstacles in your religious practices (14). Therefore accomplish that, O king, by which your son may cherish a desire leading to the well-bing of your ancestral manes (15).

MARKANDEYA said:—In the meantime the king heard the words addressed by the priest to the beggars (16). "Who wants what? What is there which it will be hard for them to achieve since Karandhama's queen is observing the vow *Kimichaka* (17)." Hearing the pirest's words the prince Avikshita said to all the beggars assembled at the palace-gate (18). "Let every one say what he wants. I shall even accomplish it with my body. My great mother is observing the vow of *Kimichaka* (16). Hear, O ye beggars, I promise that I shall give whatever you will want for the vow of *Kimichaka* is being observed (by my mother).

Thereupon hearing these words given vent to by his son the king approaching him said:—"O son, I am a beggar: Give me what I wish" (21).

AVIKSHITA said:—Tell me, O father, what I shall have to give you, even if it be very difficult to procure, whether within my power or not." (22).

THE KING said:—"If you are truthful, give me what I wish. Show me the face of my grandson seated on my lap" (23).

AVIKSHITA said:—I am your only son, O king, and am observing a life of celibacy. How can I show you the face of a grandson? (24).

THE KING said:—The life of celibacy, that you are leading, is taking you to sin. Therefore release yourself from that and show me a grandson (25).

AVIKSHITA said:—This is a difficult thing, O king; order me for some thing else. Retiring from the world I have given up associating with females (26).

THE KING said:—I have been seeing my many enemies coming off victorious. Still if you wish to retire from the world, you are an ignorant man (26). What is the use of speaking more? Give up your life of celibacy. Show me and your mother the face of a grandson (28).

MARKANDEYA said:—Although repeatedly requested by his son the king did not pray for any thing else. The son then said again (29). "Offering to give you what you will want I have fallen into a great difficulty, O father; therefore, being shameless, I shall take a wife (30). Before a female I was vanquished and thrown on earth. I shall be again the husband of a woman. O father, it is a very hard thing (for me) (31). Still what shall I do? I have come within the fold of truth. I shall do what you say; govern your own kingdom (32)."

CHAPTER CXXVI.

MARKANDEYA said:—Once on a time while roaming a-hunting in the forest, the prince, having killed deer, boars, tigers and other animals, heard all on a sudden the voice of a female, (saying):—"save me! save!" and bewailing in piteous accents suppressed by fear (1—2). Exclaiming "Don't fear! don't fear" that prince quickly urged on his steed to whence the sound proceeded (3). There bewailed the damsel in that lonely forest being caught firm by the hair by the son of Danu (4). (She said) "A non-aryan is taking me away in this forest who am the wife of the intelligent king Avikshita, the son of Karandhama (5). All the kings, Gandharvas, as well as Guhyakas are not capable of standing before him. I am his wife and am being carried away (6). He has the anger of death and prowess of Sakra. I am the wife of that son of Karandhama and am being carried away (7)."

MARKANDEYA said:—Hearing this that prince, who had the bow in his hand, thought. "How is this? My wife in the forest (8). Forsooth this is the illussion of the wicked Rākshasas who live in the forest. Or who has come here? I shall ascertain the cause of all (9)."

Going there speedily he saw in that forest a highly beautiful maiden adorned with all ornaments. She was caught by the hair by the son of Danu, with a club in his hand and was repeatedly exclaiming "Save me! Save me!" (10—11).

He said :—"Don't fear, don't fear. He is already slain. The king Karandhama governing the earth what wicked man can live here? All the kings of the earth have been humbled by his prowess" (12). Beholding him approach, with an excellent bow in his hand, that slender-made damsel said "Save me! save me! I am being carried away by him. I am the daughter-in-law of the king Karandhama and the wife of Avikshita. I have a lord but am being carried away by this wicked (demon) like one who has none" (13—14).

MARKANDEYA said:—Thereupon Avikshita began to consider the words given vent to by her. (He thought) "How is she my wife and the daughter-in law of my father (15)? I shall first release this fair one and then ascertain the cause. The Kshatriyas hold their arms for saving the distressed (16)." Thereupon the heroe, worked up with anger, said to that highly wicked demon :—"Live and go and let her alone; or else you will not live" (17). Thereupon releasing her and taking up his club the demon ran towards him. He too covered him with shafts (18). Having been covered with arrows, that demon, excited with pride, hurled his club, coated with a hundred goads, at that prince (19). While it was about to fall (on him) the prince cut it into pieces with his arrows. Then taking it up immediately with a loud cry Dama stood in the battle-field (20). Creating a down pour of shafts he discharged them at Dama He too cut them into pieces with pikes shot off his bow (21). Then the demon discharged a stone at the prince. That too, discharged by his light handedness, fell down baffled on earth (22). The prince easily cut into pieces with arrows all the weapons that the demon hurled at him in anger (23). Thereupon having his club and all the weapons broken, the demon, clenching his first, ran towards the prince (24). Thereupon cutting off his head, who fell on him, with a Vetasa leaf the prince threw it on the ground (25). That wicked demon being slain all the gods began to praise Karandhama's son saying 'well done! well done!" (26). On being addressed by the gods saying "pray for a boon" the prince said "I pray for a son, highly powerful, for encompassing the delight of my sire (27)."

THE GODS said :—"O sinless one, you will beget a highly powerful son, a lord Paramount, on this girl released by you (28).

THE PRINCE said :—I have made this promise by my sire that I shall wish for a son. But being thrown down on earth by the kings I gave up all desire of taking a wife (29). And so I did renounce the daughter of king Vishāla; she too for me has declined to take any other husband (30). Tell me then how leaving aside the daughter of Vishala I shall like, a cruel hearted person, take any other woman as my wife (31)?

THE GODS said :—She is your wife of whom you spoke so highly, the daughter of Vishala having fair eye-brows and who is carrying on penances for you (32). On her you will beget a heroic son, who will conquer the seven insular continents, perform a thousand sacrifices and who will be Lord Paramount (33).

MARKANDEYA said :—O twice born one, having said this to Karandhama's son the gods went away. He too then said to his wife :—"O timid lady, what is this (34)?" She then said to him :—"Having been forsaken by you and left behind all my people, I came here out of disgust of mind (35). Here, O heroe, having my body weakened by hard austerities I was about to renounce my life when an emissary of the gods brought me the intelligence (36). "You will give birth to a highly powerful son who will be Lord Paramount. He will satisfy the gods and destroy the demons (37)." Having been thus informed of the command of the gods by their emissary I did not renounce my life with the hope of being united with you (38). Day before yesterday, O great one, I went to the Ganges to bathe. As soon as I got there I was over-powered by an old serpent (39). Then I was taken by him to Rasâtala. There thousands of serpents, their wives and sons pleased me and others adored me; then the serpents and their females humbly prayed to me (40—41). "Show us the favour of preventing your son from slaying us who will offend him (42). The (serpents) living on air will commit offence by your son. You should pervent him. Show us this favour" (43). After I had said 'so be it' I was adorned with beautiful ornaments of Pâtala flowers, scents and heavenly raiments (44). Then I was brought here by the serpent equally beautiful and graceful as I was before (45.) Seeing me thus beautiful and adorned with ornaments this highly wicked demon caught me by the hair with a view to carry me away (46). O prince, I have now been released by the strength of your arms, O you of large arms; be pleased and take me. There is no other prince on this earth like you. I speak the truth (47).

CHAPTER CXXVII.

MARKANDEYA said:—Hearing thus her words and remembering the excellent words of his father which the king said after he had taken the vow of *Kimichaka* the prince Avikshita said to the maiden. "I have my mind always attached to you; for you I renounced all sorts of enjoyment. As I forsook you of slender body on being defeated by the enemies so I have again obtained you after having vanquished my foes. Tell me what I shall do" (1—3).

THE MAIDEN said:—Do thou accept my hand in this charming forest. The union of one willing with another equally willing, produces good results (4).

THE PRINCE said:—May good betide you. Providence is the instrument in this or why have we met elsewhere (5)?

MARKANDEYA said:—In the meantime, O Muni, Gandharva Tunaya came there acompanied by most excellent Apsaras and Gandharvas (6).

THE GANDHARVA said:—O prince, she is my beautiful daughter by name Bhāmini. By the imprecation of Agastya she became Vishāla's daughter (7). By her childish freaks she excited the wrath of Agastya who imprecated a curse (on her saying), "Be you a woman" (8). We however pleased him, saying:—"O Saint, she is a thoughtless girl. You should forgive her and show us the favour" (9). Being propitiated by us the great Muni said:—"Considering her as a child I gave a small curse; while I have pronounced it, it shall never be otherwise" (10). Then by the curse of Agastya my fair girl is born as Mānini in the house of Vishāla (11). For her I have come here. Take this princess, my daughter. She will give birth to your son who will be Lord Paramount (12).

MARKANDEYA said:—Having said 'so be it' the prince duly accepted her hand. Tamvuru performed Homa there (13). Gods and Gandharvas sang there—the Apsaras danced, the clouds showered flowers and the celestial instruments were sounded (14). There came at the nuptials of the prince all the protectors of wealth who are the givers and the agents of prosperity (15). O Muni, then they all, without any exception, went to the region of the Gandhavas along with that high-souled one. The prince and princess also accompanied them (16). The prince Avikshita enjoyed there in the company of Bhāmini. She too in his company enjoyed various objects of desire (17). Sometimes he sported with her in the garden of the city and sometimes on the hillocks; (18) sometimes on the banks of a river beautified with swans and Sarasas and sometimes in the beautiful palace situated at the terminus of the house (19). He, with that slender-made damsel and she with that high-souled one, sported day and night in various charming countries (20). The Munis, Gandharvas and Kinnaras brought for them there various edibles, pastes, raiments, garlands and excellent drinks (21). That good damsel gave birth to a son for that heroe spending his days happily with Bhāmini in the region of Gandharvas unattainable by others (22). O foremost of men, on that highly powerful son being born there took place a great festivity of the Gandharvas (23). Some of them sang, some played on Mridanga, trumpets and Anaka and some played on Venu, Vinā and other musical intruments (24). There danced innumerable Apsaras, the clouds dischanged showers of flowers and the wind blew gently (25). When there arose a great tumult Tumvura, being thought of by Tunaya, came there and performed the *Jatakarma* ceremony, O Muni (26). There came the gods and the immaculate celestial saints and the leading Nāgas headed by Sesha, Vasuki and Takshaka from Pātāla (27). And came all the leaders, O foremost of the twice-born, of the gods, Asuras, Yakshas and Gukyakas and all the Vāyus (28). The great city of the Gandharvas was agitated by all the Rishis, gods, Danavas, Pannagas and Munis, who had come there (29). Having performed all the ceremonies consequent on the birth of the child Tumvaru undertook the performance of a benedictory rite preceeded by eulogy (30). "Do thou, becoming a Lord Paramount, highly powerful, energetic and mighty-armed, rule over this endless earth for a long time (31). May Sakra and all the gods, all the Lokapālas and Rishis, do good, O heroe, to your prowess destructive of your enemies (32). May Marut do you good, and may it blow with no dust before it. And the pure southern wind shall blow gently for you (33). The Western Marut will give you most excellent energy and the northern Marut will give you great prowess (34)." After the completion of this benedictory rite a voice, without any body, said " there will be many Maruts for you as the preceptor has said." And accordingly he will be celebrated on earth by the name of Marutta (35). All the kings on earth will carry out his command. And this heroe will be at the head of all kings (36). Having subdued all the kings this highly powerful Lord Paramount will enjoy, without any obstruction, the earth consisting of seven insular continents (37). He will be the head of all the kings celebrating sacrifices and he will excell all the kings in heroism and energy (38).

MARKANDEYA said:—Hearing the words of the gods expressed through some one all the Vipras, Gandharvas and as well as his parents were delighted (39).

CHAPTER CXXVIII.

MARKANDEYA said:—Thereupon taking that dear son and followed by Vipras and Gandharvas on foot the prince went to his own city (1) Having reached his father's house he saluted his feet with reverence. And so did the bashful thin-built princess (2). Then taking the boy the prince said to king Karandhama seated on the throne of justice in the midst of all kings (3). "Behold now the face of your grandson seated on your lap as promised by me in the *Kimichaka* vow of my mother" (4). Having said this and placed the boy on his father's lap he described, in full, everything to him (5). Then seeing his grandson and having his eyes filled with tears of joy he again and again spoke highly of himself, saying "fortunate I am (6)." Thereupon forgetting every other important business he delightedly, with *Arghya*, honored all the Gandharvas who had come there (7). Thereupon there took place in the houses of all citizens a great festivity, who all thought, "A son is born to us and not to him (8)." That city being delighted and filled with the singing and and music of beautiful damsels, other women, of exquiste beauty, began to dance (9). The king delightedly made unto the leading twice-born gifts of jewels, riches, kine, raiments and ornaments (10). That boy grew up like the moon in the light half of the month. He gave delight to his parents and was loved by his people (11). O Muni, he first took lessons in the Vedas from the preceptors and then in numberless scriptures and then in the science of archery (12). He was always energetic in the use of swords and bow; and that heroe never felt tired in the use of other weapons too (13). Thereupon, O Vipra, being humble and reverent towards his preceptor he took lessons in arms from Bhārgava of Bhrigu's race (14). Having learnt the use of arms, mastered the Vedas and seen the other end of archery he became highly accomplished in all branches of learning (15). Vishāla too, having heard all of his daughter and of the proficiency of her son, had his mind filled with joy (16). Having seen his grandson and obtained his desired-for object the king performed many sacrifices and gave away gifts to many (17). Having performed many ceremonies, the king, gifted with strength and intellect (as he was) and (ever) vanquishing his enemies, piously ruled the earth with the help of his own caste people (18). Then desirous of returning into the forest he said to his son Avikshita.—"O son, I have grown old. I shall therefore) go to the forest; take from me this kingdom (19). I have no other (desire) save your installation. Do you take from me this well established kingdom which I offer you" (20). Thus accosted by his father, the prince Avikshita, having his mind bent upon going to the forest for carrying on penances, said humbly to him (21) "O father, I shall not rule over this earth. My mind does not find pleasure in kingdom.

Appoint (therefore) another man (22). Wh.n I was enchained I was released by my father not by my own prowess. Where is then manliness for me and the earth is to be governed by manliness (23). How can I, who could not protect my own self, preserve this earth? Therefore confer this kingdom upon some body else (24). How can the man, who had been overpowered by others and who had been released by you from the bow, observe the duty of his own order? How can I, who have the nature of a female, be a king (25).

THE FATHER said:—There is no distinction between a father and a son. As is the father so is the son. O heroe, you were not released by any one else but by your father (26).

THE SON SAID:—O king, I cannot change my mind otherwise. There is a great shame in my mind since I was released by you (27). He, who enjoys the riches acquired by his father, who has been saved from difficulty by his father, whose name is made known by his father, is not born in the race of mankind (28). I will follow the conduct of those who acquire riches for themselves with reputation and remove themselves their own difficulties (29).

MARKANDEYA said:—O Muni, when repeatedly requested by his father he said so the king placed his son Marutta on the throne (30). Having obtained this kingdom, with the consent of his father, from his grandfather he fully contributed to the joy of his kinsmen (21). King Karandhama too, restraining his mind, body and speech, retired to woods with Veerā for carrying on hard austerities for a thousand years and then renouncing his body the king repaired to the region of Sakra (33). His wife Veerā, covered with matted locks and impurities, carried on penances for another hundred celestial years (34). Wishing the same region with her high-souled lord in heaven, she lived on fruits and roots, resided in the hermitage of Bhārgava in the midst of the wives of the twice-born and engaged herself in their service (35).

CHAPTER CXXIX.

KROUSHTHUKI said :—O revered Sir, you have described to me in full the story of Karandhama as well as that of Avikshita (1). I wish now to hear the story of the high-souled king Marutta, Avikshita's son. I have heard he was greatly energetic, lord Paramount, noble, heroic, beautiful, highly intelligent, conversent with piety. He performed many religious acts and governed well the earth (2—3).

MARKANDEYA said :—Having obtained the kingdom from his grand-father with the consent of his father he governed it piously like a father taking care of his own begotten sons (4). He duly performed many *Yajnas* terminated with gifts and gladly carried out the command of Ritwikas and priests (5). His wheel was unobstructed in the seven insular continents and his movement was unimpeded in heaven, Pātāla and water (6). Having obtained riches, O Vipra, he duly performed his own actions and propitiated the gods headed by Indra with *Yajnas* (7). The inferior castes too zealously engaged in their respective duties, and performed, with the wealth obtained from him, Rishtha and Purtha ceremonies (8). The earth being governed by the high-souled Marutta the celestial region, with its inhabitants, grew prosperous, O foremost of the twice-born (9). He not only surpassed all the kings of the earth but with sacrifices even the king of the gods, the performer of a hundred *Yajnas* (10). His *Ritwika* was the high-souled ascetic Samvartta, the son of Angiras and the brother of Vrihaspati (11). He broke down the golden mountain Munjavan, where the celestials used to go for he had pilfered the conch shell of that king (12). O twice-born one, by giving away lands in his *Yajna* he pleased all the ascetics (13). All the Rishis sing fully the story of Marutta and read it as well (14). "There is no other king on this earth who can perform *Yajnas* like Marutta, in whose *Yajna* all the Rishis have been pleased (15). He distributed Soma juice amongst all the gods headed by Shakra and *Dakshinás* amongst all the twice-born (16). In the *Yajna* of what king like that of Marutta will the twice-born one leave aside profuse gold in houses filled with jewels (17)? All his palaces were made of gold. All the three Varnas gained something or other from him and equally gave it away (18). All those men, who had their ends achieved with the remnant left off by him, performed many *Yajnas* there-with in different countries (19). O foremost of Munis, while he was reigning and governing his subjects an ascetic came to him and said (20):—"O king, having seen a host of ascetics assailed by the poison of serpents, elated with pride your grand-mother has communicated this to you (21). 'Having governed the earth well your grand-father has gone to heaven. I too, incapable of carrying on penances, am living in the hermitage of Urvā (22). O king, yourself governing the king-dom of your grand-father, I see an irregularity (that never took place during the regeme of) your predecessors (23). Forsooth, you have been blindly attached to the objects of enjoyment and have lost all control over senses, since you do not understand who are wicked and who are not (24). Having come from Pātāla the serpents have bitten seven Muni boys and vitiated the water (25). They have also desecrated the purified Havi wirh urine, excreta etc. Perceiving your short-coming do you soon offer food to the serpents (26). These Munis are capable of consuming the serpents—but they have no right in this—it is within your province (27). O king, the children of the kings should so long enjoy as long as the water of installation does not fall on their heads (28). (They should always think), "Who are my friends? Who is my enemy? What is the measure of the enemy's strength? Who am I? Who are my ministers? What kings are on my side (29)? What man in this city or in the kingdom has been dissatisfied with me or alienated from me by the enemies? What is the matter with the enemies (30)? Who performs religious acts? Who is ignorant? Who behaves well? Who is to be punished? Who is to be protected? What persons should be looked after by me (31)? For fear of the break of treaty, a king, understanding well the time and place, should send spies to bring him intelligence (33). A king should always engage spies (to ascertain the condect of) ministers and others" (33). Having his mind daily engaged in such actions, a king should spend his days and nights and should not indulge in enjoyments (34). O king, the kings live not for enjoyment but for suffering pain and for the protection of the earth and virtue (35). If a king maintains well this earth and observes his duties, he suffers great trouble in this world but attains to supreme delight in the next (36). Understanding this and relinquishing all pleasures, O king, you should promise to undergo every trouble for governing the earth (37). This great calamity of the Rishis that has come from the serpents during your rule, you do not know, O king (88). What is the use of speaking more? Inflict punishment on the wicked and protect the good. You are the king and are entitled to the sixth portion of virtue (39). By not protecting them and subduing the wicked you will be visited by all sins. Do this if you like (40). I have thus communicated all to you. I am your grand-mother. Do this if you like, O king (41).

CHAPTER CXXV.

MARKANDEYA said:—Hearing the words of the ascetic the king was filled with shame. Then saying, "Fie on me who am negligent" and sighing he took up his bow (1). Thereupon speedily repairing to the hermitage of Aurva he touched the feet of his father's mother Veerā with his head (2). The ascetics too duly welcomed him. Beholding the seven Rishis bitten by the serpents on the ground the king blamed himself in their presence. He said—"May the entire world with gods, demons and men see how I deal with the wicked serpents who have disregarded my prowess and proved hostile to the Brāhmanas (3—5).

MARKANDEYA said:—Having said this, the king, in anger, took up the weapon called Samvartaka for the destruction of the innumerable serpents living in Pātāla (6). Thereupon O Vipra, there was a conflagration all around the city of Nagas, on its being continually burnt down by the effulgence of the great weapon (7). Being assailed by that weapon the serpents began to give vent to words as "O father! O mother! O child!" (8). Some with their tails burnt, some with their hoods burnt, taking their wives and sons wth them, keeping aside their ornaments and clothes and renouncing Patāla proceeded to seek refuge with Bhāmini, the mother of Murutta, who had formerly promised them protection (9—10). Having approached her they all, stricken with fear, saluting her, said with suppressed words "Remember what you said to us before (11). Formerly we worshipped you in Rasātala for something; the time for that is now come. Save us, O mother of heroes (12). O queen, stop your son, save our lives. The entire region of the serpents is being burnt down by the fire of his weapon (13). Save you there is no other refuge for us who are being thus consumed by your son. Have pity on us, O illustrious lady" (14).

Hearing their words and remembering her former words the chaste lady addressed the following words respectfully to her husband (15).

BHAMINI said :—Formerly in Pātala, the serpents welcoming you adressed to you some words regarding your son (16). They are now being consumed by his energy and have come here in fear. Formerly I promised them protection (17). Those who have sought my protection have also sought your protection for observing the same religious life with you I am now under your protection (18). Therefore stop your son Marutta. At your words and requesting me he will, forsooth, be pacified (19).

AVIKSHITA said :—For their great iniquity Marutta has been worked up with anger. Irrepressible is the ire of my son, I think (20).

THE SERPENTS said :—O king, we have sought refuge with thee. Do thou show us the favour; the use of arms is for the protection of the afflicted (21).

MARKANDEYA said :—Hearing the words of the serpents who came for protection and being requested by his wife the highly illustrious Avikshita said :—(22). " O gentle lady, I shall soon go and request your son to save the serpents. Those, who seek protection, should never be forsaken (23). If he does not withdraw his weapon at my words I shall oppose the weapon of my son with mine" (24).

Thereupon taking up his bow, Avikshita, the foremost of Kshatriyas, speedily left for the hermitage of Bhargava along with his wife (25).

CHAPTER CXXXI.

MARKANDEYA said :—He saw his son with a most excellent bow, his fierce weapon spreading its fire upon all the quarters, vomitting forth great fire burning down the entire earth and reaching the heart of Pātala, irrepressible and dreadful (1—2). Beholding the frowning face of the king, he said :—" You should not be angry, O Marutta; take away your weapon (3). Intelligent greatly (as you are) you have carelessly broken down the order of creatures." Hearing the words of his father and looking at him repeatedly, he with his bow, saluting him reverentially said :—" O father, the serpents have greatly offended me (4—6). During my rule they, disregarding my prowess and coming to Saptasrama, (hermitage) have bitten the ascetic boys (6). O king, during my regime, these wicked (serpents) have spoiled the *Havis* kept in the hermitages of the ascetics (7). They all have also spoiled the tanks. For this, O father, you should not speak any thing. You should not stop me from slaying these serpents, the killers of Brahmanas (8).

AVIKSHITA said :—If they have killed the Vipras they will go to hell after death. Now obey my words and restrain your weapon (9).

MARUTTA said :—I too shall also go to hell if I do not try to bring the wicked to bay. Do not prevent me therefore, O father (10).

AVIKSHITA said :—All these serpents have sought refuge with me. Out of honor to me do you withhold your weapon. What is the use of being angry, O king ? (11).

MARUTTA said :—I shall never forgive these wicked fellows who have committed a great iniquity; disregarding my own duty how can I satisfy your words? (12). A king, who punishes those who deserve punishment and protects those who are good, attains to sacerd regions. One, who neglects this duty, goes to hell (13).

MARKANDEYA said:—Although he was thus repeatedly prevented by his father the son did not withhold his weapon. He then again said (14):—"Although prevented by me you are still bent upon killing the serpents, who in fear have sought refuge with me. I shall then adopt the remedial measure (15). I have also learnt the use of arms; it is not you alone who are an expert in it. O wicked one, what is your proweess before me (16)?

MARKANDEYA said:—O foremost of Munis, thereupon Avikshita, with his eyes reddened with rage, took up the weapons of Kala (17). He then set to the bow the highly powerful and most excellent weapon of Kala capable of burning down the enemies (18). Assailed by Samvarta weapon the earth was agitated. And when the Kāla weapon was taken up all the mountains were agitated (19). Beholding the deadly weapon uplifted by his father Marutta said aloud:—"I have taken up this weapon for punishing the wicked and not for killing you. Why do you therefore discharge the deadly weapon at me, your son, observant of his own duties and always obedient to you (20—21)? O great one, my duty is to protect my subects; for whose destruction have you taken up this weapon (22)?

AVIKSHITA said:—I have made this exertion for protecting them who have sought my shelter. Thou art their destroyer; do not save me (23). Either having slain me with the prower of your weapon do thou kill the wicked serpents, or having slain thee with the strength of my arms I shall protect the great serpents (24). O fie on the life of that man who does not help him who seeks his shelter even if he be one of the enemies (25). I am a Kshatriya and they in fear have sought my shelter; thou art their enemy. Why shouldst thou not be slain by me (26)?

MARUTTA said :—He, who puts in impediments in the way of governing the subjects, be he a friend, a relative, a father or the preceptor, should be slain by the king (27). I shall thereforc strike thee, O father. Do not be offended. I am observing my own duty and am not angry with thee (28).

MARKANDEYA said :—Thereupon beholding them both bent upon killing one another all the Munis, Bhargavas and others came there (29). They said to them :—"You should not discharge your weapon at your father and you should not also kill your son of illustrious deeds" (30).

MARUTTA said :—The wicked should be slain by me and the earth should be protected. These are wicked serpents. Where is my folly, O ye twice-born ones (31).

AVIKSHITA said :—My duty also is to protect them who have sought refuge with me. O ye Vipras, my son bas committed an offence for he is about to kill my dependants (32).

THE RISHIS said :—Tell these serpents whose eyes are rolling with terror that we shall revive the Vipras who have been bitten by the wicked serpents (33). No use therefore of fighting, O ye foremost of kings. Be reconciled. Both of you are of firm promises and are conversant with your duties (34).

MARKANDEYA said :—Then Veerā,approaching her grand-son, said :—"O child, at my words you have addressed yourself for destroying these serpents (35). My object has been accomplished, for the Brāhmanas, who were dead, have regained their lives. You should therefore save them who have sought your protection (36).

BHAMINI said :—I was formerly welcomed by them living in Pātāla and therefore my husband was engaged in this work by myself (37). Therefore, O worshipful one, it is proper that there should be an end of fight between my husband and son, your grand-son and son (33).

MARKANDEYA said :—Thereupon with heavenly medicine and by taking away their poison the serpents revived those

Vipras (39). Thereupon the king Marutta saluted the feet of his sire. He too embracing him said (40):—"Vanquish your enemies and govern for long the earth. Enjoy with your sons and grandsons and may you have no enemies" (41). Thereupon commanded by the twice born and Veerā those two kings, riding their own cars and Bhāmini repaired to their own city (42). And Veerā too, the foremost of the pious ladies, carrying on hard austerities, great and chaste as she was, attained to the same region with her husband (43). The king Marutta too governed the earth righteously, vanquished his six classes of enemies and enjoyed diverse pleasures (44). The great Prabhāvati, the daughter of Bidarbha king and Souviri, the daughter of Suvira became his wives (45). Sukeshi, the daughter of Ketuvirjja, the king of Magadha, became his wife as well as Kaikeyi, the daughter of Sindhuvirjja the king of Madra (36), Sourindhri of Kekaya country, Vapushmati, the daughter of Sindhu, king and the beautiful daughter of the king of Chedis became his wives (47). O twice-born one, the king begat on them eighteen sons. The foremost and the eldest of them was Narishwanta (48). Of such energy was the highly powerful king Marutta that his wheel was unobstructed in the seven insular continents (49). Like that royal saint of incomparable energy and prowess there had been no king in the past nor will be any in future (50). Hearing the account of this high-souled Marutta, O foremost of the twice born, one gets the best birth and is freed from all sins (51).

CHAPTER CXXXII.

KROUSHTHUKI said:—O reverend Sir, you have recounted in full the story of Marutta. I wish to hear of an account of his progeny (1). O great Muni, I wish to hear of those of his children who were powerful and became kings. Do you relate it (2).

MARKANDEYA said:—Marutta had a son celebrated by the name of Narishwanta; of the eighteen sons he was the eldest and foremost (3). Marutta, the foremost of the Kshatriyas, ruled over the earth for eighty-five thousand years (4). Having governed his kingdom righteously, performed many *Yajnas* and placed on the throne his eldest son Narishwanta he retired into woods (5). Having carried on hard austerities with a concentrated mind and filled the heaven and earth with his fame he ascended the heaven, O Vipra (6). Observing the conduct of his father as well as that of other kings his son, the intelligent Nariswanta, began to think (7). "In this family, my predecessors, the high-souled kings, celebrated many *Yajnas* and righteously governed the earth (8). They gave away riches and never fled away from battles. Am I capable of following the conduct of those high-souled ones (9)? I wish to follow his actions and immitate his religious acts. If I do not do this what else shall I do (10)? What credit does a king deserve if he righteously rules the earth? For by not governing the earth well the sinful king goes to hell (11). While they have wealth, what wonder is there if the king performs great *Yajnas* and makes charities (12)? Pride of birth, shame, anger towards enemies and one's own duties prevent a man from flying away from the battle-field (13). All these were completely accomplished by my ancestors and my father Marutta. Who can immitate them (14)? What more can I do which had not been done by my forefathers? They all performed *Yajnas*, made charities, never came from the battle-field, were great warriors and manly. I shall do such works as had not been attempted by them (15—16). My predecessors celebrated *Yajnas* no doubt but they could not do so uninterruptedly. I shall do this (17).

MARKANDEYA said :—Thinking thus that king undertook a Yajna adorned with the gifts of riches the like of which had not been performed by any (18). He gave away profuse riches for the maintenance of the twice-born; the king then gave hundred fold food in that *Yajna* (19). He then conferred upon each man of the earth kine, raiments, ornaments and store-houses of corn (20). Thereupon when that king again undertook the celebration of another *Yajna* and when it was taken in hand he invited many Brahmanas but could not get any (21). Every one, of those Brahmanas whom the king invited to take up the duties of a Ritwika, said to him. "We are engaged elsewhere in another *Yajna* (22). Request some body else, O king. The riches, that you gave us in your *Yajna*, have not been exhausted as yet" (23).

MARKANDEYA said :—When the king of the whole earth did not get Brahmanas to act as Ritwikas he began to give away gifts at the outside altar (24). Still, they, who had their temples filled with wealth, did not accept them. He, then with a view to make gifts unto the twice-born with a poor heart, said (25). "Oh! it is a highly grand thing that there is no poor Brāhmana on this earth. But the treasury has grown useless and frutless is the object of those who perform *Yajnas* (26). No one will require a Ritwika for the people of the world will not celebrate *Yajnas*. We shall not be able, even if we wish, to make gifts unto the twice-born (27).

MARKANDEYA said :—Thereupon saluting repeatedly with reverence some Brāhmanas he made them Ritwikas in his *Yajna* and they began that great ceremony (28). It was a great wonder that when that king undertook that *Yajna* there were many men on earth engaged in similar cermonies (29). (So) there did not assemble a concourse of the twice-born. Few Brâhmanas came there for accepting gifts (30). Whenever the king *Narishwanta* engaged in celebrating *Yajnas* many people, with the money given by him, undertook numberless such ceremonies on earth (31). When the king Narishwanta, O Muni, undertook the performance of a *Yajna* there took place simultaneously eighteen *Kotis* of *Yajnas* in the west, seven in the north, fourteen in the south, and fifteen in the north (32—33). O Vipra, such was the virtuous king Narishwanta, the son of Marutta, in the days of yore renowned for his strength and bravery (34).

CHAPTER CXXXIII.

MARKANDEYA said:—Narishwanta's son Dama, the subduer of wicked enemies, had the strength of Sakra and the compassion and character of an ascetic (1). The king (Narishwanta) begat him on Indrasenā. The highly illustrious one lived in his mother's womb for nine years (2). As he suffered endurance by living (so long) in his mother's womb the prince will be patient by nature (3). Then his priest, conversant with the present, past and future, gave the name of Dama to the son of Narishwanta (4). The prince Dama learnt in full the science of archery from the king Brishaparva (5). He received in full the lessons in diverse arms from Dundubhi, the foremost of Daityas living in the forests of ascetics (6). He learnt the Vedas and all their divisions from Sakti and that self-controlled (prince) received lessons in *yoga* from the royal saint Arshmishena (7). Sumanā, at the Sayamvara, invited by her father, accepted him as her husband—accomplished, high-souled, highly powerful and an expert in the use of arms as he was, in the presence of all men who had come there for her. She was the daughter of the powerful Chārukarman, the king of Dasharna (8—9). The highly powerful and heroic son of the king Madra was greatly attached to Sumanā (10). And so were the great bowman and the highly intelligent prince Vapushmān, the son of Sangkrandana and the prince of Vidarbha (11). Seeing Dama, the subduer of wicked enemies, selected by her they began to consult with each other, assailed by Cupid as they were (12):—"Taking away this beautiful girl by force from him we shall go to our houses. His amongst us this fair one will be the religiously wedded wife whom she will select of her own accord, according to the rules of Sayamvara (13—14). If she, of inebriete eyes, does not like any one of us, she then must marry him who will slay Dama (15).

MARKANDEYA said:—Having made this resolution the three princes carried away that fair one from the side of Dama (16). Thereupon some kings, who were on his side, lamented much as well as some others who were the arbitrators (17). O great Muni, beholding them sorry on all sides, Dama said to them (18).

DAMA said:—O ye kings, Sayamvara is mentioned in the list of religious acts. Do ye consider whether her being carried away by force is fair or wrong (19). If (to save her) is wrong I should not take any step and must marry another wife. And if it is fair—fie on me if with my life I cannot save her by subduing the enemies (20).

Thereupon the king Chārudharma, the lord of Dashārna, making them all silent, addressed the assembly, O great Muni (21). "Do ye consider, O ye kings, what Dama has said relating to what is right and wrong so that my virtue may not suffer deterioration" (22).

MARKANDEYA said :—Thereupon some kings said to that lord of the earth :—"There is also sanction for Gandharva marriage that is brought about by attachment towards one other (23). This is good for the Kshatriyas not for Vaishyas, Sudras and Brāhmanas. Your daughter's marriage has been celebrated with Dama (24). Therefore rightly your daughter belongs to Dama. Only he, who is possessed by desire, does otherwise (25). Then those high-souled kings, who were for the words of the king of Dasharna, said (26) :—"They have foolishly said that the Gāndharva form of marriage is the best for Kshatriyas. There is another form of marriage called Rākshasa for the Kshatriyas (27). He, who has taken her away by force after slaying all the intruders, may also marry her according to the Rakshasa form of marriage (28). This is the best form of marriage for the Kshatriyas—the other one is the second. This is the duty of the Kshatriyas as laid down by Mahānanda and others (29).

MARKANDEYA said :—Thereupon the kings, who had been addressed before, again said words, maintaining their caste and religion out of regard for each other (30). True it is that the Rakshasa form of marriage is also sanctioned for the Kshatriyas. But he, of all men, was selected by that maiden as her fitting husband (31). That is called the Rakshasa form of marriage when one takes away a girl by force after having slain all the relations of her father. But it is not so when she has accepted a husband (32). In the presence of all the kings she selected Dama. How can here be then either the Gandharva or Rakshasa form of marriage? (33). Maidenhood does not hold in the case of married women. By marriage the girls are allied to (other) kings (34). They have taken her away by force from Dama; they have done this by force but it is not fair (35).

MARKANDEYA said :—Hearing this Dama had his eyes

reddened with ire. He then set aright his bow and said :— (36). "If I behold my wife being carried away by powerful men what is the use of my arms who am shorn of manliness? (37). Oh fie on me! fie on my arms! fie on my bravery! fie on my arrows! fie on my bow! and fie on my birth in the family of the high-souled Marutta (38). If these foolish and powerful men survive after taking away my wife useless is my proficiency in the use of bow (39)." Having addressed these words to the kings headed by Mahānanda, the prowerful Dama, subduer of great enemies, again said (40).

DAMA said :—How can this all beautiful maiden, of inebriete eyes and born in this family, be the wife by birth of this one or that one? Thinking this, O kings, do ye so fight in battle that ye may, after vanquishing me, make this respectable lady your wife (42).

MARKANDEYA said :—Having said this he began to shower arrows covering therewith all the kings like darkness (43). All those heroic kings too discharged arrows, Saktis, clubs, etc. But Dama cut off easily all those weapons discharged by them (44). O Muni, they too cut off the arrows shot by him. And Narishwanta's son too cut off the arrows discharged by those kings (45). When there was going on a conflict between Dama and all the kings entered there Mahānanda with a dagger in his hand (46). Beholding him approach with a dagger in his hand in that great encounter Purandara discharged a downpour of arrows like a shower (47). Those weapons and the network of arrows Mahānanda, with his dagger, immediately cut off (48). Thereupon getting in anger upon Dama's car the highly powerful Mahānanda engaged in an encounter with him (49). Mahānanda fighting in many ways Dama, out of light-handedness, discharged an arrow, burning like the fire of dissolution, at his heart (50). Thereupon taking it out of his heart which was cut Mahānanda threw a shining sword at Dama (51). Dama, with his Sakti, cut this off which was like a fire-brand and about to fall. He also cut off Mahànanda's head with a Vetasa leaf (52). On Mahananda being slain all the kings fled away. Then stood there Vapushman, the king of Kundina (53). Then the son of the king of Deccan, elated with the pride of strength, coming to the battle-field, fought with Dama (54). The light-handed heroe (Dama) cut off in battle his dreadful sword, the head of his charioteer and his flag-staff (55). Having his sword shattered he took up his club of many thorns. That too he immediately cut off from his hand (56). And as soon as Vapushman was about to take up another powerful weapon Dama, piercing him with an arrow, immedaitely struck him down on earth (57). Falling down on earth he began to tremble with all his limbs dislocated. Then the princes made up their minds to fly from the battle-field (58). Then seeing them thus disinclined to fight, leaving them behind and taking Sumanā the self-controlled Dama went away (59). Then the king of Dasharna duly celebrated the marriage between Dama and Sumanā (60). After his marriage Dama lived for some time in the city of the king of Dasharna and then with his wife went to his own city (61). Then conferring upon him elephants, horses, chariots, kine, asses, camels, female servants, and many servants, clothes, raiments, bows and vessels filled with many excellent things the king of Dasharna sent him away (62—63).

———:o:———

CHAPTER CXXXIV.

MARKANDEYA said:—O great Muni, having obtained Sumanā as his wife the prince saluted the feet of his father aud mother (1). Sumanā, of fair eye-brows, also saluted her father-in-law and mother-in-law. They too, O Vipra, also welcomed them with blessings (2). On his marriage and return from the city of the king of Dasharna there took place a great festival in Narishwanta's city (3). Hearing of the alliance of his son with the king of Dasharna and the defeat by the kings the emperor Narishwanta was greatly delighted (4). The prince Dama sported with Sumanā in gardens, palaces, forest-lands and in the valleys of the mountains (5). Having enjoyed many pleasures and grown old the king Narishwanata installed his son Dama in the kingdom (7). His wife, the illustrious Indrasenā also followed him to the forest and led with him the Vānaprastha mode of life (8). Vapushmān, the son of Sangkrandana, the king of Deccan, went to that forest for hunting followed by a small retuine (9). Seeing the ascetic Narishwanta covered with dust and his wife Indrasenā, greatly reduced by hard aurterities he asked him, "Who are you? Are you a Vipra, Kshatriya or a forest ranger or a Vaisya who is leading the Vānaprastha mode of life? Tell me this" (10—11). Theroupon the king, observant of the vow of silence, gave him no reply. Indrasenā communicated unto him everything duly (12).

MARKANDEYA said:—Being informed that Narishwanta was the father of his enemy, Vapushmān, saying "I have got you" held him by the matted locks (13). Indrasenā crying aloud 'Alas! Alas!' in suppressed words he took up his sword, and said (14):—"He is the father of Dama who vanquished me in battle and carried away my Sumanā. I shall kill him; let Dama save him (15). I shall slay the father of the wicked one who vanquished the entire host of kings assembled for securing the maiden (19). I shall kill the father of my enemy, the wicked Dama who fought with me in battle. Let him prevent me" (17).

MARKANDEYA said:—Having said this the wicked king Vapushmān cut off his head whilst Indrasenā kept up crying

(18). Thereupon all the ascetics and other dwellers of the forest said to him, "Fie on you! Fie on you!" Seeing it he left the forest for his own city (19). On his departure, Indrasenā, heaving a deep sigh, despatched a Sudra ascetic to her son (20). She said, "Go immediately and communicate to my son my words. You know everything about my husband's affair. What more shall I speak (21)? Still you should inform my son of what I say, with great sorrow on beholding the wicked condition of the king (22). He is the king, lord and the protector of the four Varnas. How fair it is that he does not protect the ascetics living in hermitages (23)? While I was crying "O lord! O lord!" Vapushmān, holding my husband Narishwanta, engaged in ascetic observances, by the hair, killed him without any fault. You have gained this reputation as a king during your rule (24—25), Such being the case, behave yourself in such a way that virtue may not disappear. I should not speak (more) in this. I am a female ascetic (29). Your father, an aged ascetic, has been killed, though he was innocent. Think what you should do in this (27). You have heroic ministers well read in all branches of learning. Discussing with them do what is proper (28). O king, this is not in our province who are ascetics; you are to do this. Hear of the conduct of other kings (29). Viduratha's father was killed by a Yavana whose family was destroyed (in turn) by his son (30). The father of Jambha, the king of Asuras, was bitten by serpents. And so by him all the serpents living in Pātāla were killed. Hearing that his father has been killed by a Rákshasa Parāshara completely destroyed the race of Rākshasas with fire (32). A Kshatriya cannot brook the insult offered to any other member of his family what to speak of the destruction of his father (33)? In this, your father has not been killed nor a weapon has struck him but methinks you have been killed and wounded with a weapon (34). Who fears him who has placed his weapon on the dwellers of the forest? Will you fear when your son is killed (35)? Therefore, O king, you should mete out a condign punishment to Vapushman along with his servants, kinsmen and friends (36).

Having despatched Indradās with this intelligence, that great lady, embracing the body of her husband, entered into fire (37).

---:o:---

CHAPTER CXXXV.

MARKANDEYA said:—Being commanded by Indrasenā the Sudra ascetic went there and communicated the destruction of his father unto Dama (1). Being informed by the ascetic of the death of his father, Dama burnt with rage like fire excited by clarified butter (2). O great Muni, being consumed by the fire of anger and pressing one hand against the other he gave vent to the following words (3). "Inspite of my existence, his son, my father was killed by that greatly cruel one, throwing an insult at my family, like one having none (4). If I forgive him I shall do so for want of manliness; my duty is to punish the wicked and help the good (5). What is the use of lamenting much as 'Oh (father)'. I should now do what should be done in this mattar (6). If I do not bring about the gratification of my father with the blood coming out from Vapushman's body I shall enter into fire (7) I shall perform the water-giving ceremony of my father with his blood slain in battle; I shall feed well the twice-born with his flesh. Or else I shall enter into fire (8). Even if the Asuras, Gods, Yakshas, Gandharvas, Vidyadharas and all the Siddhas come to his help, even them with him I shall reduce to ashes with my weapons (9). Having slain the coward, sinful and dishonest king of Deccan in battle I shall enjoy the earth fully. If I cannot kill him I shall enter the fire (10). I shall slay today the highly wicked one together with his friends, relatives, infantry, cavalry and the army, who slew the aged ascetic, observing the bow of silence, living in the forest and always extending words of blessings (11). Taking up their bow and sword, riding this chariot and confronting the army of the enemy I shall carry on an onslaught there. All the gods assembled there will see it (12). I shall lead this great army, brought up by myself, for the immediate and absolute destruction of the families of those who will help him while engaged in an encounter with me to-day (13). If the king of gods comes to the battle with the thunderbolt in his hand, the king of Pitris taking up, in anger, his dreadful rod and if the king of riches and Varuna endeavour to save him still I shall kill him with sharpened shafts (14). May the vultures be satisfied with his flesh and blood by whom despite my existence, his son, my father has been slain. He had his mind under control, was freed from folly, had his movements from the forest to heaven and used to live on fruits dropped from trees and was friendly towards all creatures (15).

——;o:——

CHAPTER CXXXVI.

MARKANDEYA said:—Having made this promise Narishwanta's son Dama, with his eyes rolling in anger, held his beards with his hand (1). Bewailing the death of his father and censuring destiny he said to all the ministers and summoned his priest (2).

DAMA said:—Tell me now what is proper. My father has gone to heaven. You have heard what the Sudra ascetic has said (3). That king was an old ascetic, was leading the Vanaprastha mode of life and observing the vow of silence. My mother Indrasenā has communicated everything to me in truth as what should be done to Vapushmān. That wicked one, taking up his sword, and holding by the hand, killed the king as if he had none. My good mother has addressed the word 'fie' to me (4—6). Having embraced the unfortunate Nariswanta shorn of all beauty she entered fire and attained to the region of gods (7). I shall to-day encompass what has been said by my mother. Arrange therefore the elephants, cars, horses and the army (8). Without vanquishing my father's enemy, slaying the destroyer of my father and carrying out the words of my mother why shall I try to live (9)?

MARKANDEYA said:—Hearing his words, the ministers with the servants and army, having their minds exercised, began to lament, exclaiming 'Alas! Alas" (10). Placing the king before them and obtaining blessings from the priests cognizant of the present, past and future, they, with the army, issued out (11). Sighing like the king of serpents and killing the army of Soumapāla and others in Jamya country Dama quickly approached Vapushmān (12). Sangkrandana's son Vapushmān was informed that Dama with his army and ministers had come (13). Without the least agitation of the mind he commanded his army and sent an emmissary out of the city (with the news) (14). "O Kshatrya, come quickly to me; Narishwanta, with his wife, is expecting you (15). These my sharpened arrows, shot off my bow, piercing your body, will drink your blood in battle (16).

MARKANDEYA said:—Hearing all this from the messenger and remembering his former promise Dama went there speedily, sighing like a serpent (17). Inviting him to battle he said "He, who is a man, does not boast." Then there arose a great encounter between Dama and Vapushmān (18). The charioteer fought with the charioteer, the elephant with the elephant and horse with the horse. There thus arose a great encounter, O saint (19). O Brahman, Dama fighting in anger in the presence of all the gods, Siddhas and Gandharvas the earth trembled (20). Neither the charioteer, nor the elephant, nor the horse could stand his arrows. Then Vapushmān's commander-in-chief fought with Dama (21). Dama struck his shaft deep into his heart. On his death the army took to their heels. Then Dama said to his master (Vapushmān) (22) :—" Having slain my ascetic father, who had no weapon and who was carrying on penances where do you go, O wicked one? Return if you are a Kshatriya" (23).

MARKANDEYA said :—Thereupon coming back the proud (Vapushmān) with his younger brother, son, friends and relatives, fought with him (24). Then the sky and the quarters were coverd with shafts discharged off his bow. He also covered Dama with his car and horse with a net work of arrows (25). Thereupon in anger begotten by the death of his father Dama cut off those arrows and wounded his limbs with his own (26). With one arrow he despatched to the abode of Yama his seven sons, brothers, relatives and friends (27). On the death of his sons and relatives the car-warrior Vapushmān fought with Dama in the battle-field with arrows resembling serpents (28). O great Muni, he too cut off his arrows. Both of them, desirous of killing each other, then fought fiercely (29). Having their bows shattered with the discharge of arrows, those two highly powerful heroes fought with each other with up-lifted swords (30). Thinking for a moment of the destruction of his father, the king, in the forest and holding him by the hair and throwing him on earth, placing his foot on his head and raising up his hand Dama said (31). " Behold, ye gods, men, Siddhas and Pannagas, I am tearing off the heart of the Kshatriya Vapushmān" (32).

MARKANDEYA said :—Having said this Dama cut off his heart with his sword. With a view to bathe in his blood the gods did not prevent him (33). Thereupon with the blood of Vapushmān he performed the water-giving ceremony and with his flesh he offered Pinda (34). He fed the Brahmanas and Rakshasas, and then being freed from debts to his father he left for his own city (35). Such were the kings of the solar dynasty as well as other intelligent heroes, performers of *Yajnas* and well read in the Vedas and religious books. I do not like to enumerate them. Hearing of their account a man is released from sins (36—37).

CHAPTER CXXXVII.

THE BIRDS said :—Having said this and left the company of Kroushthuki the great ascetic Mārkandeya performed the mid-day rites (1). We have also heard from you, O great ascetic, what you have said. This is the Siddhi without beginning described formerly by the Self-Sprung Deity (2). And which you communicated unto the ascetic Mārkandeya, sacred, and auspicious as it is and which gives longivity and the accomplishment of all objects (3). Hearing and reading the four questions which you put in the beginning people are freed from all sins (4). O Muni, you have described unto us the conversation between the father and the son, the creation of the Self-Sprung Brahmā, the origin of Manus and the history of the kings. What more we wish to hear? Hearing all these or reciting them in an assembly a man, with all his sins washed, finds himself at one with Brahman (5—6). Of the eighteen Purānas enumerated by Brahmā, the seventh is known widely as Mārkandeya (7), They are Brahmā, Padma, Vishnu, Siva, Bhāgavat, and Naradiya and the seventh is Mārkandeya (8). The eighth Purāna is Agnī and Bhavishya is the ninth; the tenth is Brahma Vaivarta and the eleventh is Nrisingha (9). The twelfth is Varāha and Skanda is the thirteenth of them; Vamána is the fourteenth and Karma is the fifteenth (10). Then follow Matsya, Garuda, and Brahmanda. He, who reads the names of the eighteen Purānas and recites them three times a day, reaps the fruit of a horse sacrifice. The Purana, that has the four qualities is called Markandeya (11—12). On hearing this, the sin accumulated for a hundred *Koti* years is dissipated. The sins of Brahmanicidi and others, as well as other inauspicious things are dissipated like cotton driven by the wind. By hearing it one gets the piety equal to that acquired by bathing at the holy shrine of Pushkara (13—14). A barren woman, or one whose child dies at birth, if she hears this truly, gets a son crowned with all marks, as well as corns, riches and the eternal heaven (15). Hearing this, a man even if he has offended the gods, is freed from all sins and flourishes in heaven (16). O foremost of the twice-born, he gets long life, freedom from diseases, wealth, corns, children and a continuous progeny (17). Hear O Vipra, after listening to this what a man should do. A wise man, after consecrating fire, should perform Homa (18). O foremost of Munis, meditating on this Purana in the lotus of the heart one should adore Gavinda with perfumeries, garlands and raiments &c., (19). O foremost of Munis, he should then worship a reciter with his wife and then confer upon him a milch cow with its calf (20). O Vipra, the kings should, as much as lies in their power, make gifts of corn-fields, gold, silver, villages and beasts of burden (21). Having pleased the reciters he should pronounce *Swasti, Swasti*! Without having pleased the riciter if one listens to even one verse he will never attain to piety. Such a man is designated by the wise as the purloiner of scriptures. The gods are not pleased with him and the ancestral manes do not accept the things offered by him in Srāddhas. The thief of scriptures does not reap the fruit of bathing at holy shrines and is censured by the reciters of the Vedas (22—24). After the completion of Markandeya a wise man performs a festival and makes a gift of a milch-cow for being released from all sins (25). He also gives away clothes and jewels unto the twice-born with their wives, as well as golden ear-rings, turbans, clean-beds gold-coins, seven sorts of corns, brass vessels for taking food and vessels for clarified butter (26—27). Doing this, O foremost of the twice-born, a man achieves all his objects. Hearing the reciting of all these Puranas duly a man reaps the fruits of a thousand horse sacrifices, and a hundred *Rajashuya* ceremonies. He does not stand in fear of death or hell (28—29). Being freed from all sins he purifies the present and future generations; forsooth the continuity of his family is never disturbed (30). He goes to the region of Indra and the eternal region of Brahmā; there spoken of highly he will again be born as a man (31). Thus by listening to the recitation of Puranas one attains to most excellent yoga. Gifts should not be made unto an atheist, adulterer, villifier of the Vedas, unto him who speaks against his preceptor, him who breaks his vow, forsakes his parents and steals gold; unto him who shall disregard an honourable man and speaks against his kinsmen. No gifts should be made unto these even if vital breath comes up to the throat (32—34). If out of avarice, ignorance or fear one reads it or makes others read, forsooth does he go to hell (35).

JAIMINI said:—"O ye birds, you, out of friendship, have removed that doubt of mine, the solution whereof I did not find in Bharata. Who else will do it (36)? Do ye live long freed from diseases and gifted with wealth. And may your understanding grow in Sankya Yoga (37). You will be freed from the curse of your father."

Having said this he left for his own hermitage (38). Thinking of the noble words of the birds the great Jaimini adored the leading twice-born ones (39).

THE END.

A PROSE ENGLISH TRANSLATION OF MARKANDEYA PURANAM

EDITOR
MANMATHA NATH DUTT

A Prose English Translation of Markandeya Puranam by Manmatha Nath Dutt is a scholarly work that renders the ancient Sanskrit text of the Markandeya Purana into accessible English prose. This translation makes the religious, mythological, and philosophical teachings of the Purana available to a wider audience beyond Sanskrit scholars. Dutt's careful and respectful approach preserves the original's spiritual and cultural significance while promoting understanding of India's classical heritage.

Manmatha Nath Dutt (1855–1912) was an Indian scholar, writer, and translator known for his contributions to Bengali and Sanskrit literature. He specialized in translating classical Sanskrit texts into Bengali and English, helping to make ancient Indian literature more accessible. Dutt's works often bridged traditional Indian culture with modern literary forms, playing a key role in the Bengal Renaissance and the revival of interest in India's classical heritage during the late 19th and early 20th centuries

GYAN

GYAN PUBLISHING HOUSE

email- books@gyanbooks.com

Distribution Network:

www.gyanbooks.com

India, USA, Canada, UK, Australia & France

Price : ₹ 1000

ISBN: 978-93-7169-122-2

9 789371 691222 >